ECCENTRIC GENIUS

An Anthology of the Writings of Richard Kitzler, Master Gestalt Therapist

FOREWORD BY DAN BLOOM
EDITED BY ANNE TEACHWORTH

GESTALT INSTITUTE PRESS
METAIRIE/NEW ORLEANS, LA USA

Copyright 2008, 2009
Gestalt Institute of New Orleans, Inc.

First printing in July, 2008
Second printing in May, 2009

Library of Congress Catalog Number: 1-197806956
ISBN: 1 889968 00 5

All rights reserved. No part of this book may be reproduced, stored in a retrieval system, or transmitted in any form or by any means, electronic, mechanical, photocopying, recording, or otherwise, without the prior written consent of the publisher, except in the case of brief quotations embodied in critical articles and reviews.

Cover Photograph by Anne Teachworth

This book was printed in the United States of America.

To order additional copies of this book, contact:

THE GESTALT INSTITUTE PRESS
433 METAIRIE ROAD
SUITE 133
METAIRIE, LOUISIANA 70005 USA

Phones: 1.800.786.1065 or 504.828.2267
24 Hour Fax: 504.837.2796

Website: www.gestaltinstitutepress.com / www.teachworth.com

E-mail: ateachw@aol.com

TABLE OF CONTENTS

ESSAYS BY FRIENDS AND COLLEAGUES

ARTICLES BY RICHARD KITZLER

RICHARD'S FAVORITE POEMS

Dedication

In appreciation to my dear friends,

Dan Bloom and Anne Teachworth

who urged and sturdied me.

They are the real architects of this book.

Acknowledgments
for Pre-publication Support

Frank Bosco   Susan Jurkowski

M'Lou Caring   Burt Lazarin

Carl Eden   Philip Lichtenberg

Silvie Falschlunger   Charles Myzwinski

Frank Fink   Peter Philippson

Seán Gaffney   Mary Lou Schack

Judith Graham   Gary Yontef

Robert Harman   Lee Zevy

Martha Helliesen

Foreword: A Reader's Guide to *Eccentric Genius*

Dan Bloom

If ever a reader needed an introduction, it is you.

You are about to begin a journey through the terrain of one of the most inspired, original and undisciplined thinkers in the world of gestalt therapy. Go ahead and thumb through the pages of this book, read some prose at random and come back to this introduction.

Our guess is that you found sentences whose imaginative verbal acrobatics and idea-play caught your eye and started you thinking; our guess is that you also started grinding your teeth at some impenetrable or confounding phrases. Be assured: The treasures you will find in Richard Kitzler's writings will reward you despite any irritations resulting from your stumbling over eccentricities beyond your tolerance — or taste.

Richard Kitzler is an eccentric genius, gestalt therapy's eccentric genius, and this collection of his writings is a record of his eccentricity — and proof positive that Richard has been making an important contribution to gestalt therapy. Truly eccentric, Richard follows no straight line, nor even a consistent curve; his thoughts leap and lurch, dip and weave, fly and dazzle. Read this book. You will see. Richard's writings here are "Richard Untamed." Here are his words as he intended them, and only minimally edited. You will be getting a full-on Kitzler experience.

This introduction is an orientation to Richard Kitzler's previously unpublished writings; it will be your guide. It will direct you to the development and shape of Richard's concerns, much as the lines of longitude and latitude might organize a traveler's journey. This introduction will also give you conceptual "toe-holds" so your journey on the cliff of Richard's sometimes merciless prose might be less "perilous."

Along with the personal reflections of his friends and colleagues interspersed in this volume, this introduction will also try to personalize this eccentric genius. We who have known him during these last decades know him as a friend and inspired teacher. Perhaps this will come across to you.

1. A child of Elizabeth, New Jersey: A few paragraphs about origins

Since one of Richard's games is to play with words and names, it is impossible to resist this: *"Kitzeln"* is German for "to tickle" and *"Kitzler"* is that part of the female anatomy whose orgasm Freud refused to recognize. Think of this as you read him, and be tickled.

Richard is a child of Elizabeth, New Jersey, where he was born almost 81 years ago. If you listen closely to his speech, you can hear the local music of the region, quaintly humble overtones amid the notes of his exceptional vocabulary. His father, a child of German immigrants, was a minor functionary in the infamous Elizabeth political machine. Richard's mother, according to Richard a suffering spouse with formidable personal powers and impressive physical girth, was of an old New York family. Richard was raised along with two brothers and a sister.

This was his family-of-origin. Yet Richard comes from someplace far deeper and wider, his writings announce his erudition — and he carries it with him to this day in a memory that simply cannot forget anything, unless it is the name of a friend, or the day of the week. He would call it, "the riches of the Indies." We call it the riches of his eccentric genius. We turn to his ideas, here, as a guide to his writings.

2. The archeology of his thinking

Richard's ideas, as he might say, are like Gaul, "divided into three parts."

a. Parts One and Two

Part One marked his time with Frederick (Richard refuses to use the nickname, Fritz) and Laura Perls, and of course, Paul Goodman. This was also his time with the other members of the so-called "professional group," who in New York from the 1950s through the 1960s, were the originators of the foundational model of gestalt therapy. These were the early days of the New York Institute for Gestalt Therapy (NYIGT). Richard became a Fellow of the NYIGT and remains a conscientious member of its community.

Part Two is marked by his teaching *Gestalt Therapy, Excitement and Growth in the Human Personality* by Frederick Perls, Ralph Hefferline and Paul Goodman (*PHG*), as the only text for the understanding of gestalt therapy. He taught this in a weekly study group in which *PHG* was read aloud, line by line. Difficulties in understanding the text became opportunities for group "experiment" — that is, gestalt therapy interventions designed to personalize the reading in a group experience. This period is also the time of his development of gestalt therapy group process, culminating in his claimed invention of process groups.

We can mark the height of this period as beginning with his speech at Laura Perls' *Festschrift* (1987) and cresting with his significant role at the NYIGT first groups' conference. (1991). His speech at the Laura Festschrift started his summation of gestalt therapy and his inquiry into its bases. This conference was the high water mark of Richard's advocacy of the foundational model of gestalt therapy as an implicitly social theory expressed through group process.

Richard also played a role in the founding of the Association for the Advancement of Gestalt Therapy (AAGT) during this time. He brought his understanding of group development and the function of small groups as intrinsic to the whole — which was his theory of process groups — to this new international organization.

Parts One and Two have a single arc of intellectual development. They share Richard's mature understanding of gestalt therapy group theory, which developed from his understanding of gestalt therapy's theory of self functioning. Beneath the surface, though, were difficulties he was about to discover, which would soon crack across fault lines and begin Part Three of his thinking.

b. Part Three

This period began in the early 1990s and continues as this collection is being published. As Richard describes it, one day he returned to his exploration of the bases of gestalt therapy (which began at the *Festschrift*) and asked himself, "How do we know what we say we know?" He began an excursion back to Aristotle and then forward, almost century by century, to the present.

One day, while reading an entry in a dictionary of philosophy, he innocently found a cross-reference to American pragmatism and George Herbert Mead; his curiosity was engaged. At first, it seemed a simple thing: a common use of the word "contact" by *PHG* and Mead. This happens all the time. He continued to read and thus, a chain of thought began which led him to question, *challenge, PHG's* discussion of "contact."

This questioning was as if he had found a loose thread in the fabric of foundational gestalt therapy — or at least the "solid" garment of the Goodman model he had so loyally taught for years. He started gently to tug at it; and then not so gently to tug. The whole fabric unraveled in his hands.

Those of us who studied with Richard during Parts One and Two knew him to propone Goodman's theory as exquisite, perfect, flawless; not a word out of place, it ticked with the precision of a master's timepiece. He referred to *PHG* as Paul Goodman's *tour de force*. He knew Goodman and revered him as one of a handful of people whose erudition intimidated him. Now Goodman's perfect model for human experience became a thin, inconsistent, poorly thought-through, insufficiently established jargon-filled muddle on which many gestalt therapy practitioners have been trying to anchor their praxis.

When these icons, Paul Goodman and *PHG*, toppled in the mid 1990s, if there could have been a sound to their crashing commensurate to the impact it had on the firmament of Kitzler's universe, it would have deafened thousands. Goodman fell, *PHG* fell, and so fell that perfect world of gestalt therapy theory. All this is clear in Part Three. With the fall of the "perfect model" and the bohemian intellectual who created it, that on which it was supposedly based — gestalt psychology — took on a rank odor, and Kitzler set his hounds upon it, without mercy.

These three parts of the Kitzler intellectual terrain, then, are Kitzler the Standard Bearer of the Perls-Goodman Model, Kitzler the Innovator of Gestalt Therapy Group Theory, and at last, Kitzler the Iconoclast who shattered the statues of his mentors, Perls and Goodman. And now raising up a new standard, he is Kitzler the Advocate of the American Pragmatism of William James and George Herbert Mead.

3. The Wednesday Group: An important amendment
Richard chuckled when we mentioned this three-part schema to him. And he immediately corrected it by making sure we added this amendment. Central to the development of all his thinking has been a core of colleagues and students — his Wednesday Group. This group started in the early 1970s, and its membership changed as people came and went. Yet, like a keg of vintage sherry to which new wine is always poured and from which one regularly drinks, this ongoing group aged over time along with Richard's own thinking.

Richard says that without this group's support, he could not have so intensely studied gestalt therapy nor had the energy to challenge its established ideas. The Wednesday Group has been at the core of

Richard's work and has served as proof of his own belief that the personal is social, in every shape, manner, and form. His work, his self, is incomprehensible except as a function of the social world.

4. A restless "Eccentric Genius"
At so many points during his life, Richard could have rested and taught from what he already knew. Many teachers do that. But that was never enough. He has never been content with static ideas. He has shown us that no belief goes unchallenged, however widely held, even if they are his own.

5. Now to some of the ideas
If a complex idea can be stated sufficiently without complexity, then it wasn't complex in the first place. So we are not faced with much of a challenge here. Since many of Richard's ideas *are* complex, as you will see when you read his essays, we do not have to spend much time reducing them into simpler forms. They will stand for themselves and will demand your attention. They seem to defy traditional techniques of comprehension, as if they were four-dimensional, needing to be rotated in our own minds, "seen" from different angles, and "held" so their meaning can develop over time. His style is elliptical, so he doesn't offer too much help, either. Yet, we can try to help.

6. Parts One and Two: Richard as *PHG's* advocate and formulator of gestalt therapy group theory
This book contains nothing from Part One of his intellectual terrain. Part One was the time when Kitzler began his Wednesday Group, his line-by-line hermeneutic reading of *PHG*. His students probably have annotated copies of that book disintegrating at the back of their bookshelves, each bearing evidence of the close reading, pen in hand — lines marked, pages turned down, scribbled notes. If he wrote anything himself, he didn't save it.

By Part Two, we have his 1987 speech at Laura's *Festschrift* and written preparation for the NYIGT and AAGT conferences for which he was principal designer of the group facilitator training. For better or worse, his ideas here are as straightforward as Richard gets. We draw your attention to his description of process groups in his documents prepared for those conferences. The lofty expanse of his Laura *Festschrift* speech is the launching pad for his later mission to excavate the deepest foundations of gestalt therapy — which mission became no less than his version of the cleansing of the Augean Stables, the mythical Fifth Labor of Hercules.

7. Part Three: Richard the Iconoclast — the deepest intellectual waters.

Here Richard takes on Perls, Goodman, gestalt therapy, and most aggressively, gestalt psychology, with the passion of a party to a failed marriage.

a. American pragmatism

This is not so much a theme as an architectonic of his thinking. In a period of a few short years in the middle to late 1990s, American pragmatism became the underlying framework for all his ideas, replacing every shred of Goodman's gestalt therapy. At first, William James' *Principles of Psychology* guided Richard through a preliminary step-by-step re-organization of his own consideration of experience.

For example, James' considerations led Richard to challenge the sufficiency of gestalt psychology and consequently its privileged place in gestalt therapy. Compared to James' thorough analyses, Goodman's discussions became thinner and thinner to Richard. Compared to James, Köhler was a sham — or worse. This will be discussed in a little more detail, below.

To many, John Dewey was the most influential American pragmatist. His influence on Richard, however, seems minor. Dewey's analysis of the reflex arc as a circuit *including* the arc, hence, a complete whole circuit of the organism and the stimulus, not a mere automatic response of a body, is integrated throughout Richard's understanding of pragmatism as a sound basis for his own version of gestalt therapy's monism (that is, non-dualistic holism).

Although it was mostly uncredited by Goodman, Richard discovered that American pragmatism is a central engine to *PHG*'s model of human experience. It was no surprise to Richard that the deeper he plowed the earth of American pragmatism, the richer bases for gestalt therapy he found.

b. George Herbert Mead, "The Mantra," self

George Herbert Mead was the inspiration for nearly all of Richard's latest thinking. His ideas are background to Richard's, much as actual paper bears a nearly visible watermark. If Mead's writings lacked for Richard the clarity and scope of Dewey's which were composed over a longer career, and it is an understatement that they lacked the elegance of James', Mead's *Philosophy of the Act* contained a methodically reasoned, experientially based model for human experience for which Richard had been searching.

Mead took James several steps further, and perhaps, took Dewey several levels deeper. James and Dewey are "easy reads"; James' philosophical heft is almost done-in by his lyrical prose. Ironically, Richard replaced one famously opaque text, *PHG*, with nearly an equally opaque text, *Philosophy of the Act*. The Wednesday Group brought its line-by-line method of reading to sections of that book that Richard provided as handouts until group members were able to locate their own used copies.

He taught group members to replace the "organism/environment" quotations from *PHG* with the following "Mead Mantra," a Kitzler paraphrase: "The organism 'logically' determines the environment through its senses and susceptibilities; the environment causally determines the organism through its opportunities; the two are mutual, not convertible."

This mantra, according to Richard, in one sentence, more fully and completely describes the relationship of organism and environment than anything written in *PHG*, or elsewhere in the gestalt therapy literature. The mantra elegantly accounts for the whole process of organism-environment adjustment, without the need of further explanation. Such is Richard's enthusiasm for Mead.

Mead's self is not unlike the self of gestalt therapy. Both are emergent of social experience. Yet where *PHG* describes self-emergence through a hodgepodge of complicated, inconsistent, arcane and contradictory passages that sometimes simply make unsupported assertions of gestalt therapy dogma, in Richard's view, Mead carefully describes the development of self through a *social* process whereby a person ultimately takes the perspective of the "generalized other" through a process involving vocal gestures and play. Self both comprises and is of the social world. Here was a sound basis for Richard's gestalt therapy: A perspective in which individual and group are indistinguishable.

c. An assault on gestalt psychology
Armed with James' and Mead's philosophically and scientifically grounded approaches, Richard went after gestalt psychology — the supposed basis of gestalt therapy and which was the discipline from which it derived its name. The scientific method of Köhler and Wertheimer? To Richard, unkindly, sharply, and shockingly, they were "fraudulent." (See *Three Lectures.*) Part-whole and figure-ground? To Richard, they were suspiciously thin constructs that needed to be looked at more closely.

You will see these densely argued by him in *Three Lectures, Bases of Gestalt Therapy: An Evolutionary Restatement, The Bases of Gestalt Therapy: A Synoptical Restatement, Gestalt Therapy Theory: A Perspective from Pragmatism* and *Ecology of Contact.*

i. Part-whole, figure-ground
What can be wrong with these axioms of gestalt therapy? Simply, and our simplification butchers Kitzler's complexity. Part-whole and figure-ground are clumsy abstractions from direct experience. We do not experience separable parts. Perhaps, and only perhaps, they make some

sense in the simple visual perception experiments performed by the gestalt psychologists and others, but when considered from a pragmatist or phenomenological perspective (Richard's analysis includes references to Husserl, Merleau-Ponty, Marcel, and Ricoeur), these axioms of gestalt therapy fall apart as failing to account for actual multi-dimensional embodied experience.

Instead of figure-ground, Richard borrows from James and suggests core and fringe as one single experienced unit. We not experience parts and wholes; we apprehend wholes that we "rotate" within the differentiation process of experiencing. Gestalt psychology had it wrong for many reasons, Richard claims. The gestalt psychologists' perspective was flat without the *chiaroscuro* to reflect the dimensional world as experienced. How then, could it provide a sufficient basis for an experiential psychotherapy?

ii. Contact

It was Richard's discomfort with "contact" that started his unraveling of gestalt therapy as he had known it. That was the word he was reading about when he found the cross-reference to Mead's use of the exact same word. By now, you know the structure of Richard's disillusionment with Goodman. Where *PHG* spins an abstract model of contact, full of holes, inconsistencies, or thin reasoning, Mead places his concept within a fully worked out philosophy of the act and within an embodied, social world of self-development and action.

PHG purports to offer a meta-theory for gestalt therapy's experiential psychotherapy and world-view. Instead, according to Richard, *PHG* offers barely supportable abstractions. *PHG*'s contact is the nucleus of experiencing, the process whereby a human organism orients in the world, creatively-adjusts, and assimilates novelties necessary for survival. Its indivisible (whole) process is heuristically partialized into forecontacting, contacting, final contact, and post contact. *PHG* describes these, and again, to Richard, does an insufficient job of making these abstractions relevant to lived experience.

Mead describes how human beings, by taking the perspective of others, get to the insides of things, see as if through one another's eyes to fill out the dimensions of the physical world. The world of objects is the world of social objects, not a flat impersonal world. Even more, this world of things, social things, has its own feel and this is the feel of resistance, the sense of the world's substance that gives us direct experience of the insides of things.

Mead seems to approach this from *within*, observes Richard, that is, from within the experience of the act. There is nothing abstract in Mead's description of his own, coincidentally, four-part description of the act — impulse, perception, manipulation, consummation — as a direct depiction of human action. This description of the act has flesh and bones: It is the peopled world of selves in society. Mead's contact is an expression of his complex yet specific philosophy of the act. For Richard, *PHG* offers a thin soup of an alternative.

iv. "Contact," further steps
Richard was not entirely satisfied with "contact" even now that he resituated it within Mead's world of social acts. *Ontology of Action* contains Richard's most recent development of contacting. In this paper, Richard repeats his conversion of the flat figure-ground model into the plumper multi-dimensional core-fringe model, where the object of perception holographically emerges in consciousness.

Now he adds a dramatic concept from Merleau-Ponty. "Contact," to Richard, is a chiasm of experience, a crossing of the known with the not-yet-known in the moment of experiencing. This crossing, this chiasm, is fully situationally embodied, in the sense intended by Merleau-Ponty. But Richard takes Merleau-Ponty's concept back into Mead's social world of objects and yet further back into Richard's re-formed gestalt therapy.

8. A re-formed gestalt therapy
This is the final point we will make in this introduction. Despite what may appear to be the unreachable loftiness of Richard's intellectual

excursions, our simplifications truly do not do them justice. Above all else and consistently, Richard is a practicing gestalt therapist. Throughout most of his essays, you will find dozens of invitations for the reader to *do* the work of his ideas, right now, to put his suggestions into action, and to find meaning not by reading his words, but by *doing* his words. Richard's work is the *praxis* of gestalt therapy, that is, ideas in action. "We do theory."

9. Conclusion

We cannot offer a final assessment of Richard's contributions to gestalt therapy. His work is not over. Neither is it fully understood. Yet of this, we are confident. He discovered and addressed the *ad hoc* dilettantism of both Perls and Goodman who certainly were gifted innovators, visionary if not prophetic in their own ways, and helped re-established gestalt therapy on firmer ground. Of course, Richard has not been alone in this process, but he has been one of its leaders. His essays bear his special stamp and for that, he stands out from the rest. He stands out still further by the depth of his thinking and the mysteries of meaning hidden in the labyrinths of his eccentric method.

This collection of the writings of a person whom we have dubbed an "eccentric genius," and for whom we fully intend such a title, is an audacious venture. Eccentricity is by its nature unpredictable and erratic, of an odd or whimsical orbit. For us, the challenge has been to assemble these writings and to hold them steady enough to be tamed enough to be published ... it is called "to be edited."

For you, the reader, the challenge will be to grasp the excitement of our genius' mind and imagination, despite and because of these eccentricities. We are offering this introduction to assist you in this challenge.

Dan Bloom, JD, LCSW

Postword to the Foreword

A Personal Voice by Dan Bloom

Our publisher, Anne Teachworth, read my *Foreword* and regretted my omission of personal details. I thought such details would have distracted us from the principal mission of the *Foreword*. It belongs here, briefly.

Thirty years ago, I anxiously climbed the stairs to Richard's second floor office for my first psychotherapy session with him. The hallway was darkish and faded in the way so many rent controlled older apartment buildings were in the 1970s. There might just as well have been the smell of various dinners lingering in the barely ventilated stairwell. I must have knocked on his door or rang his buzzer. Since I was anxious, I may have done both.

Later, he would teach me that the first impression of a clinical situation contains all there is to know, all that can be known, and all that will ever happen, collapsed in that one instantaneous act.

I forgot what that first moment was like, other than that he was tall, and rude, perhaps even annoyed that I was there. I spent what must have been an hour in my protracted lamenting state, which had become my art.

He asked me if I had high fevers as a child.

I denied it. (What child does not have high fevers, I wonder now?)

"Then why those eyes?"

"Contact lenses."

"Oh."

(What on earth was that about?)

Well, I came back.

The psychotherapy lasted for about six years.

Then I started studying with him. I left the practice of law, became a psychotherapist, went to social work school, started teaching and training gestalt therapists myself, and began writing.

I never stopped studying with Richard. He is a best friend.

Dan Bloom, J. D., LCSW, is a psychotherapist in private practice in New York City. He studied gestalt therapy with Laura Perls, Isadore From, Richard Kitzler, and Patrick Kelley. He teaches, supervises, and lectures internationally. Dan is a member of the adjunct faculty at the Gestalt Associates for Psychotherapy, and of the core faculty of the Gestalt Training Institute of Bermuda.

He is the Past-President and a Fellow of the New York Institute for Gestalt Therapy and President-elect of the Association for the Advancement of Gestalt Therapy, an international community. Dan is also a full member of the European Association for Gestalt Therapy. His writings have appeared in various professional journals and books in many different languages. He is Editor-in-chief of Studies in Gestalt Therapy: Dialogical Bridges (www.studies-in-gestalt.org) and a member of the editorial board of the Gestalt Review.

dan@djbloom.com

Early Photos

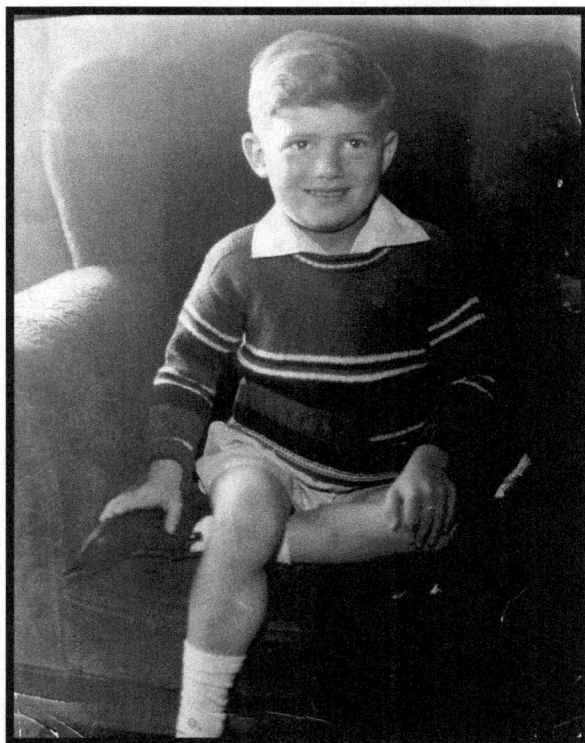

Richard at 3 years old.

Joseph F. McCrindle
March 27, 1923 – July 11, 2008

Richard at 7 years old
3rd grade

**Richard at 7 years old with his mother,
Elizabeth Mae McGuire Kitzler, 35 years old
Point Pleasant Beach, New Jersey**

Richard at 14 years old
Junior High School Graduation 1942

Richard's passport photo, Ibiza, Spain 1961

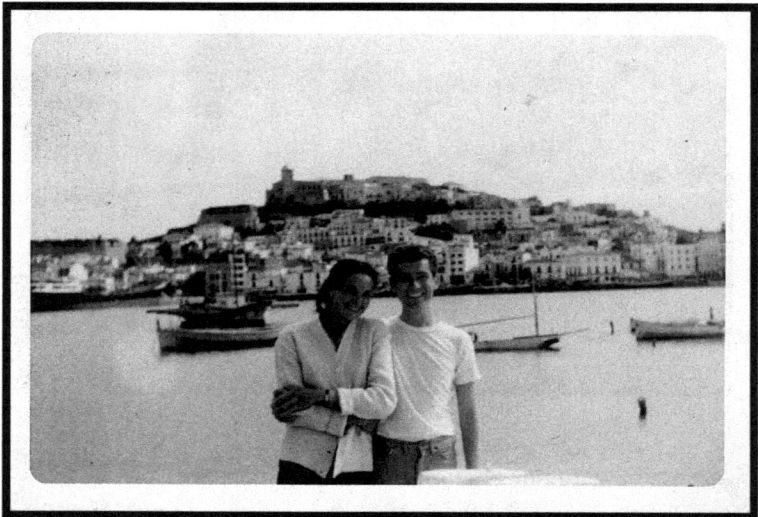

**Ina Schlagter and Richard on Richard's boat, The Lady Ana,
in the Balearic Islands off the coast of Spain 1961**

Richard in Madrid, 1961.
On the left, is a high-level French Military officer, retired.
On the right is a French Count.

**Richard onboard the QE II from Cherbourg, France
to New York, 1986. Notice the ring he is wearing,
a Cartouche of Tuthmosis III, the Warrior Pharoah.**

Autobiography

Richard Kitzler

When Mark Twin was born in Florida, Missouri, in November of 1835, the town had a population of one hundred souls. He later remarked his birth increased the census by one percent, a fact of which not many could boast.

When I was born in November, 1927, a triple Scorpio, the population of Elizabeth, New Jersey, was at one hundred twenty-five thousand, the seventy-fifth largest city in the country. Mine was a political family, my father the alderman of the then almost totally Italian ward, where his German father had been a political leader. Under the earlier commission form of government, my grandfather had rotated through every post in the commission firmament: Mayor, Fire, Police, and Parks. You get the idea.

My maternal ancestors, the Van Pelts, came to New Amsterdam in the early Seventeenth Century and like the Bourbons, never learned anything or never forgot anything, except a sturdy duteousness of which the central motif was DON'T. But the blessings of an Italian gang culture and its natural ease in foolish matters produced in me and my two older brothers a counter-DO! Have I remarked that I am the youngest son of a youngest son for three generations?

Of course, in the neighborhood I was ashamed of *my* parents because they couldn't speak Italian. My playmates were ashamed of *their* parents because they couldn't speak English. But the miracle of reading and

33

education burst upon me and the universes of travel, adventure, and fantasy insulated me from the DUTY and the DON'T. And of course, I was a hopeless athlete, left-handed, with illegible handwriting and totally clumsy. I still can't tie my black tie without closing my eyes and making believe I'm tying a shoelace.

One fond memory and example of real education occurred in kindergarten with the Misses Newman and Rekemeier who had been my parents' kindergarten teachers! I couldn't get how to skip! Yes, I said, "Skip!" Whoever had to be *taught* such a thing?

Well, Miss Newman was skinny as a rail and Miss Rekemeier, fat as a house. They banished the rest of the kindergarten to the side of the room near the block box and made space. They took respectively, my left hand, then my right hand. "NOW, STAND ON ONE FOOT! NOW, HOP! NOW, STAND ON THE OTHER FOOT. NOW, HOP!" We hopped together.

I was skipping in three hops. Let's analyze it. They held my hands and gave a clear instruction for something I wanted to learn. They held, pulled and supported me against gravity; we did it together. How is that for training in psychotherapy, and group psychotherapy at that? Nothing in any subsequent education, including two ABDs came close.

Have you ever tried to "change the sign of the subtrahend and proceed as in addition?"

A profound and civilizing education came by way of my mother's somewhat fanatical devotion to the High Anglican persuasion of the Episcopal Church. I began as a five-year-old altar boy right out of Norman Rockwell…pale freckled skin, intense strawberry blond hair (more strawberry than blond). I had been at Father Hoffman's 7:30am mass on Wednesday with Miss Prevost and Miss Ogden as worshippers (Both D.A.R.). Miss Ogden lived a block away on Boudinot Place (Declaration of Independence). Afterwards, the Reverend and his wife and I breakfasted in the rectory. I learned there how to eat a four-minute egg from an eggcup and all that went with it: toast from the silver rack, porridge, (not oatmeal), and well-done drained bacon.

And of course, on the seventh day of (rest!), Sunday that is, came the real goods: again, early communion mass; breakfast in the parish hall; Sunday School where we studied the Word; then High Mass from 11am to an interminable homily ending at 1:15pm more or less, usually more. There then had to be the endless High Church socializing leading to Jane Austen-like hellos and good-byes. And so finally, home to eat.

With all this, comes the magnificent rhythm and diction of King James which, lo, even as we speak manifests, comes to pass, in my literary efforts. Cumulatively, further vehicles of civilization are driven in Bach, Palestrina, and the Hymnal; Gothic arches and statues of the saints and stained glass.

But no belief! I knelt alongside our bed and prayed my father would stop his outrageous and violent drunkenesses. He didn't stop and I stopped praying. Because of this, therefore after this, the old logic of *post hoc ergo propter hoc* was reversed.

The Word became sacred to me and I now think, somewhat magical. And indeed, it is! I found myself typing excerpts of particularly on-turning literature on the best bond paper I could afford and accumulating the sheets like Fagin counting his silver. It was my treasure: *First Corinthians*, speaking with tongues, angels, charity, sounding brass and tinkling symbol; Churchill's "Never surrender" speech which we heard on the shortwave; Hamlet's *Soliloquy* and Macbeth's *Tomorrow and tomorrow and tomorrow,* Bryant's *Thanatopsis*, Handel's *Messiah* and the Hallelujah Chorus, and don't forget, Emily Dickinson's *I'm Nobody. Who are you?* — but we shouldn't tell on the penalty of banishment, you know.

In my words and worlds, I sailed on silver and also wine-dark seas in privateers of the Revolution and the barks of Homer, and drove my family crazy because I could not be pried from my latest book to come to dinner. The other truth was the routine family insanity at that table that made me burp and prefer to eat later in solitary splendor, with the peace and quiet broken only by my mother's necessitous preachings and scoldings. She was being affectionate. And then there were the scholarships.

I won a four-year scholarship to Rutgers on the basis of a competitive exam. My father had fits. *He* had had to make an appointment with his father to go to High School, a permission that was granted only on condition that the money he forfeited by not working would come back to the family when he graduated. My father finessed it by taking a commercial course given only in the Girls' High School, where there were three hundred and fifty women and only twelve men. As my mother would say in her exasperations, "He was like a pig in shit."

The university was running under the Harvard Report which required all courses for a sound education in sciences, humanities, language, English. A student was allowed one elective per semester, all this for two years. With extras, gym, military, chapel, etc., etc., I calculated I accomplished 27 credits per semester. Classes began at 8:30am and ended at 5:30pm.

I rescued myself by enlisting in the United States Regular Army Infantry where ironically, one could find peace and quiet. All one had to do was stand at attention and breathe. They did everything else. I ate in a mess hall that served nine thousand meals a day on metal trays and I never burped once until I came "home" on my first leave. *Res ipsa loquitur.*

In 1949, having uncovered the incredible concentration of artist, intellectual and the downright liberation of the Village, I also discovered a highly functioning, flattening and pernicious classical detachment. Through David Sachs, a philosophy instructor at Rutgers and an acolyte (later to be profoundly disabused) of Paul Goodman, I made my way to Frederick S. Perls and gestalt therapy, and with them, recovered a life and a career for which I am forever grateful and irritated. Dr. Perls sent me my first patient in 1953 and was my supervisor. Renate Perls reminds me it is fifty-six years since first we met in the Farmer's Market, Los Angeles.

There was a disastrous year at the McCarthyite UCLA Law School where I made and got into trouble; a scholarship at the New School for Social Research for my Master's degree in Experimental Gestalt Psychology; and another with Columbia University psychiatrist Allison Montague, another patient of Perls. I became a staff psychologist at the Columbia Health Service and kept a private practice, while I wined and dined and carried on until closing at the famous, perhaps notorious San Remo Bar on Bleecker Street, alas, now long gone. *Sic transit gloria mundi.*

I cannot think of another person who has completed two All But Doctorates, ABDs, one at Columbia, the other at N.Y.U. There were various assistantships and instructorships of which it is best to say little, but which allowed me to develop and refine my thinking in groups' interaction both in task and in process as a powerful organizational and educational tool. This thinking ultimately lead to what is now known as the New York Model of the New York Institute for Gestalt Therapy, my home for more than a half century and to the good people of it. They have been vital, generous, and severally brilliant supports and supporters in good and bad times, and especially in recent and painful financial catastrophes. Of such is the kingdom of Heaven.

On February 21, 1961, I boarded a Yugoslav freighter, the *Bovec*, bound for Tangier, nine days for $90. My colleague and old and dear friend, Patrick Kelley, shared a cabin. An utterly transformative experience enveloped me as the ship sailed past the Rock of Gibraltar at 3am and we entered the harbor of Tangier, ablaze with neon lights, all in Arabic. G.K. Chesterson's comment on Times Square became a reality: "What a sight this must be for a man who cannot read."

That very day the King of Morocco died and there were demonstrations. The owner of the Hotel Marmora in the Medina would not let us out of the hotel: "These are very excitable people," he said. They were very excitable times with new sounds and images rampant. Upon referrals from Tennessee Williams and Paul Goodman, Paul Bowles invited us to meet at the Café de Paris at the top of the hill. We were invited to dinner at their apartment house where he and Jane Bowles had apartments.

We later discovered that Jane was being systematically poisoned at dinner by her lover, the viciously jealous Fatima. Paul had a separate apartment with three layers of oriental rugs running three feet up the walls. There he sat *djellaba* and *fez* and smoked his hand-rolled *kif.* He sat cross-legged in a hypnotic fog while Pat floated forty feet up in a cloudy blue-green eyed dream. Since I had never smoked *kif* or otherwise, except for un-inhaled cigars, Paul opined I would have to settle for the candy or brownies. I passed, though I must confess, it was the only time in my life I could dance before the beat was in, just such an un-embarrassable state.

Having just received a check from home, I treated myself to a civilized dinner in the good restaurant in the French quarter. The waiter approached and told me that that a nearby table of men wanted to buy me a drink. I told him to thank them but say "No." "But you must. It is the King's brother! He said you were worth fifteen camels!" I found out later that one camel cost about a thousand dollars. I hope I was misinformed.

The trip became very much the Grand Tour for me: Spain and the bullfights; The Prado and Toledo and El Escorial and Alhambra. Then France, then fleeing Paris, which I found cold and isolating (except for the winged victory of Samothrace looming over the stair case at the Louvre), to hospitable Barcelona to find that the French army had made a *causerie*. The border had been closed as I slept on the overnight train back to Barcelona where I lodged, unknown only to me, in a whore house.

As the train to Rome rounded a curve, there, suddenly filling my eyes, was Michelangelo Dome of St. Peter's. I wept, feeling I had come home. The Italians were *so* Italian! In Venice, I stayed the first night in a wonderful and cheap *pensione* on the Salute. I spent the next night and remainder of my time in Venice in the Palazzo Dario, one of the five remaining private palaces on the Grand Canal. The toilets were sculpted from a solid block of (brown) marble and the palace gondola from mahogany, and the gondoliers were dressed in the colors and stripes of the house. I think they did double duty with their white gloves and uniforms in the palazzo and in the splendid dinners at the walled garden to the rear. There was an all-night party in the balconied music room with candles and harpsichord. The sunrise and retired instruments were as sculptures hanging on the walls. I was living a Thomas Mann novel!

In my first trip to Spain, I wound up in Ibiza in the Balearic Islands where I met Mariano Tur de Montis, a descendant of the Monte Pope Julius III. He lived in a grand and Renaissance *casa seigniorial* replete with the old masters and his own paintings of his spacious garden which brought the bouganvillea and hibiscus right into the house. I rented the Lady Ana, a retired Dutch canal boat in the harbor for eight dollars a month. Señor Sardinas rowed out every morning and replenished the water tanks. It was equipped luxuriously: living room/library, kitchen and stove, sitting deck. I never felt such privacy!

Leaving my second ABD at NYU, I went directly to Formentera, the smallest of the Balearics that is habitable. It had a thousand people and eleven centenarians and thirty-five estranjeros. I carried a trunk with me that contained a Remington noiseless typewriter on which I was going to — and did — write my unpublished novel. Eileen, whom I had met on the first trip, followed with her two children, renting a gloriously old farm house five minutes to the rear of mine. The living room had a floor of living rock and a fireplace one could be roasted in, or before which one could celebrate rites of sexual liberation and also, I'm afraid, of abandon.

Every evening, we four rushed to the pine forest behind the house to pagan-like watch the fiery and cooling sunset. For a moment, one could see the silhouette of Valencia across the Mediterranean. These were religious events. Far, far different from my dinner burps in New Jersey.

In perusing this document which I find very much in the style of an *apologia pro vita mea,* a defense of my life, I am in wonder that what would ordinarily be seen as important events are completely left in darkness. I am referring to enormous successes in business (read money) and as a result, frequent returns to just those islands where I had lived on $80 a month. I can only think those chords of so-called "reality" sound in my soul as flat and oddly unprofitable. Though, of course, there are moments of touching fidelity and loyalty that nothing can extinguish, although the agents of those moments are now long dead. Still with us, though gravely ill and incommunicable, is my dear friend, J. F. R. McCrindle, perhaps a strong and faithful older brother.

Richard Kitzler, New York City, June 2008.

Note: On July 12, 2008, after this autobiography was written, my dear friend Joe died at 85 years of age. (See our childhood photos on pages 26 and 27) *Ave atque vale.*

ESSAYS BY FRIENDS AND COLLEAGUES

I'm Nobody! Who Are You?

I'm nobody! Who are you?
Are you nobody, too?
Then there's a pair of us - don't tell!
They'd banish us, you know!

How dreary to be somebody!
How public like a frog
To tell one's name the livelong day
To an admiring bog!

— Emily Dickinson

Richard Kitzler,
My Family, My Friend

Renate Perls

We met in Los Angeles soon after the birth of my youngest daughter in 1951. Richard claims it was at the Hollywood Ranch Market, but orange crates and suitcases in the living room of my house surrounded my first memory of him. However, since Richard has always had a fantastic memory, I'll have to agree with him. He never fails to surprise me when relating events of what occurred in my family which either I had forgotten or didn't even know existed. Sometimes, I believe he even knew my parents better than I did. That couldn't possibly be true ... but after all, Richard worked with both Fritz and Laura at one time or another and thus became, and still is part of our family history.

Although Richard and I didn't see one another often for many years after I came back to New York, we began our personal friendship when I joined the New York Gestalt Institute several years ago. This has little to do with the Institute. We now occasionally meet on the street in Greenwich Village, talk on the corner, sit on somebody's stairs, and dine with friends, or just plain yak on the phone. Basically, we talk "family." His, mine ... things seldom shared with others.

I had always been somewhat in awe of Richard, something passed on to me from my mother who was a bit afraid of him. She didn't like to argue, and he stood up for what he believed. He was and is extremely eloquent.

He let his views be known on whatever subject in which he was involved. Of course, he's not always agreed with, and this might lead to some sort of confrontation. I believe this was what frightened Laura. Being her daughter, I, too, find it difficult to be confrontational, but I love Richard's mind and find him most fascinating and am now very comfortable with him.

Richard Kitzler is admired and respected by gestalt therapists in Europe and America. There will be words of appreciation and praise for his work as well as his vast knowledge on a variety of subjects.

From Fritz and Laura's daughter and granddaughters, we send you greetings with love and joy at our long and cherished friendship.

Renate Perls *is an Associate Member of the New York Institute for Gestalt Therapy. As she says, "My life began at the age of seventy-four, so there is not much to write about in a bio of only two years, but here goes ..." The daughter of Laura and Fritz Perls, she was born in Berlin, grew up in Johannesburg and came to the United States at the age of sixteen. Renate is a citizen of both Germany and the U.S. and calls both countries home. The mother of two daughters, she was for many years an agent in the classical music business, and like many people in the last years, has become interested in the psycho-spiritual field, in the richness and awareness of the metaphysical and the interconnectedness of all things. Presently, she studies and does serious research in this area.*

renateperls@yahoo.com

Gestalt Therapy: From New York to Scandinavia

Sheldon Litt

I first met Richard Kitzler (RK) in 1961. He was traveling with Pat Kelley, two very tall impressive New Yorkers. I was just a young, naive psych grad from Washington D.C.

The Yugoslav freighter sailed from NYC to Tangier; $99 for twelve days. So we had time to get acquainted. There were several interesting characters on this epochal voyage, including a well-known author, but RK was my favorite. He was impressed by my academic background: early-entrance scholarship at the University of Chicago, and I liked his wit and his poise, both of which I lacked.

By chance, we met up again in Paris. All I recall of this brief meeting was that his hotel room was full of empty wine bottles strewn on the floor. I knew I'd look him up when I returned to the USA.

In spring of 1962, I began gestalt therapy (GT) with RK at his Jane Street apartment. I had found a sublet on Cornelia Street. Thus began a long training in GT. About a year later, RK went off to Spain, and I was turned over to Isadore in Hoboken. Later, I was in one-week workshops with Fritz, and also a weekly training group with Laura Perls.

But Kitzler was the better therapist. In the typical Fritz group, the leader focuses on one person with the group as background, a kind of classical

45

Greek chorus. But RK insisted on group dynamics as part of the gestalt therapeutic process, each person gives input. The "go-around" was built in as an important part of the process. One might call it "first among equals" — RK vs. the "Fritzian Guru Style." Fritz was a fascinating therapist, a cross between Rasputin and Santa Claus, achieving many "instant breakthroughs" with professionals. RK, on the other hand, worked more for small increments of growth. His goal was to gradually increase awareness for each person in the group which I found to be a superior method, and one that I incorporated into my group work in Scandinavia.

Of course, at times, RK would amaze the group with his razzle-dazzle quick insights. How can I ever learn this, I wondered in those long-ago days? His answer was Kitzlerian gestalt... "Be open and the answers are there." At the time, I had no idea what this meant. Later, I was able to see that I could also possess some of these mysterious magic powers.

In 1961, I went to the New School where Professor Mary Henle, a follower of Max Wertheimer was the doyenne of gestalt psychology (GP). RK advised me to study with her. I became her top student and assistant but soon learned she was not interested in Perls. She considered gestalt therapy (GT) to be a blasphemy. As one of the few (including RK) who studied with both Henle and Perls, I took on the challenge of exploring how GT was related to those ancient gestalt theoreticians.

In October 1978, I wrote to the *American Psychologist*, the first time a serious mention of Perls appeared in this journal. My point was that GT is not an exact derivative of the work of the gestalt psychologists, but as Paul Goodman wrote to W. Köhler, GT is not irrelevant to GP, but a contribution in that psychology. Richard now rejects the idea that GT was influenced by GP.

During my first week teaching at Stockholm University, a young fuzzy bearded wild man from the North strutted in. I don't recall if he was wearing furs, but he should have been! After five minutes he yelled, "This is not gestalt!" and stormed out. Apparently, he had been influenced by one of the "circuit riders" — RK's term for some therapists, often from California, who fly into Europe to lead weekend workshops, use aggressive emotions to achieve "instant breakthroughs" which cause introjections, and in many cases, future work for me when the short-term "transference cures" wear off.

There were many "little Fritzes" running around at that time, adding to the myth that gestalt therapists assault patients' defenses with sadistic thrusts, following no principle or guideline, other than the need to dominate. This, as I pointed out in the *Swedish Journal of Psychological* in 1973, is more the personal expression of a particular therapist than any inherent rule of the gestalt method. But still, there are unshaven pseudo-gestaltists imitating the style of Fritz the Guru, without his substance, which is, of course, an introjection of him as an authority figure.

I have met many gestalt therapists in Northern Europe; few have any awareness of Perls' "chewing exercise." RK insisted that this was the most powerful tool in GT's armory. Difficult to do, therefore, it is often neglected. As the head of a Swedish anorexia clinic, I found the gestalt chewing exercise to be crucial. An article I wrote about this work, *On Anorexia,* was published in the *Swedish Medical Journal* in 1992.

It's been a long, fantastic journey from New York City to Stockholm. I often return to take part in RK's groups, recharging my batteries. I leave you with his keen admonition to keep in mind the limitations of our knowledge and ability — perhaps what therapists need is humility to balance (in RK's words), "...the arrogance that we can make a difference in their lives."

Sheldon Litt, Ph.D. *has trained professionals in Northern Europe for more than thirty years. He taught at universities in USA and Scandinavia, following years of study at the NYIGT. He is the author of one book and many articles and is currently living in Stockholm, Sweden.*

sheldonlitt@yahoo.com

Regarding Richard

Karen Humphrey

"Excitement and growth" is part of the sub-title of our foundational text, *PHG*, the bible that Richard Kitzler whittled at for years. He was the big hound baying in pleasure, his nose to the ground while we, the rest of the pack, yipped and ran to keep up. Richard's excitement when on the track of a developing intellectual trail has organized the New York Institute for Gestalt Therapy for much of its history, certainly since its reorganization in 1988. His excitement, a glittering attractant, gives the lie to the split between thought and passion.

Richard gave his heart to our text, *Gestalt Therapy: Excitement and Growth in the Human Personality*, by Perls, Hefferline, Goodman (*PHG*). He taught from it with a pleasure more commonly associated with aesthetic or gustatory experience. When he finally came to understand that seeming contradictions in the text were inherent in "Goodman's flawless argument," he fell out of love. His disappointment was massive. I came to understand that what I had taken to be intimidation by Richard's "arrogant" style, was really an anxious wish not to be the cause of such profound disappointment. Without his excitement, it seemed the sun was eclipsed.

Perhaps there is a lesson here, because Richard not in thrall to Goodman, has become a focused scholar, channeling his excitement into the longer patience required to explicate his thesis. This thesis, at its simplest, is that gestalt therapy is firmly supported, but differently supported than commonly assumed, at its theoretical base. Further, gestalt therapy, theory and method, forms a bridge between modern and postmodern philosophical and psychological thought. He began where Goodman began with Aristotle, trying to wrap all of western intellectual history in the confines of a paper delivered at a meeting celebrating Laura Perls' eightieth birthday. In the aftermath of his re-evaluation of Goodman's text, he started a deconstruction of our easy acceptance of gestalt psychology as fundamental to our developed theory. With less love lost in this pursuit, he fairly quickly demonstrated the areas of inadequacy generated by the gestalt psychologists' determination to mime physics' certainty. It was not the end of a love affair, but still it left a void.

The sun returned with Richard's "accidental" encounter with George Herbert Mead. The American pragmatists, and especially William James, have proved (thus far) worthy of this affection. Once again, we are the beneficiaries of Richard Kitzler's intellectual excitement as an organizing force of our growth. Appetite and excitement tempered by experience.

He embodies the radical holism of gestalt therapy, mind and senses inseparable.

Karen K. Humphrey *is a Fellow of the New York Institute for Gestalt Therapy. She has been a member since 1962. Currently, she is pursuing an interesting cross-fertilization of gestalt therapy process/field theory and phenomenological performance theory.*

khumphrey@verizon.net

Breathe, He Said

Carl Hodges

I had asked him what was the answer to my problems, my insecurities, my anxiety (I was twenty-nine).

"Breathe," he had said. And I knew he was a charlatan, a phony, a snake-oil salesman.

Of the six therapists I had "interviewed" so far, he was the most irritating from the moment he had opened his door.

His place was so White. The fireplace with the crystal on the mantel, those layers of oriental rugs, the antiques, and all those paintings of the English countryside, the seascapes, and the prints — all screamed out a non-verbal message of: "I am White and upper class." (Later, I would learn he grew up in the oil-refinery town of Elizabeth, New Jersey).

And him: tall, red-haired, and erect, in modern metal-rimmed glasses, a crewneck sweater, khakis, and penny loafers.

I also noticed, however, the dust-balls rolling across his floor like sagebrush across the prairie.

"Your mother had obsessive concerns with cleanliness?" he half-asked, casually blowing his cigar smoke toward some imaginary target on the ceiling of the session room. Already, *my mother*, I thought to myself; I haven't even had time to roll out my usual introductory remarks yet. He would have none of it, and continued to bring us back to the here-and-now.

I told him about his *White thing*, his *Gay thing*. "I'm not your ego ideal," he stated with no sense of guilt whatsoever and blew more smoke.

He also asked me if I was interested in doing an experiment. He invited me to shut my eyes (on him), to breathe, to have a fantasy. My fantasy was of a journey where I was my own guide on my own adventure. I forgot about him, until I "returned"…and found him there, present with me. There and here all along.

My "irritations" were compelling: I decided to give him another chance and two weeks later returned to begin therapy with this Richard Kitzler. He had an annoying way of re-casting my "constructions" into his terms, and into my own experiencing and creating.

After about a year in the therapy, I came to a session one day and complained, "I feel more comfortable every place else now, but not here!" He smiled, took a puff from his cigar, and said emphatically: "Good! Then at least *here* there is still a chance for you to grow."

The Black/White issue kept coming up, and tired of me being tired of hearing his White experience of Blackness, he invited me to close my eyes, breathe, and find my "own blackness," the center of it, the core of it. I did: it was the center aisle of the church built by my great-great grandfather where my great uncles and aunts were deacons, ushers, teachers, where they sang and prayed and found their strength and pride and stubbornness. From that core, that bedrock, that deep place in me, I spoke my voice to him, to me, to all.

When our first baby died, the devastation and sorrow were monumental beyond words. In the session with Richard, at some point, he left the room and returned with two antique crystals, fragile and eternal, holding Laphroaig. And I, too, felt held: in the darkness, in the silence, in our breathing, in our tears.

After reading *PHG* line by line several times in Richard's study group, I wanted to learn more about gestalt psychology and it was he who suggested that I take Mary Henle's course at the New School in NY. Richard had studied at the New School with Henle (Köhler's assistant), with Arnheim, Wallach, Asch, and Schutz (Husserl's assistant), had read Gurwitsch, and was one of the few people I knew who had actually graduated from there.

This became an embarkation point for my interest in gestalt field theory and its application to groups, organizations, communities, and diversity. It was certainly part of the foundation for the unique group process that is so much identified with the New York Institute. We did not always agree. There have been shouting matches in the streets, but we seemed to always ask each other the hard questions that would lead to the next steps.

"And why *can't* you go to England? Breathe, please."

So Kitz,
For all the times you gave me ground to make the next step;
for being inextricably and inexplicably part of my life;
for being there, and here, all along,
my thanks, my gratitude, and my deep appreciation.

Love, Carl

Carl Hodges *was the second President of the New York Institute for Gestalt Therapy, following Laura Perls. He is in private practice, does supervision and training, teaches periodically at the Gestalt Centre London, and has taught at the Istituto di Gestalt in Italy, Hunter College, and Fordham University.*

CWHVOSGE@aol.com

A Riff on Working
with Richard Kitzler

Lee Zevy

> *RIFF: a melodic phrase, often constantly repeated, forming an accompaniment or part of an accompaniment for a soloist.*

There was always beauty, style, elegance and genius when the study group met in Richard's office on Wednesday afternoons. Sprawled on the antique Oriental rug, gently perching on a Seventeenth or Eighteenth Century chair or sinking deeply into an old couch amidst the dust of antique objects and paintings, we listened to Richard reading a text. Words, language and meaning are to Richard Kitzler as air is to breathing and gestalt therapy theory is to practice.

In the early 1970s, a small group of new therapists came up the metal and marble staircase, one flight from Pat Kelley's practicum, to Richard's office in an old Chelsea brownstone to learn theory. Some of us arrived via Identity House, a new concept of peer counseling and psychotherapy for gays and lesbians designed by Pat and others on gestalt therapy principles. Pat was also a Fellow of the New York Institute for Gestalt Therapy and a close friend of Richard's. He graciously donated his office downstairs and we began to counsel clients and study. Identity House found larger space nearby, and a number of us moved into the neighborhood to be near Richard and Pat, joined the NYIGT, and a community was born.

For many years, we read Perls, Hefferline and Goodman's *Gestalt Therapy: Excitement and Growth in the Human Personality, Part II (PHG),* as the text. We sat, so to speak, at the master's feet with Richard reading each word and the punctuation. We studied the old-fashioned way, learning taking place on the cellular level. We studied the founders, the poetry and elegance of Paul Goodman's writing, the therapeutic artistry of Fritz Perls' and the intelligent and somatic wisdom of Laura Perls.

Questions from the group would elicit stories, stories would form experiments and in turn, awareness. Everything brought examples from Richard's life and his seemingly unlimited knowledge of literature, psychology, philosophy, history of the Institute, art on the walls or early period chamber pots. Everything was grist for the learning of theory and practice.

Although he did not suffer fools easily and could be critical, Richard had infinite patience when it came to working with any of us as clients or the group itself. His specialty was always to focus on the small experiences that build to a body of awareness. In addition, he had infinite faith that if opportunities were available, growth would occur. He eschewed therapeutic techniques in the belief that experiments arise out of the work if we are trained to co-create them.

In one famous example, he asked the women in the group if they would create a birth canal for a member of the group who was particularly bloodless in his energy and demeanor, so much so, that no one wanted to touch him. Richard first worked with him for some time on building awareness of his body and breathing and then encouraged this man to physically experience on his skin and organs, the pressure of these caring walls.

When *PHG* had been digested sufficiently, Richard's attention moved backward toward the beginnings of philosophy. He read Aristotle and the Greeks to us. Moving forward period by period, we examined each philosophic theory in relationship to gestalt therapy. Simultaneously, the

Institute was changing and as the leadership began dropping away, a vacuum emerged and Richard encouraged rebellion.

Now his students became the learners, teachers, and writers. Richard led us to Europe and the dialogue expanded. Under Richard's tutelage, the core concepts of *PHG* were re-examined and then revitalized by scientific presentations and the study of other theories. As we became a teaching/learning community, our membership expanded widely and after much coaxing, Richard joined others to write and publish his continuously evolving ideas. The room was the same, Richard still read the texts and discussion became extraordinary.

Richard's gift to us is his loyalty to gestalt therapy coupled with his continuous yearning for knowledge and the scope, depth and adaptability of his thinking. In the 1990s, he turned his dissatisfaction with gestalt psychology as the foundation of gestalt therapy and looked to the pragmatists and other philosophers for a more meaningful foundation.

Richard is always the soloist who announces the theme, yet absorbs the melodies that follow. Playing back to us a new theme or an old theme with a new twist, we still have the privilege of accompanying him in the song.

Lee Zevy, LCSW, *is a full member and Past-President of the New York Institute for Gestalt Therapy. After graduating from Fordham School of Social Welfare, she trained with Richard Kitzler for many years, eventually becoming a colleague and friend. She has been in private practice as a gestalt therapist and teaches, lectures and writes on gestalt therapy topics. Six years ago, Lee received her certification in Integral Coaching from Ventures West.*

lzevy@verizon.net

On Richard's Seminar

Joe Lay

Any collection of Richard's papers could not adequately capture his genius as a mentor, therapist and scholar. While his papers trace his experiencing, learning, and changing over a thirty-five year period, unfortunately, they only hint at his process of thinking/learning/teaching which is far more lively and fun. Richard writes seriously, with occasional puns and high-level sarcasms, to a highly selected audience who are expected to expend time and effort to understand his ideas. (This is no more effort than Richard himself expends as he often reads relevant philosophical texts four or five times and selected pages dozens of times.)

Richard's written phrases and words are carefully chosen and are occasionally deliberately poetic, with an example or two of creative syntax used to convey a precise meaning. They are excellent monuments to a particular place and time in Richard's own curiosity, growth, and integration of novel ideas. In contrast, his weekly seminars, while also serious, are gossipy, witty, provocative, supportive, and frequently turn into group therapy. They are also a weekly window into his own curiosities and development.

I first joined Richard's seminar in the fall of 1972 and have been in the weekly seminar for twenty of the last thirty-five years (with time off for grad school and a long-distance relationship). There are six or seven others who are long-term members of this community. What keeps us coming back year after year? I will give a personal answer. Principal structures of the group are readings that are explicated line by line in an almost Talmudic fashion.

For many years, we read the theory chapters of Perls, Hefferline, and Goodman (*PHG*). It was only through these repeated readings that I (and others) began to grasp a working knowledge of gestalt therapy theory. (Richard's last note to himself indicated his nineteenth line-by-line reading.) The theory chapters were supplemented by other chapters from Paul Goodman, Fritz and Laura, and the early gestalt psychologists. We also read Rank and Harry Stack Sullivan.

Richard, however, was never satisfied with the philosophical grounding of our theory. After a few years, we began a many years' long study of relevant philosophers. These were also often read line by line with commentary and discussion. At Richard's direction, we read Whitehead, Husserl, and Heidegger. Then back to the Greeks: Socrates, Plato, Aristotle. Forward to commentaries on the Greeks: McKeon and Randall. And most importantly, the American pragmatists: William James, John Dewey, George Herbert Mead. There were commentaries and biographies of these great men. As is the nature of true scholarship, one set of readings would lead to another. Even now, there is no end.

To give you a hint of the real nature of those meetings, I pulled down several journals (from a shelf of notes) and settled on Fall 1984 to Summer 1985, and will lift a few anecdotes from that time. It was a difficult year for us. AIDS was beginning to take a toll. Patrick Kelley, a Fellow of the Institute and a downstairs neighbor of Richard's, had recently died. Some of his furniture was temporarily stored in Richard's apartment. Michael Altman, a member of the group, was living with HIV. During these months, Richard and his partner were in complex real estate negotiations to buy a block on Eighth Avenue between 16th and 17th Streets.

Different than his writing, his regular Wednesday seminar is an intellectual/experiential free-for-all. First the setting: the walls of the living room in his New York apartment are floor-to-ceiling paintings and furnished with a baroque overstuffed couch and chair which sit close to the floor. At various times, other pieces of furniture come and go, most significantly, an over-scale Georgian sofa now in his office. Oriental rugs are three-deep on the floor. Richard loves auctions and often buys and sells. So part of the fun is discovering what has disappeared and where is the latest haul.

Papers are stacked on the tables and floor. Light pours in from two large windows overlooking the street. Richard, in sweater and wool hat, ambles in with a 16-ounce Pyrex measuring cup of tea and plops in the Baroque chair, seat low, knees high. He adjusts his glasses and scans the room, getting an intuition of the group. After some challenging banter, he begins the Johnny Carson monologue, usually some reading with the subtext of how could someone write something so stupid, or so obvious, or so failing in awareness.

Richard searching through the stacks: "Where is that book?"
Young Member of Group: "There, second from the bottom."
Richard: "There is a use for youth. They know where things are."
Young Member: "They know where other people's things are."
Richard: "Yes (smiles), and that is the instinctual theory of youth."

Reading the Times, "Says we're going to clone a mummy soon ... (grins)."

Richard, lamenting his neighbor, "The man next door would play lovely classical music, Chopin, etc. But since the fire, he's flipped. He now plays only pop music of the *Smoke Gets in Your Eyes* variety."

Richard had a motel in Key West and there was always good gossip: "He was a decorator with good taste. He stole three lovely urns from the Key West Cemetery."

Richard described his elderly father, "He's all the world like a dog with his muzzle out the window. To get out of the house and find a moment of sanity, my stepmother buys groceries a piece at a time in different stores."

To a Group Member: "You look ten years younger. Isn't this marvelous! Only a Christian martyr could have his life in shambles and look radiant."

Richard: "Congratulations on your beginning, middle and end (of a minor flirtation). It often lasts only a few days. You may not believe it but I've known whole families who have been in love for weeks."

Gestalt Gossip

Fritz and Jacob Moreno at the Psychodrama Institute mutually influenced each other although Fritz would deny it. Once Fritz, Moreno and his wife, Zerka, were at a conference together. (Richard was there.) Zerka was the principal speaker. She was amputated at the wrist. At the end of her talk, Jacob Moreno jumped up, held up his wife's arm and said, "Give her a hand." A hand was the one thing she didn't have.

"Fritz is reported to have said that therapy is a combination of brains and despair."

On Therapy and Therapist

"Based on the therapist's shortcomings, the therapy reaches an impasse. This is a false proposition. Correctly stated: Based on the therapist's aware shortcomings, there are new important opportunities for experiment."

"Therapist must be both inside and outside the values of society."

"For the artist, failed creativity means the loss of immortality. Living begins to feel like dying. There we have the notion of immortality as the basis of neurosis."

Patient: "I'm falling apart here in therapy."

Richard: "Good. Let's try to do it deliberately now. Let's see if we can do it with awareness and creatively. I won't let anything too difficult happen. I'm in control." (Of course, the patient will become quietly furious.)

Richard: "In your work in therapy, you will routinely feel elements of unreality, major segments will not come together. You will feel — and this is OK because you have been taught it — that this is a catastrophe. It is not. This is a part of the process of reintegration and is to be expected."

Group member: "I have this new patient who will just fall silent."

Richard: "Yes, the patient falls silent. After some time has passed, describe the quality of the silence, the tone, rhythm, density of it, your hunch about it, and that they may creatively sink with it, and that you will attentively wait. Then wait."

"The nothing is not merely nothing, but a creative nothing."

"One of the most obvious qualities of a paranoid person is the flatness of affect as they describe their persecutions. The immediate job is to find a way for them to include their suffering."

"Is it the purpose of psychotherapy to creatively sabotage?"

"This therapy may be unique. When do you ever have the experience of sitting with philosophers who believe a theory and then apply the same?"

On Our Own Group

Richard: "How to explain the ongoing life of the one who is no longer here, but is yet present ... Pat Kelley is dead, and yet he is here. The field is ongoing. The empty chair is not merely a chair and it is not empty."

Group Member: "That was not made clear."

Richard: "That was not made explicit. It was made clear."

"The authority problem here is called 'sweeping under the rug.'"

"There is often this phenomenon of premature resignation before real defeat."

Following question after question from a group member, "I feel like I am on a rolling ball and falling backwards."

Richard: "People are stressors."
Michael: "Cats are stressors."
Richard: "Cats are people. In fact, what is not a people?"

On His and Our Relationships

Richard to Visitor: "Where did you get your tan?"
Visitor: "It was given by heaven."
Richard: "Yes, from Puerto Rico. That, of course, is where all the angels are."

"I can go on for weeks and not see an interesting human being. I might as well be on a desert island. The minute Paco (his long-term partner) arrives from Key West, Friday's footprint appears in the sand."

Richard to Group Member: "What do you do these days, now that the lover is gone?"
The group member mimed masturbation.
Richard: "Motion carried."

"An eternal law: For one to live, the other has to die."

"When I asked Sammy (a lover), why he let them do that, he echoed an old sentiment, 'One would like to be put upon every now and then.'"

"It's a rule of existence: You always give in order to get."

On disciples, "Their job is to make things their own. But from their betters, they quickly meet the equivalent of the Circumlocution Office."

"When you can make a complete ass of yourself with utter equanimity, then you have reached adulthood."

In going through my notes, I realized there were many, many quotes from both high and low cultures. Richard is encyclopedic in his range of literary and cultural knowledge. He makes no distinction as to time period. He seems always in constant dialogue with the larger human family. They are all alive for him. In the interest of brevity, I will not give the quote but give a partial list of his sources:

Martin Luther, Loretta Bender, Carson McCullers, George Washington, Hemingway, Voltaire, Dr. Johnson, Mary Henle, Jimmy Walker, Louis XIV, Anatole France, John Stuart Mill, Ruth Benedict, Mark Twain, Shakespeare, W.C. Fields, Plutarch, Ford Maddox Ford, Descartes, Cervantes, and the lyrics of various operas and Broadway musicals, and many others.

It is my (and others') great good fortune to know a mentor of such great ability and resources. At eighty years old, Richard still fills his day reading the philosophers, thinking/doing theory, engaging in therapy, and cruising the avenues. He is still someone to admire. I never expected it all to be so much fun.

And to give Richard the last word (which he manages to get in any case):

Caller: "Promise me you won't change."
Richard: "I won't change."
Caller: "Promise me that I will always be in your thoughts."
Richard: "That will be a change."

Joe Lay *has spent his adult life within the New York Institute for Gestalt Therapy community, except for a few years away to complete a Ph.D. in Clinical Psychology. He has served as President of the NY Institute as well as President of the Manhattan Psychological Association. His interests have included community building, couples therapy, Daoism, Buddhist philosophy, political activism, and group therapy. While also owing a great debt to Laura Perls and Isadore From, Richard Kitzler has been Joe's primary mentor since 1972, and he thanks Richard for his inspiring scholarship, his sharp insight, his warmth, his humor, and his rigorous approach to teaching gestalt theory.*

joelay@earthlink.net

His Influence on My Work, His Contribution to Gestalt Therapy

Perry Klepner

Richard has been my therapist, teacher, colleague, friend, creative artistic muse, and supporter. Hence, he's had many influences. From our first contact, he helped me appreciate seeing and being seen. His respectful, if not intimidating gaze, and discerning response to my experience, and our struggles in therapy with confusion, anxiety, hope, despair, loving and being loved, taught me valuable lessons in the power of support, recognition and contact.

Richard prompted me to explore the vantage point of an elevated horizon where my perception was supported and fueled with experience, and possibilities loomed. I could know where I was located beyond my ground, make choices and take directions not previously possible. This, along with his championing his own opinions and precepts of courage, along with breath in the face of mounting anxiety, contributed to my discovering and inventing my own entitled voice and faith in creative contact as a person, client, student, therapist, teacher and colleague.

Richard's presence, bearing, and creative ideas in theory/practice inspired my own aspirations and values. I found guidelines for practice in his sensitive probing analysis of our unfolding process; his relying on the experimental method, structured analysis, aesthetic criterion, support, truth, and love; and, perhaps most powerfully, his abiding respect for the integrity of each individual in his/her unique creative organization of experience. As a teacher, he conveyed valued lessons in patience preceding with word-by-word analysis, openness to new ideas, persistence examining confusion, and abiding belief that interest and creative inquiry will lead to beneficial learning.

His brilliance and courage in following his creative impulse inspired my writing/presenting on contact and its interruptions, process groups, intimacy, and awareness. He modeled the leader exemplar as a scholar, equal member, supportive colleague, teacher and student to his pupils; and championing the novice in learning and the minority viewpoint in organizations. He was inspirational conveying his appreciations for art, music, poetry, language, philosophy, aesthetics. He demonstrated "contact" that I could aspire to by his talent, integrating his self/other experience in gesture, glance, thoughts/ideas, evoking a deep pathos of feeling, thinking and insight.

Contributions to Gestalt Therapy

Richard's contributions to gestalt therapy have been seminal and are pervasive. As a client of Fritz and Laura Perls, and an associate of Paul Goodman, Isadore From and other founders of gestalt therapy, Richard has been a provider and guardian of gestalt therapy's oral history. As a Fellow of the New York Institute, he has been a guiding force in its development; the principal trainer-supervisor of its leading members and responsible for developing its worldwide membership of accomplished practitioners.

He has illuminated theory/demonstrated practice at conferences worldwide. Early on, he fought against those who would hybridize gestalt therapy by integrating it with other approaches or minimize the contributions of Paul Goodman and Laura Perls and the comprehensive theory presented in *Gestalt Therapy* (*PHG*). He argued for a radical conservative perspective — radical in the sense of proceeding from the foundation or roots of gestalt therapy, while preserving what is fundamental and conservative by applying detailed examination to guard against uncritically adopting new theory. His influence is seen today in the emphasis given to critical review of gestalt therapy theory; in the recognition of basic theory presented in *PHG*, even as gestalt theory grows beyond it; and in the continuing attention and interest in the contributions of Paul Goodman and Laura Perls.

His written works are powerful and inspirational in their depth of understanding, his unique vision, and scholarship. They have a special quality of being not only illuminating but in their syntax, lyrical poetic style, reference and affective expression provocative of feelings and thoughts streaming together. The influence of his written work may be hampered by his telegraphed associating style and encyclopedic reference. His papers require concentrated reading and rereading. Their full value has not yet been realized. In particular, I would cite his most recent work, *Ontology of Action, 2006,* which provides new insight into the theoretical ground of gestalt therapy's phenomenology, and extends its theory by new connections to the psychological field outside of gestalt therapy.

Richard was an early proponent for a gestalt community which led to the organization of the Association for the Advancement of Gestalt Therapy, AAGT. He was a strong voice formulating its egalitarian principles and valuing the minority perspective. While shunning leadership positions, except for chairing the Braking and Watchdog Committee, he has been a supportive private voice to its leadership and a public vocal voice to its membership to aggress conflicting viewpoints so contact could be made, an association forged.

Richard has long been involved in developing the theory/practice of gestalt therapy in groups. His *Gestalt Group* is an important contribution to gestalt group therapy literature. At the New York Institute's Groups Conference in 1991, he introduced the "process group" as a way to utilize gestalt therapy principles in small and large groups. He introduced process groups to AAGT where they became a valued approach to understanding and integrating the emerging novelty of the conference, fostering new orienting, learning and a community in contact.

I end these brief comments with regret as a more comprehensive review of Richard's contributions is beyond the scope of this critique.

Perry Klepner, MBA, LCSW, *is a full member and Past-President of the New York Institute for Gestalt Therapy, 1993–1995, where he studied with Laura Perls, Isadore From and Richard Kitzler. He is in private practice in New York City and Kingston, NY, providing training, supervision and individual, couples and group therapy. He has been on the faculty of several institutes and is consulting psychotherapist to the Bard Graduate Center, NY. He has written papers, authored articles for the Gestalt Journal, and has made numerous conference and workshop presentations in the U.S. and abroad on gestalt therapy including intimacy, contact, aggression and conflict.*

Perry302@aol.com

The Pearl in the Oyster

Gail Feinstein

We are seated at our favorite bistro. I notice that we're comfortable and easy with each other. There's an excitement knowing that we're about to embark on one of our preferred pastimes. We wonder if the Malpeque's or the Prince Edward Island's or the Hama Hama's are the freshly shucked oysters being offered tonight. "You order the wine," he says. I'm fairly familiar with this extensive wine list that is void of pretense and I'm glad to make the selection. I am moved by his trust in me and I savor the moment.

As oysters are an acquired taste, so too, my relationship with Richard took many years of unfolding, developing and cultivating.

We met in 1978 at the institute. I'm young and impressionable. Across the room, I see a strikingly handsome, elegant and postured man. He is extremely articulate; I barely understand a word he says. I attribute this to being a beginner in the gestalt world. I'm struck by his intelligence and find myself intimidated by him. With a mixture of repulsion and attraction, I know I want to train with this formidable man.

He greeted me at his door, poised and contained. As I enter, I'm surrounded by art — loads and loads of art. There are three rows of paintings on the walls and some are resting on the floor. Maria Callas is singing in her colorful and dramatic style and a Louis XVI chair sits in the midst of it all. I'm overwhelmed — too much to take in at once (just like Richard). I must slow down, pause and take time to chew and digest the wealth that is before me. I sense Richard's joy in the beauty of his paintings and music and antiques; and most especially, gestalt therapy. I want to stay connected. This extraordinary man has much to teach me. I wind up spending a lot of time here and learning even more.

The turning point in our relationship came one night at an institute meeting many years after we first met. When I simply ask Richard how he is, he quickly responds in an intellectual, tangential manner. This being familiar, I feel frustrated. I decide not to let him off the hook this time. I repeat the question, "I just want to know how *you* are." He grabs the arms of his chair with both hands, digs his feet into the floor, pushes back and exclaims how he always feels backed into a corner by me because he knows when I ask him how he feels, I am really interested in knowing. With assistance from our astute colleagues, Richard and I flesh out our interruptions and de-structure the projections and introjections. I'm greatly relieved to be doing this meaningful work together.

Thus, our visions clear and deeper layers are revealed. I could always see his brilliance and wisdom; and now, I see his vulnerability. He is no longer just my mentor, trainer and colleague, he is my friend. We have traveled a great distance together and our relationship continues to blossom. I'm so grateful. Richard is a gem with abundant riches to offer.

He holds a significant portion of history of our gestalt community and often shares stories. Once, while I was complaining to him about my struggling with preparing a presentation, he said to me, "Ah, yes, my dear, Paul (Goodman) always use to say the 'agony of erudition' is well worth it." I could finally get what a great fan Richard was of me; and the women of the institute — especially the Women's Caucus, the group that changed the shape and course of our history. He was/is so enthusiastic, supportive and proud of us.

With my new clarity, he has become an inspirational presence; one that sees beyond the usual and demands that of me, too. He has a special ability to perceive my talent and beauty, my essential nature; and encourages me to be sharper, wiser and bolder. He challenges me to welcome what I do not know and to see for the first time, more than once.

I am one of the fortunate people who have gotten to know Richard. And in so doing, I am deeply rewarded by touching and being touched by his gentle soul, and his tender and noble heart.

I have found the pearl in the oyster.

Gail Feinstein, LCSW, LMT, *is a student and lover of gestalt therapy. She practices in New York City, co-creating with groups, couples and individuals. She is the Past-President and currently, on the faculty of the New York Institute for Gestalt Therapy as well as other training institutes. She has also taught and trained in Europe, Canada, Mexico and Australia. Her practice includes supervision, training, workshops and retreats. She splits her time between city and country living; loves gardening and creating visual and ritual art.*

Ursa Luna@aol.com

Richard Kitzler, A Generous Supporter and Friend

Sylvia Fleming Crocker

The time was the early 1980s and the place was Cape Cod. I was attending my first Gestalt Journal Conference, having only recently begun the process of becoming a gestalt therapist. Just as I was finishing my presentation of a dramatic method of doing gestalt dreamwork, I heard an unfamiliar voice coming to the front of the group, clapping and saying, "For the first time in twenty-five years, I've seen something new that is pure gestalt!"

I had no idea who this person was, although he spoke with an air of authority. Of course, I was immensely flattered by what he said and, naturally, I wanted to find out more about this person, Richard Kitzler and I learned that, indeed, he was (and still is) an important person in the gestalt community.

The reader can imagine how I must have felt at being affirmed and praised by such a person since I had only recently entered the field of gestalt therapy. I saw myself as a "nobody from nowhere," Sylvia Crocker from Laramie, Wyoming. I could hardly believe that I had anything I could contribute to the field, and yet here was an important person telling me what I had demonstrated was both "new" and "pure gestalt." That was the beginning of my good friendship with Richard. Richard has encouraged and supported me ever since we met, even telling me when he read an early draft of the book I was writing, "Don't let anyone or anything stop you from writing this book!"

I always feel somewhat inferior to Richard's intellect and knowledge. Sometimes I don't understand some of the things he says to me, and yet, he treats me as a peer. I'm still awed by that fact! And yet, I think that in many ways Richard and I share a common vision about what-is, how human change happens, what constitutes living well, and the contributions gestalt therapy can make, not only to those persons who come to us for help, but to the field of psychotherapy itself. And thus, we are kindred spirits.

When I used to entertain doubts about myself, way out in Wyoming without colleagues to talk with about gestalt therapy, Richard's support and appreciation gave me the assurance and the courage I needed to keep stretching out into the field. He has been a wonderful and generous friend to me and many others, and I am deeply grateful to him. He is a marvelous man!

Sylvia Fleming Crocker, Ph.D., is a gestalt therapist, trainer and author, living in Laramie, Wyoming. She trained with Miriam and Erving Polster and at the Gestalt Therapy Institute of Los Angeles in both Los Angeles and Europe. She has Masters Degrees in Comparative Religion and Counseling, as well as a Ph.D. in Philosophy. She had authored numerous articles in gestalt journals and a book, A Well-Lived Life: Essays in Gestalt Therapy, now in its third printing. She is currently writing a book on dramatic gestalt dreamwork.

CROCKERSF@aol.com

In Gratitude

Stella Resnick

Though I've spent most of my adult life since graduate school in California, I moved back to New York City in the fall of 1974 for just two years while my mother was fighting cancer. I was already a gestalt therapist, having studied with Fritz at Lake Cowichan on Vancouver Island in Canada. At that point, I had also taken a number of trainings with Laura at the San Francisco Gestalt Institute where I was on the training faculty. Laura did a professional training there once or twice a year and, as I was sharing a house with Elaine Kepner at the time, we had the good fortune to have Laura stay with us and to share some personal time with her.

When I told Laura I was coming to live in New York for a while she invited me to join her weekly study group and to attend the New York Institute for Gestalt Therapy meetings. I gladly accepted. That's how I met Richard.

It was not an easy time for me, and to be frank, I don't remember many details. I remember meeting Richard then, along with Bud Feder and Dan Rosenblatt. What I recall most of Richard during that period was how straight he stood and what a wicked sense of humor he had. He had a formidable presence and I felt strangely shy and deferent towards him. But Richard was to endear himself to me forever for the kindness he showed me at the meeting in Chicago where the Association for the Advancement of Gestalt Therapy was born.

I had been trying for years to get accepted to do a presentation at the only annual gestalt conference that was then being offered. Year after year, though I was well known for my writings and seminars on gestalt therapy, my proposals were consistently turned down. In 1989, when a gestalt conference was being held at the Congress Hotel in Chicago and my presentation proposal was once again rejected, I was determined to attend and I contacted Jo Lief who was running the Gestalt Institute of Chicago. Jo was delighted to have me and arranged to sponsor me for both a public talk and a professional workshop. That paid my expenses and made the trip worthwhile, especially since an article on my public talk appeared the next day in the Chicago Tribune.

Maybe that was what emboldened me at the gestalt conference the next day during the Town Hall meeting. The focus of the discussion was the question, "What can we do to restore interest in gestalt therapy?" We were all aware that gestalt was not enjoying the popularity we once had and people were raising their hands and offering suggestions as to how to promote awareness of the value of this work. I thought our problems went deeper.

When my raised hand was recognized, I stood and said that I thought our predicament was a reflection of a lack of collegial warmth and inclusiveness among the different gestalt centers, and that since I left the San Francisco institute I myself had felt shut out. I thought that we should heal our own larger community and that perhaps a new spirit of connectedness among ourselves would make us more welcoming to others. Unfortunately, my comments were summarily dismissed. I sat down feeling like a fool.

Suddenly, a hand from behind me squeezed my right shoulder. I turned to see Jim Kepner in the seat in back of mine, nodding a silent approval. I reached back and touched his hand in gratitude. Down the row of seats to my right, Judith and George Brown leaned forward to catch my attention and Judith raised both thumbs and smiled. I was not as alone as I feared. A little further down the row sat Alan Schwartz who suddenly sprang to his feet in support of my remarks. At that point, a powerful energy swept the room. I was amazed at the bottled up feelings that were suddenly released as people started to corroborate my observations.

I was appreciative for the unexpected acknowledgement, but it was when Richard raised his voice in my support that I felt like I had hit the jackpot. Richard stood in the back of the auditorium and in a commanding voice intoned, "I, for one, am grateful to Stella for her courage in speaking up. She's absolutely right and whoever else wants to express their gratitude, let's meet her in the back of the room and give her some hugs." Wow, I went from the depths of being a *persona non grata* to the heights of acceptance — getting a hug from the once intimidating gestalt giant, Richard Kitzler. From that time on, Richard has occupied a permanent place in my heart.

For several years, there had been talk about creating an independent gestalt organization but nothing had been done up to then to implement its establishment. With the passions stirred up in the room, someone else rose and said, "All those who want to be involved in creating a new gestalt association, let's meet in the Lincoln Room. After receiving my hugs, I blissfully floated off to Lincoln Room where I joined a good forty or so committed gestaltists to participate in the birth of what was to become the Association for the Advancement of Gestalt Therapy (AAGT).

With his commanding presence, Richard Kitzler's imprimatur bestowed valued legitimacy to our gestalt fledgling, AAGT.

Stella Resnick, Ph.D. *is a clinical psychologist and body-based gestalt therapist in Beverly Hills, California specializing in couple's therapy, relationship issues, and sexual enhancement. She is the author of* The Pleasure Zone: Why We Resist Good Feelings, *a Past-President of the Western Region of the Society for the Scientific Study of Sexuality, and an AASECT Certified Sex Therapist and Clinical Supervisor. She trained in gestalt therapy with Fritz Perls at Lake Cowichan on Vancouver Island, B.C. Canada and with Laura Perls in New York and San Francisco. She has written magazine and journal articles, and chapters for books on gestalt therapy, including an early cover story article on gestalt therapy for* Psychology Today *magazine. Her work integrates attachment research, sexual health, and embodied gestalt therapy. She can be reached through her website* www.drstellaresnick.com.

StellaRes@aol.com

My Mentor

Ruella Frank

It seems an impossible task to pay tribute to my mentor, Richard Kitzler, in just a few paragraphs. In order to best do so, I decided to write of our first meeting. Just as gesture holds the greater meaning of the moment — the first words exchanged between two people often reveal the general feeling tone of what is and what will be.

It was the winter of 1987. That previous fall and just after graduating from a four-year gestalt training program, I joined Laura Perls' Tuesday theory/practice group. Working with Laura opened me to the incredible beauty of gestalt therapy and I wanted more.

According to several group members whom I respected, studying with Richard Kitzler would provide a good next step in my learning. I was told he was brilliant and quirky which both excited and intimidated me. At that time, I was the most junior member of our group and I thought, perhaps I might need a better understanding of theory before I studied theory. In truth, I wondered if I was smart enough to study with someone so smart. Mustering my bravado, a useful substitute when supports are not available, I called Richard and made an appointment.

A week later, I was at his doorstep ringing the downstairs bell. Once inside his building, I climbed a spiral staircase replete with black lacquered banister and red carpet and landed at his door. With as much aggression as necessary, yet as little as possible, I knocked. Richard, tall and handsome, welcomed me, and gracefully led me to a small, dark room whose walls were overwhelmed with paintings, and whose furniture and floor were covered in piles and piles of books, magazines, and journals.

Richard seated himself in a high back regal-looking chair, which was angled to the front and side of a small sofa whose springs were long gone. Having cleared away several pens, a huge dictionary, a few old newspapers, a crumpled throw and even a spoon, I removed my shoes and sat cross-legged at the sofa's edge.

Richard looked at me for what felt a long while, took a deep inhalation, gently placed his hand onto his chest, exhaled slowly and asked with great authority, "Picasso! What period?"

"Blue," I smiled, "his blue period."

"Yes, of course," Richard said.

It wasn't so much a matter of Richard seeing me so immediately and so clearly that invited me to him. Rather, I just loved his audaciousness. To be so wonderfully inventive and bold in the moment — I knew I had met my teacher.

Ruella Frank, Ph.D.*, has been exploring early infant movements and their relationship to the adult since the mid-1970s. She brings many years of experience to her work as a gestalt psychotherapist; professional dancer, yoga practitioner/teacher, movement educator, and student of Laura Perls. Ruella is Director of the Center for Somatic Studies, a faculty member of both the Gestalt Associates for Psychotherapy and the New York Institute for Gestalt Therapy, also teaches throughout the United States and the world. She has written numerous articles and chapters in various publications, and is the author of a book, <u>Body of Awareness: A Somatic and Developmental Approach to Psychotherapy</u>, which is available in four languages.*

ruellafrank@nyc.rr.com

"Pusillanimous Twaddle"

Charlie Bowman

> *Pusillanimous: lacking courage and resolution: marked by contemptible timidity*
>
> *Twaddle: something insignificant or worthless*

This is a phrase only Richard would use in conversation. He first expressed it in an AAGT community meeting when, I believe, he felt the community was trending towards premature pacification of a conflict! It could refer to "making nice," for instance. Several of us grew quite fond of the phrase after he uttered it!

I have received several such gems from Richard over the years that illuminate his character in a way I feel privileged to witness. I was the third President of the Association for the Advancement of Gestalt Therapy (AAGT), an organization to which Richard is attracted more than I suspect he will admit. During this period of remarkable struggling, fighting, growing and general turmoil that marked the early years of AAGT, I was persistently at wits' end. The harder I worked, the crazier the organization became. More factionalized, more parochial and political, with too little support for too much aggression. I can feel re-traumatized at the mere recollection!

Richard and I grew fond of spending social time together during AAGT gatherings and we found ourselves drawn to many of the same workshops, if not the company of the same barkeeps. I experienced

83

enough support to begin to pour out my dilemmas and trepidations regarding the exasperating and boundless job of AAGT President. With exquisite timing (that which defines one's experience of contact with Richard), he offered, "My dear Charlie, the President presides." That sentence was peculiarly reassuring. The more I dwelled upon this idea, the more my need to control everything melted away and was replaced with a sense of witnessing that was truly relieving. Of course, I understand that Richard's support in that moment was more meaningful than his words.

During the planning of AAGT's First International Conference in New Orleans, Richard and I worked on the plenary session *Generations in Dialogue*. We worked hard on this plenary — more so than I had anticipated because Richard insisted on the process design flow from the theory of gestalt therapy as presented in Perls, Hefferline and Goodman (*PHG*). This was exactly what I wanted and why I wanted to work with Richard on the project.

Long before my attraction to Richard led me to a friendship with him, I was deeply interested in the study of *Gestalt Therapy: Excitement and Growth in the Human Personality* (*PHG*). After reading the book three or four times, I joined a peer study group and we mimicked what we understood to be the New York Institute for Gestalt Therapy's method of studying the text. After another year of this, I started leading study groups for graduates of gestalt training programs. I thought I knew the book and the theory reasonably well. Of course, my upcoming study with Richard would redefine "reasonably well."

For several months, we collaborated on this project. I would suggest that dialogue might flow in a particular way and Richard would suggest otherwise, backing up his ideas with Perls, *et al*, text, chapter and verse. I offer the following recollection, accurate in spirit if not content.

"Richard, if we set up the plenary session in this fashion then the issues will surface between the generations … it will become interpersonal," I said.

"If you will recall, Charlie, we are not as interested in the interpersonal as we are in field disturbances and the contact boundary," Richard proclaimed. "We're saying the same thing, Richard, 'interpersonal' and 'contact boundary' are ways of expressing the same idea," I said with certainty.

With finality, Richard suggested, "If you are familiar with 'Conflict and Conquest — Section 2,' you will note that the contact boundary is more fundamental than intra or inter." End of discussion. Sure enough, he rendered the essence of the transcript practically verbatim.

If you know Richard, you likely don't see that as remarkable. What I found remarkable was that these conversations often took place late at night while I was on the road calling from my bread-box sized "mobile" phone (it was 1995). He didn't have the text in front of him and he would at times excuse himself to go get it (I assumed more for comfort than for accuracy). Further, he would recall from one session to the next those theoretical issues I had struggled with, how that was applicable to the task at hand, and usually a comment as to the disturbance in me leading to my misinterpretation of the text.

I had mixed responses to such rich teaching. As I have matured, and these teachings have settled, what I am left with is the generosity of the man who took the time to walk with me through very difficult intellectual and emotional work while standing our ground, with Richard neither refusing to compromise his knowledge or integrity nor settling for less than the very edge of my capability.

Charlie Bowman *is Past-President of AAGT, Co-President of the Indianapolis Gestalt Institute, and a gestalt therapist, trainer and author. Charlie is Director of Verizon Communication's Work/Family programs and maintains a small gestalt therapy practice. He and his wife, Ann, live in a quiet town in mid-America where he enjoys time with five children, four grandchildren and his Harley.*

aagt1@sbcglobal.net

In Richard's Presence

Zelda Friedman

My friendship with Richard is an immeasurable gift, both small and large, not frequent, yet continuously reliable, honest, loving, assuredly mine and consistently life-affirming. In other words, ours is a gestalt friendship.

I came to know Richard through gestalt events and conferences and later, I found my way to the New York Institute for Gestalt Therapy where I saw him more regularly. In the beginning, we were both active in related committees when the Association for the Advancement of Gestalt Therapy was coming into being. Richard and I shared in the effort to have the theoretical, philosophical and political implications of gestalt therapy inform the creation and ongoing nature of the association.

At a point in this history, I was asked to take over the chairmanship of the Philosophy and Purpose Committee. Within a few hours after I said that I would, I found myself unexpectedly expected to facilitate a meeting of that committee in a large room where we met along with many other committees, to be followed by the chairpersons reporting for their committee to the whole. I did as best I could, listening and attending to individuals and group interaction above the whirring soundlessness of my anxiety. I jotted down a few notes and said what I could to the large assembly the sense of our group at the time: that gestalt ideas were not welcomed openly in institutions which were the surround of our lives, and how much gestalt had to offer to that surround that could not hear us.

The next day, Richard came to me in passing and said, "I liked what you said yesterday, and I especially liked your quaver." This moment between us is the core of our friendship. In Richard's presence, I stand between knowing and not knowing, affirmed as I am and so freed to try more, learn more, and say more. In this spirit, I offer my appreciation of Richard and the treasure of his work that you hold in your hands!

Zelda Friedman has been a gestalt therapist for over thirty years. She is a member of The New York Institute for Gestalt Therapy and of The Association for the Advancement of Gestalt Therapy — An International Community. She has written and presented on Gestalt Theory with a special interest in its political aspects and its relevance to feminist issues.

zelnorm@aol.com

I Want to Reach You, Rich

Margherita Spagnuolo Lobb

(The most convinced "outsider" I've ever met)

The first time I met you was at the conference dedicated to Isadore From which Joe Wysong organized in Boston, 1996, where I gave a keynote speech. Soon after my speech, you came forward to make a public comment. You approached me from the left side of the audience, and from the way you arrived at the microphone, it was clear to me that your style was that of an outsider. So I said: "Oh, an outsider!" And you replied: "Always!" One of your comments to me was: "Thank you for that beautiful moment of silence!" It was love at first sight.

From this beginning hence, there was the music of your words; yet I couldn't understand much of what you were saying. Still, I appreciated the melody of your music and I could get some of your speech. Soon, I got in touch with your content, the nuances and depth of your speech.

In the meantime, you met me: you have been the first and probably one of the very few who read the content of my first *International Journal of Studies in Gestalt Therapy*, and understood it, although it was written within a very different culture from America. Rather complex and pregnant with meanings, it was difficult to understand fully, even for psychotherapists of the same culture.

You immediately understood those articles and supported them at the NYIGT. Thanks to you and to those who joined you in that interest, and a fruitful transatlantic dialogue between our two institutes started. You nominated me for full membership in the NYIGT, and I am proud to be such a full member today. You understood that the work that had been done in my institute in Italy was a hermeneutic one, and that it was important to include this work within the NYIGT. I believe that both the institutes have gained from that.

Finally, I came to meet your fragility more fully, and to appreciate you for it. It's not that you don't show your fragility. You do it well with nonchalance as an ingredient of your upper middle class intellectual style. I mean that I got to know it better. There is a moment in your meeting the others when the event is full of your sophisticated, deep and flying discourse, when it would be obvious that you could keep the energy of the moment and bring it forward towards a co-created completion.

But in that moment, you seem to surrender the central position that you have gained. You simply don't keep your energy while you intentionally lose your ground. So your figure is never grandiose, rather it is always critical of yourself. Your eyes are continuously wide open to see incongruent and humorous aspects of others' grandiosity. It seems that at that point, you purposely sacrifice your possible and obvious emergence as an enlightened figure. I have always wondered why.

Is it an act of generosity that leaves the ground to the other? Or is it an attempt to demonstrate that anything, including you, is vague? Or is it your way to be coherent with the core political principle of gestalt therapy by embracing minorities as you avoid becoming an icon? Or is it rather because you feel compelled to repeat a relational pattern where you disappear at the end? I don't have an answer. In some way, it seems to me that to have an answer would be impolite. However, it's clear that this is your fragility and consistency at the same time. It's your style.

Our meeting has been beautiful and incomplete enough to let me hope for more interesting things that could still happen. (For instance, I could see your needs better, besides our intellectual chats.) There are enough secrets between the two of us that might be discovered, and this makes our friendship alive.

I have a beautiful picture of you in Palermo (during the Sixth European Association for Gestalt Therapy Conference in 1998) standing in the night in all your length, with your arms wide open in the posture of a huge embrace. You seem to embrace the whole world, singing. I like your capacity to embrace the world — meaning everybody and what they feel — from the position of your intelligence and grace. I wish to continue to be hugged by you as you have always done in our relationship. I wouldn't mind if you allowed yourself to shine in front of me without diminishing yourself in the best moment of any meeting, and this — I'm sure — wouldn't disconfirm my richness or that of the others.

That's why I want to reach you, Rich! I want to reach you, Rich, in your richness.

Margherita Spagnuolo Lobb is the Director of the Istituto di Gestalt HCC Italy, since 1979, and an international trainer and supervisor. She is a full member of the New York Institute for Gestalt Therapy. Former President of: European Association for Gestalt Therapy (EAGT), Italian Association of Psychotherapy Methods (FIAP), Italian Association for Gestalt Therapy (SIPG). Editor of the Italian journal, Quaderni di Gestalt since 1985, and Co-Editor (with Dan Bloom and Frank M. Staemmler) of the International Journal Studies in Gestalt Therapy, Dialogical Bridges. She wrote about one hundred articles and chapters, edited a few books, one with N. Amendt-Lyon titled <u>Creative License: The Art of Gestalt Therapy</u>, is now translated into German, French and Italian.

training@gestalt.it

Going Toward the Quarter

Eric Werthman

> *My present field of consciousness is a centre*
> *Surrounded by a fringe that shades insensibly*
> *Into a subconscious more. I use three separate*
> *Terms here to describe this fact: but I might as*
> *Well used three hundred, for the fact is all shades.*
>
> *And no boundaries. Which part of it properly*
> *Is in my consciousness, which out? If I name what*
> *Is out, it already has come in. The centre works in*
> *One way while the margins work in another, and*
> *Presently overpower the centre and are central*
> *Themselves.*

> — William James

These days it goes pretty much like this: Werthman ascends the steps of one of the four exits of the 14th St. subway station at 7th Ave. Like his mentor, he has resigned himself to giving up coffee so he searches for a non-herbal but decaffeinated cup of tea. Only the local diner provides what he needs and hot cup in hand, Werthman goes the familiar two blocks, makes the familiar right turn, and walks a quarter of the way up the block to 140 West 16th St. Werthman has been making this same trek to visit Richard Kitzler since 1981.

He presses the bell for 2E and waits. In the beginning, Werthman waited longer then he does now. Over the years, he has come to understand that Richard was either in the back of his long apartment making himself a Rob Roy, or trying to end a phone call that irritated him, or fussing about in his Bowery-furnished bathroom, which is what always made him seem a bit tardy in ringing the buzzer.

That is to say, in July of 2007, he answers promptly. There are no more Rob Roys. The phone doesn't ring as much and the bathroom is just one more necessary bore. Richard has probably been sitting in his living room. The daily pages of pragmatism, usually no more than three at a time, sit next to him on the couch. In the old days, he probably sat in his "consulting room," with faded towel over the cracked leather of his chair, the cracked window pane behind his head, the piles of books scattered around the floor, reminiscent of W.C. Fields' office in *Never Give a Sucker an Even Break.*

In the old days, that is where we usually sat together, but now we are out front in the living room. Many of the paintings and some of the furniture have been sold off. There have been financial difficulties of late. An old trusted lover and partner has behaved badly. He is still behaving badly. But Richard fights off his bouts of depression: "Look at it this way: who else gets to begin again at eighty? This is a great opportunity." How else, short of suicide, can one look at it?

We discuss the news of the Rialto by way of the NY Times. The schemes of the political class always give us great pleasure. I may recount a recent "adventure" or offer up a case for his supervision, which in turn, may make for some speculations on his part. But it usually comes down to something that I have said that sends his arms reaching to the floor, then a book appears in his hands and the pages are turned, the paragraph is found and he begins to read. In the old days, it was "Dr. Johnson" (as Richard always referred to Samuel Johnson) and/or Paul Goodman and then, very much better, Alfred North Whitehead. Sometimes, it was Aristotle or Immanuel Kant, but in recent years, it was either William

James or George Herbert Mead, or a secondary text on American pragmatism. The next three hours were spent on these pages.

Somewhere around 9 or 10, we decided that dinner was in order. In the old days, we would stroll the boulevards: into Chelsea, or over to Houston street, or descend into Soho all the way to Grand. Another kind of conversation would take place then: bawdy, romantic, tough, ribald, grandiose, tender, sensual: down-in-the-gutter or high in the aesthetic hemisphere, and always, always hilarious: Hal and Falstaff, Stephen and Bloom (and who was who?) wandering through the "parade" of the Nighttown. But I will return to all that a bit later.

We are still in the living room. In the old days, when we sat in the small "consulting" chamber, the work was always about cases and my reactions to them. Sometimes, I dispensed with the cases, and the sessions were about me. He would do little tricks like telling me my mood from the way I rung the doorbell to the sound of my footsteps coming up the stairs. I thought that was really hot shit. But now, in my 66th year, I can do it, too. It's a way of dazzling clients, but I do it very rarely, partly because I don't have the self-confidence that Richard has.

In comparison to other supervisors, I was struck by his disinterest, at least at first, in the history of the client. When I went into the usual information, "he/she was born in and grew up in etc., etc.," the pained expression on his face stopped me cold. "Just tell me what happened in the last session?" Richard was after what he called "the structure of the situation": What did the client look like, how did he sit in his chair, how was the rhythm of his breathing, how did he speak and then, finally, what did he say? And conversely, the same questions were asked of me, until the two of us had created the context in which the session was taking place. From this context, Richard would put together a biography of the client that was extraordinarily accurate (there were few times that he would miss) and I would fill in the details I thought were germane. But a lot of the extraneous information so beloved of "casework" was put aside.

This was in contrast to Isadore From who insisted much of the time that he couldn't make an accurate "clinical" description (in gestalt terminology) of the client because he just didn't know enough information. In fairness to Isadore, he certainly was able to make accurate observations about Werthman, albeit in that world-weary sigh that always seem to imply how commonplace I was, but I found it all loveable since it always felt like a style that he created very early: See Christopher Isherwood's letters.

You could say that Richard's insights about clients and the "situation" of the sessions was part of that illusive definition of "talent" that combines hard knowledge with intuition. I prefer to think about it more as the painful consequences of his upbringing. This is not the space for a biography of the young Richard Kitzler...*Portrait of the Genius and Grand Master Psychotherapist as a Young Man AND Dog*...but the near constant humiliations of his youth. An indifferent lack of support from anyone in the family for his intelligence and the growing realization of his bisexuality in the Singer Sewing Machine dominated working class town of Elizabeth, New Jersey, helped create a man who had to be very careful, and very guarded (this is the 1930s), in order to survive at all.

There are tales, many of them excruciating to listen to, but for our purposes here, it is not the content of the tales that is important but what the young-therapist-to-be was to make of the human heart and all the vast and loveable, but more importantly, self-deluded, unaware (and aware), devious ways the heart has created to make human beings act in the way they do. All this knowledge went into his "insights" as a supervisor.

Since he knows I am trying to write this memoir, he asked if I might specifically write down a piece of supervision he did (over the phone) about a client who had called me to tell me that the open window in her living room was "calling her" to jump. She lived on the top floor of a 6-story apartment house. I had recounted this supervision at dinner during Richard's 65th birthday celebration but he wanted me to write it down.

I was just in my second year of private practice when a troubled but very intelligent client called to tell me that she was sitting in her apartment staring across the room at her window trying to ignore what the window was saying to her, but finding the window's clear voice very seductive and attractive. The voice seemed to be calling her into a place of warmth.

Shaking, I asked if she could hold out for a short time, and she assured me she could. She wanted to be "called back" in both senses of the phrase. I called Richard feeling quite unsure what to do but sure that I would get the answering machine. I had had a number of cases in the clinic of clients who heard voices but those cases had been in a place where I had instant support of colleagues and hospital backup. In my private office, I felt very alone.

I guess there is a God after all: Richard picked up. Very carefully, he suggested an experiment that I could do over the phone. His suggestion felt very bold to me and I was not sure whether I could do it. I was also not sure whether I believed in the experiment. But I had nothing else. She was still sitting across from the window when I called back.

What I asked her to do, after making sure that I had her permission every step of the way, was to imagine herself walking to the window. I asked her to describe as fully as she could what she saw and what she experienced. I asked her to see if she could be on the ground in front of her apartment house. Then I asked her if she could imagine herself standing on the roof of her apartment house. After she completed this work, I asked if she could be on the ground again. She said yes. Next, I wanted her to stop and look into the windows and describe what she saw and what she felt at every floor she passed on her imaginary journey up the outside of her apartment house.

She described the people she saw and the activities they were engaged in, what she "smelled" and how she felt at each window. I always made sure that she "felt done" with each floor before she went on to the next one. This was a point that Richard paid special attention to: "Don't rush!"

he'd say (which is a variation of Laura Perls' patient work of creating support for awareness before moving onto the next stage.)

As she moved up the apartment house, her voice went from a spacey, trance-like quality to a clearer, stronger tone. Passing the final window, she landed on her feet inside her living room. She felt enormously relieved. I asked if she wanted to come in to see me that night but she felt strong and we scheduled for the next day. I felt enormously relieved.

The experiment made tangible and therefore available what the fear, engendered in my client by the windows "command," had frozen. Though the voice of the window had offered relief, the idea of a "final peace" had struck unaware terror in the body of my client. Correction: not totally unaware. She had made the phone call. Of course, all the held in unaware background (or at least, some of it) was released to the surface and made aware during the experiment.

I placed a call to "my supervisor" since he claimed a rooting interest in what might happen.

His supervisions were filled with detailed examinations of small parts of sessions backed up by gestalt theory. He encouraged us to try together most of our suggested experiments for clients. A close friend of mine, who was in therapy with Richard, told me that half the time, he would have to end the session himself since they would go on for so long he would be late for his next appointment.

***

Now it was time for dinner. The points under discussion had been exhilaratingly discussed. The page of George Herbert Mead had been exhausted.

> *When one of them moved through the marketplace of Selefkia*
> *Just as it was getting dark-*
> *Moved like a young man, tall, extremely handsome*

With the joy of being immortal in his eyes,
With his black and perfumed hair-
The people going by would gaze at him,
And one would ask the other if he knew him,
If he was a Greek from Syria, or a stranger.
But some who looked more carefully
Would understand and step aside;
And as he disappeared under the arcades,
Among the shadows and the evening lights,
Going toward the quarter that lives
Only at night, with orgies and debauchery,
With every kind of intoxication and desire,
They would wonder which of Them it could be,
And for what suspicious pleasure
He had come down into the streets of Selefkia
From the August Celestial Mansions.

— C.P. Cavafy

On those early summer nights of long ago, with a slight breeze blowing from the East River across town to the Hudson, Richard and I strolled down the avenues looking with aesthetic approval and occasional lust at the near naked bodies of the Empire City. Richard showed no gender bias when it came to "buns." Men and women equally caught his eyes. Alas, as Joe Lay once said to me: "Eric, you are hopelessly heterosexual," and so my attention tended to focus on women's legs: sometimes sleek and slender, sometimes magnificently muscular, sometimes white with slight outlines of blue veins running down the thigh, or a rich, earth colored brown with barely perceptible light colored hair reflected in the glow of the street lights.

In Richard's early thirties, he closed his practice and made the long desired trip to the land of his intellectual foundations: Europe. It was the common practice for intelligent, gifted, alienated young Americans in the first half of the Twentieth Century. But after a first trip with Pat Kelley, replete with Moroccan boys and a few meals with Paul Bowles, Richard went alone.

Sitting in the public parks or on benches facing the wide boulevards of the Cities of the Plain, dark, mysterious cars would pull up to the curb. A chauffeur would approach. Usually a gentleman of considerable wealth sat in the back seat. The discussions with the chauffeur were not about "trade." It was obvious that the man seated on the bench was a person of some distinction. One look at Richard's passport photos of the period offered explanations for these situations.

In the corridor just off the kitchen in Richard's apartment is a photograph of a man dressed in a black cape smiling mysteriously at the camera. His old world good looks slyly emerge from the black and white shadows. Mariano de Montis, a descendant of the Renaissance Pope Julius III and oldest heir to a family that acquired the island of Ibiza from Phillip II, was a formidable painter with a large family. Richard's lovers have always tended to be married men. Near the end of the bliss of their union, Richard, momentarily tired of the island life on his beloved Formentera, had made for a small hotel in Barcelona.

Mariano was devastated at Richard's sudden departure and the messages he sent to Formentera produced the hotel's name. Traveling by overnight ferry, Mariano arrived at the hotel desk demanding to know the room where "Dr. Kitzler" was resting. Unfortunately, due to Richard's familiarity with the hotelkeeper, Richard had neglected to sign in so the poor clerk at the desk had no record. The clerk was also a professional and not allowed to show the registration book to strangers. Mariano's voice rose, exasperation apparent in his tone of voice: "a kingdom for my..."

This entire racket awakened Richard who happened to be in a room on the floor above the desk. He recognized the voice. He was not sure he wanted to deal with a near-crazed lover but he felt sorry for the poor clerk. As he walked down the stairs, he heard Mariano proclaim that he had had enough of all this ignorance and would simply buy the hotel and find Richard himself. How much was the man asking? When Richard reached the desk, Mariano's checkbook was already on the counter.

By this time, Richard and I had reached the row of restaurants on 6th Ave. between Bleecker and Houston Streets. We had once split a $200 bottle of wine in one of these establishments and it was quite good. Agreeing we were not yet ready to sit down to the table, we moved on further into the outer reaches of Soho. Richard gently pushed me to the outside of the sidewalk. He never walked on the curbside. If one of us was going to die by some crazy out of control car, it was not going to be him.

To our right, we saw the marquee of the Film Forum. I had pushed Richard to see the director's cut of *Rocco and His Brothers* because I knew he liked to look at the young Alain Delon, but what really interested him in the film was that the Italian family that had migrated from Sicily to Milan were part of the same group of Italians who had settled in Richard's hometown, Elizabeth, New Jersey. ("Growing up, I just followed the 'guineas.' The guys had sex with women and then with each other in the back of the poolroom.")

One Friday night, at his insistence, we had seen *The Big Sleep* with the supplemental alternate scenes. We agreed that the actress (cut from the original version) who played the wife of Eddie Mars had just the right look and attitude: blonde, regal in a proletarian way, and surprisingly tender. A few years later, for obvious reasons known to people who have seen the film, we saw *The Conformist.*

My favorite Richard story: Somewhere in Europe, Richard had met Charles Briggs and his companion, Raul. Briggs was the heir to one of the automobile tire fortunes in Akron, Ohio. His family had bought him off with an income if he promised to move from the States and stay on the continent. Charles insisted Richard must visit the Palazzo in Venice across the canal from Peggy Guggenheim's. The arrangements were made.

A gondola picked Richard up on the docks and brought him down the Grand Canal. Just as Richard saw the number of the palazzo from the water, a gate opened and the gondolier steered the vessel through the watery hidden passageway to Charles' front door. There was live music for dinner (shades of Kierkegaard's banquet) and young men serving. Richard admitted to me the conversation was boring…"Where would we go next season?   Should we live in San Remo instead, or possibly Capri?" They liked that Richard was a psychologist.

Before dessert, some young man, barely dressed, danced for the dinner guests. Richard was sure that he had finally cast his eyes on Antinous, the tragic, young lover of Hadrian who had been described by Marguerite Yourcenar in her novel. *The Memoirs of Hadrian* was beloved by both of us.

Slipping off the boat into the water in the middle of the night, because he had feared, correctly, that Hadrian was tiring of him, Antinous had let himself drown. Hadrian was devastated by the suicide. Statues were erected in Antinous' honor in every part of the empire. ("This is what you can do if you have money," Richard would say). I actually saw one of these statues in the waiting room of Tolstoy's house in Moscow.

The evening came to an end. Richard retired to his bedroom in the palazzo amid the antique furniture and expensive art that hung on the walls. He was awakened from sleep when he heard the door open. Softly, but quickly, "Antinous" tossed the blankets aside and slipped into Richard's bed. The dancer had all the moves.

"That is one I'll never forget," Richard smiled as we made our way down West Broadway. "Of course, after I left, I am sure they pumped the boy for information. How was I and all that? Charles and Raul, now he was something, came to New York once. I showed them around. The city was too much for them."

On Grand Street, we picked a restaurant with a small staircase that put the restaurant up a bit from the street. We also liked the statue of Toad from *Wind and the Willows* that graced the entrance.

There was a woman in Formentera. She had a son and daughter and for two years, Richard was a father. The woman still lives in Spain and some years ago, Richard received a letter from her son who was now a barrister in London. The letter was one of the most beautiful I have ever read. Her son wrote that he had asked his mother for Richard's address so he could finally communicate to Richard what Richard had meant to him after all these years.

Of all the men his mother had been with, Richard was the one the son remembered most fondly. He was the one who had given the child books, encouraged his pursuits and supported him when he felt troubled. The young man had never forgotten Richard and all that Richard had meant to him. The prose style of the letter was impeccable. As for the mother, well ... a woman for Richard was finally insupportable.

The restaurant was only half-full giving us a chance to stretch our legs. In those days, Richard drank wine and Werthman drank Scotch as they talked about the New York Institute, the people in it, Margherita and Giovanni, and Richard's great friend, Joe McCrindle, who had nothing to do with gestalt therapy, and so on into the night. Somewhere in the conversation, Isadore From appeared.

After Isadore's death, his ghost seemed to mysteriously hover over Richard. The more he brooded about Isadore, the angrier Richard seemed to be. When I started attending Institute meetings, Isadore From was one of the two other master gestalt therapist-teachers in the Institute. Laura Perls was the other. They were all geniuses together but, alas, only Paul Goodman, whom I met only once in a 1960s political context, could be said to be a writer.

Of Laura, Richard paid only the highest compliments (though she told me once that she could be quite terrified of Richard herself. I didn't tell her I didn't believe her. Richard later said to me, "Why didn't you?") Between the two men, Richard and Isadore, there had always been great theoretical differences. When I started attending Institute meetings, Isadore appeared only sporadically and then stopped going altogether.

I only heard from others about the exhilarating arguments the two of them used to have. Joe Lay and Dan Bloom both told me that the highlight of their month was coming to meetings to see the two men wage theoretical battles. What everyone learned!

After the meetings were over, many of the assembled crowd went out for drinks. Richard and Isadore could be seen laughing together over wine far into the night. But Richard was never comfortable in Isadore's house. He sensed that Isadore seemed embarrassed in his presence. Through the years, as Isadore grew intellectually smaller in Richard's eyes, Isadore's presence seemed to grow bigger in Richard's mind.

In this collection of Richard's essays, there is a critique of Isadore's actions and thoughts that sums up some of Richard's intellectual ideas on the matter. But there was a wound there, a hurt, which did not seem to go away.

Isadore was not threatened by Richard nor Richard by Isadore. They both were too intelligent for that. But the core of the differences between them was more than theoretical.

There have been many such wounds in Richard's life. Men and women who could not compete with his intelligence found him irritating or threatening in public and turned their back on him. I once said to him, "You don't understand that people don't know what you know." He was flabbergasted at first as though this thought had never dawned on him. And indeed, it hadn't. Of all the things I have ever said to him through the years, this was the one thing he was the most grateful for.

***

These were the men of NY:

Stunning Sammy, who I met, alas, near the end, his body ravished by drugs. I could not recognize the man I had seen in pictures. Richard created an altarpiece in his apartment and the candles burned for a few days...

Equally stunning Jose; Richard hung the black and white picture of this Puerto Rican man flexing his muscles on the wall facing his dining room for a while ...

Sweet, hopeless E: he still drops in...

Jim, the Karate master and businessman from New Jersey, now dead of cancer...

"The Writer," the one who deserted Richard. Much to his later regret, Richard had told Fritz not to touch that subject in therapy. The pain of his departure was the background for an infamous summer night in the forest behind the dunes on Fire Island. Feeling utterly alone, Richard had been first startled and then surrounded by a number of hands and bodies that moved to places that space or modesty does not allow me to describe. As Richard said of that night, "I realized I could be loved."

Paco... and the men of the night.

And then there was Pablo, whose body once lay twisted on the Brooklyn streets with his motorcycle on top of him while men from the bodega frantically tried to lift it off him. Years later, after visiting Richard, Pablo, unable to hold onto the stairway banister, slipped, his paraplegic body falling to his death in the foyer below ...

Key West... the sudden appearance on the beach of boyhood friend, Frankie Merlo from Elizabeth, New Jersey, the celebrated lover of Tennessee Williams. According to Maureen Stapleton, the one Tennessee should never have left. There were dinners with the great playwright, not all of them happy...A wonderful night spent pub-crawling with Tallulah Bankhead...

Captain Tony...and all the other denizens of Richard's sometime Southern retreat...the wonderful madness supported by Key Lime Village, the motel that Richard co-owned with Paco, where my family spent a wonderful week in the early 80s. Richard had a room reserved for him on the second floor of the main house. But Key West was for another night, another walk in the city.

At Grand and West Broadway, I hailed a cab to Brooklyn. Richard would walk back home alone. He did not take cabs. "The drivers were clearly unstable."

***

> *What interests me in any man is ... certain characteristics*
> *Which express not so much an individual personality as*
> *A particular relationship with the world ... The human*
> *Mind invents it's Puss-in-Boots and its coaches that change*
> *Into pumpkins at midnight because neither the believer nor*
> *The atheist is completely satisfied with appearances ... this book*
> *Is haunted, often in the midst of tragedy, by a presence as elusive*
> *And unmistakable as a cat slipping by in the dark: that of*
> *The farfelu ...*

— Andre Malraux

In the translator's footnote in the *Anti-Memoirs*, Terence Kilmartin explicates that one of Malraux's favorite words, "farfelu," was spurned by the major French dictionary, Littre and Robert, but was now in fairly widespread usage. The word's meaning was many: whimsical, eccentric, dotty, bizarre, and fey. Its etymology is obscure. Malraux used the word not only as an adjective but also as a noun. *The Baron Clappique of La Condition Humaine* is Malraux's most famous creation illustrating the word.

"From time to time" — pointing with his forefinger —
"A European minister sends his wife a little parcel
By post, she opens it — not a word..."
His forefinger to his lips: "...it's the head of her lover.
They still talk about it three years later!"

When I first met Richard Kitzler at the wedding of Charles Myzwinski, I had heard about him from others. Richard was there with Pat Kelley and because Pat went off to dance, Kitzler and I sat alone on the back steps of the Brooklyn Ethical Culture Society. If Richard had gone off to dance and Pat Kelley had remained on the steps, my life would have been very different. We talked for some twenty minutes. I had just gone into private practice and needed a supervisor. I called him later that week. He forgot our first appointment. Since I had been told he owned a fish market on 8th Ave., I walked down. Richard was cutting fish on the front counter.

From the first moments until now, I have always felt there was something of the farfelu in Richard. He struck me as so self-created that there was always a quality of parody about him. The parody sometimes made him seem foolish but he was always serious in the artifice. The farfelu was cunning and wary but extravagant in gestures and speech. The farfelu acted the way he did because the world as presented to him tried to disguise a hypocrisy he could not ignore since it was apparent on the surface.

As I was to find out, Richard as farfelu was a deep, extraordinary adventurer of the mind and a daring adventurer of the body. For all his guards, he was naked most of the time because he had nothing to hide. And yet, there was always the quality of a shade right at the surface.

***

On a recent July night in 2007, we dined round the corner. Whereas, once we would walk for miles, now our walk was reduced to blocks. Richard never finishes his dinner these days. There is always a doggy bag. I thought the take-home food might last him for a number of days.

We parted in front of the restaurant, kissing each other on the cheeks. I started for the subway but instead of descending the stairs, I kept on walking.

At Greenwich Ave., I turned East needing more time to think. Richard means as much to me as any man/woman I ever knew. He understands me in a way that allows me an extraordinary ease in his presence. Norm Fyuchter once said to me: "What will we all do when he is gone?" But because of who he is and how he relates to the world, combined with all time we have enjoyed together, I knew that I would continue to stand if Richard passed before I did.

Walking down 6th Ave., I turned left on West 3rd to stop and look in the front window of the Blue Note. In my high school years, this building housed the first striptease club I was ever allowed into. Dressed in my adolescent suit, I must have passed for eighteen just because the owners probably needed the money. Now I was walking up Bleecker St. past the NYU faculty housing towards Mercer St.

Whenever I'd worked with Richard, I thought he was a living demonstration of "stream of consciousness." As one thought was in progress, another thought intruded, sometimes in the middle of the first thought. One had to have patience to follow him, and I decided in our first meetings not to interrupt unless he used a word that I did not know. (Being respectful of my dyslexia, Richard was always extraordinarily kind and not exasperated when he gave me the meaning). The flow of his words and ideas, and sometimes images, slowly began to cohere as his meaning rose over the horizon.

Yet this infusion to the center from the margin was sometimes why he lost his place or forgot a name even though the person was sitting right in front of him. He'd say, "Where was I?" or "What's your name again?"

I walked down Broadway through the downtown streets of Soho. A stunning Asian woman passed me and I stopped to watch her turn down Spring St. Balthazar was still open. Two men laughed then hugged each other on one of the benches next to the entrance. Standing beside the take-out doorway, a black man with a gold chain around his neck pressed his thigh into a white woman whose skirt ended above her knee.

Richard's power is that he had showed me that one could live a life refusing the subjugating power of the received beliefs of our culture. But it was a struggle that had sometimes brought me to my knees. And then I'd get up and walk past "them" and go on.

For his companionship, I love him in a way that I feel for no one else.

Eric Werthman, CMSW, *is a gestalt psychotherapist living in Brooklyn, NY. He has been a member of the New York Institute for Gestalt Therapy for over 20 years. He was the Program Director of the Institute for about 8 years and the Director of the Kings County Counseling clinic for 10 years (1981–1991). Before that, he was a tenant organizer and social activist. Three years ago, his life took a detour and he made a 35mm feature film called* Going Under, *about a psychotherapist who has a relationship with a professional dominatrix. His film played at numerous film festivals and opened theatrically in three cities. The film is now on DVD and can be found in independent video stores (and NetFlix).*

ewerthman@aol.com

Later Photos

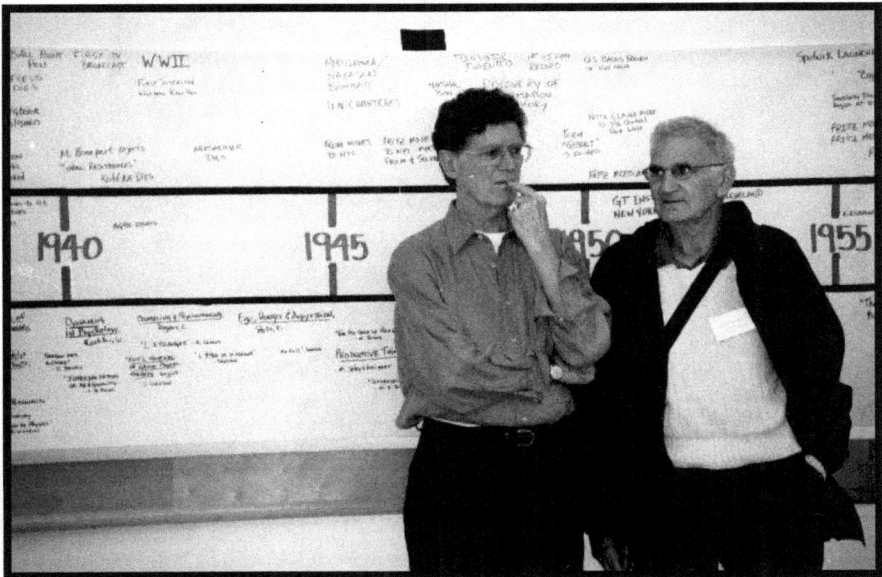

Richard Kitzler & Philip Lichtenberg standing in front of Charlie Bowman's gestalt history timeline at the New York Institute for Gestalt Therapy's Golden Anniversary Conference. New York 2003

Richard at Parthenon in Nashvile, Tennessee 2007

Dan Bloom, 2007

Richard, Renate Perls and Anne Teachworth
New York City 2007

**Richard at his 80th birthday celebration
November 2007, New York City**

Richard at home
New York City 2008

Editor's Note

Anne Teachworth

Richard Kitzler is my dear, dear friend and a superb teacher. I have absorbed so much wisdom from him that listing all of those instances would be another book in itself. It was this progressive enlightenment that prompted me to encourage Richard to collect his unpublished articles and allow me to honor him by publishing them in a book. Dan Bloom joined me in this quest and together we campaigned. *Eccentric Genius* is a culmination of our goal. You are about to venture into Richard's magical intellectual forest.

From the beginning of this project, my aim was to make Richard understandable to everyone … a mighty task considering that on my first read of his papers, I found most of his writings incomprehensible myself. I had to reread these articles a minimum of three times to truly value the full depth of Richard's immense philosophical wisdom and gestalt heritage. Many times, I needed to phone Dan to guide me back onto the pathways of comprehension.

Interestingly, I had not found Richard's teachings difficult to understand during the many hours he and I had visited together. Of course, when I was with him, I had exercised the luxury of interrupting him at any point to ask what a word or Latin phrase meant. Patiently, without ever a hint of frustration, he always graciously stopped and explained, responding to me as if I was a student he was teaching at Columbia.

Perhaps you will experience some interpretive difficulties as I did at first. But do take hope. I have gone through each article several times now, editing for your reading ease. However, since the joy of Richard is partly in learning his vocabulary, I have made as few changes as possible to the content of the text, concentrating in the beginning more on simply shortening his sentences. Shades of *Finnegan's Wake*!

Let me give you a few hints to help you find your way through the philosophical woods you will be entering. Richard uses many words that you may not understand on first read. Or second. Some of you may think them "typos" … they are not. Incidentally, my web guy, Phil Dodson, commented that "spell check" went crazy while he was formatting Richard's book. So we crosschecked with Google and Wikipedia and Dictionary.com. Surprisingly, we discovered each one was a real word. As a result, I chose to add a Lexicon at the back of the book for you, the reader, not as a projection defining your linguistic abilities, but as an admission of my own limitations, with which some of you might readily identify.

I take full responsibility for adding all the commas which I call "breathers," and also the periods which are "full stops." On my second read through, the commas and periods gave my inquiring brain enough of a pause to comprehend the depths of what Richard had written. "Breathers" were absolutely necessary as I travelled blindly along the road of his brilliant six-or-seven-line sentences, peppered with many, many semi-colons. Most of these I changed to "full stops."

These interludes were the lost-in-the-woods moments when I would have asked Richard a question had I been sitting with him in person, but he was not sitting here with me as I wandered on, only his words were. So I began the editing challenge alone, leaving a trail of bread crumbs as I went in.

My next editing adventure was to shorten the paragraphs and give the eye some wide-open space between philosophical insights. Whereas my Lexicon at the back of this book lists real words that only Richard knew the meaning of before this, it does not mention my favorite three words that he used in the text. These are words that Richard obviously made up when nothing else in his vast linguistic repertoire would do...namely, "thumpingly," "insidedness" and "outthereness." I choose to leave them in. After all, it's an editor's job to retain the author's true voice, isn't it?

As the editing progressed, I began to recant my earlier comma additions and began deleting many of my previously well-placed "breathers." Gradually with each read through, my capacity for enlightenment increased. I called Richard and Dan less as I began to hear Richard answering my questions in my head. I've always been mesmerized by William Buckley, Jr.'s orations, regardless of whatever he was saying. Richard's voice carries a similar hypnotic quality. At this moment, I am contemplating producing an audio CD of him reading *Eccentric Genius.*

Richard Kitzler is a wordsmith of the highest order, eloquent in elocution and yet somewhat overwhelming for an ordinary thinking/speaking human mind to comprehend. His is a truly extraordinary human mind. Dan Bloom appropriately named this book, *Eccentric Genius.* My mind was expanded by going deeper into the intellectual terrain of Richard's. I followed my trail of bread crumbs out. These articles are no longer a wilderness for me. I love this book. I hope you will have the same experience. I invite you to journey along with my dear friend, Richard, on the following pages.

Anne Teachworth *is Founder and Director of the Gestalt Institute of New Orleans/New York and Gestalt Institute Press. In private practice since 1976, she is now specializing in couple, parenting, and family sessions. In 1996, she wrote* Why We Pick The Mates We Do, *describing her own Psychogenetic System, a transgenerational approach to re-imprinting introjected interactional patterns. She is a Fellow of the American Psychotherapy Association and an Associate Member of the New York Institute for Gestalt Therapy. She was a student of both Laura Perls and Richard Kitzler.*

ateachw@aol.com

ARTICLES BY
RICHARD KITZLER

Never Surrender

We shall not flag or fail.
We shall go on to the end.
We shall fight in France.
We shall fight on the seas and oceans.
We shall fight with growing confidence
and growing strength in the air.
We shall defend our island, whatever the cost may be.
We shall fight on the beaches.
We shall fight on the landing grounds.
We shall fight in the fields and in the streets.
We shall fight in the hills.
We shall never surrender.

— **Winston Churchill, Prime Minister of England**.
His famous speech was given in the House of Commons, June 4,
1940, following the evacuation of the British and French Armies
from Dunkirk as the German tide swept through France.

Talk at Laura's Birthday Celebration

1985

Toward the latter part of the Eighteenth Century, a Reverend Dodd preached a sermon to his brother convicts and the Sheriff of Newgate Prison, the night before he was to be hanged for forging a bond on his former pupil, the Earl of Chesterfield.

The world doubted that a man in such extreme straits was capable of the composition. The friends of Dr. Samuel Johnson, "Dictionary Johnson," fairly certain by internal evidence that he had done the composition for the luckless clergyman, charged him with it. Johnson adamantly maintained Dodd had written the sermon, saying, "Depend upon it, Sir. If a man is to be hanged on the morrow, it concentrates his mind wonderfully."

In preparing these remarks, I frequently felt I was concentrating my mind, not wonderfully, and not before brother or sister convicts who wrote prior to their being hanged. This was the same Earl of Chesterfield who wrote the celebrated moral letters to his natural son. Johnson's remark on them was, "Sir, they teach the morals of a whore and the manners of a dancing master." Two qualities I did not feel in this preparation, having passed the embrace of one and abandoned the agility of another.

The Eighteenth Century was the high point of the English enlightenment — Galileo (not English) was born, and had already died by the time Newton was born in 1642. Newton's Law stating the relations of physical bits of matter acting on other bits of matter in space had transformed physics and philosophy. And philosophy, developing the logic of Aristotle's substance and thus, it's primary and secondary qualities in Descartes through the efforts of Locke and Hume, had teased the laws of cause and effect; materialism, simple location, subject, object, *res extensor*, *res cogitans*, time and matter, and determinism was awaiting the *Critique of Pure Reason* while it struggled with the curtain of the ideal that George Berkeley had set before the world.

That's the problem of the perceived without the perceiver, and, therefore, those endless trees falling in endless forests unwitnessed, endlessly silent, infinitely removed, all organized, and perceived ultimately in the great eye of God. I've wondered how a man felt, who'd climbed out his window, and looked in his room to see if he was still there. Reflection? Johnson, himself no small thinker and baffled by Berkeley's logic, asked by Boswell how Johnson would refute it. He responded immediately, "I refute it thus and kicked a great stone violently away," providing, as Boswell noted, a very portrait of Jean Bulle Philosophe vigorously asserting common sense intuition against airy metaphysics.

Boswell also stated in action, this split of *the vita activa, the viva contemplativa,* a great compelling life of the world, actor vs. thinker, theoretician vs. clinician. Newton, of course, would have none of this metaphysical nonsense, and since all his systems were go, spectacularly accounting for all that technology could so far predict or measure, he would, outside them, frame no hypothesis. And so, it more or less proceeded doer-less, mind and matter somehow interacting, a great one, somehow representing different aspects, according to some sublime cosmic harmony.

Now, this is unsatisfactory. Humans crave, by definition, to reach out for meaning, and the study of metaphysics, the study of beliefs about reality, epistemology, cosmology, onotology of being has been a source and solace of this craving. But if the great questions upon which practical life in the world remain irritating to common sense, a suspension of belief follows that teases the soul for more nourishing answers, and, of course, what science of mind or psychology merge, it's up for grabs. The individual scientist finds the theory he deserves, so to speak, on which to found his belief. In this case, I will later in all cases with belief, find the theory. But the bifurcation of nature was complete.

The survival aspect of Darwin's evolution to neglect the creative aspect, and the miracle of Nineteenth Century technology which practically completed the Newtonian Revolution, and sowed the seeds of its destruction as it pressed on, nudging the consciousness of the era to the acceptance of different ways of viewing nature. Particles, waves, electromagnetism, electrons, protons, quantum-relativity, and at last, the observer, and the observed included. There was a rebellion against the Newtonian fixity early on, from, of all places, the romantic poetics — namely, Wordsworth, the favorite of Paul Goodman's at the barricade. Personally, today, *The Intimations of Immortality from Recollections of Early Childhood* is an adequate source for an escutcheon on which is emblazoned a glory that has passed from the earth.

Alfred North Whitehead summarized the anti-position. "Nature gets credit for this romantic position, which in truth should be reserved for ourselves — the rose, for its scent, the nightingale for his song, the sun for his radiance. The poets are entirely mistaken. They should address their lyrics to themselves and turn them into odes of self-congratulation and the excellency of the human mind. Nature is a dull affair, soundless, scentless, colorless, merely the hurrying of material, endlessly, meaninglessly."

Whitehead was cogently insistent in his belief that the imagination and intuitions of mankind conquered all these transcendentals for the way of a philosopher, the way of imaginative realization. "Philosophy is the melding of imagination and common sense into its restraint upon specialists." Some gave imagination from the poetic insight of ours, as a source of the categories for cosmology from Process and Reality in 1929. Of course, process is reality or reality is process.

Michaelson-Morley had happened in 1887, Einstein in 1905. Absolute was out, and relativity was in. In psychology, the teutonisms of the just noticeable difference and scientific method as standard procedure, the death knell of philosophy, according to Whitehead, contrived more intricate and elaborate experiments in perception, sense physiology, animal studies, and so on. These were carefully designed to avoid contaminating the results by including the experiment, in spite of relativity, and based on the mental physics of associationists and reflex psychologists. A physics of the soul was, and is, established. Psychology snuggled next to science and begot its bastards.

Prior to the Whitehead's synthesis, Edmund Husserl developed phenomenology and the transcendental reduction or *epoché* whereby consciousness is elevated in all experience, admitted as intuitive, purely descriptively in all aspects, and deriving the relations of those possibilities. He criticizes the gestalt psychologists, who are beginning to publish at the turn of the century, for their insistence on "scientific principles in a demonstration of organization as given in experience not built up." Their method is itself, non-inclusive, in the phenomenological sense. This activity is at high-pitch in Germany, as a legacy of that country's triumph of specialization in its schools and industry.

But the professional concentration on a narrow field in experience building units of knowledge, resurges the narrowness and morals, that will drive its best unitary minds from it. Freud, the specialist/neurologist turned psychiatrist, who had admitted to the power of the unconscious through Charcot's "penis envy" as a prescription for its repressed sexuality, invents the physics of the libido and the reflex arc threshold of psychology conscious/unconsciousness.

The duality again is the struggle of the individual against the social represented in the censor as the libido pushes through its pipes and valves under more or less pressure with transference as the faucet. The libido speaks in the parables of the unconscious through the agency of the interpreter. The "talking cure" is born. So is Frederick Perls. With Laura Posner Perls, they publish their dissatisfaction with psychoanalysis.

In 1942, in *Ego, Hunger and Aggression*, their basic effort was to arrive at a unitary therapy based on the zero point differentiation to opposites through Hegel or Friedländer, itself a kind of dialectic from Plato, to a therapy that arrives at truth through the synthesis from previous positions prior to polar, thesis, or antithesis. The point being that no position is conquered, but only progressively moved to a new place, including the prior views now reduced. It is a kind of foreground/background analysis or view, one that was later so fateful to gestalt therapy.

The developmental theory of dental aggression is included "biologically." That's in quotes because Perls insisted on using biology imbedded in quotes to ground himself. He used it in many senses, one of which was confusing — as an organism which biologically bases the therapy. Perls will have no apparent truck with metaphysics or cosmology. Only a stasis from Cannon's organization, structure, field, wholes, part foreground/background are taken over from gestalt psychology.

Reich's amazing insights into the muscular character as he formulated it included the active ongoing activity of the ego self-expression, with more than and prior to defense, the logic of the here and now. All of this is translated to an active concentration method involving the unitary or holistic approach; self, social, biological, verbal, and non-verbal aspects within the unifying theory of contact, as more and more bound energy is released to a temporary zero point of meaning and peace and the aim — growth.

Frederick Perls is an adolescent with the horrors of the 1914–1918 War and the Iron Cross before him when Paul Goodman is born. Goodman's father abandons the family. Paul audits at Columbia, is influenced by

Morris Raphael Cohen at City College, and influenced in Dewey's Chicago. His notions to admit all experience (while he consults his deepest impulses) is probably the debt he acknowledges to Husserl. The admission to Husserl is the impulse to write. His notion that a logical conclusion leads to actions is from the instrumental pragmatism of Dewey. He has published a May pamphlet in 1945 or a little earlier, stating his active passivist principles and his protest against the social coercion of a man's nature and calls on all to resist such unnatural coercion.

In the blow against the hesitation of the timid, perhaps the obsession of neurosis, he urges any movement, however small, in that direction since the direction one wants to go must be known. He already knows that one thing leads to another. Later, he will say, it is man's nature to lead to trouble with prudence.

Perls and Goodman collaborate and *Gestalt Therapy and Excitement and Growth in the Human Personality* (*PHG*) is published in 1951. I think it's safe to say about therapy, as such, that there is nothing in the book that is not found in Perls' prior work. In this context, I quote Whitehead, yet again, "The safest general characterization of the European philosophical position is that it consists of a series of footnotes to Plato." I do not mean the systematic scheme of thought which scholars have doubtfully extracted from his writings. I allude to the wealth of general ideas scattered throughout them but a dialectic discussion to the meaning of language taking the combination with this shrewd observation of the actions of man and the forces of nature. This last [RK] must be in my view what psychotherapy ultimately is, with some qualifications.

What is not found in Perls, however, is, I think, a proper emphasis of the side of evolution that is not survival based as in the engine of his biological theory, namely, the notion of dominance. Natural selection has also, as to its organic internal relations, created activities of the community of organisms that create the special affects or environments needed to nurture and recreate those environments. Thus, nature is brought into organism and flows out from it.

Even here, Perls has spoken of the alloplastic and autoplastic organic functioning in the environment, but I cannot overcome an intuition of reluctance on his part to remain in the discipline of his unitary view of nature. It is as though, his criticism of the false split, insidiously bases itself in a false split.

Goodman structures form a coherent whole and logically orders the relations of gestalt therapy on a firm, theoretical foundation. His treatment of the theory of self is the logical centerpiece and masterwork of the book. It could probably not otherwise have been worked out than in the hands of artist and philosopher. This is the first time that the creative process, itself, first worked out by Rank's *Art and Artist* is introduced. Perls had seen him only as past-bound in the trauma of birth.

The consequences of assimilating the novel to the self, aggressing contact, restructuring the elements in creative adjustment in an organism environment field, are fully deduced. The scope is panoramic. Gestalt therapy has everywhere something to say and criticize, and necessarily so, since it is obviously not an adjustment, but a unitary and process therapy, and especially so, in a taxonomy and anatomy of these splits, awareness represented by mind and body, personal and social, conscious, unconscious, infantile, mature prose, poetry. A contextual method of argument whereby the conditions of experience of the listener are changed, not the treatise of the argument, is the emphasis.

Goodman need not so candidly admit the contextual method is an *argumentor ad hominem*. It has already been done by Socrates. He does it to Meno, then or later. However, since "All Gaul is divided into three parts," he boldly adds, "What is new? Gestalt therapy?"

First, the expectation of anxiety is unaware breathing. Excitement has been taken over from *Ego, Hunger, and Aggression*, not to be cured or alleviated, but therefore to be enhanced that states immediately the "here and now" in all the possibilities that are or forever could be. Excitement is heightened in the service of the ongoing aware process of the reality of the self as experienced within the typology of the activity of the self; pre-contact/contact/post-contact, excitement to growth, confluence to aftermath in the secondary physiology. Whitehead talks of a tri-partite learning, romance, unstable shaking out of the terms, a stability of generalization of concrescence. I think that they would both agree the growth or learning is not otherwise than the musculature.

Secondly, Goodman analyzes for all times, the neurosis of normality, staking out boldly the position that it is not from the study of the normal that one should deduce the standard of behavior, Freud, et al, and still have "done in" its contractual relation with the world, since that behavior, and its background is already hopeless. But it is precisely in the therapeutic hour, where the true human self is struggling to find itself in a process ego function that the true intrinsic self is reached.

Goodman and Perls are convinced by similar experiences that the human race is turning its aggressions on itself, rather than making do in the environment, and gone collectively mad in the grip of the assumed projections and the gospel of hate. Whitehead has said this is the inevitable result of specialization that builds only extrinsic knowledge in abstraction. For example, macro events are predicting special macro events, Newton's laws, and reducing reality from them. Even the exactness of mathematics is a fake, says Whitehead. This is his famous fallacy of misplaced concreteness and probably an example of Goodman's criticism of anthropology that has abandoned human beings and tools and culture that go along with human nature, and seeing them as, instead of, human nature.

And what is human nature? It can be found only in the concrete stubborn fact. It is certainly social, and probably quotes both "individual" as an abstraction in the concrete prior given community. Thus, Goodman's famous line, "Show me your Jews, Queers, and Niggers, and I'll show you your society." Well, here we are. Of course, this is part and parcel of the part-whole to have a partial analysis; the minority is always a repressed part of the majority.

Remember the criticism of the normal. But if the minority stays repressed, how is the majority to be informed? If the self will not awarely take back in awareness its repressions, where will the fullness of spirit in growth come from? Even if we were all hatched at twenty-one years old, the awareness work would still have to be done. Now even with every pill in the world that they are going to invent or think they are going to invent — the work still has to be done. So psychotherapists may have some income in the coming decades.

So gestalt therapy states its political aspect: emotions, those value statements of self, finding the kindred souls who band together to press for change in the social field. Alas, the strength of the movement is known only by its martyrs. It is a tough book. An example, as it always must be, of also what it purports to say. Whitehead, said, "Whenever a textbook is written of real educational worth, we may be quite certain some reviewer will say it will be difficult to teach from it." Of course, it will be difficult to teach from it! If it were not...if it were easy...the book ought to be burned, for it could not be educational.

In education, as elsewhere, the broad primrose path leads to a nasty place; this evil path is represented by a book or set of lectures which will practically enable a student to learn by heart all the questions likely to be asked at the next external licensing examination.

Gestalt therapy has been held by some to be incomprehensible. That's the book. I shall never forget my delight, when in the history of the psychoanalytic movement, Freud commented on Jung. Freud said he must confess that he found it incomprehensible. Exactly my experience! Except mine was by a confusion of tongues and Freud attributed his to the revisionists' refusal to aggress infantile sexuality. This, I suppose, still fuels the instinctualists versus the inter-relationists, specifically, in object relations theory. I would think, however, that prior to re-parenting would come de-parenting on which to build the analysis and undoing of retroflection.

Volume One repeatedly cautions that before...before...before the "breakthrough"...the meaning of the clench in its fullest, moment by moment, millimeter by millimeter, experiences must be traced. The danger is a premature resolution that leaves much unfinished and therefore much in the limbo of the repetition compulsion, especially including endless, humanistic peak experiences.

Of course, there is a point at which interpretation is crucial in gestalt therapy. Interpretation is the meaning to the individual of what he is saying and what he is doing, and it states what he is to him. It is not, however, the work itself. We'll have this discussion another time. They do, however, give the experience hope. That's the humanistic experiences.

Paul Goodman thought that sex held out the hope of paradise. We would be therefore, its priest and votaries. I must say, that I, until that moment, did not understand religion, but back to gestalt therapy. Contact and the spontaneity of the creative process itself are grounded in the contribution of Rank who analyzed the work of the artist as the action impulse itself, the working of the medium and the technique. This is also found in the play of children and the dream material. At least as illusion, Rank takes over from Schiller the notion of the play instinct. But what is an instinct?

Schiller, of course, is one of the great German romantics. You will remember at least, in *The Ode to Joy from the Ninth Symphony, Tochter aus Elysium*, Perls quotes Schiller in connection with Perls' experiences as a teenager. "Until the day when philosophy will rule the world, it is being regulated by hunger and love." I think that means sex.

"Philosophy is a drag," says Fritz in *Garbage Pail*. This is of course, the problem of surpassing or rising above the animals or primitives and places the problem at the dualism that engenders Rank's analysis. The impulse of life, however you mean it, against the structures of life leads to fear, leads to Will by a voluntary resolution. The Will that ego and art created. At first in the art, it is a religious illusion. Thus, the work is abstract. Next, as in the Greek, social to humankind, is the reference of art in its objects.

When the belief and the social breakdown presses worldly events, perhaps with the stars blindly running, the romantic artist emerges, creating religious and social within itself in a high individualized style and work, triumphantly resigning our situation, as we do with Saskia. A neurotic is a failed artist. That said, the analysis of art, working as a unifying concept, is also derived from aggressing and destroying the novel and creating a new heretheto unknown gestalt or organization in the "here and now."

But the problem with aggression is precisely of the unknown from which we shrink. We cannot risk the leap of fate as Kierkegaard's "knight of despair" into the fertile void, the great Tao of the buzzing forward movement of the background poet. We, from shock and anxiety, back away. Charisma is scrutinized and we are back to the bits of matter acting on other bits of matter which we disguised elegantly in words like stage, clinical, projection, system, introjection, and blah-jection. Difficulty of apprehension leads to the constellation of resignation to authority. Poetic becomes a pejorative.

Gestalt therapy holds that Max Weber is not inevitable; the teeth need not be drawn. The retreat is a failure of aggression. But if this is so, then we have failed in developing and supplying the tools of the work and the background supports that give rise to the foreground aggression. There is no good psychotherapy that is not revolutionary. Ask Laura Perls. The book is hard. For example, Page 416:

> In final contact, the self is immediately fully engaged and with the figure it has discovered and invented, momentarily there is practically no background. The figure embellishes the concern of the self and the self is nothing but its present concern, so the self is the figure. The powers of the self are now actualized so the

self becomes something. [Thought you had it?] But in so doing, it ceases to be the self. [So far, so good.]

But since gestalt therapy is an awareness therapy, let us consider the nature of an awareness that there is no environmental or body background. For awareness is a figure yet to ground. Such awareness is possible only of a whole and parts, for each part is immediately experienced as involving all the other parts in the whole, and the whole is just of these parts. The whole figure could be said to be the background for the parts, but it is more than the ground for it. It is at the same time, the figure of the parts, and they are ground.

To put this another way, the experience does not allow for anymore possibilities because it is necessary and actual. The actual is necessary. This thing at this moment cannot mean anything else.

"Through the examples at the moment of insight," Goodman has just derived how a thing can be itself and another thing at the same time. He states, of course, the Thou of experience, the exististential reward, not from the general shittiness of things, or to riding the ocean of despair on the crest of a wave of an absurd exstistential surfboard underneath in ever-shifting support, but in faith in the shared inquiry, in the meaning that is meant that will provide a solution as the background to fill the apparent void.

I think that Perls was right in 1969, when he said individual therapy was dead, and it was only in group work that the true growth could take place. He was also ignorant. In my arrogance, sixteen years before, I had informed him he knew nothing about groups. From the catch in his breath behind me as I lay on the couch as he sat on the throne, I knew he felt hurt. But he really didn't know anything about groups! It isn't necessary to reinvent the wheel.

One's competence and contempt can lead to isolation, pride and impatient novelty from the tedium of informed structure. So, for example, Lewin and Ziegarnick, who experimentally validated individual closure, had been tried in group function in the Fifties with effects in preparing the individual and the group, and within the group, focusing on individual prescription, perception of group goals with the closing effect. I think it's an intricate thing, and I don't want to tease myself trying to figure it out.

George Homans' *Human Group* came out in 1952 demonstrating activity in the formal external system leads to sentiments of a liking that leads to interaction in the informal, internal group. But that the progression in the small group, on the basis of such interaction, will, if the larger system is not ready, result in blind attack and suppression, why movements fail. "When one considers in its length and its breath, its import as the question of the nation's young, the broken lives, the defeated hopes, the national failures which result in the frivolous inertia with which it is treated, it is difficult to restrain within itself a savage rage. In the conditions of modern life, the rule is absolute. The race which does not make and value intelligence is doomed. Not all your heroism, not all your social charm, not all your wit, not all your victories on land or sea, can move back the finger of fate." That's Whitehead from *Aims of Education,* 1929.

Well, how are we to educate and whom? I remember the question with Frederick and Laura Perls, Elliot Shapiro, Paul Weisz and all the rest of us. We agreed they had said that gestalt therapy could not be taught in a lecture way, but probably only by demonstration. There was, at the time, interest being shown in the world, and brave souls were asking for the word. Cleveland was, in fact, happening.

It goes without saying; we were talking of the education of therapists as we are talking now. How to give them the tools of therapy is one of the basic tenets of gestalt therapy with patients. Even in sharing equality, the argument holds that if something X holds to any person, and A and B are particular persons, then it holds for A or B. As Perls said in his 1969 introduction to *Ego, Hunger and Aggression,* hunger in aggression is the context of misplaced aggression. Bloody unlikely!

There is a touching story of Aristotle. His mind a blank, searching for an example of his form, he stares at a painting of Socrates on the rear wall of his lecture hall, and his eyes fall on his pale and musical student, Corsicas in the front row. His X needs an A. A stubborn irreducible fact. You remember that God first made the animals and then he named them.

Remember, it used to be in gestalt therapy that we got our co-seekers in shared inquiry after they had knocked around elsewhere for years. Now it appears, we teach them in courses. Did you notice the confluence there? Some organizations, for example, Identity House in New York, which based its format on peer counseling, have seen its members so transformed in the process. They have gone on to skills and training and accreditation in exactly the reverse of the usual model, "First know, then you do." They are now struggling with death and dying in their groups, and the existential loneliness of the position is restated. What is it?

As the ellipses of the spiral of my arguments swirl out and back, I hope they would snag on, and on each loop, there would be some little nugget there. I've been developing the notion that the method of teaching psychotherapy is the method of dialectic from philosophy that have shared the social inquiry, the method of Socrates where the truth is already in the student and needs only to be brought out, not by example or precept, but by romance.

I think the existentialists are wrong when they say their issues of death and dying ultimately involve areas where one is alone. Precisely, the opposite is true. Shared inquiry involves all in experience together, ultimately and elsewhere, called group contact for lack of a better teaching term. But on page 39, we are now far from bits of matter and solipsism to the spirit that Goodman called the "Creative spirit by whom and with whom we meet as called."

Note from Renate

It was Laura's 80th birthday celebration and she couldn't come because she was in the hospital in New York with a broken pelvis. She sent me instead. I wasn't going to go because what I had written to say there was for *her*. She read it in the hospital, smiled, but didn't tell me she liked it… just said, "I want you to go." So I went.

My mother was born August 15, 1905. The celebration where Richard gave this talk, as I recall, was in October of 1985, because Laura was always in Germany on her birthday. Poor darling. She so much wanted to be at this celebration, and had been looking forward to dancing there. Unfortunately, she was the only one who was unable to attend.

Death and Dying

1987

How are we different? The issues of death and dying are always there. What is not always there is the faith and the shared inquiry of the horrors that people face. This might be the classical instance of "backing away" from a dread experience and "talking about" it!

I think you will have absolutely no trouble dealing with death issues if you take a deep breath and just talk within your groups about these issues. Namely, if you get a shared inquiry going, such as, "Why are we here? We know why we're here. We're dying." So let's begin there and the thing will take off. I don't see any difference in dealing with that issue than any other treatment procedure, except one of faith.

Out of the concrete of the supports and emotions of love and basic human togetherness, faith will help us all let go. Not like quarry slaves to our dungeons, but sustained and soothed by an unfaltering trust, we can approach our graves and wrap the draperies of our couches and lie down to pleasant dreams.

Who Died?
Michael Altman's Eulogy

1989

It is only now, now after the appalling swiftness of his travail and death, that we are able to make peace with that passing, add process to cruel abruptness and make fitting our consolings.

Many Michael life themes were touched at his funeral, deeply yet lightly touched: the relentless psychotherapist, an honorable calling; apocalyptic terror as creative companion; the questing, somewhat quixotic lust for truth from the background of casting probabilities within equable confusion. These we knew and were familiar teasing figures for our Michael; yet we were unable to capture his spirit as a whole, much was left unsaid, perhaps unsayable. How indeed to utter what we so much took for granted and perhaps sometimes not quite so seriously as death's focus forces.

He was there, to the side as usual, next to the light-as usual. Was his light yet again hidden under his own bushel; yet again being so still for his own dear self that others were to shine?

I kept looking at his coffin. This made no sense. Why were we the center of attention? Was he again teaching the great lesson of his learning, the Socratic deliverance as midwife of his pupils' learning as he stood out of the way? I thought excruciatingly for both of us: when will it be your turn, Michael? Your turn alone to shine with your own light without question, without fear and trembling, in the sure and certain hope of your worth.

I longed to say but I had not the Hebrew: "Michael, Michael, son of Micha, if not now, when?"

Focus Groups

1991

The focus groups are conceived as the ongoing processing organ of the conference. They will begin with experience, aggress and "chew" it, make that experience their own and then support the individuals in the group in their special process of assimilating. In so doing, their experiencing will affirm the group conference and its theory as approaches to gestalt group psychotherapy theory and practice. The conferees will be assigned to their focus groups as a tool for furthering new associations rather than pre-existing ones. Late-comers will be sequentially assigned.

In getting started, foremost is the task of immediately involving the group in its own process. Practically ground work actuality, post-beginning points, matters such as seating, distribution of new material and information, if any, introductions and so forth, selection of the individual duties: group/rep/recorder/volunteer, for example. Further, the conferees come with expectations based on the program literature: experience, discovering and inventing, finding and making.

These are not housekeeping grounds' details, but grounds that go to the soul of gestalt therapy and which are the task of the focus group. Thus, we come to our "go-arounds" building adequate support for the individual's new experiences as they come from the workshops and share the new contact possibilities, reciprocally re-organizing and re-integrating their focus groups to ever more cohesive or figural levels.

In our working together and in our administrative work together, we have tried therefore, to make available the widest possible experience potential and have it quite organized, and which offers the optimal opportunity for incremental growing in the experience, supporting and integrating, preceding step-by-step to movement and growth.

Ruth Ronall's reading of Laura Perls' *Woman in the Dunes* combines the conference ground and figure. We have elected (assigned to groups) to be here together (ground), and how do we experiment (figure), to resolve that "end-directness of process" (being) — unfinished business — creating both its space and time in action.

The reps will meet after each focus group as an essential element of the bold experiment as messengers from their groups, bringing feedback from the focus groups as a whole to their individual groups and the conference as a whole to its reps (Bud, Ruth, Carl?). Thus, the loop completes itself as an instrument of change, in itself, the *Bold Experiment* is affirmed.

New Conference Training

1991

Generally, what has been introduced into the theory of conferencing known as the New York Model is the instrument of process groups known as the teeth of the conference: chewing, de-structuring, assimilating and co-creating the novelty that the conference would become. It stands directly on the ground of the theory of dental aggression, an axiom of gestalt therapy theory. At Frederick Perls' memorial, Paul Goodman described this theory as Perls' "unique contribution" to gestalt therapy.

It is fitting that this theory of dental aggression has been almost totally neglected in recent decades in favor of the more phenomenalistic, existential ("intersubjective"), conservative ("sensitive"), cognitive emphases in gestalt therapy, in a new theoretical development in groups, as they refer to large group development and organization.

As instrument and moving power of the organism known as the conference, the process groups together and individually function to move from individual conferees to small group interaction to large group interaction to the novelty of the conference-as-a-whole, necessarily emergent and unknown, the surprise of contact. It is not therefore surprising that the process groups have been called the self of the conference. How to train for this process?

It is an imperative of this new approach that the training group be aware that the conference has already started, significantly more so as they

145

begin their work. It is imperative because only in this way can the support of the conference, already underway and organizing itself around, within and perhaps, even in spite of them, be available for ground on which to stand.

Prior to this model, the instrument of the unrestricted go-around was the method of choice, a simple procedure where each person in order has a chance to have a say even if (and preferably in large groups) it is one sentence. This can evoke a storm of protest, especially among the most experienced. Apparently, the embarrassment of being and becoming and their reciprocal commingling in mutual "self protection in the Sahara of sensitivity" ignites near explosive unfinished dynamite. It is so simple, but as Paul Goodman said, "Life is not complicated and hard; life is simple and hard."

But we are not doing group therapy in the classical sense, which in one of its extremes is individual therapy in a group context. Nor are we working the apparently less structured earlier group model (almost client-centered) where leadership is largely facilitative and standing out of the way as the group evolves and structures its own reality, a strong and difficult process as the group experiences its existential angst and struggles step-by-step along its developmental way — from theater as form via director to Tao standing out of the way.

The more available aesthetic is literary, specifically the poem and our choice of the form in which we will write our experience: ode, sonnet, haiku? What we are striving after is the form that requires a beginning, middle and end and makes its point creatively: the poem has its say, and that within a structure of rhythm and sound (words) that the form demands. We are freed for our best creativity by an edifice into which we are invited and to which we agree as guests to join. This is obviously support in the best sense; I prefer to believe in the sense of Laura Perls.

Within our view of the theory of conferencing as aesthetic and its freedom within structure as poem, we can easily understand the form, say sonnet, as leadership, its structure sequentially leading the way to the next development as it makes its point. We experience the quandary, state the theme, restate the new development and wind up in an elevating platitude. The experiment of shared personal metaphor is a prose form of this leadership aesthetic.

We find ourselves in a difficult contretemps: to suit our purposes to our words, we must first discover our purposes in our words. The embarrassments in language are deep and facilely trustworthy, and excessively touchy. As Paul Goodman says, to attack one's speech is deeply personal. It is here that much of what is meant by "sensitive" is generated. The perhaps unknown true sensitivity is shielded by a hyper-irritable rationalism, in a largely impenetrable thicket of words. Institutionally, in our organizations and groups, certainly in our politics, these false figures are further defended in an appalling bureaucracy. These bureaucracies are elevated to theory which then reads, thus creates, structures off it. The true conflict is suppressed.

False conflicts of objects in the foreground careen and collide; premature pacifications emerge in solutions from *Robert's Rules of Order*. A failure of aggression, of pressing on to the next resistance, a fundament of gestalt therapy is the pacifier. The split is maintained. Only the whole person is free, and that also politically. A therapy that envisions the whole person, as gestalt therapy, is obliged to find the support possible to bring us into closer and closer contact. We have tried to do this in our groups/structure interaction in AAGT as a democratic model.

We will investigate in our dialogue how we have failed.

New Conference Training II

1991

In the first installation of this work, we discussed the organism of the conference we are approaching and the theory of conferencing that we have been evolving that has come to be known as the New York Model. We made the points that the process groups are the self of the conference; that they are the points of contact and the intersections of the movement to large group figure/ground development and the surprise of contact. Most important, we stated the imperative that the conference has already started, that it manifests in the training and developing support of the process group leaders. The issue: How to do the training is the further imperative.

Approaching this challenge, we tried to see the conference from an aesthetic point of view, in this case literary, a poem, i.e., a sonnet. The point was to see the liberating effects of firm structure within which one, with the release of concern for building the structure, is free to create, and co-create, the work.

Taking as a rough approximation of beginning, middle, and end of the poem, our bodies, minds (thoughts?), and emotions as guides to our interaction we introduced the notion of value as an amplification and significant statement of the union of body and mind in emotion. It is significant in that we are guided in our activity as a group, not merely as a statement of individual concern.

It is in that sense a creative group achievement of shared experience to which we have therefore aimed. The last sentence of the notes in the prior paper was a parenthetical: "(In contact, it is clear we are here in group experience, nibbling at the cookie of contour)" The sentence should have also concluded: We are stating the unity of experience.

There are some who prefer we do without words and use a music model to touch souls more directly without the leadership tyranny implicit in who does the talking. That is a fascinating experiment and I thought of asking Susan Gregory to work something up for us as a training and perhaps conference tool as she did so well with *Frere Jacques*, but even so what would the theme be?

If we took as the material of our poem or composition, *Issues of Theory/Field/Contacting/Self/Evaluation/Gestalt Group Theory,* I think we might have the *abba abba* of our poem, non-rhyming though they now be. Of course those words would have be placed on our bodies, in our thoughts and in our emotions as experiences to arrive at our creative effort. Sounds crazy but deserves the experiment.

The Good, the True, and the Beautiful have occupied philosophers for millennia as direct experiences. It is clear that they express morality — what it is right to do — and the study of that is ethics; how are we to behave, what is right conduct. Obviously value, that to which it is worth aiming underlies conduct, in other words action. We are aiming at the value of worth arising out of group interaction and addressing the further value expressed in background structures of our common experience and agreement on the grounds of our grouping arising out of interest, communication, language, as against other fields, e.g., of rest and motion.

New Conference Training III

1991

In the first two installments of these papers, we made the points that in this training the conference is recognized as already importantly launched; that a structural approach aesthetically may be a fruitful way to proceed and suggested the poetic form, in this case a sonnet; and that a statement of value, i.e., the worth of activity may be a more direct aim of the training. That is, if as we say, morality, what it is right to do, is the result of creative social contact, how can we best aim the training work to that end.

We further stated the conference theme as providing the raw materials, or perhaps the ground against which the figure of the training could emerge; that is, that contact which would lead to a clearer sense of who and what we are in the conference. This is demonstrably a clear inference from *"Evaluation"* and implicit as well in *Issues of Theory*, certainly in *Field, Contact, Self,* and since it is what we will be doing, *Group Therapy Theory.*

Perhaps all the above merely means to ask is: How do we construct the experiment or experiments that best move along the contacting process at the level most appropriate to the present state of the group, or to say it another way, that the present and just about to be future can support?

Another emphasis is the more traditional the way New York has done its group conference work, that is, "Just let it emerge," thereby obviating any hint of oppression from the leadership to sully the process. This has the virtue of making available the possibility of a less mediate leadership emerging from the group and thus the aim of the conference, conferees becoming the leadership as a whole, facilitated. How to lead without leading?

But if it is agreed that the conference has already started in the training aren't we also now doing it? And if we're doing it can we not say what it is we are doing? And if we say what we are doing is our creative work and that work is in that sense aesthetic can we not say, e.g., we are making a "poem"? And if we can do that are we imposing leadership or cooperatively working to the creative surprise of contact? If art is the "un-bought language of delight" — we did not have to work at it — what is the objection to handling the medium, in this case speech in the field of communication?

Last week we understood that Kant felt he had to write a third critique, *The Critique of Judgment,* the first two treating Reason, since he could see no way that Reason had anything to do with the joy of art.

I suggest we do the experiment of the two points of view: mere emergence radically as against a more structured approach. I offer the possibility of role-playing them sequentially and having fun with them and let's see where we get.

The Process Group Approach

1991

Perry Klepner has organized this forum as a creative discovery-and-inventing activity to "chew" the Process Group approach to conferencing that evolved to what he has called, since 1991, the New York Model. He has asked me to speak somewhat on background and philosophy out of which the model is evolving and is founded and as you will see, I have, as usual, interpreted his request perhaps too broadly.

In a larger sense, the history of the New York Institute, of which the process group is an epitome, can be seen first as a choppy though fairly uniform evolution to first, the context, then of course, the group in therapy in a traditional, perhaps conservative format. ultimately, or at least at the present stage, it has evolved to the process group itself, mutually and reciprocally, that is, in a whole and parts relation as well as with the larger group and the polis.

Secondly, though far more important, the process group embraces not only the figural, the movement from individual-to-group, but also illustrates the pragmatic principal that novelty — in the sense of the problem — is at first a biographical referent. The individual or minority sees what the others do not yet see. Their hypothesis is an advanced experiment within the hypothesis and of course, within what is already known by all, the results evaluated.

If the hypothesis is demonstrated, the effort moves into what is common against its polarity (private or biographical), and the experiment becomes knowledge. Knowledge, as opposed to information, is of course, social; that is, based on reflective intelligence.

There are problems. The format hypothesis/experiment/demonstration is ideally appropriate to so-called "scientific" pursuits. It has not proved workable in psychological science except where the conception of humankind has been primitivized to where the unknown can be isolated as in the infra-human studies. This is another way of saying in reverse a principal tenet of gestalt therapy. That is, the hypothesis must be tested in the unquestioned world that is there. Gestalt psychology has proved its conditions, i.e., it is out there, but it did not establish itself philosophically as they had hoped to do. Gestalt therapy focuses on the interruptions (the "hypothesis") and immediately, the conditions of the interruption (the world that is there unquestionably) and the reality reveals itself (the demonstration) and this is self-demonstrating. The general hypothesis is proved: unity, or better, self. Further, as Sylvia Crocker puts it…"and this is good science."

If we keep these two flows in mind, the stream of gestalt therapy itself within the river of its developing awareness of its place in the roots of the Chicago school of pragmatism, we will have the clarity of parallel development with support and robustness of intellectual cross-fertilization that removes the sand bars to theoretical progress and guides us even farther from the pseudo-clarity of the wilderness and ontological desert that is systems theory.

I will begin with the prehistoric past. I say "prehistoric" since I note in the *Gestalt Review* that gestalt group psychotherapy, at least in theory, began in the Seventies. Other revisionists, one has been informed in Sicily, have gone so far as to maintain that gestalt therapy itself began in South America or perhaps even in California. In the broader view, a process that is now called the New York Model began at the New York Institute for Gestalt Therapy in 1952. Let me take you there almost a half century ago.

A stubborn group of brilliant and near geniuses, perhaps with a few real geniuses, originally gathered around Frederick and Laura Perls, formed an organization to do what such things do, give classes, seminars and so forth. They ranged from offering supervision and demonstration to education and writer's block. The latter two, education and writer's block, were respectively Elliott Shapiro's and Paul Goodman's. All also did individual psychotherapy.

Then when Frederick Perls opined he wanted to do groups, we formed a group and did group. As in their individual therapies, supervision, and demonstration, the work was individual, one on one, and the context defined, or better, named the activity. Thus, for example, Perls would start the group with the famous: "Ja, who wants to work?" He would then do what he did routinely, individual therapy, while the rest of us awaited in various states of anxiety/excitement, panic or stupefaction, our turn.

Much later, he acknowledged the context and began using the other group members as projection screens for the victim patient's productions. I believe that emerged as he began his circuit riding and developed his famous demonstration style.

So to the biographical within gestalt therapy as first practiced, circa 1952. After returning to New York from Los Angeles mid-1952, I asked Perls about the possibility of becoming a therapist. He was encouraging, but said I should complete my graduate degree at the New School where they "had a good program in gestalt psychology." I did that, completing the requirements in 1955. Perls sent me my first patient in 1953.

At the New School, my teachers were Hans Wallach and Rudolf Arnheim in perception, Helen Block Lewis in personality, Mary Henle and Irvin Rock in experimental, Solomon Asch in social psychology and Alfred Schutz in philosophical anthropology. Asch had done his pioneering group pressure experiments in the late Forties. Our class room text, Ash's *Social Psychology*, was published in 1952. Lewis had taken Zeigarnik's and Rickers-Ovsiankana's adaptation of Lewin's original work on quasi-needs, perhaps quasi-instinct, from the memory for unfinished tasks to the completion of those tasks not as originally with the individual but with pairs and thus a group context.

Perls was familiar or perhaps acquainted with "the memory for the unfinished" in Lewin, indeed had cited it in *Ego, Hunger and Aggression*. He had however, a delight in not reading anymore, preferring to have others do it for him, listening closely to their reports for his background information. From my studies, I told him "He knew nothing about groups," to which he agreed. "Ja, I do not read; I have no referential knowledge." At first, I regarded this as a defensive boast. Finally, I thought it a wall against new information in a man driven to be original. It is not novel that the energy goes out of an idea if someone else has already thought it.

Notwithstanding the introduction to the 1969 edition of *Ego, Hunger and Aggression*, where Perls listed the contributions that had been accepted from gestalt therapy over twenty years, e.g., "awareness" had been accepted in sensitivity and T-groups, individual therapy "was dead," he echoed an announcement he had made at an APA conference somewhat earlier. Perls dismissed his former work as obsolete and was determinedly pressing the "impasse" or breakthrough of the "death layer" in the larger group demonstration setting.

The rhythmic pulsation of figure/ground, individual to group/group to individual, individual/group/large group/culture had no place except perhaps a despair that his truly revolutionary insight which was that aggression could be brought back into the field of the biological activity of the human organism, be not projected into infinitely destructive and savage wars.

The New York Institute has met and continues to meet monthly since its inception. It became clear as a function of several accepted though critically unexamined axioms of the theory of field, not field theory, that those axioms were not a supportive presence at those meetings. For example, if contact at the boundary in the here and now is a unifying and central concept in gestalt therapy; if the group and its members are the here and now reality thus obviously the field of contact; if individual work, that is therapy, that is contact-making is attempted thus ignoring the group context and its dynamics, obviously, the reality is fractured and enormous potentialities, forever to be undiscovered novelties, un-operated, remain underground.

Not having learned the mistakes of present and future history, we were condemned to repeat them. Specifically, authority/dependent, rivalrous, scapegoating forces are fostered and festered. In short, all the transferential elements that are typical of a primitivized field are elicited. I would go further and say just such a field is the supporting ground of transference and the theory of transference makes no sense without a basis in a truncated reality.

Of course, therapist and patient are a field of contact and not exceptional in this analysis. That band of "blessed and rebellious outcasts," as Elliott Shapiro called them, could not seem to complete its revolution within themselves and that tradition clung to our meetings as an unstated group norm. Several things had to happen first...What happened?

The apparent converging of psychology/science and psycho/therapy in 1952, diverged, again split, into psychology versus psychotherapy.

The most recent issue of *The American Psychologist*, calling for "relational science" in psychological research, traced the retreat from the emerging social emphasis regressing to the so-called individual to the entrance on the stage of Leon Festinger's *Cognitive Dissonance*. I feel compelled to remind you that "cognitive" restates, of course, "individual," itself a projection of the secondary experience of isolation within the primary social.

In the Institute, as more and more members came with backgrounds in group therapy or especially field group work, the divergence between individual and group emphasis became clearly marked. In particular, Patrick Kelley, a patient of Laura Perls, who was fleeing gray flannel

Madison Avenue, became a youth gang worker, completed his graduate work and joined the faculty of the Human Relations Department at NYU. He is the author of *Reaching the Teen Age Addict*. He brought his democratic faith and fierce zeal for the underdog to everything he approached. I have him with his first rate intellect in mind when I say the conflicts were cosmic and creative and mirrored the professional split within the Institute.

The split was clear: the members who wanted "structure," represented by Isadore From, who clung to one-on-one therapy in or out of the group context, also held foundational the stages of contact and its interruptions in the traditional theory of contact and its revisions in the Cleveland systems or cycle of contact theory. I suppose I led the process oriented members who saw the stages of contact as Goodman stated them as the typology of a single behavior for purposes of the therapist's "scientific conception."

Further, that the "here and now" contextual interaction was crucial which then included group as rhythmically figure/ground or ground/figure and the emerging objective awareness of group contact as a perception in the field. This split was, of course, not limited to the New York Institute. It mirrored the movements in psychotherapy in the general field and restated the varying devolutions within gestalt therapy as its holistic logic, and Frederick Perls' "gestaltist attitude," bumped against the fortress of the building block theory of knowledge and thus the atomistic bias that yet remained in gestalt psychology.

In the many attempts to "integrate" these splits over the years, the best that can be said is that they used the tool of the bed of Procrustes universally. If the whole did not fit their outlook, then it was snipped until they could rest comfortably on the pallet of semi-gestalt therapy that yet remained. And so, the various institutes revolved around their axes sweeping the same arcs of micro-cosmic dust into the black holes of their swirling centers.

Again systems and the process group model remained, developing at the cutting edge, as it carried along with and in front of itself, the novelties brought about by taking the group seriously. Work product became better support for further dissolution of underlying conflicts. Nature of experiment, relation to process groups, meant risk, hence, process groups emerged as a vehicle for safe emergency from the novelty arising out of group, large and small, and the group interaction as a whole.

The Question Is

1992

The question is: How do we operate the general principles in the conference that we addressed in our first fax? That is: *Bringing Us Together; Diversity; The Advancement of Gestalt Therapy* and so forth. We agreed in our conference calls on the basis broadly outlined in that statement.

The conference is so far, designed as a loop which will flow on its ribbon presentations, invitationals, demonstrations, papers; groups so far perhaps thought of as process groups, whose function is to relate the conference to and within itself, the presentation part, in operation, seems obvious — you just do it, always provided that the offerings are within the conference call and as always, move the conference along. Here the position of the presentation, its space/time relation within the program is crucial. This depends on a careful analysis of its content and underlying thrust by the people authorized to do such things in the conference in New Orleans.

This brings us to the ticking time bomb in the conference, the groups. It is here that the real work of integrating the experience of the conference begins, that is to provide the base then for its wind-up as a coherent whole, including also the routine era of good feeling that arises in such a convocation.

We have already agreed that two leaders are crucial for the groups. More accurately, again based on the difficulty of training this kind of process

161

group leader and our experience that more senior people are more successful in this leadership, we have concluded it as a base, and thought a co-leader, perhaps one of the Young Turks, who could energize our tired bones is also needed. Moreover, we realized that routine leadership methods or even styles seem not germane, though perhaps, a benevolent eclecticism is a *desideratum*. (That is what we get in a senior person; it's called style).

The conference kicks off. There is a keynote. Depending on the program, there are various sessions. The groups meet. The questions are: Who are we? What are we here for? What do we/I hope to get/contribute? Where do we/I stand? Who are you? What is your/our place (relationship) and what will it be? What is your skill level?

The inside question for the leaders is: How do we become an enlivening pulsation of a coherent whole, learning and contributing on a meta-level — a level that levels up not down, that generates a tide of interaction whose currents and eddies lift and turn and make and gradually float together gently downstream depositing fertility within us the delta of the generous loam of growth?

The answer is a leadership that quickly sheds to function as the strength of each individual makes itself known and is supported while the grounds of support are temporarily bounded by that leadership. The technique is an equally valued and made opportunity, particularly with some variation of the "go-around." (Perhaps for example, a variation I have used: each group member pairs with a neighbor as a dyad. After a given interval, the group as a whole reforms and each person introduces the other, stated as him/herself. We're off and running.)

There are many further possibilities; I'd like to walk them through. It would be snazzy to try it on ourselves first!

Hands Off!

1993

In 1991, the New York Institute for Gestalt Therapy sponsored a group conference, *A Bold Experiment*, which attempted to bring the unitary theory and process of gestalt therapy to demonstration. The aim was for the conferees to generate their own theory as it arose from the group process and ultimately for them to create the unfinished remainder of the conference which had remained un-programmed. This was a "bold experiment."

There were many structures built into the process, the most important of which were the so-called focus groups which were conceived as the self of the conference: aggressing, chewing, and ultimately assimilating the groups' interaction. To this end, the group leaders were extensively trained, both wide and deep, to the aims, goals, hopes and fears of the bold experiment. The emphasis was on intense group leader interaction in the training group as an example of the hoped for elaboration in the *Bold Experiment Conference* itself. As such, there was perhaps a blurring of individuality in the service of the experiment, inevitable in any developing group loyalty.

Realizing this somewhat homogenized cast, the sponsors sought to present a varying picture at a subsequent conference which is now in the planning stage, tentatively titled *Leadership Styles in Gestalt Group Therapy*. Obviously here, idiosyncratic turns and conceits in the leader's work would be stressed as the group moved to cohesion. One will recognize a long tradition of dramatic interactive styles in gestalt therapy, one of the supports for the criticism is that gestalt therapy technique bound.

This writer is persuaded the criticism arises from ignorance: the technique works but the critic knows not why. The test is this: can the leader, perhaps while under pressure, say, and precisely so, why? Style is a murky concept. Like pornography, one knows it when one sees it. The concept in part owes its provenance to Laura Perls who frequently said there were as many gestalt therapies as there were gestalt therapists.

Presumably, she meant effective gestalt therapists. However, we can analyze her meaning thus: gestalt therapy is concerned centrally with contact and support in fostering the flexible sequence of figure/ground formation through present experiment which is the work of the self. Creative figure/ground formation creates strong selves, themselves highly idiosyncratic.

It is a maxim of gestalt therapy that healthy people are quite eccentric as compared to the neurosis of normalcy, which is flattening, stultifying and deadly. They, the healthy ones, will be flexible and various in their styles. Such a one, as group leader, will be a powerful influence in the group development toward cohesion, that background which will support the creative efforts and failures and successes of its members. Hence, *Leadership Styles in Groups*.

Quod erat demonstradum!

Reflections

1994

I have known Isadore for a half-century. It is no easy thing to have held such a friendship and to be so miserably bereft at his death. Hence, the tense: "I have known," for I think he is with me always. What is still with me is his gentle praise and blame, intense, often irascible intellectual rigor, and his humanistic grace: the legacy of his Continental Renaissance *nachas*. He was our Prince Valiant. Where now do we turn? Perhaps to Isadore's unique contribution to gestalt therapy...

Paul Goodman in his eulogy at Frederick Perls' memorial opined Perls' contribution as "the theory of dental aggression." Isadore took the section on *Contact* in *Gestalt Therapy: Excitement and Growth in the Human Personality,* tore the genitals out of it and restated that theory in more linear approachable steps rather than stages. He thus became the apostle to the Gentiles and gentled many conversions. Chary of writing as a bow to his excruciatingly demanding standards, his Epistles are written by the hand of his congregations, often in ways he dreamt not of, nor did he always approve. Who can control the inheritors when the estate is settled?

Hunt, Isadore and I emerged from a church in Sarlac in his beloved Dordogne into the brilliant sunshine. Directly *en face de l'eglise*, the carving over the door of the presenting building proclaimed it to be the birthplace of Etienne de la Boetie, the beloved of Montaigne's *Essay on*

Friendship, the tone which was echoed in Dewey's memorial to George Herbert Mead:

> Since I lost him, I doe but languish, I doe but sorrow: and even those pleasures, all things present me with, instead of yielding me comfort, doe but redouble the grief of his loss...There is no action can betide me, or imagination possess me, but I hear him saying, as indeed he would have done to me: for even as he did excel me by an infinite distance in all other sufficiencies and venues, so did he in all offices and duties of friendship. His mind was modeled to the pattern of other best ages. Goodnight, Sweet Prince.

First AAGT Conference

1995

The first question is how can we achieve in the New Orleans AAGT Conference the goal inherent in the name? *Bringing Us Together in Diversity, The Advancement of Gestalt Therapy* is so far designed as a loop which will flow on its ribbon presentations: invitationals, demonstrations, papers; and groups so far perhaps thought of as process groups whose function is to relate the conference to and within itself.

The presentation part in operation seems obvious: you just do it, always provided the offerings are within the conference call and, as always, move the conference along, {Here the position of the presentation, its space-time relation within the program is crucial}. This depends on a careful analysis of its content and underlying thrust by the people authorized to do such things again in conference.

It is in the process groups that the real work of integrating the experience of the conference happens. These groups provide the base for the conference's windup as a coherent whole, including also the routine era of good feeling that arises in such a convocation.

Two leaders are crucial for these groups. More accurately, again based on the difficulty of training in this kind of process group leadership and past experience, it seems that senior people are more successful in this type of leadership so a senior leader is recommended. A co-leader, perhaps one of the Young Turks who could energize our tired bones, is also needed. Moreover, routine leadership methods seem not germane, though perhaps a benevolent eclecticism is a *desideratum*. (That is what you get in a senior person: it's called *style*).

The conference kicks off; there is a keynote and depending on the program, there are various sessions. The groups meet and the questions are: Who are we? What are we here for? What do we hope to get/contribute? Where do we/I stand? Who are you? What is your/our place (relationship) and what will it be? What is your skill level? The inside question for the leaders is: How do we become an enlivening pulsation of a coherent whole learning and contributing on a meta-level, a level that levels up not down, that generates a tide of interaction whose currents and eddies lift and turn and make dizzy and gradually float altogether gently downstream, depositing fertilely the generous loam of growth with us on the delta?

The answer to the second question is a leadership that quickly sheds itself to function as the strengths of the individuals makes itself known and are supported, while the grounds of support are temporarily bounded by that leadership. The technique is equally valued and the opportunity, is made available, more particularly some variation of the embarrassing "go-around." (Perhaps, for example, a variation I have used: each groups with the other to the left of him/her.

After a given interval, the group as a whole, reforms and each member reports who the other is (new twist: state report as him/herself). We're off and running.

There are a lot of further possibilities: I'd like to walk it through. It would be snazzy to try it on ourselves!

Gestalt Group Psychotherapy: Theory and Practice

1995

Query: Richard, we are allotted so little time to do our work for the process groups.

Richard: Time for what? Very little time to train people to do the thing? Very little time for people to learn the thing? Very little time for people to do the thing in order to learn it? Yes, that's all correct. There isn't time to do the usual kinds of groups. There is only time to set the grounds to bring forward new grounds as the process moves along.

Q: What do you mean by "set the grounds"?

R: In two important ways, grounds are set already: The "social" exists before the "ego." Here in this group, I can feel myself aware as "we." All that you asked to do has been happening already. Everyone involved in the planning and in the program has set for themselves the same tasks as we all face now. We have been meeting as a group and have been at this work of awareness. You are in an ongoing process. The conference began some time ago. (This is an example of the "social" realizing of the past, present, and future.)

Q: I'm still trying to understand what we are to do as facilitators.

R: To continue: Your specific work as a facilitator is to be part of the ongoing support process — or ground — for contact.

Q: Yes, and how do I do that?

R: To answer, let's go to Kurt Lewin. A basic tenant of gestalt psychology is "contour." How would you describe contour in the group? It is a circle. We are a circle. (One experiment is to hold hands, and we can immediately feel the circle moving through our bodies.) Now Lewin points out that the contour can be located in specific coordinates such as space and time. This is "topology."

We can also speak of the group as a "force field" whose amplitude and index are indicated by specific qualities such as energy level, sense of cohesion, palpable direction, excitement, common destination and faith. Your task is to be aware; to sense the changes in the force field.

Q: And how do we do that?

K: The contour of the group requires a method that acknowledges the circle. That is why we use the "go-round." The "go-round" progressively states the field. The topology of the group is "here and now." This "here" and "now" is itself in motion.

To go back to Lewin, the group is a quasi-stationary equilibrium, which is always moving toward the new equilibrium. Any problem of the group will self-correct if awareness is brought to the present experience in this novel field. (Incidentally, since experience presents itself as a whole through contact, we are speaking of contour, topology and force-field all at once, since the whole always states the field.) And finally, the changes in the qualities of the force-field can be noted by the facilitators or by anyone else in the group. Here it is good to remember Paul Goodman's statement that "emotions are the only evidence of the actuality, and there is no other."

Here, emotions are taken to be primarily wholes of sensation. It is important to let go of egoism and allow yourself to be open, at first, and experienced as vulnerable. In your vulnerability, you will be closest to the actuality of the field and through vulnerability, therefore, most powerful, a paradox! You may find in your "go-round" that there are several groupings or whole experiences of feelings. As we all can state our feelings, we each can better know who we are. This act, in and of itself, supports growth.

Q: I begin to understand. Now you can help me know how to begin. I still feel that I have an enormous task.

R: It may help you to remember that we are not doing "big" things. There is nothing "big" that you must make happen. In fact, there are good theoretical reasons to go to the tiniest experience you can have together with your group. One of the simplest and most basic is to breathe together. And breathing can become a group experience. An experiment could be to pair off in the group and have the one on the left be with and breathe with the one on the right. And then reverse it. In a "go-round," you can ask how they experienced breathing with the other. There will have either been too much or too little air. If too much, they were dizzy, high, spacey, etc. If too little, they were choked, confused, etc. The experience becomes: "I'm feeling you presently in the group and you are feeling me, and together we state the field."

Q: Doesn't this promote confluence?

K: Confluence is a problem if unaware. We are here building increasing levels of awareness. You may want to say to the group members, "OK, take your own breathing back now."

Q: What if someone refuses to cooperate?

R: Let's say that a group member refuses to do the "go-round" until they know what the goals of the group are. This person attempts to pull the facilitator into a question and answer. So remember: 1) contour, 2) topology, and 3) force-field.

The contour of even these questions is a circle. This is a whole group dilemma, not just the group and the facilitator. How do you bring this back to the group?

How is this a "here and now" occurrence? How does this event somehow state the present or perhaps an avoidance of the present? The force-field is best described by the qualities of experience: emotions, energy level, clarity of figure, etc. This is best known by inviting vulnerability within the group and going to feelings. The group member can soon know who else may have similar feelings (not necessarily similar questions).

Exactly how you proceed is an expression of your personal style. My own reply may go something like this: "There are three or four ways to talk to your concern. However, my sense is that this is not only our issue to talk about. We have ten other people present and learning, and we need to creatively include them. Where we are going is not completely known, but the ground is known. *Here* is the ground, we can know *here*, and that's positive. And I promise, we will not make one move until you are satisfied.

"Importantly for the group, your coming in with your question just now is right. We can only know where we are if all stop and say so. If you'll say what you are feeling right at this minute, the rest of us will be better able to say where we are as well. We can see who else is feeling what it is that you're also feeling."

Q: What if the person continues to refuse?

R: I noticed I could have gone to a more vulnerable place personally, so I might say: "Let's assume that both our positions were defensive. When I go to my present feelings, I am..." (Then I may ask permission to include the group.)

Q: That's helpful, but what are the goals of the groups? Where would you like us to end up?

R: The goals are the process ones that we have been discussing. I do not know where we will end. For those people who always know where they're going, they cannot be where they are. Where we are now is at the boundary (the circle) where all there is or ever can be, is. That is the meaning of group.

Preface

1995

Introduction
The conference is seen as an organic whole, each element within it reinforcing and developing thematically and structurally, the aims of the conference thematically and structurally, as well as providing and demonstrating an *in vivo* episode of large group contact experience.

 If the conference can be seen as an experiment that reaches an essential fundament of gestalt psychotherapy therapy, namely, that therapy is experiment and experiment is *meant* and is a *meeting*, it follows that the conventional notions of leadership are maladapted. That is, in an experiment where the client *has made available and takes the tools of psychotherapy* in an equal status interaction, he or she is able to find and invent solutions that are spontaneous, sharply contoured and contactful. This is, indeed, excitement and growth in the social personality.

Method
To provide materials for experimenting and chewing, the conference has built a formidable array of presentations, from demonstrations to didactic content, to witness the events and themes central to gestalt therapy and its development. They are made flesh in the oft-repeated themes: *Bringing Us Together; Inclusion, Diversity, Outreach, Developing Gestalt Therapy*.

The instrument for taking these experiences and making them part of the individual's integrated experience of the conference is the process groups. It is here that the work of the person is accomplished in making the information of the conference and the experience of the other conferees. It is obvious then that the traditional models are not apposite and that a different type of training experience is a *desideratum.*

I suggest below a series of questions to be presented to each group before each process group experience that can serve as an evaluation and guide to the group, perhaps to reinforce where they are and how they should be aiming in their conference experience. The questions could be "Guttmanized" in a quasi-scalable way. This is worked up in *The Handbook of Social Psychology,* 1954, pages 353–358.

In this way, some statistics could be generated when the results of the conference are worked up and reported to all the conferees as closure, leading perhaps to a new conference. The point is, however, in the guidance, not the numbers we get. The questionnaires are to be completed and handed-in after each process group. This routine activity can be part of the introduction after the first fifteen minute group get-together on Thursday, and at the first Friday meeting after the *Bridging Generations Conference* begins.

Rate First and Second Groups Accordingly:

1. Agree Strongly

2. Agree Moderately

3. Agree

4. Neutral

5. Disagree

6. Disagree Moderately

7. Disagree Strongly

First Group Feedback Form

1. The leader moved quickly and directly to include us all in the group process.

2. I began to feel part of the group and integral to it.

3. My contributions were equally supported.

4. Considerations of status and authority rapidly became secondary as we worked.

5. The formal components of the conference, e. g. presentations etc., became early materials for the work of knowing each other.

Second Group Feedback Form

1. The conference began to demonstrate a coherent direction.

2. I felt part of that direction and wanted to join or perhaps change it.

3. Within the conference as a whole, my personal goals and needs began to be clear.

4. The demonstrations and presentations were secondary to the process groups for my needs.

5. My voice was heard and respected.

6. I felt empowered.

Third Group Feedback Form

1. Express appreciations

2. Regrets

3. Resentments

4. Say goodbye.

Gestalt Therapy Theory:
A Perspective from Pragmatism

1997

You have heard well-wrought and elegant statements on issues of theory. Carl Hodges on *Field*, Lee Zevy on *Contact,* Dan Bloom and Ken Meyers on *Self.* It is left for Carl, me and you to state the general tone and direction of gestalt group psychotherapy theory, its agreements and area of disagreements as it has emerged, and also as it is emerging today in our work together; for we are serious that this process can open up more and more as we move to closure.

With the work of the gestalt psychologists, Carl has developed group and large group work here and abroad to an estimable level of expertise and has succeeded in re-introducing the strength and liveliness of the work into gestalt therapy and theory. His efforts and the support he has received indicate the power of the theory and the thirst for sources that had been somewhat grown over. Perhaps, I should say "hunger" for sources since that would keep us in the "chewing" mode so necessary for hard texts and difficult meetings. He would be the first to say he could not have done it without the exciting, even dramatic, support and interaction arising out of the series of experiences that the Institute set in motion these past years, and of which he is so much a part.

I have found myself pulled more and more toward the pragmatism of the Chicago School, however, arising from a growing unease with the implications for fundamental theory that gestalt psychology assumes. This first arose in my studies for the Anniversary Conference in honor of Laura Perls in 1987. There is no doubt that experience is of structures and that they exist in the form and the environment, and their trenchant and elegant analysis of elementalism is beyond praise. The postulation of a psycho-physical parallelism in isomorphism as axiom to account for the interaction seems philosophically untenable to me.

That began and continued a process into which I am afraid I dragged some reluctant Institute members for an examination of the so-called bases of gestalt therapy. We thought our basic text was fundamentally a philosophical psychotherapy and so we began by examining Aristotle who conceived the vocabulary and we continued to wherever we would lead ourselves.

This is hard work but since misery loves company, it kept us at it and together for some years. I have forty-six video tapes gathering dust in my office to give testimony to the work and to give grief to some poor graduate student of the future unfortunate enough to try to base a dissertation on some previously unplowed dust bowl. We took seriously our thesis that we were in this together, that we were sources for each other, that we could learn together what we could not learn separately, that pooled aware ignorance, hence conflict, is a very intellectually stimulating state.

Preparing for the seminar one day at the graduate library of the New School, I was struck with "meaning." I found myself in increasing clarity of my ignorance of the meaning of "meaning," and promptly took myself to a dictionary of philosophy. Of course, in serendipity, it was the entry just after George Hebert Mead, which I began scanning. The usual I, Me and generalized Other were there as we all experienced in sociology, and then put aside

But I was riveted by the following:

His view of perception marks out a path somewhat similar to that whereby gesture led to symbolic meaning. In the case of perception, his point is that the consummatory phase of perception is contact, so that perception can be said to be implicit manipulability. Thus, the idea of substance is generalized from the sense of resistance. Space, time and mass are derived from contact experience.

Stressing the importance of the present, Mead stressed also "the ubiquitousness of novelty" both in the emerging present and the past and future, which likewise became novel of terms of the unique character of that present.

His view of sociality led to a perspectival theory of the universe, centering in the act in which the present moment is pluralistic due to the multitude of perspectives taken with respect to that moment by different individuals. On the other hand, however, the individuality of these perspectives is reduced by the fact that each of us has the ability to also take the viewpoint of the other. (Reese, W. L., *Dictionary of Philosophy and Religion*, 1996).

I have described this moment as one in which my hair stood on end. So it was all there and had been. Paul Goodman was at Chicago eight or nine years after Mead's death and although there is a direct reference to Dewey in his philosophic provenance, there is no mention of Mead that I've come across yet, in spite of startling similarities. Of course, Mead himself thoroughly credits Dewey's article on the reflex arc as influential in his own thinking, manifest in the *Definition of the Psychical* of 1903. Incidentally, both Dewey and James, in epistolary confidences, found that one to be tough going, though James said he would have another try at it.

What was there was the development of speech through the vocal gesture as the infant babbled back and forth with its mother and itself, naively taking the roles of the others, then responding to the roles in play, stimulating the attitude of the other that he stimulated in himself, then responding to that response in the game, ultimately taking the attitude of the generalized other and its symbols in communicative speech. The process was alive, the mechanism as stated. As Ken Meyer has indicated, there is then solid ground for the social nature of humankind that Paul Goodman stressed so strongly as prior to the ego and the individual in his cry against the increasing isolation of the neurosis of normalcy.

The unit is the act. The act is in four stages: impulse, perception, manipulation, and finally, consummation or contact. The first three are involved in distance perception and implicate sound, taste, odor and color, the classical secondary characteristics. Therefore, perception is a collapsed act that is not yet completed in consummation or what we would call contact.

In prior contexts, I have made a parallel with the four phases of contact in gestalt therapy theory. But the general notion that action takes place in and creates a social world, that the capacity to stimulate an attitude in another that one stimulates in oneself, then to respond to that response as an object, creates a self among selves who, as in the rules of the game, can then take each part in the whole and so behave, is a foundation of a conception of self that is firm and ontic. It is also capital for group theory and extends the reach of gestalt group psychotherapy theory, giving texture and intellectual satisfaction to what was perhaps known intuitively, merely.

For example, we have held from *Ego, Hunger, etc.* and *Excitement and Growth, etc.*, the expectation of anxiety as excitement which is aroused as the possibility of contact or finishing the unfinished business is stimulated. This comes from the notion of the present as not merely the "here and now" of present practice but that cone of experiencing that includes the past, at least, as pattern and the future as emergent and novel but somewhat unpredictable. The about-to-be is anxious but with the movement of the act, it is necessary in what it means to be and do. This is far different from neurosis and is firm ground for a healing theory of anxiety.

Further the notion of resistance as putting the insides to things, not merely as divisible surfaces, is essential to the act. The mechanism is especially the action of touch, principally of one hand upon another as we feel pressure, but from the inside, and in perception, that resistance is experienced in the object and in ourselves. We could restate the theory of the erogenous zones as a partial activity within the theory of resistance that Mead developed. Seen as social, we see its power in our work in therapy on an everyday basis. It gives solidity to the statement that had been previously based on another experience of feeling and as such invites experiment and analysis.

Since the unit is the act and that which moves to completion is valued, we have a direct theory of the way to behave in the relation to the generalized other, the community one makes and is a part of. This is an inclusive statement of the social criticism of gestalt therapy theory and a firm ground for it as it arises out of "the aftermath of creative social contact."

Finally, the insistence on aesthetics and persistently returning to the term "philosophical psychotherapy" was made by Laura Perls, whom I have come to see as the seminal thinker in gestalt therapy. She said:

> Music was most important (in her early training). My mother played quite well. And I heard her playing from the cradle on. I started to play myself when I was five. I could read notes long before I could read anything else…I didn't know anything yet about anything else. But I got more interested, really, in philosophy, languages, and psychology and all kinds of other things.

Daniel Rosenblatt commented:

> The creative nature of resistance and the way of working with it, I think, is one of the revolutionary aspects of treatment in gestalt therapy.

Laura responded: (as in interpretation)

> Actually, in identifying with the activity of his resistance, the client can make his own interpretation. It becomes immediate experience.

> The basic concepts are philosophical and aesthetic rather that technical. (Laura Perls, *Living at the Boundary: The Collected Works of Laura Perls*. Gestalt Journal Press. U.S. 1991)

Welcome and Orientation

1997

Welcome to the *Trans-Atlantic Dialogue* Conference of the Istituto di Gestalt and the New York Institute for Gestalt Therapy. The conference has been designed as an interactive one in which, as it progresses, the participants become more and more the conference discoverers and inventors. To that end, process groups are created and function to chew the experiences and learning that evolve with the conference. In that sense, they become the self of the conference as they contact their ongoing activity and share it within and among the groups/conference.

Your program has the following paragraph:

> Our process groups are an evolving New York Institute Model of gestalt group theory and provide a unique conference experience. In contacting, de-structuring, and grouping, each person enters a co-creative process. Each of us is changed by and changes the conference as a whole.

After the first papers, *Field* and *Contacting*, you will move to your process groups, meet your facilitators and your work and fun will begin. The conferees have been assigned to their groups as heterogeneously as possible for maximum interaction. Your facilitator will probably suggest an opening grounding experiment. Frequently, this is the familiar "go-around" with the "Who am I?" and "Where am I?" and perhaps "What am I?" as foreground. Perhaps some other issue will be of immediately concern, but the point is that each person feels an equal opportunity to participate, even to decline to participate at first.

Other tools are dyadic, triadic or larger group interaction within the process groups, including the "fish bowl" interactions. You are all familiar with these experiences and we hope you can move in and out and through them if they happen gracefully.

We have used the term "facilitator" advisedly, since we mean just that in consistency with our theory of leadership. Leadership is seen as function, not position! It is that level of interaction that calls out in its members the roles that the trending equilibrium appears to demand.

For example, a group member may be exquisitely tuned to field events such as draining energy, unsupported hilarity and so forth, and find her/his voice needed. Another may be susceptible to interpersonal perturbations and may need to point out the background conflict concealed by a false conflict of objects in the foreground, and so forth.

Evaluation and diagnosis is a major theme of the conference and, for heuristic purposes, may be seen as process/contact versus naming/evaluating on a hypothetical continuum. The Istituto di Gestalt has made a significant contribution in its analysis of the temporal dimension of contact and the dual nature of diagnosis and evaluation within a developmental therapeutic/situational, relational/personal field and its hermeneutics. An introductory *précis* is available as is their periodical, *Quaderni di Gestalt*, which we urge you to buy.

Welcome, and all aboard!

The Bases of Gestalt Therapy: A Synoptical Restatement

2001

In a previous paper, I pointed out the salient features of group as a gestalt configuration. As experience, it is perceptual as well as exhibiting all the classical features of gestalt psychology as proximity, distribution, similarity, direction, atmosphere, coherence/closure, and group pressure, all as a dynamic of figure against ground (figure/ground formation), i.e. the individual and group or subgroups as "partial structures."

Further, *prägnanz*, the effort to reach the simplest equilibrium and cohesion, is present. The elements of the autonomous criterion as brightness, clarity, grace, harmony, closure, aware contact excitement and energy are manifest. My attempt was to address, indeed counter, the notion that group therapy experience and theory had no primary place in gestalt therapy, a position that had been held strongly.

At the time, I was not yet ready to assert that not only does gestalt group psychotherapy theory hold a primary place in gestalt therapy but that working and theorizing in that field supports a more thorough ongoing analysis and leads from building on the insights of gestalt psychology to a perhaps firmer ontic base for gestalt therapy theory to stand.

This position, arising out of the work of the Chicago school of pragmatism, is most adequately supported in the work of George Herbert Mead, principally in *The Philosophy of the Act*. This seminal work became the basic text after the long and perhaps difficult and arduous study for a seminar that began in 1992 and culminated in a paper, *The Bases of Gestalt Therapy: An Evolutionary Restatement*, in the New York Institute's series of papers under the leadership of Joe Lay. The paper itself, I presented in December of 1996.

At best, *Bases*, was a cooperative effort for the seminar's imagined audience and myself to chew our way into the difficult world of process. It involved recasting all the ways I had come to think of the foundations of gestalt therapy and the therapy itself. It is difficult to insist on wholes of experience in the act of perception as figure/ground formation within the momentum of a contacting process, which is itself the unifying concept of gestalt therapy theory.

Part of the difficulty is that the work of the gestalt psychologists has been largely bypassed in current and long recent past in the training of therapists. Their insistence on field, process, structure, perhaps their aesthetic humanism, had been traduced to the hypostatizations of a systematic theory of contact and its linear development that had been originally "the typology of a single moment of experience" as a bridge to "the therapist's scientific conception."

The future in the sense of the "about to be present" is unpredictable. Therefore, the bearer of novelty is constrained within a novel definition of "structure" that strangles process and drains excitement and growth. It is the future of thought not action.

Now I think it imperative to reaffirm our philosophy of process and experiment, to support the anxiety that is rewarded by the emerging excitement of contact and novelty, to reject the corners of doctrine which have wrapped themselves protectively around the shoulders of "gestalt-and" practitioners and their schools, to press on, to aggress the next resistance, the ever-present tendency to collapse to authority in the face of anxiety and shock.

The lesson that anxiety is to be greeted, hence, supported by the excitement of joining the reality that is already in motion that we can take part in, especially "as yet unknown" is not an obvious truism, though none-the-less true. "Life is not complicated and hard; it is simple and hard." The defense of complicating life into multiple abstractions or elements or cycles and attacking the stubborn advocates of process is famously obdurate.

To move along this argument that gestalt therapy is well served and uniquely serves group psychotherapy, I want to restate many of the traditional notions of group psychotherapy theory at least as they seem to operate and have developed in the ongoing group work of the New York Institute. Those notions are centrally:

1. Experiment (as activity)

2. Group process (as opposed to individuals in groups);

3. Leadership as function not position;

4. Language (as communication of significant symbols restating the generalized other, thus the group as self, as a root notion);

5. Value (as the examination and outcome of action within the group, thus, wonderful to say, morality)

6. Finally, within morality, Aesthetic (as the experience of the good, the true and the beautiful to the senses relaxing in the middle mode).

The model for this restatement will be to parallel the notion of the act as the unit of experience with the same design in the phases of contact in gestalt therapy theory as process, the process itself in Mead's terms as the expression of intelligence in the world. From a somewhat different aspect, philosophical psychotherapy can be seen on a continuum from empirical/experimental to phenomenal/conservative.

From foreground, possibilities in the experiment as the process moves and moves to conserving the grounds that surface as they make themselves more and more aware, going from, on the one extreme, a Reichian hands-on body vegetative emphasis to a Rogerian client-centered positive regard hands-off on the other.

The aspects mirror the therapist's scientific conception and determine the activity of the above "traditional notions." There is a parallel in the cognitive, existential, phenomenal. They presume what they are looking for in the first place, in the schema, the dialogue, the appearance. At bottom, there is an abandonment of the boundary and a retreat to abstraction that presumes a transcendent reality behind the experience, e.g., the *noumena*, God, un-thought thinking, the Bracket.

Husserl said: "The famous phenomenologist was too addicted to certain abstractions for that," (To do an experiment is the center and aim of gestalt therapy. It presupposes present equal opportunity activity which is the aim of interaction to perform. The present problem is balked in its completion by competing solutions or hypotheses, the members are baffled, surprised, uneasy, individual (the group is partially structured in multiple).

The pressing oneness is constricted, as is the breath. Impulse is aimed but split; perception is clouded, perhaps fixated. Manipulation has its grasp just beyond its reach. The questions are: "What do I/we do next? Where/who is my support?" Perspectives are experienced with minimal generality.

Group process becomes manifest as the background of the tentative foreground efforts as the obvious support for the differing experiences that begin to shape themselves structurally similarly. The hypotheses as they are grasped and crumbled widen to include more (less fixed), more process. An answer is felt: "I was right. Some of us somewhat share somewhat like experiences." Shared perspectives develop.

Leadership is implicated in the awareness of shared experience as polarities: that is, it is the process that is the reality that supports the extremes of the continuum of apparent difference and similarity. It is the demand of the process that elicits the functional leadership including the initial facilitative leadership support. The imperative and most difficult task is to shed leadership to the group.

We could declare the following speculation: In the parallel statement of the phases of the act as impulse, perception, manipulation, consummation (to the gestalt therapy theory of the stages of contact): fore-contact; contact (a), appetite etc., contact (b), movement toward/away; final contact; post contact; we have a restatement of the dynamics of the group in firmer terms.

That is the developing phases of the act are perhaps equal to the dynamics in the groups as indicated by the individuals' readinesses in assuming leadership roles as needed. The effort is to place oneself in the other's shoes, experience the generalized other, indicate it to himself as object, respond to that response and act as required by thus clearer rules of the game.

Such action states the equilibrium of the group at the time, and structurally always supports the individual/group relationship and reciprocity which in turn states the equilibrative ongoingness of the group act. This is a restatement of what has been in "Feeling" terms called group contact.

Language arising out of the vocal gesture, the infant "soliloquy," in process with play, the game, self and the generalized other, the response of the indication of the other to the individual and the response to that stimulus, restates the possibility of different perspectives in communication by significant symbols.

Differing individuals have somewhat different views. It is the probability of experiencing that difference in the shoes of the other that generates communicative sociality. We see and we can grasp what we see from a slightly different perspective than the other sees. An utterly novel event could not be experienced.

So resistance, the insides of things, not indefinitely divided surfaces, arises from the infant experience of exploration, principally, the reciprocal pressure one hand on the other.

In the perception, we put insides to things as perception becomes a "collapsed act." We perceive as in contact which still awaits consummation (phenomenology of direct experience); Husserl's dualism of sensation and feeling: "...Husserl's dualistic account (which he seemed to take for granted while declaring his presuppositionlessness." (See Pgs. 13, 23) "Neither (of his lectures or his writings) satisfied me.

Husserl seemed naive in his basic program, partly as he did to Heidegger, because of his idea that we can achieve absolute evidence, utter clarity and distinctness, by suspending belief (bracketing) and attending to the given." (See pp. 22)

Contrast: "If we must settle for a non-theistic view, (in metaphysics) then I question if Dewey and Mead have been surpassed." (pp. 531) The self-reflexive examination, individual within group, group within individual, and the awareness of that attitude and the perhaps layered self-consciousness within it, is the essential of faith in the continuity of our process and of that process. A group perspective emerges.

Value as the aftermath of creative social contact restates the characters of morality, loyalty, rhetoric in *Excitement and Growth in the Human Personality*. How one is to conduct oneself, to act, is central. Group perspective adequately shared by definition leaves room for everyone, as human, to be as one is. One's creativity is at stake in the creative support of the group.

With room to be, implicit in a perspectival view of perception, action and conduct, how one behaves, becomes indifferent but not without weight. Indifferent in that sanction within conduct is a minimal group instrument;

weighty in that the act is and means itself and is seriously considered. The exculpatory lightness of a shared significant symbol in communication developed in the groups is blessed. The wheel, always to be invented is reinvented as a matter of course. It is not a big deal.

The group resting in its accomplishment and relaxing in the warmth of consummation is in contact and peace. There is no further effort of knowing. Available and neither here nor there, the unity of experience including the unity of the senses, is direct. The "unbought language of delight," the expression of the unity of nature in the process of the emotions granted by the artist or the artistry of the group work, its creative drama, supports us all.

Experiments
Appropriate experiments suggest themselves correlative to the phases above. It is useful to let them develop themselves systematically. To make aware the grounds of the individuals who will be in the group thus providing appropriate support for experiment within the group:

- Permission for experiment.

- Eyes closed, focus on the seeing of the eyes; await breath which will indicate a space for next.

- Touch thumb and fingers of each hand. Make light rubbing and crumbling motions. Identify the feeling as compared to the same act with both hands together. For a moment shuttle from your fingers/hands back to your eyes. What registers?

- With hands together (Praying hands?) press one against the other. Which is doing what? Where is the Resistance? Inside or outside or no-side? Who is it?

To increase directly the experience of sociality and refine the notion of the social nature of the individual touched on above:

- As a group hold hands, neighbor to neighbor in the circle. Repeat the first experiments. Get the sense that this experiment is in the context of the first thus making comparisons possible. You will be doing, repeat doing, abstraction. That is, not merely abstracting but also accounting for the process which is the reality. The abstraction as such is an emphasis on which side of the process you are making the election.

- Breathe.

- Again to your visual and tactile shuttle.

To sharpen the sense of self and other and more poignantly that of other and self that the group makes available:

- Still holding hands, look around the group silently. At first, a gentle gaze. Note where your eyes seem to rest or on whom.

- Return to that place; simply gaze and rest, do not work, you are doing it. Breathe.

To make clear that self/other is fundamental and prior, that self alone is defensive and states the individual yearning:

- Locate the other person that your gaze also rested, rested on.

- Look through her/his eyes at the first one on whom your gaze rested. (Or perhaps who for you is now figural.) The point is to note again as you hold one position of comparison the difference from another (who is also you), and that your activity takes for granted and is supported by the background activity, which at this point may be a group phenomenon.

To make this place an area of support by consolidating its learning and directly taking the role of the other:

- Count off or group to triads; rapidly repeat the above; note your breath, physical and emotional feelings in your body.

- That integrated, dyads face each other, the third person of the group observes. Thus, A & B, with C observing. Reserve your observations.

- "When I look at you, I notice": ("In my body: pressure, thermal, movement, pleasure/pain. Sharpening emotions: Calm, excitement of whatever emotions. Moving toward contact: I expect, hope, want, think, etc., for or from you.")

- Then B & C, with A observing. Then A & C, with B observing. Has everyone tried each role?

- Share observations. A moment of rest as triad/group.

- Breathe.

Regroup to secondary group perhaps six or nine. The task is to build on the earlier experiences and to make clear the sense of self as and in group, to shuttle from self as individual to self as group, in short to notice group process and one's freedom, therefore leadership, within it:

- Breathe.

- Brisk go-around or interchange: What is now foreground for you? From what background of the earlier experiments, have they have made a difference or an irrelevance?

- Breathe.

To sharpen your awareness of your language and communication and the significant symbols that state the generalized other precisely because your perspective is not the others' significant symbol, means an area where agreement can be reached that also includes your difference:

- Reflect on the changes of whatever kind that marked and are marking your transitions from the earlier experiments and contexts. Do you notice movement? Stasis? Are you breathing?

- "Reflect" does not mean "think." In this context you are being asked to include your whole self, body, mind, group, as process, not habitat, and let your transitions come to you not you to them.

- Do you notice any differences for you in your apprehension of communication and language? Do you search for the right word? Can you try for the language that as adequately as you can says your say. Can you "try" as a group task?

- Regroup to group-as-a-whole.

- To discover how in your process and where you now find yourself perhaps as a result of your experimenting how you do act and want to act: what is your theory of value?

- To appreciate aesthetically the good, the true and the beautiful you have created together.

The above pair is beyond experiment.

From The Beginning

2001

From the beginning, gestalt therapy has understood that human experience speaks a varied language. That understanding was both the source and energetic thrust of its eclectic embrace of theory. Wilhelm Reich's revision of Freud, Frederick and Laura Perls' restatement of aggression as oral, was, from the very beginning, the theory of dental aggression.

Paul Goodman's formally theorized within aggression and indeed, language, as well as reclaimed the boundary of contact from the orgone, where Reich had projected it, to interacting in the organism/environment field. All spoke to lively contact and growth in the field known as the human organism.

Inevitably, as the creators are gone, the theses begin and there has been a long trail of devolving theory in gestalt that has treated the themes in greater detail and that is, as in a glass darkly, for example, Frederick Perls' abhorrence of verbalizing with its empty mirrors of existence. His feeling "here and now" thesis emphasized the mind/body split by treating only the body, its energies and currents and its practitioners' manipulations. Understandable. Laura Perls and I insisted that there is contactful thought, and her thrust was always to support whatever was going on, including thinking, especially, thinking. Support meant the platform, the essential ongoing relation to the earth of which the individual is a part. Nature does heal.

There have been many variously tuned attempts at integration. They have not succeeded and have fallen on the swords that felled the exclusively relational, (read sociological) and love-conquers-all conservatives; the completely instinctual as primal, utterly embodied as movement, unifunctional as breathing, (which is, of course, of air). Cognitive held up the other end of the seesaw. Goodman lamented, "Will there be nothing left of the instincts?"

What has been missing is a theory of therapy that understands the unfolding human/organism/environment field, holistically, that is, a whole-and-parts relation that is controlled by a whole process in nature in its widest context, which is perhaps, life. This is a humbling experience akin to Bergson's catastrophe when, after much puzzlement and searching, one intuits infinity, the bottom falls out and time is existential — in duration — rather than spatialized.

Such an experiencing is clearly what Dr. Ruella Frank has brought to her work from her own development and her developmental theory. She has understood the body as a physical thing and that the language of the organism/environmental field is "there from the beginning," and that its vocabulary, grammar, and rhetoric spring from "the organ of speech," i.e. the field. Further, that communication is there to address and be called a true existentialism.

Dr. Frank's restatement takes seriously the functional identity of the contents of resistance of the body and the object in the field, chiefly, the social objects. It is thus that touch and movement and distance "pull" the therapist and client into perception and contact, with a pause at manipulation. The varied language of the organism/environmental field thus reorganizes from the development of a unique instrument of communication, that is, the therapist, Ruella Frank.

Her approach is communicable and teachable. I said in another context of her somatic therapy: "It is a rare person in my experience who can say: 'This is what, how, and why we did what we did'…Ruella Frank's work gave me joy…as it wove in and out of case examples. It has theory and personal, yet reflexive, involvement: For the therapist, her work is essential, for the lay person, excellent self-help, and also a hardy tradition in gestalt therapy from the beginning."

The Bases of Gestalt Therapy: An Evolutionary Restatement

2002

The genesis of the thought for this paper arose from a personal and uneasy awareness that I didn't know what I was talking about — both insofar as a background and at the present edge of the future. This is a situation which will not be unfamiliar to the many of you who joined with me in our communal study of Perls, Hefferline, and Goodman (1951).[1] There is a note in the frontispiece of my copy of *Gestalt Therapy* that reads: "Nineteenth reading for seminar workshop, 1972." And further: "3/17/76 Completed theory section for Monday night seminar as we have *every* Monday night for past three years. Beginning to understand."

Pondering this ignorance and with developing certainty that it was a shared, though suppressed, background to the many *cognoscenti* in the gestalt therapy field, I dreamed up the following: The theory we had been reading was written by a philosopher with philosophic sensibility, language and vocabulary. The theory's background was essentially Aristotle's and if we wanted to understand we would have to make a beginning with Aristotle, to subject our basic vocabulary and axioms to as rigorous an examination as we were able and so bring ourselves to a

---

[1] *PHG*

new understanding and support level for developing theory and practice —
that is, the praxis of gestalt therapy.

We set as our task to examine the simple linguistic currency of our
gestalt therapy discourse and to see if by an intellectual Gresham's Law,
we could drive out by our good coin, the counterfeit that was — and
remains — in circulation. We would begin with Aristotle, who:

> ...thus approaches every subject matter from the standpoint of
> living, of life as the foreground of nature; from the standpoint of
> knowing, of the way in which the mind grasps it, of the
> intellectual instruments it employs; and from the standpoint of
> talking, of the ways in which knowing proceeds, by means of
> language, making distinctions, arriving at an understanding, at a
> statement of what it can be said to be.[2]

Living as the foreground of nature; knowing; talking.

That process itself was what Aristotle in a far loftier effort accomplished
when he surveyed and summarized what was basic to all preceding
philosophy and therefore what all agreed upon as a foundation for
developing his own. That "first philosophy" again set the language of
discourse that we today chew to understand. So the desire to know leads
to the activity of knowing in the power of selective response to the object
of desiring; with the arrogance of defended ignorance assimilated to the
humility earned in hard chewing and its eclectic gusto, we would go as the
yellow brick road leads us to the Emerald City and the great Oz! Thus the
journey of our seminar, *The Bases of Gestalt Therapy*, began in 1992,
continued formally until 1995, and continues informally to this day.

> Gestalt therapy is a psychotherapy that concentrates on
> the present functioning of the organism/environment field.
> Experience is the activity of the boundary of that field. The
> unifying concept is contact and the method is experiment in the

---

[2] *Aristotle.* Randall, p. 8. 1960.

here-and-now. Self is the activity of the boundary in figure/ground formation as it unceasingly moves in its function of creating wholes of experience.[3]

One has said and heard this so many times that it is almost rote. Yet with a fresh skeptical or examining attitude, those four sentences took ten minutes to put on paper. There is not a word or phrase that is not thorny and difficult. We know from Carl Hodges, the difficulty of field and event and eventually the requisite faith in and of the field with its event/events-continuum, rock to person. Lee Zevy has put contact in perspective in her usual clarity and elegance, but there remain many puzzlements. For example, Zevy shows Theo Skolnick, who while pointing out that gestalt therapy is the only organized therapy whose fundamental model is based on *The Relation Between,* believes that it is not a theory but a "Meta-theory outlining what psychotherapy ought to be about." Incidentally, Aldous Huxley, too, thought *Gestalt Therapy* the only book on existential psychotherapy "worth reading." But Skolnick seeks the compelling ontological argument that persuades the world of the centrality of contact in life. It is the same query that set us on the yellow brick road.

These puzzlements are not so much ignorance or lack of treatment in our basic texts but a growing sense that fundamentals have been treated roughly as with a coarse grater. That is, concepts have dropped through the holes and have been accepted, not uncritically, but with an unstated agreement that we will not push our demand for where, what, why, when and how.

That push itself can be irritating and invite an attack since an examination of basic assumptions is as well an exercise in goring someone's ox. Paul Goodman warned of this when he spoke of the dangers of the contextual method of argument, i.e., that it was a form of the argument *ad hominem* which not only points out your opponent is wrong but generously offers to

---

[3] *PHG*

help him correct the personal conditions that got him there in the first place.

Since this was a task we were doing by and for ourselves and with a foundation of humor and agreement of shared ignorance as nexus, we pressed on to a general understanding that mostly our difficulties were in stripping processes from the terms that had been assigned them and experiencing the processes as such (including the conception of them) to the extent we could. Perhaps, then a restatement could be essayed which would give us a place to stand within an "experiential, experimental, and existential psychotherapy."[4] That is, our definitions themselves would arise from shared experience in the field.

Thus in the statement of gestalt therapy above, there are many terms: present; here-and-now; gestalt; contact; experiment; experiential; existential; self; organism; environment; organism/environment; field, and so forth. Let us take one, "present."

What does it mean when we say "present?" More closely, what, after inquiry, do we mean arising out of our experience which also includes our texts when we say "present?" "Present" implicates "past" and "future" and without them is unintelligible. Gestalt therapy says the past is invariable, the future not yet and without organic need can vary in every conceivable way; and the present, here-and-now. We will try to analyze the present more closely later on and come to an understanding of the fluidity of these concepts within experience.

For Aristotle, a basic notion arising out of his theory of substance was the act. Paul Goodman's footnote:

> Imitating Aristotle, modern psychologists (especially of the Nineteenth Century) start with the mere physics of the *objects* of perception, and then switch to the biology of the organs, etc. But

---

[4] L. Perls

they lack Aristotle's saving and accurate insight that "in act," in sensing, the object and the organ are identical.[5]

In the opening chapter, *The Structure of Growth,* in the section, *What is the Subject-Matter of Psychology?* he says:

> ...psychology studies the operation of the contact-boundary in the organism/environment field. This is a peculiar subject-matter, and it is easy to understand why psychologists have always found it difficult to delimit their subject.

Then the foregoing footnote appears. But the total of the section is a discussion of boundary culminating in the startling:

> ...the contact-boundary is not so much a part of the organism as it is essentially *the organ of a particular relation of the organism and the environment.* Primarily... this particular relation is growth.

But what is *Growth* in *Excitement and Growth*? He divides the *"single whole,"* that is contact, into the sequence of grounds and figures as fore-contact; contacting; final contact; post-contact. Then in a brilliant exegesis:

> It is the organism and not the self that grows. Let us speculatively describe growth as follows: (1) After contact there is a flow of energy, adding to the energy of the organism the new elements assimilated from the environment. (2) The contact-boundary that has been "broken" now reforms, including the new energy and "the organ of second nature." (3) What has been assimilated is now part of the physiological self-regulation. (4) The boundary of contact is now "outside" the assimilated

---

[5] *PHG* p. 229

learning, habit, conditioned reflex, etc., e.g., what is *like* what
one has learned does not touch one, it raises no problem.[6]

Aristotle analyzed the power of selective response or sensing as a
function of the power of the sensing organ, for example, the eye with the
power of vision, and the power of the object to be seen as colored. Both
powers are potentials to be actualized in the operation of the sensing act.
So in the classical example, the power of the eye to see white and the
power of the wall to be seen as white are actualized in a single process.
In the cooperation of the two processes, "seeing the whiteness of the
wall, the locus of the color is in the seeing of the eye,"…but the color is
the same in both object and organ.[7]

That the act of seeing of the eye and the object seen, seem never to have
been separated, is crucial for a metaphysics that takes the act itself as
ontic and the basic unit. However, for now it is major that the boundary is
not between mind and body as in Descartes but in Aristotle's famous
definition "man is a rational animal": between sensing the particular and
knowing the universal; by life, discourse and dialectic; by living, talking,
reasoning. Thus man is a political animal: in society, he can make his
opinions known and shared and create the conditions of mutual existence
in community.

Incidentally, from motion, rest, figure, etc., Aristotle also derives the
laws of association as similarity, frequency, contiguity, and so on, that
the empiricists will use two thousand years later to deny mind at all. Of
course, they denied it within the framework of *logos*, or discourse and
dialectic that Aristotle had developed in the first place. Thus we have come
full circle. You will remember the quote from the first page:

> Aristotle thus approaches every subject matter from the
> standpoint of living, of life as the foreground of nature; from the
> standpoint of knowing of the way in which the mind grasps it, of

---

[6] Ibid. p. 428.
[7] Randall, p. 82.

the intellectual instruments it employs; and from the standpoint of talking, of the ways in which knowing proceeds, by means of language, making distinctions, arriving at an understanding, at a statement of what it can be said to be.[8]

For example, from *The Structure of Growth,* Goodman tries to demonstrate the unity of experience, thus healing the split in the primary and secondary qualities:

> Experience occurs at the boundary between the organism and the environment, *primarily the skin surface and the other organs of sensory and motor response"* and experience is also, *"the function of this boundary ... We* speak of the organism contacting the environment but it is *the contact* that is the simplest and first reality.[9]

Then in the first and great experiment in the theory section, we are urged to close our eyes:

> You may *feel* this at once if, instead of merely looking at the objects before you, you also become aware of the fact that they are objects in your oval field of vision, and if you feel how this oval of vision is, so to speak close up against your eyes, indeed, it *is* the seeing of your eyes. Notice, then, how in this oval field the objects begin to have esthetic relations, of space and color-value. And so you may experience it with the sounds "out there": their root of reality is at the boundary of contact, and at that boundary they are experienced in unified structures.[10]

In your experiencing this experiment, make an effort to get to the experiencing itself of your seeing. As Paul says, "the seeing of your eyes." Then, prior to object-forming, thus distance objects, perhaps the words closest to the experience would be, "pressure, tension,

---

[8] Atistotle, Randall, p. 8. 1960
[9] PHG p. 227
[10] Ibid.

movement, light and dark, scintilla, shapelessness." But remember, this experiment is intended to explicate the notion of contact-boundary that of the organism and the environment, but the contacting is the simplest and first reality. Here apparently, the seeing of your eyes is the simplest and first reality. "We use the word 'contact' as 'in touch with' objects as *underlying* both sensory awareness and motor behavior ... and where there is (good) contact, one can always show the cooperation of sense and movement (and also feeling)."[11]

That is, in contact as such, the subject/object split with its primary and secondary qualities, the bifurcation of nature is healed in unitary experience. And contact is the condition of that experience, therefore, it cannot be explained by itself, is thus ontic in Skolnick's sense.

I don't think we can say that yet, certainly not based on this experiment, although I had always accepted the experiment as fundamental and illustrative and it is. But what it demonstrates fundamentally, I think are the subtleties within the concepts of "organism" and "environment." Paul speaks of the developing objects in the oval field of vision and their "space and color-value," their aesthetic relations. Also in a different experiment, "with sounds 'out there': their root of reality is at the boundary of contact, and at that boundary they are experienced in *unified structures.*"[12]

He apparently intends the experiment to demonstrate the interaction, the organism/environment, the field, the boundary, the unity, that is, contact. Better, we may say: interaction, organism/environment, field, boundary, unity, therefore, contact. But he seems to be demonstrating the activity of contacting in its early phase leading, of course, to perception in organized structures as against building up the perception from "stimuli" or elements or parts to make the whole. The perception, as the gestalt psychologists proved, is of a whole, and is relational and contextual. So far, so good.

---

[11] Ibid, p. 228
[12] Ibid, p. 227

But if the seeing of the seeing is a step on the way, where are we when we take that step? If the experiencing possible in the experiment is of pressure, tension, resistance, what is the interaction in the organism/environment field? Clearly, it seems the experiment is demonstrating the organism also as a physical thing and the environment is the individual itself, in this case, contact of the oval of vision. It is a prejudice that the experience has to be "out there" in what we routinely think of as distance.

Here we are talking of close surfaces where distance as extension is immeasurably tiny, but as human beings with the capacity of reflective experience developed to the point of reaching the universal, it is nonetheless as a mile, though intimately close. We are seeing distance with our eyes closed! With a re-analysis of contact and the act itself as ontic, distance values become the "root of reality."

The gestalt psychologists themselves, bedeviled by the solipsistic problem of the subjectivity of the senses, resorted to "isomorphic parallelism" to dig themselves out of the trap. They postulated a structural equivalence in neurology the object "out there." And now with CAT scans and MRIs to show levels of brain activity with certain stimuli, the brain itself is becoming more and more mapped. For example, new research demonstrates the brain difficulties in dyslexia and is providing ingenious treatment opportunities for this vexing educational malady. Of course, I would make the point that it is the education that needs the treatment. Incidentally, they have yet to make the screens light up when an animal reads.

About seven or eight years ago in an interview, I opined that psychophysical seemed the most plausible of the possibilities for explaining the unity of experience. I had struggled for some other solution but this seemed the only way. It was still unsatisfactory to explain how the activity of the object out there gets into the neurology in here?

Köhler has done some good experiments with the figural after effect, which is, after all, "in here," as it is projected "out there," apparently reversing the process. They are buried in the proceedings of the American Philosophical Association in Philadelphia and if I can't get to a library before the time mandate for this paper, at least, in introduction, that's where they'll stay. At any rate, I haven't heard that they went anywhere.

The discovery for me of George Herbert Mead's work, opened finally ground on which to stand for my faith in the work and theory of gestalt therapy. Here at last, beyond Goodman's reworking of Aristotle — who would have found the splitting unintelligible — was a thinker who began at beginnings that made sense in experience. Unlike Husserl, who was total consciousness, Mead stood solidly in experience with the act as ontic, and, parsed, the unit of experience; the ongoingness of it through its phases: impulse; perception; manipulation; consummation; constituted all human activity. Consciousness itself is a phase within the act when the individual can be an object to himself and respond to that response.

Mead's work in social psychology is seminal and we have all been exposed to I-Me, the generalized other, "taking the role of the other" in our sociology and psychology courses at college. As you see, the phrases have become cliché. I had no idea that in the revolution, Mead accomplished in his account of the social genesis of self that he had satisfactorily established a genuine ontology of experience that solved the problem of the so-called "secondary qualities."

The general difficulty is the ease with which I-Me, etc., is learned and the tough chewing required in the more basic of his texts. That is, *The Philosophy of the Present,* which was written directly by him as a social psychology versus *The Philosophy of the Act*, which was pooled from lecture notes, various papers and stenographic student notes and is notoriously difficult.

Mead died in January, 1931, after delivering the *Carus* lecture at Berkeley in December. That lecture was the basis for the *Philosophy of the*

Present. Time after time, in introductions, prefaces, and so forth one reads; "It is regrettable that Mead did not live to develop his ideas more systematically. It would be sure to make his work more available to ..." (the general public?).

We have read the *Philosophy of the Act*, cooperatively in our seminar, and cover to cover by my solitary self; this paper is a further effort to integrate material that has driven me to despair in the effort required to limit it. It is 667 pages. I am certain that the lament of Mead's lack of systematization is a rationalization for the wish that at least, some of it could be pre-chewed. But as Paul said of writing works like *Gestalt Therapy*, essentially a kind of phenomenal prose: "It is the devil ..."

> Experience is prior to the "organism" and the "environment," which are abstractions from experience. It is prior to and "that there", which are abstractions. They are plausible, perhaps inevitable abstractions, except for moments of deep absorption. They are said by every natural language, and it's the devil to try to invent a phenomenological language that avoids them. But we must be careful not to forget the matrix from which they are abstracted. There is no function of an organism that does not essentially (in essence? — RK)[13] involve its environment — we breathe air and walk by gravity and ground.

> No feeling does not address the environment — anger that there is an obstacle to reaching, or an insult to organic integrity; grief that there is a hole in the environment, or a loss there that must be mourned through. If emotions did not signal something about the environment, they would not have been inherited and have survived; they tell the relation of organism and environment, and they spur us to cope.

---

[13] Strange locution. RK

Eccentric Genius

Conversely, the actual environment, the place, is what is selected, structured, and appropriated by the organism.[14]

Experience is neither subjective nor objective. Its proper nouns are Here, Now, Next, Thou, We, rather than I, It, Past, Future. It is impossible to talk such language, but it is the genius of literature to recapture primary experience by combining narrator and narrative in ongoing plot.[15]

Among academics, insistence on the value-neutral feels like chronic low-grade spite.

Incidentally, thirty or so years ago, Sheldon Litt, who at one point wrote encyclopedias, said of *Gestalt Therapy*: "It is hard to read and it can't be paraphrased." I sympathized and rejoiced as Joe Lay suffered in his preparations for his monthly seminar. He, too, tried to outline the material. I think the experience is as Sheldon said, except to add: "And nothing can be left out."

The latter half of the Nineteenth Century saw the heyday of evolutionism and physical science and its mechanics. As in the machine, cause and effect were separated and in psychology, this was replicated in the stimulus-response reflex arc which became the unit of study. Many ingenious experiments demonstrated its power, and in Germany under Wundt, psychology as sensations, physiology and tuning finely stimulus and response were the elementalisms that the gestalt psychologists rejected.

William James had pointed out "the insurgent character of the organism," and Dewey's paper on the reflex arc had analyzed the basic point: When on the level of naturalistic science when "organism and environment have taken their places in a world neutral to any observer, it often seems as if the environment produces, stimulates and controls the

---

[14] CH & FE, p. 31.
[15] Ibid, p. 32

organism."[16] But in general, it is the impulses that are largely "attentive" to what will express them. This is the meaning of "dominance" in gestalt therapy.[17] Dewey said:

> ...the distinction of sensation and movement as stimulus and response respectively, is not a distinction which can be regarded as descriptive of anything which holds of psychical events or existences as such. The only events to which the terms stimulus and response can be descriptively applied are minor acts serving by their respective positions to the maintenance of some organized co-ordination...It is a circuit not an arc...(and this) circle is a coordination...which needs reconstitution. The stimulus is that phase of the forming co-ordination which represents the conditions which have to be met in bringing it to a successful issue; the response is that phase of one and the same forming co-ordination which gives the key to meeting these conditions, which serves as instrument in effecting the successful co-ordination. They are, therefore, strictly correlative and contemporaneous ... It is the *circuit* within which fall distinctions of stimulus and response as functional phases of its own mediation or completion.[18]

Dewey had been appointed to the chair of the Department of Philosophy and Psychology at the New University of Chicago and George Herbert Mead joined him in 1893. The Chicago School of Pragmatism was born.

---

[16] PA, GH Mead, p. vii.

[17] Although Fredrick Perls was obviously persuaded of the field, he persisted in a "biologistic" leaning in his language which tilted in the direction of body or rather organism (appetites, urges, drives, etc.) that tend to keep the split he is trying to avoid. This is patent in *"Ego, Hunger, and Aggression."* In his last years, he seemed to bring it all together in an ontic fascination with *gestalt*, in *"In and Out of the Garbage Pail."* Paul Goodman's tilt is clear in his lament against the neo-revisionist social therapies (Washington School, etc.): "Will nothing be left of the *instincts'!" Five Years.* I have the clear and distinct idea that he meant the complex of sexual drives. RK

[18] JD, *Psychological Review III* (July, 1986)

Ten years later, Dewey came to Columbia and in 1934, Richard McKeon, Paul Goodman's teacher at Columbia, went to Chicago where Paul followed.

C.S. Peirce's pragmatic maxim: "Consider what effects, that might conceivably have practical bearings, we conceive the object of our conception to have. Then, our conception of these effects is the whole of our conception of the object." Restated by William James: "The meaning of any proposition can always be brought down to some particular consequence in our future practical experience, whether passive or active."[19] The basic notion is action (conduct), ideas having meaning as part of a larger field, namely their consequences. Thus, the act itself becomes central.

> Now this assumption of the pragmatist that the individual only thinks in order that he may continue an interrupted action, that the criterion of the correctness of his thinking is found in his ability to carry on, and that the significant goal of his thinking or research is found not in the ordered presentation of the subject matter of his research but in the uses to which it be put, is very offensive to many people, and, I am afraid particularly so to the historian.[20]

Dewey had "the will, the idea, and the consequences all placed inside of the act and the act itself placed *only* within the larger activity of the *individual* in society."[21] Mead analyzes the act itself into four phases, impulse, perception, manipulation and consummation which is contact (!) But for Mead the basic act is a *social* act:

> ...the basic act is a social act that involves the co-operation of more than one individual, and whose object as defined by the act ...is a social object. I mean by a social object one that answers to

---

[19] DPR, Reese, p. 453
[20] PA. p. 97
[21] PA, p. ix

all parts of the complex act, *though these parts are found in the conduct of different individuals.*[22]

To return to *Gestalt Therapy*, we repeat the four (!) phases of the process of contact as a "single whole whose sequence of grounds and figures" are divided as follows:

1. Fore-contact: the body is the ground, the appetite or environmental stimulus is the figure. This is what is aware as the "given" or Id of the situation, dissolving into its possibilities.

2. Contacting:

    a. excitement of appetite becomes ground and some "object" or set of possibilities is the figure ... There is an emotion.

    b. there is the choosing and rejecting of possibilities, aggression in approaching and in overcoming obstacles, and deliberate orientation and manipulation. These are the identifications and alienations of the Ego.

3. Final Contact: against a background of unconcernful environment and body, the lively goal is the figure and is in touch...a spontaneous unitary action of perception, motion and feeling. The awareness is at its brightest in the figure of the You.

4. Post-Contact: There is a flowing organism/environment interaction that is not a figure/background: the self diminishes. [23]

Contrast the above with an example of Mead's four stages:

1. Impulse: The hungry animal has an impulse to eat;

---

[22] Ibid.
[23] PHG, p. 403

2. Perception: this impulse in turn determines what stands out as a distant stimulus to guide the ongoing action;

3. Manipulation: the object that is approached is clawed, bitten, downed;

4. Consummation: with eating, the impulse reaches its consummation.[24]

Contact (b) would seem to correlate with the manipulatory phase in Mead's schema.

> It is of importance that it is not the character of tactual or contact experience in itself that carries with it perceptual reality. It is the successful completion of this portion of the act initiated by the distance experience that gives reality to the physical thing in the manipulatory area...perceptual reality is a mediate field within the entire complex act...The physical thing is seen, and that which is seen has been realized in contact. The contact, however, is not simply a pressure, not simply a hardness or roughness. It is primarily a resistance. The contact experience that constitutes the reality of the physical thing comes from the inside of the thing, and it comes from an inside that can never be reached by subdividing the thing. This reveals simply new surfaces. It is an inside that springs from the co-operation of physical things with ourselves in our acts. We are seeking the sort of resistance that we ourselves offer in grasping and manipulating things. *We seek support, leverage, and assistance.*[25]

Of course, resistance was a central concept in classical psychoanalysis and was much discussed in the early gestalt therapy years. Classically, it was "resistance" to the interpretation, later embodied by Reich in the character armoring. The bio-energetic therapists saw this as a blockage,

---

[24] PA, p. ix
[25] Ibid, p. 143

but as Laura Perls used to say: "Resistance is the life of the patient." ⚹
Therefore, it was an opportunity for therapy.

There seems a perfect segue here: If resistance is what we offer ourselves
in grasping and manipulating things and that is support, leverage, and
assistance,

> ...The mediate act (in the sequence) is completed in the
> resistance of the thing. It is the sort of resistance which one hand
> offers to the other." (!) "Now what we mean by an inside as
> distinguished from that which can be revealed by removing
> something spatially exterior (Interpretation?), which then
> becomes an outside, is action as it is going on ... Resistance is
> action.[26]

Perhaps in our restatement, we could attempt the following: Find in the
person where the interruption of experiencing is. That is, find which
areas need support, leverage, and assistance for the on-goingness of the
act and by experiencing the pressure in the client/therapist field in our
action together, as for example, the pressure one hand offers the other,
increase the action on the inside. The therapy gets on.

> To reach a "now," the result of the act must be present as a part
> of the activity which excites it. It is this which renders resistance
> of so fundamental importance. The resistance of the thing we are
> about to seize can be excited in the individual who will grasp it
> but the attitude must have been assumed before either the thing or
> the organism can appear as object.[27]

> It is impossible to start off with the organism as an object and
> project its contents into other perceptual objects. The organism
> becomes a perceptual object only after the act is in some sense
> located outside the organism. This is, of course, the basis for

---

[26] Ibid, p. 144
[27] Ibid, p. 146

reflective activity, in which the organism becomes an object to itself. Resistance as an activity is a fundamental character which is common to all physical objects, including the organism.[28]

The unity of the act is not given in a permanent space abstracted from passage, until the "now" of the ongoing process in the animal becomes identified with the spatiotemporally distant stimulus through *acts of identifying itself with the stimulus*, thus enabling the stimulus to share in the resistance which is the reality of the percept in the manipulatory area.

In the manipulatory area, both the distance promise and the resistance contact fulfillment unite in a percept, but the percept does not become an object except in a situation within which the organism is also an object. It is this involvement of the organism in the perceptual situation as an object which we denominate as consciousness, i.e., consciousness as *awareness*.[29]

Thus the "now" of the experience is the datum of the organism, i.e., not as "experiencing the object but as a perceptual object essential to the situation." So we are taken back to the earlier question: What does it mean when we say "present?" It is clear that the present must contain the distance stimuli which prepare the organism for the action that will lead to consummation. In that sense, the present contains futurity and as future it cannot vary in every conceivable way, but is constrained by the present whose future it is. In general, let us say that the form or pattern of the activity is relatively structured to the on-goingness to whose present the actuality belongs and to whose past it will become.

The present spreads before and after the percipient event. This is a far more finely analyzed present than the "here and now" so routine to gestalt therapy. As such, the opportunities for a closer figure/ground examination in the ordinary events of the therapy process are available.

---

[28] Ibid, p. 145
[29] Ibid, p. 147

This must lead to a more richly textured experimental selection and experience.

Mead analyzes more closely:

> To reach a present experience that takes on the form of a present, a "now", which contains the distance stimuli, a number of conditions must be met:
>
> 1. The act itself must be inhibited; this can take place if alternative processes of carrying out the act arise in the organism.
>
> 2, There must be stuff of experience of which this present can consist which is irrelevant to passage not only because of the repetition of an identical pattern but also because it belongs to the same phase of the act in the various alternative completions of the act. It must *be functionally* identical if the present is to contain different alternative present possibilities. This can be found in the organism's contact experience of things which serve as means to final consummations.
>
> 3. To have a temporal character identical with the organism, that it be a "now," it must be content that does not simply attach itself to the distance stimulus taking on its temporal character, but it must be something that the organism calls out in itself, so that it has the temporal character of the organism. *This can be attained if the organism excites itself to respond to itself as the distant stimulus would respond to it if it were at the completion of the act, i.e., were in contact with it* .(!—RK)."[30]

Thus Descartes' analysis that places the so-called secondary qualities in the mind reverses the actuality. "If the resistance of things, their inner matter, is to be dated simultaneously with the organism, this resistance must be excited in the organism, and

---

[30] Ibid, p. 148

thus wrench temporally distant stimuli characters out of their futurity ...[31]

Mead has spoken of the resistance the organism receives from things being of the same nature that it can excite in itself, and that this is therefore, the "social character of the perceptual process." "While in a perceptual world, the ultimate test is the handling of what we see, we stop far short of this in most tests of the reality of things. We depend upon the substantive meanings of what we see, that is, upon the universalized social responses which implicate experimental data but do not demand them."[32]

Perhaps, we could make a speculative leap over a not very high hurdle and in therapy not depend so much on what is conceived to be universalized social responses, stated in the symbols of language, but as in the emphasis here, focus on the unitary approach of a therapy that has as its center the experience of whole-functioning in the organism-environment field. Gestalt therapy is well-founded in the philosophy of the act.

The experience of correlation of what goes on "outside" with what goes on "inside" is the experience of parallelism and as we have seen boils down to the arbitrary cut mind/body, psychical/physical and further carries the implications of conscious/unconscious. It must be kept in mind that subjective and private are not synonymous. Private is polar to common and they cannot be understood apart. What is private is not as yet available but is on the way to be part of the world of shared experience.

Individual is, of course, an abstraction from earlier social experience and is not otherwise intelligible. And of course, the neurology is as indicated earlier an abstraction and projection as an environment, though the environment side is not acknowledged.

---

[31] Ibid, p. 148
[32] Ibid, p. 151

While the metaphysical psychologist, perhaps unconsciously, (!) is placing the occurrences in the central nervous system parallel to the experience of the perceiving individual, *the actual parallelism lies between the neurological occurrences and experiences which are referred to the self in the social process of reflection.* Thus, the physical mechanism presents a series of phenomena that answer to the so-called sensations which are referred to the *self* as a social object.[33]

This self which has in it attitudes and impulses which are counterparts of the hostile and friendly conduct of things is not the individual of immediate experience … (in which) are embedded the impulses, attitudes, memories, the social values, etc., which are not in immediate experience. The self is a social object like other social objects and is reconstructed like other objects in reflective experience… if one undertakes to introduce consciousness into the process, (it) is stated in neurological terms, while back of this neurological expression of being conscious, would lie another state of consciousness of this that is going on in the system…consciousness appears in experience when the social or physical individual appears as an object and exists for the perceiving individual.[34]

It is possible by a *tour de force metaphysique* that the individual perceiving and the individual as object — the social self as object as above — of the perceiving be "identified" but parallelism is what is introduced to resolve the predicament. Mead gives a detailed analysis of his meaning of the experiences "referred to the self in the social process of reflection" and the parallelism with the neurological occurrences. Since this will lead to a general statement of the genesis of the self, I will give the example and discussion entire.

---

[33] Ibid, p. 156
[34] Ibid, p. 155

The illustration...is that of the recognition of error in the perception of the apparently bent stick in the water. This calls for the comparison of the stick as felt with its apparent bend as seen. The comparison is either between the anticipated bent contour and the felt contour or between the anticipated seen contour when grasping it in the water and its seen bent contour. It comes back, therefore, to a conflict between an *image of the result of an act and the experienced result.* There is a conflict because the experienced result calls out a different response from that which an object would have called out which was what the so-called image indicated.

One *acts* in a different way toward a bent stick and a straight stick, in particular, one acts differently toward a straight stick that can be depended upon to remain straight and one that treacherously becomes crooked when partially immersed in water. *The immediate undertaking is to state the straight and the bent stick as one, in that one may act with reference to it.*

This can be done only in so far as direct values for immediate experience are canceled and one can substitute for the stick of one's immediate vision an inferred object of molecular structure reflecting motions of ether that reach and influence the retinas of the eyes and so affect the central nervous system. From this standpoint, the stick is the same, and its straightness and its crookedness are stated in the same terms and one's reaction to these stimuli is stated in the same molecular terms. It is a method which inevitably puts the object and the perceiving individual and his world on one side and the corresponding physical and so-called psychological states parallel to each other.

The perceiving individual and his world of immediate experience, however, is that in which the explanatory statement must find its test, if conduct is to go on. Both the physical and the psychical series are, however, referred to this individual of immediate experience, but they cannot be stated in terms of immediate experience.

The parallelism is an expression of the relation between the erroneous perception as a fact referred to the individual — the self — and that statement of the object which abstracts from the reaction that the character of the object demanded, e.g., reaching for the bent portion of the stick in the water, and could never lie between these series and the world of immediate experience; that is, when this is undertaken — when we state the real world is the mechanical order of corpuscles plus the stream of consciousness of the self and that the world of a world which is not itself the direct subject of observation. This is a recognition of the attitude of so-called common sense...

The independent reality of the physical corpuscle and of the imagery, of significant symbols, and affective contents as contents of mind, pass into the full reality of immediate experience, and in that immediate experience these elements, into which the object was analyzed when conflicts arose in its meanings, lose their independent character... It is important to recognize that the value of the experimental test lies in the fitting-in of the hypothesis into the world of conduct — the rendering of continued action possible. ... This world changes ... its permanence is relative to the immediate situation.[35]

Individuals differently implicate the succession of the same event. We see an approaching car; it is near me before it is near you, the identical experience but "fundamentally different" in its site in differing "spatio-temporal planes." This represents the individuality of these objects "in behavior." The apparent timelessness of our spatial world:

---

[35] Ibid, p. 157

...is due to the consentient set which each one of us selects.[36] We abstract time from this space for the purposes of our conduct. Certain objects cease to be events, cease to pass as they are in reality passing and in their permanence become the conditions of our action, and events take place with reference to them. Because a whole community selects the same consentient set does not make the selection less the attitude of each one of them. The life-process takes place in individual organisms, so that the psychology which studies that process in its creative determining functioning becomes a science of the objective world.[37]

In evolution, "natural selection," new forms therefore, differing "spatio-temporal environments" as above have arisen, but also new characters ... answering to the sensitivities and capacities for response...It is as impossible to transfer these characters of the habitats to the consciousness of the forms as it is to transfer the spatio-temporal structure of the things to such a so-called consciousness.

If we bring things into our immediate contact experience (give them the date of our organism or a now), they take on the character of tangible matter ... they are what they would be if we were there and had our hands upon them...This instantaneous view has the great advantage of giving to us a picture of what the contact experience will be when we reach the distant object, and of determining conditions under which the distance (or so-called secondary qualities) characters arise.

If the world at an instant did exist in experience all individuality is lost and everything falls apart. Further, we would need a place like consciousness to stuff the secondary qualities. Therefore:

---

[36] "Consentient set" is, I suppose, the unity of conscious experience of space within some (unaware) process of agreement among individuals. In Mead's spirit, one's mutually taking the role of the other as regards "space." RK
[37] PP. p. 176

> If consciousness in evolutionary history has an unambiguous significance, it refers to that stage in the development of life in which the conduct of the individual marks out and defines the future field and objects which make up its environment, and in which emerge characters in the objects and sensitivities in the individuals that answer to each other. There is a relativity of the living individual and its environment, both as to form and content.[38]

This is coming at the solution of the problem of consciousness, not from perception as such as in the example of perceptual error (the bent stick in the water) but from its utility in answering to the on-goingness of conduct in the life process in evolution.

To account for "mind" and "self" in the evolutionary development of conduct, Mead develops an analysis of the social development of invertebrates and vertebrates parallel to the possibility of their internalization of a "social object."

> I wish, however, to restrict the social act to the class of acts which involve the cooperation or more than one individual, whose object as defined by the act, in the sense of Bergson, is a social object. I mean by a social object:
>
> 1. One that answers to all the parts of the complex act
>
> 2. Though these parts are found in the conduct of different individuals
>
> 3. *The objective of the act is then found in the life-process of the group, not in those of the separate individuals alone.*[39]

---

[38] PP, p. 178
[39] PP, p. 180

He compares the social conduct of the Hymanoptera, the membrane-winged insects (bees, wasps, termites, etc.), with sub-human vertebrates (here, cattle), and humans. Although the Hymanoptera carry out social activities of vast complexity with a common goal, so much so it is said of them, "They are not unmixed with intelligence," the varying functions of the group are accomplished by individuals of varying physiological differentiations:

> In the complex life of the group, the acts of the individuals are completed only through the acts of other individuals, but the mediation of this complex conduct is found in the physiological differentiation of the different members of the society. As Bergson has remarked of the instincts, the implements by which a complex act is carried out are found in the differentiated structure of the form.

> There is no convincing evidence that an ant or bee is obliged to anticipate the act of another ant or bee, by tending to respond in the fashion of the other, in order that it may integrate its activity into the common act. And by the same mark, there is no evidence of the existence of any language in their societies.[40]

As to the sub-human vertebrates, while there is "little or no inherited physiological differentiation to mediate the complexities of social conduct," the social activities of "the wooing and mating of forms, the care of the infant form, the bunching of animals in migrations, and fighting, about exhaust vertebrate social conduct." They call for no "more than inherited physiological adjustment and beyond these seasonal processes vertebrate societies hardly exist till we reach man."[41]

---

[40] PP, p. 179
[41] Ibid

Therefore, the "full social object does not exist" in the insects or lower vertebrates where the "objective of the act is then found in the life-process of the group, not in those of the separate individuals alone."[42]

There are two further implications as Mead continues to develop the emergence of mind and self in evolution:

1. Only selves have minds, that is, the cognition only belongs to selves, even in the simplest expression of awareness." (He means awareness usually not as "consciousness of," remember, but more closely "consciousness of itself.")

2. And, further, "this development (above) has taken place only in a social group, for selves exist in relation to other selves, as the organism as a physical object exists only in its relation to other physical objects.[43]

But if we remember that the individual should have present in his "organism the tendencies to respond as the other participants in the (therefore social) act will respond," we see Mead's aim in the insect/vertebrate comparative analysis. He needs to get a mechanism co-inside the individuals which can accomplish the functions that are outside the individuals in the physiologically differentiated insects, and physiologically adjusted vertebrates. That mechanism will define humans who have minds and are selves. And he finds this in the cortex of the vertebrate central nervous system which enables the different responses of (these) individuals in the complex acts (which) could be found in the separate individuals (that) render them sensitive to the different values of the object answering to the parts of the act: *impulse, perception, manipulation, consummation,* as you will recall.

The activity of the cortex in its "indefinite number of possible actions" represents many acts competing, thereby inhibiting each other as the

---

[42] Ibid
[43] Ibid

conduct proceeds which is the genesis of the "problem" of organization and adjustment. Perhaps we would say in the developing field the event of the clearer and clearer figure against an emptying ground until a gestalt, or whole of perception is achieved, is the perceptual experience.

Mead says further:

> Answering to these adjustments (so that overt conduct may proceed) are the objects organized into a field of action, not only spatially but temporally; for the tendency to grasp the distant object, while already excited, is so linked with the processes of approach that is does not get its overt expression till the intervening stretch is passed. *In this vertebrate apparatus of conduct, then, the already excited predispositions to thousands of acts, that far transcend the outward accomplishments, furnish the inner attitudes implicating objects that are not immediate objectives of the individual's act.*[44]

We have to imagine the human infant "goo-goo-ing" and "ga-ga-ing," lying in the crib. It is moving about, looking about, "reaching with its mouth" as Ruella Frank says. Its earliest experiences must be the experience of pressure, of effort, especially one hand against the other, the activity of which develops the sense of the organism as physical thing and is the genesis of "resistance" as we have seen which puts the insides to things. Things are no longer, or are not, Aristotle's bounded surfaces, bounded on the inside border, or Democritus' agglomerations of atoms as solids into which the knife blade sinks into the void as it cuts, which yields further surfaces. Thus we have the social aspect of things including the organism.

Moreover, as the field responds with parental "goo-s" and gaa-s" and the infant's vestibular apparatus is excited and stimulated within and without by the vocal gesture, it excites the conversation with itself, perhaps as child, plays in conversation, and excites in itself ultimately the attitude of

---

[44] Ibid, p. 183

the other as the child moves from play to the game where it must internalize the expectations and co-anticipations of others and itself as it identifies with the generalized other and assumes the roles of the others. The ball, from catcher to third to first is seen from every perspective.

Early on, there is the Me (the other), and the I which is the spontaneity and in the interplay with the possibility of novelty or the emergent as the I grows around the conservative Me; and then the I-Me. With the generalized other and the game over against it, there is the self developing as the individual calls out the response in himself that he has called out in the other and then responds to that response as conduct proceeds. How well Mead puts it:

> The earliest behavior of the human infant is social, that is, it is called out by behavior of other organisms in answer to inner impulses, and the characters, and especially the movements of these other organisms, are determining stimuli to the infant. Among these stimuli are the sounds which the infant hears and to which he replies. He attracts by his cries the attention of those about him, and they reply not only by care but with answering sounds.

> *The infant calls out in himself sounds of the parent-forms by his own vocal gestures, and reaches the point of thus conversing with himself, though at first, this conversation is but the play of sounds calling out answering sounds in the babbling of the infant. There is as yet no social object and no self. The two appear together, and they emerge from a behavior that antedates them. The self speaks to itself with the voice of another, but it cannot do so until it speaks with its own voice.*

The essence of the other must have become the self in order that the self may exist. And the other cannot exist as an object except as the essence of that other is the self.[45]

To look at the "character of psychological interaction" from the point of view of a social psychologist, let us take the following, which describes activity developed beyond the infant and child stage grounded in those stages:

In full interaction, each participant refers his action to the other and the other's action to himself. When two people, A and B, work jointly or converse, each includes in his view, simultaneously and in their relation, the following facts:

1. A perceives the surroundings, which include B and himself;

2. A perceives that B is also oriented to the surroundings, that B includes himself and A in the surroundings;

3. A acts toward B and notes that B is responding to his action;

4. A notes that B in responding to him sets up the expectation that A will grasp the response as an action of B directed toward A.

The same ordering must exist in B. It should be noted that the field of each participant *is highly objectified. The other person is not simply part of my psychological field, any more than I see myself simply as part of his field. Instead, each perceives the facts as shared by both.* (This capacity) is the first requirement for the formation of a social field of a *group relation* at the psychological level. It is a remarkable

---

[45] PA, p. 199.

achievement, which involves transcending one's own viewpoint by bringing it into relation with that of another.

> This transcendence is, however, a process that occurs *in the individual*; it is a product of his activity. This has perhaps been the fact most difficult to grasp about psychological interaction: that it is a process with an intrinsic social direction that has its locus in individuals. Phenomenally, we objectify the process of transcendence by placing it in the field of action. As a result, we tend in theory to distort the character of a social act in one of two opposed ways: to consider it either as the sum of individual acts or as a new product that transcends individuals.[46]

This view from social psychology was published thirty years after Mead's death. We see from him that precisely because he put the social back in the field of action that it was objectified and therefore the tendencies to distort theory in the direction of elementalism or transcendent consciousness were unwarranted and sterile. This point underlies his critical analysis of parallelism above.

To return to the discussion precisely of the point of the two-way distortion as a result of seeing the group relation as a *transcendence* that occurs in the individual, that is idealism/transcendence versus empiricism/elementalism, let us continue with Mead's developmental notion of self that began: "There is yet no social object and no self. The two appear together, and they emerge from a behavior that antedates them. The self speaks to itself with voice of another, but it cannot do so until it speaks with its own voice.

The essence of the other must have become the self in order that the self may exist. And the other cannot exist as an object except as the essence of that other is the self." Then he proceeds with a subtle analysis similar to his deconstruction of parallelism that corrects the distortions *as fundamental* in each direction as above:

---

[46] *Social Psychology*, Asch, p. 162.

This (self/other reciprocity as object) appears in the *form of perspectives in nature*. The nature of the environment of the biological form is its relationship to the form, what we term the *logical determination* of the environment by the form. On the other hand, the form is that which the environment does to the form, what may be termed the *causal determination* of the form by the environment. The spatial mapping-out of the world from the standpoint of the physical thing is the setting and bounding of it, while the volume of the thing is the effect of this setting and bounding in the thing itself. A similar statement may be made of the interrelation of any mass or embodied energy and the system of masses or embodied energies that is essential to the existence of energy.

What is involved in all these situations is that the content of the object is that statement of the thing in terms of other things, the content of the object is the statement of the thing in terms of other things, the content by which it can affect other things, while the content of other things by which they can affect it is in terms of its susceptibilities to them.

The logical determination of the field by the individual, of the environment by the biological form, of the consentient set by the percipient event, results in the appearance of objects (the phenomena?) *which would not otherwise exist.* They exist in the perspectives. The most concrete form of these objects is that of *social individuals in human (!) society.*

An *abstraction* of these is the environment of the biological form in which appear objects determined by the physiological nature of the living form. A further abstraction is the consentient set in which appear objects at rest and in motion, determined by the relation of here and there of the percipient event.

Now it is evident that the appearance of objects in the world of human society is responsible for the actions of human individuals. They are objects because of the susceptibilities of the human individuals.[47]

Human individuals behave toward goals such as "wealth, beauty, prestige" and so forth, since these are objects because of the human susceptibilities, which are determining factors and the "springs of conduct." At the level of the biological form, the environment has equal determinative value in the animal susceptibilities of food, danger, sex, and parenthood. This is routinely the stuff of behavioristic psychology in its experimentation as its throws up its hands at the complexities of human individual conduct. Finally, there are physical objects:

> ...which are in motion because of their determination of the here and the there of the percipient event because they fall within the consentient set of a certain individual. If a body is in motion, it has certain physical characteristics which it would otherwise not possess. The doctrine of relativity has shown that these characteristics include not only momentum but also the configuration of the form and the duration of its changes. This latter situation introduces a fundamental transformation into the theory of determination.

> As long as one assumed that the physical changes (those of the objects of the physical sciences) were independent of the logical determination of the environment by the individual, it was possible to present a series of changes of ultimate physical objects determined by their laws which would be identical in whatever consentient set (or biological environment, or social world); and the nature of these objects which arise within these different perspectives would be relegated to the experience of the forms themselves, while the physical configurations, and the spatio-temporal changes, and the quantities of energies involved would remain identical, whatever the point of view from which they were regarded.

---

[47] PA, p. 201

> Thus, the conduct, for example, of a human individual in pursuit
> of wealth or political preferment, expressed in terms of every
> action of the man, would be analyzed into movements of the
> ultimate physical particles constituting the man and his
> environment.[48]

Therefore, we would then have the familiar determination of every act of
the *universe* and its analysis in terms of the previous positions of its
collections of physical particles and chemical processes which contain
none of the characters that make life worthwhile. But:

> If, however, we assume that every system determined from the
> standpoint of the individual thing is an aspect of the universe that
> is objective; that this objectivity involves even the configurations
> and spatiotemporal changes and quantities of mass and other
> forms of energy as belonging to this system; that the universe is
> an organization of such aspects, then all objects and all processes
> suffer the logical determination that belongs to the perspective of
> the object, and this determination belongs to nature as revealed
> in the abstract physical sciences.
>
> Above these perspectives, stands the human social perspective
> with a character which these do not possess. Those below this
> human perspective are shut within themselves, just because they
> are perspectives. Each is a prehension of the universe within
> which the whole universe is mirrored. It is an aspect of the whole,
> and, because it is an aspect of the whole, there is no footing in it,
> no point of view, from which *another* aspect can appear.
>
> If such a point of view of another perspective did appear, it would
> not be in this prehension. But it is just the character of human
> reflective experience that it is social, i.e., that the individual
> regards his own perspective from the standpoint of others. If he
> so regards his own perspective, the field is simply there for the

---

[48] Ibid, p. 202

individual and excludes the individual himself. *He could not be both determining and determined.* But, if he can regard the perspective of another, he must enter into the other to reach his perspective, and yet, as it is another for him, he must be regarding the other as well. This must be equally true of his experience of his own perspective and of himself in the role of another, or of others. We call this *self-consciousness.* [!—RK][49]

Mead's analysis of the technique of this is in his discussion of the community development of the bees, etc., in which the varying perspectives on the basis of the physiological differentiations make a community perspective. His point here is that the individual perspectives are so sharply differentiated on the basis of the susceptibilities to their environments, that the "peculiar characteristic of human intelligence is presented with equal definiteness." Again, that is a matter of self-consciousness.

Then in a brilliant peroration Mead declares,

> The precondition for such a development on the human level is that there should be such a community perspective, that there should be objects which exist in their relationship to the group, that is, that there should be common characters which exist for all the members of the groups, though they exist also within the perspective of each individual. A further precondition is that different responses of the different individuals in corporate activities should be such that they can be called out in all the different individuals, i.e., specialization cannot go so far that the tendencies to perform the varied acts in the community activities cannot be in some degree initiated in any form.

> In such a situation, if one individual stimulates another individual to his part in the common act, and if that stimulation can affect himself as it affects the other form, it may place him in

---

[49] PA, p. 202.

the attitude of the other through initiating in him the response of the other, and thus place him in his perspective in so far as there are common objects. Thus a cry which arouses another to assist an individual in danger may act as a stimulus to the same act to the one who cries out.

The further requisite is that this commencing to act as the other does should itself become of value in carrying out the common act, so planning a common undertaking arises. Through this type of social conduct, the individual becomes all members of the group, and thus in some sense, the group itself over against the group perspective, but he does it by both entering into the attitude of the other and finding himself in this attitude with its perspective within his own perspective.

It is a deliberative attitude in which the individual indicates situations to himself by indicating them to others in so far as he assumes the attitudes of the others as the result of his own gesture. It is a process by which he puts an inside into the other who is otherwise only a distant social object[50]

Self-consciousness is consciousness of self. Since it is social it is likewise the awareness of the attitude of the other — of course, within the self, for wherever can awareness be? — as expressed in communication through significant symbols, i.e., language. All of this arises through the stages of the act: impulse, perception, manipulation, and finally consummation, which states the operation and field of conduct. And conduct ultimately implicates value — those shared aspirations which guide and make coherent the on-goingness in our nature.

In the intersection of the "technical and the final" is the experience of attempting to grasp the joy and experience of the "language of delight" that is the aesthetic attitude. It is an experience that is without science in the sense of knowledge gained through the experience of the full act in

[50] PA, p. 204.

its four stages. In that sense, it is an attitude, an aesthetic attitude, and prior to knowledge as such.

The aesthetic attitude tries to "catch the joy of consummation...to so enter into it in nature and art that the enjoyed meanings of life may become a part of living is the attitude of aesthetic appreciation."[51] That is, in the pragmatic attitude of imbuing means and ends with common process and reciprocal ongoing adjustments, something of the joy, the emotion, the spirit informs the means that the end is not so far distant though not to hand; that the greatness of what it means to be human can be shared by the group. [The separation of this in the division of labor is what brought the ultimate collapse of Marxism]. The shared creative experience brings the sense of unity, inclusion, a shared whole and parts, the parts making up the whole, the whole giving purpose to the parts.

It is this aesthetic attitude that is the gift and essence of gestalt therapy. It was Laura Perls' gift to us so to approach it and Paul Goodman's basis for the criticism of the neurosis of normality which gestalt therapy specifically addressed and which became the theoretical basis for the social criticism of the Sixties.

They approached the artist in us, the power to make the operations more and more aware in the experiment so our dream with them became our drama and we and they, the dramatist and audience. With them, we entered into the others' awareness and created artistically the avenues that made a path through and about our isolation. What a feeling to have created a drama! And it was serious. We attended to our awareness together and our together awareness and we became the artists of life; felt our creative powers, in them sharpening our tools, sculpting the life of self, bending our torsos and limbs to the appreciating form as we, in the peace, regarded the statuary of our form and structure to our oneness in the simultaneity of our co-awareness.

---

[51] Ibid, p. 455

Eccentric Genius

The method, finally, is the Tao. Paul Goodman's unique contribution to gestalt therapy theory is his notion of the ground emptying itself into the figure, giving its energy to the sharp figure against an empty ground. This in itself is a statement of boundary but it requires the notion of contour, the line belonging to the figure. I have been unable to find in gestalt psychology, the notion of the ground giving its energy to the figure; nor for that matter, that notion in the early basic gestalt therapy literature: *Ego, Hunger and Aggression.* Although it is in *Gestalt Therapy*, the mechanism is not stated. But it is made clear in *Here, Now, Next, Final Essays of Paul Goodman,* in the essay, *Within My Horizon,*[52] written twenty years after *Gestalt Therapy*:

> Surrounding finite experience must be what is not experienced. (This is an article of faith). (Mead thought, as we have seen, it was an obvious *condition* of the field of experience). What, if anything, can be said about it from what is actual in experience?
>
> In awareness, there is a boundary of which one is still dimly aware, Husserl's "horizon." Let us consider this in two different ways. First, if I turn to *it,* then what is *beyond* the boundary enters awareness. (We saw from the oval of vision experiment that the "boundary" is not experienced as such. This must be what Paul means by "dimly aware": perhaps, a "something other." The "it" that one turns to is far less than that and has within its experience much of what he called "faith.") Whichever way I move, "it" comes into being *new space…*(!)
>
> To attend to the boundary is a standard device in psychotherapy: if there is an absence of feeling, trace the boundary of what *is* felt; for example, the air in the nostrils; then how far can you feel beyond (!) the previous boundary, for example, air in the sinuses.

---

[52] *Crazy, Hope, and Finite Experience: Final Essays of Paul Goodman.*

> Awareness itself seems to generate energy. They tell me there is a neuro-physiological basis for this effect.[53]

But remember, tracing the boundary of what is felt is against the contour of the encroaching and retreating numbness. If there is "new space," it is immediately a field and a field of event/experience and states the reality of the human percipient event.

> But the contrary tack is even more remarkable. If I withdraw further from the boundary, (i.e., beyond Husserl's "horizon"), by concentrating on the center then the emptier the background is, the brighter and more structured the figure in the foreground. I take it that this is the idea of Yoga concentration. *For my own theoretical purposes, I feign (!) the hypothesis that energy flows from the emptying background and vivifies the figure in the foreground.*
>
> *I rely by an act of faith, precisely on what I do not experience.* Tao says, *Stand out of the Way.* The implication is that there is a *new* energy, and theoretically, I like to deny the conservation of energy. But *perhaps,* it is energy that we have dammed up and now set free, (the approach of *Gestalt Therapy*), the tack that Horatio takes in *The Empire City:* "Let go, and it will move."
>
> If in either case, attending to the boundary or withdrawing from it, the void is fertile, then it is very well that experience is finite.[54]

I want to couple Goodman's approach through *Standing Out of the Way,* with Mead's more thorough-going analysis:

> The present is the combination of the future (the horizon) and the past in the process that is going on (the figure or in Paul's

---

[53] Ibid
[54] Ibid.

sense the "center")...What appears in the *a posteriori* formulation is nothing but ultimate physical particles.

> ...A point of crucial importance here is that the selection is responsible for an actual succession of events in nature which would not obtain if no selection were made or if another selection were made; but I am confident that no selection is conceivable without the appearance of a process which I have attempted to define in its highest abstraction as a spatiotemporal extension of events which is, in some sense present in all its parts. *Life seems to be the earliest illustration of this. Another example of this, to which Whitehead is fond of referring, is a melody, though it stands on another level.*[55]

And so are full circle, contact, life, aesthetic, music.

The point of gestalt therapy is that experience is event/field and cannot be understood otherwise. As such, the splits in experience that are justified by a partial approach in science and psychotherapy and are institutionalized, must be reconsidered in a new approach that takes the whole functioning of mankind as its criterion. The healing of these splits is psychotherapy and health (which is unanalyzable but is a value) is the task of *Gestalt Therapy*. The method of experiment in the here and now is a sturdy and adequate instrument of this task and through half a century has proved itself thumpingly.

But there has been always an uncertainty in spite of Paul Goodman's tremendous work in formalizing gestalt therapy theory, that there are gaps at the construct level filled with the stuff of faith (in my view, a singular virtue). To the tough-minded, a reliance on art and artists and an aesthetic does not intellectually support the practice. It is here that reliance on so-called technique generates the couplings "gestalt therapy and ..." which undermines Laura Perls' insistence on integration which she saw in the accomplished and integrative *style* of the therapist.

---

[55] P.A., p.350

This is not a position unique to gestalt therapy. It is endemic in our culture and science. It is the center of the effort of American pragmatism to address, especially that of the Chicago school out of which Paul Goodman comes.

Although George Herbert Mead died in 1930, six years before Paul came to Chicago, it seems inconceivable that there is no public statement of Mead's influence on him. Dewey, Mead's close friend and predecessor as Chairman of the Department of Philosophy, is always acknowledged. This is even more puzzling when the schema of contact is frequently compared with almost identical language.

Yet, it is Mead, with his astounding analysis of experience as social, the self arising out of the vocal gesture and finally, the generalized other and communication through significant symbols, (significant because social), that a solid basis for the unity of experience, who finally grounds us all.

For example:

> Is this capacity for placing ourselves in the plane when we are on the earth, or on the earth when we are in the plane (the ability to be cogredient with the landscape or with the train while we are traveling) due to some power that belongs to thought as such, or is this power of thought due to the capacity to place ourselves in the attitude of the object which presents itself in experience?

> The doctrine which I am advocating is the latter, that meaning as such, i.e. the object of thought, arises in experience *through the individual stimulating himself to make the attitude of the other in his reaction toward the object.* In the case of physical objects, this attitude is resistance though the mechanism by which this power of placing the activity of the organism in the distance stimulus has arisen in the conversation of gestures with other social individuals in the same co-operative acts.

> Meaning is that which can be indicated to others while it is by the same process indicated to the indicating individual. In so, as the individual indicates it to himself in the role of the other, he is occupying his perspective, and as he is indicating to the other from his own perspective and that which is so indicated is identical, it must be that which can be in different perspectives. It must, therefore, be a universal, at least in the identity which belongs to the different perspectives which are organized in the single perspective; and, in so far as the principle of organization is one which admits of other perspectives than those actually present, the universality may logically be indefinitely extended.[56]

In the participation and communicability of this social analysis, we have satisfactory foundations. For instance, "dominance," a central notion arising out of evolution, is no longer grounded in such things as hunger and thirst, and certainly, the fundamental notion of "unfinished business" now gets a solid basis in what it means to be human rather than in an neurological tension state that demands equilibrium.

Certainly, the rich development of gestalt psychotherapy group theory is released from the strictures and inadequacies of the Lewinian systems model and has direct application from Mead to the group work that has become known as the "New York Model."

What was done intuitively is now done in light; in power, now clear to its style: experience, therapist/patient as above, awareness, Tao. Mead and the objectivity of the universe (thus in the Tao), are also the inhibitions of alternate courses of action on the phase de-emphasizing the notion of choice.

---

[56] PA, p. 546

Theoretical Responding

2002

Let me try to state a series of (tentative) propositions without much explication because it would require a restatement of the problem more lengthy than now possible.

Organisms DO contact. We are talking at that level of plants and fauna even at the cellular level within the category of extension, that is to say, space and matter. (Touch, touching; but not IN touch). That however is not the contact — obviously — we are talking about. The human organism as a physical thing is not also what we are talking about, but is the necessary condition for "experience" which may be a description of an appearance of things or phenomenology but which may not be experience unless you are willing to state a belief in *noumena*, the things in themselves.

Noumena are unknowable and have no place in experience except as you bifurcate nature *ab intio* into the classical primary and secondary (sensuous) qualities, subject-object, mind-matter, etc. And the instant you do that there is no reason that consciousness or "mind" hypostatized does not swallow everything up including extension and matter. This is where Kant came to grief. He tried to wriggle out of it with "transcendental."

What would we call the (human) organism when there is no self? Anesthetized? Or dead?

We cannot work on experience, or in an experience therapy like gestalt therapy, WITHOUT talking about self. It is stated and restated in every definition: Contacting at the boundary in the organism environment field; the self function; also figure/ground (one word!) forming (not formation); the AGENCY of growth which takes care of the existential "in between." You are NEVER NOT WORKING "SELF." All the definitions are reciprocal, convertible, and actual. And demonstrable (Present in every moment). All this is qualified with "structure" to avoid particularization but none of the above could operate without that as an essential condition. The river has to run between banks.

And it is the duty of every gestalt therapist to be able to present this part/whole relationship in every therapeutic moment. Perhaps not to DO it, that is a technical question of timing which with enough awareness and support that the moment can bare, the patient can, like interpretation, do for herself/himself.

By the way, an outstanding example of the presentation of this relationship was Margherita Spagnuolo Lobb's noble and courageous address to the Sicilian EAGT conference. I am told that if the blade of the guillotine is sharp enough, one feels nothing. I have always experienced dull guillotine blades. You will let me know the experience when your head is on the block. I guess it is then we will know unlike the Bourbons who "learned nothing and forgot nothing" the price of saying what we believed and the price to pay. Was it not Hemlock for Socrates? Well, you see where a low grade fever gets me.

The Beginnings
of the Gestalt Controversy

2002

In a contemporary treatment of *The Gestalt Theory and the Problem of Configuration*, we have an exhaustive examination, theoretically, empirically, scientifically and ultimately philosophically, by Bruno Petermann:

> The beginnings of the gestalt controversy are, as a matter of fact, still concerned with nothing further than questions of detail. Even in so far as they take their stand, and as a matter of course, independently of actual psychological work and more upon logical grounds, Mach in 1861, G.E. Müller in 1890, Husserl in 1891, and von Ehrenfels in 1898 still have as their essential objective, the further extension of our knowledge of the phenomena. Even as with von Ehrenfels, this phenomenological analysis might result in emphasis upon the singularity and irreducibility of the gestalt facts, the cardinal significance of this with regard to the systematic attention. (The "old" psychology.)

> As yet, the conceptions of the time receive no attention. The same is true even of the delicate researches of Schumann in 1898, where for the first time, a more thorough inquiry into certain fundamental manifestations of the gestalt problem is systematically carried out by means of careful experiments; or

even the first precisely set out theories, the Production theory, (cf. e.g. Benussi), or the Coherence theory, (G.E. Müller).

In its subsequent development, however, a narrowing down of the gestalt problem to questions about underlying principles ensues.

The most far-reaching claims in this direction are made by the school of Wertheimer, Koffka, and Köhler; to them the word "gestalt" has become the *symbol for a basic reorientation.* So much so, that they put forward their theory, as a fundamentally "new psychology" in radical opposition to all the other work which has been done in psychology.

But as indicated above, there was a progressive development in the old psychology: Cornelius and Lipps (*Gestalt-quality, Complex-quality*); Krueger ("wholeness" characteristic of psychic phenomena, 1905); and Volkelt's revision in "Complex-quality", 1912. Goetz Martins had already criticized Wundt's work as an atomistic-synthetic psychology and

> ...in 1912, formulated in principle, at least, the *central point of the present gestalt controversy,* viz the cleavage between the atomistic standpoint of the refuted theory, and the characteristic closure (!), which the phenomena of form-perception manifest.

It is perhaps thus time to close this treatise and I hope to do it somewhat in the manner of falling off a precipice. (Why didn't I say "cliff?")

Gestalt psychology has no original or even new foundation; its works had been experimented, studied, explicated and published under the "old psychology" as far back as the mid-19th Century. The effort in the main as I see it, had been to dress up the old in the gaudy garb of new labels in an unintelligible rhapsody. It cannot support itself. It certainly cannot support a psychotherapy to which it bears only a relation of figure and ground expressed otherwise as "figure/ground."

Note in the Goodman transformation this is and is seventy-times-seven-intended, meant as *one word* in spite of the reams of scribble reading otherwise. Absent that awareness and its foundational connotations, gestalt psychotherapy has no meaning. I expressly do not mean the technical meaning of the word itself. I do mean it as an expression of that holism the psychotherapy was developed to fertilize and grow in a field otherwise sown to apparently irreconcilable splits.

The irony is that Frederick Perls had it right in the first place. In the introduction to *Perls, Hefferline and Goodman,* he pointed out that to understand the book, the reader had to have the "gestalt attitude;" but to have the attitude, he had to understand the book. Further, that the attitude was not unique but was the natural way of mankind, then sundered by the splits.

But Fritz Perls' "lament" for ontology and his pitch for it in gestalt psychology was an example of a classical collapse to authority of a not untypical rebel whose ears and eyes were closed to "thinking" and for whom all the world was a stage.

We will see in the next lecture how his partner in the effort, Paul Goodman, in his most brilliant exegesis, as well cut and pasted and fudged, embraced contradictions and ignorances and perhaps unintelligibilities from time to time in the guise of wisdom.

But in the main, for them both, the "center of their vision," as William James says, was grand and true, fundamentally sound and stirring, a call to life in a saner and just society, where again after James, "something is doing in the universe."

FOOTNOTE

History and Systems of Psychology, Spring 2002, Three credits, Staff

This is a review of a number of the main historical systems in psychology from instrospectionism through functionalism, from behaviorism and gestalt psychology to modern cognitive approaches. The purpose of the course is to acquaint students with the recent history of psychology and to help them identify important systematic trends in contemporary writings and their underlying assumptions. (*Catalogue, The Graduate Faculty of Political and Social Science*, New School University).

Three Lectures

2002

The inspiration for this series swooshed in my mind at a retreat of the New York Institute for Gestalt Therapy in 1999. It became clear to me that I could best sum up in lecture form what had been partial; and I so stated it in a "go-around":

1. Gestalt therapy as I understood it and its bases.

2. Where we are now in its development, and,

3. Where I hope it to be in the next fifty years.

It all came trippingly to my tongue but to organize and structure the material balked me until recently, when I saw that many articles and plans for papers I had contemplated and even started were, in fact, connected as history, theory, case history, speculation and example.

Thirty years ago, Fritz Perls lamented in his autobiography, *In and Out of the Garbage Pail,* the lack of a firm ontic base for gestalt therapy:

> I had to take all responsibility for my existence myself...I had trapped myself. Through being preoccupied with psychoanalysis in Frankfurt, I remained uninvolved with the existentialists there: Buber, Tillich, Scheler. This much had penetrated: existential philosophy demands taking responsibility for one's existence. But which of the existential schools had the Truth with a capital T?

> Skeptically, I searched further and this is where I stand now. In spite of all the anti-conceptual and pro-phenomenological bias, no existential philosophy stands on its own legs. I am not even talking about the typical American existentialist who preaches and bullshits about existence but walks the earth as a dead conceptualizing computer. No, I am talking about the basic existentialists. Is there anyone who does not need external, mostly conceptual, support?

> What is Tillich without his Protestantism, Buber without his Chassidism, Marcel without Catholicism? Can you imagine Sartre without support from his Communist ideas, Heidegger without support from language, or Binswanger without psychoanalysis?

And then almost plaintively:

> Is there then no possibility of an ontic orientation where Dasein — the fact and means of our existence — manifests itself understandable, without explanatoriness; a way to see the world not through the bias of any concept, but where we understand the bias of conceptualizing; a perspective where we are not satisfied to take an abstraction for a whole picture — where, for instance, the physical aspect is taken as all there is?

And then the apotheosis to Discovery:

> Indeed, there is! Surprisingly enough, it comes from a direction which never claimed the status of a philosophy. It comes from a science which is neatly tucked away in our colleges; it comes from an approach called gestalt psychology. (Perls, 1969)

That the direction never claimed the status of philosophy is questionable; that the direction is a science is a further question. Indeed, it was the hope of Köhler that gestalt psychology could be seen as a "young science" that would approach the strong foundation on which physics was built which, of course, did not happen.

> I had to take all responsibility for myself. I had trapped myself. Existential philosophy demands taking responsibility for one's existence. Truth. Anti-conceptual versus phenomenological. Ontic existentialism. Abstraction versus the whole picture. The physical aspect is (taken) as all there is. Gestalt psychology.

I will revisit these asseverations as Perls' loose language in the service of excellent ends; but also as in a man of undoubted genius, whose grasp was beyond his reach; whose intellectual tools were not merely lacking but unwanted. In another context, I have described this as a gust for originality so intense as to deny himself the information that perhaps might prove otherwise. It is formally related to Procrustes and akin to revisionist historians of gestalt psychotherapy. It has lamentable provenance in the question, what is gestalt therapy? and the deserved metaphysical twaddle that wraps itself into such discussions.

Presently, let me say that taking all responsibility for oneself with the trap that springs in isolation released only in the contact demanded in horniness is the cynical conceit of the inconsolatory loneliness of adolescence. Given the social nature of humankind, it is an impossible doctrine; given the opportunities to inform himself except for a stubborn pride in "having no referential knowledge" and "I do not read," it is *jejeune.*

Also, to restate as the antithesis of an abstraction, "the physical aspect," is to refute your own argument. How is it less an abstraction? Moreover, it reveals Perls' relentless antipathy to thinking, or rather conceptualization, understandable in the displacement of feeling to thought of his time. As if there is not contactful thinking.

Frederick Perls had brusqued the same conundrum in the introduction to *Gestalt Therapy* in 1951:

Indispensable — both for the writing and the thorough understanding of this book — is an attitude which as a theory, actually permeates the content and method of the book. Thus the reader is apparently confronted with an impossible task: to understand the book, he must have the "gestaltist" mentality, and to acquire it, he must understand the book.

Fortunately, the difficulty is far from being insurmountable, for the authors have not invented such a mentality. On the contrary, we believe that the gestalt outlook is the original, undistorted, natural approach to life; that is, to man's thinking, acting, feeling. The average person, having been raised in an atmosphere full of splits, has lost his Wholeness, his Integrity.

To come together again, he has to heal the dualism of his person, of his thinking, and of his language. He is accustomed to thinking of contrasts — of infantile and mature, of body and mind, organism and environment, self and reality, as if they were opposing entities. The unitary outlook which can dissolve such a dualistic approach is buried but not destroyed, and, as we intend to show, can be regained with wholesome advantage. (*PHG*, pp. vii)

Three points should be made here: the excerpt is pure Perls on the internal evidence; and indeed, except for Paul Goodman's amazing restatement of the body of Perls' work and Goodman's section on Verbalizing and Poetry in the theory section of the book, so is the rest of the work. Broadly indeed, there is nothing in Perls, Hefferline and Goodman (*PHG*) that is not in *Ego, Hunger and Aggression.* Secondly, we have the basis for their attack and criticism of the "neurosis of so-called normalcy" which, if gestalt therapy is to go anywhere in the next fifty years, must exhaustively to go there. Third, the healing of splits becomes the restatement in the theory section as *The Plan of This Book.*

There is a further semi-point which I insert and intend also to revisit. Explicit in Perls' words is that his audience wants to heal their splits, do the hard work of the dental aggression, and indeed, are able to bear the suffering of loosening the grip of the linear so-called education in the *Gulag.* Or, more theoretically, to loosen the grip of the false identifications to which we still remain loyal. How could it be otherwise?

I have attempted to locate gestalt therapy in time and space a half-century ago and in New York City. Apart from the plain truth of it, there is a method in my madness: that is, to try to find a way that one can feel included while learning, supported in the apparent wilderness of learning, to have faith that one will get it, without having to chuck the whole thing up and reinvent one's own school in the name of "accessibility," or perhaps "integration," to avoid "being dumped on," and in the revision, to place the origin of gestalt therapy in the late 60s or 70s in California, Europe, or even South America.

There is authority for this amputation in the gestalt body. It comes from Perls himself who, when he rediscovered the "impasse," announced that his previous work was "obsolete," embraced and brought with him the taped work — an audio of *Gestalt Therapy Verbatim,* along with film and video from the Esalen period. *Excitement and Growth in the Human Personality* was hung on the line to dry.

Laura Perls circled the wagons in New York. The logic, implications and experiments growing out of classical gestalt therapy there remained ever in focus. Self as contact at the boundary in the organism/environment field; creating the figure of contact, not the figure it creates; technique, therefore, as an expression of fully integrated process out of which it emerges, not for its own sake; the social nature of the field, and field itself taken seriously.

Perhaps, most importantly, gestalt therapy is profoundly a philosophic activity, and within that, emphatically an aesthetic one. Although for fifty years, these themes and contexts were worked and reworked, taken seriously and experimented, there were many changes.

In the early or perhaps mid-50s, Isadore From had worked out his exegesis from the phases of contact that Goodman had "conveniently divided" from a single contact episode on Page 403 of *PHG*, Perls, Hefferline and Goodman. He worked arduously at the logic and implications of this schema and brought it to Cleveland where it found a welcome reception even as Isadore took as his task to be the shield and guerdon against easily introjected gestalt therapy.

With the phases, fore-contact, contact A and B, final contact and post-contact with their typical accompanying behaviors, Isadore taught a careful and meticulous gestalt therapy. The magnitudes and vectors implicit in Lewin's unfinished business — cited in *Ego, Hunger and Aggression* — carried with them a systems perspective that became the "cycle of experience" in Cleveland. Intra-personal, interpersonal, and group systems in a market driven whole became the synopsis. Isadore himself regarded group therapy very much in a Tavistock model, almost phobically, as that model replicated the pain and horrors of the family.

Indeed, the model of evolution in New York was from individual gestalt therapy in a group context to a figure/ground individual/group context as the Institute opened itself to the full implications of field and context, as members who had trained in group awareness, and were sensitive to the field, displaced the earlier approach. As we continue, a more complete analysis of this evolution and the New York Institute as a case history generating its self-development will be apparent.

The method of these papers will be: exposition, as in the foregoing analysis or restatement; and finally experiment. In every case, I will try to bring the work to these three partial integrations so the lectures themselves evolve to examples that I am trying to develop: that is, exactly gestalt therapy theory, standing on its own two feet.

Imagine you are in a group of several groups, perhaps in a conference such as the one the New York Institute convened in 1996, entitled *Transatlantic Dialogue*. Suppose further, one of the tasks is precisely to heighten awareness of the perspective/object continuum and its social nature as follows:

> For example, I ask you to close your eyes; working from that Act:
>
> 1. to the experience of seeing;
>
> 2. to the development of imagery;
>
> 3. to present physical experience;
>
> 4. to your group's awareness;
>
> 5. to the large group situation and awareness; and, almost finally, to the difference from first to last with and in the integration.
>
> Thus, our analysis will not be a "dissolving force" but a unifying experience viewed from differing but not separate perspectives, proceeding "next to next" in the rhythms we call contact sequences but which I shall try to restate within a theory of the Act.

The sequence is not linear but circular and spiraling to a point. It is thus that we avoid tautology which is circular and linear and does not open itself to novelty as does our theory of experiment and our experiment itself which we approach with the expectation of novelty: something there that was not there before to which we open ourselves — and the summit of integrity — to which we say we are available.

It has been said that when the figure of contact has been achieved the gestalt is completed, the unfinished business is irrelevant, that it sinks into the background or is merely forgotten. Within the theory of the Act, we can sketch a more complete analysis, but not an explanation, of the process. Where there are problems, the process leading to the completion of the act through the stages of Impulse, Perception, Manipulation and

Consummation becomes "checked" as competing hypotheses for the solution of the problem emerge. Finally, when all fits, the problem — the Act — moves to Consummation or Contact.

In gestalt therapy theory, we would say the process moves through the four stages, fore-contact, contact A and B, final contact and post-contact to the gestalt of contact, the Whole where all the terms are known, and there is nothing that is unaccounted for. All is flowing in the figure of the Thou. The segue to Buber's dialogic existentialism is immediate. It does not get us far ontologically, however.

Generally, we are taken to American Pragmatism of the Chicago school, specifically, James and Dewey, whom Goodman affirms as his philosophic forebears. We hear not a word of the social philosopher and social psychologist, George Herbert Mead, though the schema of gestalt therapy and his analysis of the theory of the Act seems from time to time uncannily identical.

The gestalt psychologists stated perception as wholes of experience and demonstrated the gestalt in shining experiments effectively eliminating summative elements building up to a bundle of perception in the Humean tradition. They founded their work in an isomorphism or psycho-physical parallelism later which posited equivalent dynamical relations in the neurons with the objects of perception experienced as the wholes of experience. They demonstrated the conditions of the gestalt in such classical areas of experimental psychology in the various constancies, size, color, shape and so forth, including movement, as in common fate and goodness of fit.

The fundamental condition was *prägnanz*, "that grouping that tends toward maximal simplicity and balance, or toward the formation of good form." Köhler specifically warned of the problem of social perception and little was done on it except for the classical work of Solomon Asch's *Social Psychology*, especially his group pressure experiments.

Of course, Lewin's original work was essentially social and so it developed as those experiments went from memory for unfinished tasks which so impressed Frederick Perls, to the completion of unfinished tasks themselves to those effects in group pairs.

I will restate those effects from the pragmatic point of view as we get more deeply into that work. For now, let us just say that in gestalt psychology, after again failing to continue the social emphasis toward what is now being called relational psychology, Leon Festinger and cognitive dissonance were embraced, and in gestalt psychology, cognition again prevailed. The dust bowl was easy to the plow and so the mule and psychology trudged on in its furrow of tedium and apathy with returns at monotony.

"Thus the reader is apparently confronted with an impossible task: to understand the book, he must have the 'gestaltist' mentality, and to acquire it, he must understand the book." (*PHG,* pp. vii) This throw-away line indicates the grief that has led legions of students and trainees to crack their teeth and despair of ever learning the theory of gestalt psychotherapy.

(Of course, it then is a rationale for neglecting the rich experiments section of the book, pure early Perls and "beyond praise." That rationale has led also to major devolutions which have attempted integrations of the two sections to heal a split that does not exist. The surgery has produced the stitches of the scar called cognitive therapy which within its broad reach becomes Rogerian or so-called "client centered" therapy, which the more one chews, the further one is driven to intellectual despair. For starters, what is "a" (or) "the client?" The client is the field).

To return to the theme, not half in jest but certainly in satire, I was tempted to title it, and now do:

On Not Getting It

To stitch further my reference to American Pragmatism, let me refer to William James' *The Meaning of Truth:*

> We should never have spoken elliptically. The critics have boggled at every word they could boggle at, and refused to take the spirit rather than the letter of our discourse. This seems to show a genuine unfamiliarity in the whole point of view. It also shows, I think, that the second stage of opposition, which has already begun to express itself in the stock phrase that "what is new is not true and what is true, not new," in pragmatism is insincere. (James, 1970, pp. 181)

Then, in a mixture of barely suppressed irritation and perhaps lofty patrician patience:

> If we said nothing in any degree new, why was our meaning so desperately hard to catch?

In the introduction to *The Meaning of Truth*, Ralph Ross says:

> William James was surely one of the masters of English prose. His style was masculine and terse, yet fluent and at times lyrical, a New England style in the tradition of John Adams and with many similarities to that of his boyhood friend, Oliver Wendell Holmes, Jr. How was it, then, that throughout this book, as throughout his life, he complained that his writings were misunderstood? (M.T., pp. v)

I, a founding member of the "Incomprehensibility Club," have no pretensions to a Jamesian style. I do, however, completely understand the personal incredulity of being misunderstood one more time, and one more time, feel the rage, embarrassment and humiliation, yes and the existential loneliness that accompanies, not being a foreigner in your own land, but the glimmer and the blaze of awareness that they are doing it to me.

And so did Paul Goodman. I was witness to such scenes frequently. He was often goaded to protest he was not the village idiot. He did have a "masculine and terse, yet fluent and at times lyrical ... New England style." (He is buried in New Hampshire next to Matthew and his sister.)

To return to Ralph Ross on William James's complaint of misunderstoodness:

> The answer, I think, is that any philosopher who makes a difference, because he has something new to say, is misunderstood, at least for a time ... New themes require new types of statement and it is (as) difficult for a reader to fathom the new prose patterns.
>
> He was a psychologist with firm grasp of ordinary human behavior, and he assumed that a description of what men did in solving problems went a long way in philosophy. (James, *The Meaning of Truth*, pp. vi)

The dilemma is not insoluble. That is, the dilemma of "having to know before you know." It is not even a dilemma. It is a false split, the foundation of Perls, Hefferline and Goodman (*PHG*) as the *Plan of This Book*. Let me give what is not so much an example but an example of one:

> "If we said nothing in any degree new, why was our meaning so desperately hard to catch?" This has, to repeat, frequently been otherwise said: "The book (*Gestalt Therapy*) is inaccessible, confusing, incomprehensible, polemical; it must be integrated, reconsidered," and so forth, and so forth.

But of course, if you have flies in your eyes, how can you see the flies in your eyes? The bedrock of gestalt therapy is the experiment, or rather, experimenting. In New York, we discovered and invented the group reading of the book as an experiment. What are the elements of experiment classically? It is at first private, an idea that must be proven in the world that is there, the only possibility of any proof whatever.

Experiment has elements of equality, mutuality, opportunity and support. And it must be meant. That is, we must go where it takes us. So the book invites group study where the leader is at best facilitator and sometimes first among equals. This redefines "leadership" and leads directly to a theory, and the praxis of gestalt group psychotherapy, of which more comes later.

We have been so trained in the educational *Gulag,* precisely, to think, to take responsibility, individually to know before we know or could possibly know, that this alien identification we defend as our true I. The defensive armamentarium bristles with spikes eager to explode the mines in a lonely and unnavigable sea. And so one collapses against the wall of authority, anxiety and confusion.

It is a painful adjustment which soon becomes familiar and numb, like bad posture, one's relation to the only world. The entire picture was beautifully presented and analyzed in John Dewey's wildly popular Gifford lectures at Edinburgh in April 1929, subsequently published as *The Quest for Certainty.* That quest, he said, leads inevitably to dogma and authority and self and social oppression. And on and on.

The influence on Goodman is direct and supports this. Indeed, he restates it in his description in *Gestalt Therapy* "of intrinsic as against extrinsic" standards, that which moves the process and that which constricts it. Or, to restate its source in Dewey, *A Study of the Relation between Thought and Action,* which says it all.

There is a further invitation in experiment. That is, the support for anxiety, individual and institutional, which follows from equality, opportunity and mutuality. Reading *Gestalt Therapy* together is both the example for experiment and justification for refusing. Because we expect and invite anxiety, we are creating therapeutic anxiety and inviting, therefore, and also cultivating, institutional support for breath.

Such a creative adjustment is not easy but hard; not complicated but simple. With its achievement, the protection of isolation and inaccessibility and the economy of an inconsolable individuality is exposed to process, novelty and change. Genuine responsibility, self/other enlightenment and action take the place of, "I had to take full responsibility for myself." What ultimately becomes clear is the projection off the secondary isolation of the so-called adjustment of that, the abstraction we call the "Individual."

On page 4, I spoke of the method of these papers as analysis, or restatement and finally, experiment and guided (!) imagery as an example. But the meta-example was these lectures themselves and this process as it now develops and changes. We now witnessing "new themes requiring new types of statement (and how) difficult it is (for a reader) to fathom new prose patterns." (M.T., pp. vi) The foregoing paragraphs were an attempt at the "example of the example" and perhaps the spiraling I spoke of also on page 4. We are attempting a language of awareness without resort to the aesthetic of poetry which is perhaps, and indeed likely, impossible. We can, however, be poetic.

How did we get to this point in the discourse? We presented the problem of the bases of gestalt therapy and the frustration of the Perls et al, at the incompleteness of the ground on which to stand for their new therapy; and spoke to the attempts to fill this need, indicating the various schools and revisions that seem to me to have nibbled around the edges in futile attempts to gnaw a niche in which to operate on the body gestalt, but apparently lacking the second set of teeth adequate to do more than gum the job. What is that task and what is or was or continues to be lacking?

For an introduction, and again a meta-method and meta-example, let us take a short history of the New York Institute as the patient and derive what we can clinically from its examination.

We will find generally that we didn't know what we were talking about. Certainly one of the glories of an awareness therapy is that with good will and presentness, you can in enlightened ignorance bring about movement and change in the field and "with support, the patient can make his own interpretation," as Laura Perls was wont to affirm. But it is nice, within the aura of experiment, supported by its meaning, to see light within the patient's and your co-creating.

A forum had been organized as a creative discovery — and — inventing activity to chew the Process Group approach to conferencing evolved to what, since 1999, has been called the New York model. I had been asked to speak somewhat on background and philosophy from which the model evolved (and is evolving) and upon which it is founded and as you will see, I have as usual, interpreted the request perhaps too broadly.

In a larger sense, the history of the New York Institute of which the process group is an epitome, can be seen first as a choppy though fairly uniform evolution to first, the context, then of course, the group in therapy in a traditional, perhaps conservative format; ultimately or at least at the present stage, to the process group itself mutually and reciprocally, that is, in a whole and parts relation, or better, organization, as well with the larger group and the polis.

Secondly, though far more important, the process group embraces not only the figural, the movement individual — to group, but also illustrates the pragmatic principle that novelty in the sense of the problem is at first a biographical referent. The individual or minority sees what the others do not yet see. Their hypothesis is advanced experiment within the hypothesis and, of course, within what is already known by all, and have the results evaluated. If the hypothesis is demonstrated, the effort moves into what is common over against its polarity (private or biographical), and the experiment becomes knowledge. Knowledge, as opposed to information, is social, that is, based on reflective intelligence.

There are problems...

The format of the hypothesis/experiment/demonstration is ideally appropriate to so-called "scientific" pursuits. It has not proved workable in psychological science except where the conception of humankind has been primitivized to where the unknown can be isolated as in the infra-human studies. This is another way of saying in reverse a principal tenet of gestalt therapy. That is, the hypothesis must be tested in the unquestioned world that is there.

Gestalt therapy says focus on the interruptions (I prefer "interruptings") (the "hypothesis") and immediately, the conditions of the interruption (the world that is there and the reality) reveals itself (the demonstration) and this is self-demonstrating. The general hypothesis is proved: unity, or better, self. Further, as Sylvia Crocker puts it..."and this is good science."

If we keep these two flows in mind, the stream of gestalt therapy itself within the river of its developing awareness of its place in the roots of the Chicago school of pragmatism, and we will have the clarity of parallel development with support and robustness of intellectual cross-fertilization that removes the sand bars to theoretical progress and guides us even farther from the pseudo-clarity of the wilderness and ontological desert that is systems theory,

I will begin with the prehistoric past. I say "prehistoric" since I note in the *Gestalt Review* that gestalt group psychotherapy, at least in theory, began in the 70s. Other revisionists, as I have been informed in Sicily, have gone so far as to maintain that gestalt therapy itself began in South America or perhaps, even in California.

In the broader view, a process that is now the New York model began in New York at the Institute for Gestalt Therapy in 1952. Let me take you there almost a half-century ago.

A stubborn group of brilliant and near geniuses, with perhaps a few real geniuses, originally gathered around Frederick and Laura Perls, and formed an organization to do what such things do give classes, seminars and so forth. They ranged from supervision and demonstration to education and writer's block. (The latter two, education and writer's block, were respectively, Elliott Shapiro's and Paul Goodman's). Everyone also did individual psychotherapy.

When Frederick Perls opined he wanted to do groups, we formed a group and did group. As in their individual therapies, supervision, and demonstration, the work was individual, one on one, and the context defined, or better, named the activity. Thus, for example, Dr. Perls would start the group with the famous: "Ja, who wants to work?" He would then do what he did routinely, individual therapy, while the rest of us awaited our turn in various states of anxiety/excitement, panic or stupefaction. Much later, Perls acknowledged the context and began using the other group members as projection screens for the victim/patient's productions. I believe that emerged as he began his circuit riding and developed his famous demonstration style.

So to the biographical within gestalt therapy as first practiced, circa 1952 ...After returning to New York from Los Angeles mid-1952, I asked Dr. Perls about the possibility of becoming a therapist. He was encouraging but said I should complete my graduate degree at the New School where they "had a good program in gestalt psychology." I did that, completing the requirements in 1955. Dr. Perls sent me my first patient in 1953.

At the New School, my teachers were Hans Wallach and Rudolf Arnheim in perception, Helen Block Lewis in personality, Mary Henle and Irvin Rock in experimental and Solomon Asch in social psychology. Asch had done his pioneering group pressure experiments in the late 40s. Our class room text, Asch's *Social Psychology* was published in 1952. Lewis had taken Zeigarnik's and Rickers-Ovsiankana's adaptation of Lewin's original work on quasi-needs, perhaps quasi-instinct, from the memory for unfinished tasks to the completion of those tasks not as originally with the individual but with pairs and thus group context.

Perls was familiar or perhaps acquainted with the memory for the unfinished in Lewin, and indeed, had cited it in *Ego, Hunger and Aggression*. He had, however, a delight in not reading anymore, preferring to have others do it for him, listening closely to their reports for his background information. From my studies, I told him he knew nothing about groups to which he agreed. "Ja, I do not read; I have no referential knowledge." At first, I regarded this as a defensive boast. Finally, I thought it a wall against new information in a man driven to be original. It is not novel that the energy goes out of an idea if someone else has already thought it.

Notwithstanding the introduction to the 1969 edition of *Ego, Hunger and Aggression,* he listed the contributions that had been accepted from gestalt therapy over twenty years, e.g., "awareness," which had been accepted in sensitivity and T groups, and said individual therapy "was dead," (echoing an announcement he had made at an APA conference somewhat earlier)

Perls dismissed his former work as obsolete and was determinedly pressing the "impasse" or breakthrough of the "death layer" in the larger group demonstration setting. The rhythmic pulsation of figure/ground, individual to group and group to individual, individual/group/large group/culture had no place except perhaps a despair that his truly revolutionary insight — that aggression could be brought back into the field of the biological activity of the human organism and not projected into infinitely destructive and savage wars.

The New York Institute has met and continues to meet monthly since its inception. It became clear as a function of several accepted, though critically unexamined axioms of the theory of the field, not field theory, that those axioms were not a supportive presence at those meetings.

For example, if contact at the boundary in the "here and now" is a unifying and central concept in gestalt therapy; if the group and its members are the here and now reality, and thus obviously, the field of contact; if individual work in therapy, that is contact-making, is attempted, ignoring the group context and its dynamics, obviously, the reality is fractured and enormous potentialities, forever to be undiscovered novelties, are un-operated and remain underground.

Not having learned the mistakes of present and future history, we were condemned to repeat them; scapegoating, authority/dependent, rivalrous forces were fostered and festered.

In short, all the transferential elements that are typical of a primitivized field are elicited. I would go further and say just such a field is the supporting ground of transference and the theory of transference makes no sense without a basis in a truncated reality. Of course, therapist and patient are the field of contact and not exceptional in this analysis.

That band of "blessed and rebellious outcasts," as Elliott Shapiro called them, could not seem to complete its revolution within itself and that tradition clung to our meetings as an unstated group norm. Several things had to happen first.

What happened? The apparent converging of psychology/science and psycho/therapy in 1952 diverged, again split into psychology versus psychotherapy. The most recent issue of *The American Psychologist*, calling for "relational science" in psychological research traced the retreat from the emerging social emphasis regressing to the so-called individual, to the entrance on the stage of Leon Festinger's *cognitive dissonance*. I feel compelled to remind you that "cognitive" restates, of course, "individual," itself a projection off the secondary experience of isolation within the primary social.

In the Institute, as more and more members came with backgrounds in group therapy or especially field group work, the diremption between individual and group emphasis became clearly marked. In particular, Patrick Kelley, a patient of Laura Perls, who was fleeing gray-flannel Madison Ave. He became a youth gang worker, completed his graduate work and joined the Human Relations Department faculty at New York University. He is the author of *Reaching the Teen Age Addict*. He brought his democratic faith and fierce zeal for the underdog to everything he approached. I have him with his first rate intellect in mind when I say the conflicts were cosmic and creative and mirrored the professional split within the Institute.

The split was clear: the members who wanted "structure" represented by Isadore From who clung to one-on-one therapy in or out of the group context and who also held foundational the stages of contact and its interruptions in the traditional theory of contact and its revisions in the Cleveland systems or cycle-of-contact theory; led the process-oriented members who saw the stages of contact as Goodman stated them — the typology of a single behavior for purposes of the therapist's "scientific conception." Further, the "here and now" contextual interaction was crucial and included group as rhythmically figure/ground or ground/figure and the emerging objective awareness of group contact as perception in the field.

This rift was, of course, not limited to the New York Institute. It mirrored the movements in psychotherapy in the general field and restated the varying devolutions within gestalt therapy as its holistic logic and Frederick Perls' "gestaltist attitude" bumped against the fortress of the building block theory of knowledge and thus, the atomistic bias that yet remained in gestalt psychology.

In the many attempts to "integrate" these splits over the years, the best that can be said is that they used the tool of the bed of Procrustes universally. If the whole did not fit their outlook then it was snipped until they could rest comfortably on the pallet of semi-gestalt therapy that yet remained. And so the various institutes revolved around their axes sweeping the same arcs of micro-cosmic dust into the black holes of their swirling centers.

Why was it so hard to get?

When Cleveland was about to happen, Frederick Perls queried the professional group in New York how best to approach teaching gestalt therapy to a serious group of Mid-Western professional psychologists. He was concerned about scaring them off with the New York "somewhat in-your-face" direct approach. The consensus was that an existential therapy could not at first be taught with the usual teacher-led lectern technique. It could at best be demonstrated with the didactics to come afterwards. This was, of course, the teaching method in the professional group that became the New York Institute.

The fuzzy concept was that, in a stunning reversal, if there was a problem in the therapy (when is there not?) the stuck point was not in the patient who, after all, had come for exactly that reason, that he/she was stuck. Since there were you and the patient, the problem had to be largely in you. Now, how to work with this in the professional/supervision group in New York?

Let me show you the scene. A brave soul, after a long group silence, ventured that he/she was balked/stuck/frightened or generally in the dark with a specific patient and wanted help or support or enlightenment. The therapist was invited into the circle and usually lay on the floor. (The foreshortened view of pairs of shoes, legs, ultimately head and neck with its implications of prostration before the "Great King" was not considered. The therapist/victim then "became" the patient.

Let me repeat: since the patient was not there and the therapist was, under the theory, of contact at the boundary, here and now, in the organism/environment field, it made sense as a teaching instrument to "role play" the patient. There were not yet the intellectual tools to understand the multiple role takings normally there in every person and as well, the specific sense of group-as-a-whole and its pressures.

So there were individual offerings and "therapies" from each group member for the therapist/patient/victim accordingly as the process rotated to an area of his/her concern or interest as he/she was persuaded or coerced or bullied, perhaps exhorted into believing where he/she had gone astray. Now, if you had the guts, this is not bad. Moreover, to stand the therapeutic relationship from doctor to patient, therapist to client, teacher to student, individual to individual, on its head was a half-century ago, not less than astounding.

The step to learning from the patient was obvious and not at all unstated, but much more honored in the breach. Perls himself still sat on his "throne" behind the couch on which I lay and interpreted away right and left. "Ja, something inside is trying to come out." Or, "How did you cope with such a *rochet de bronze*?" That was my mother.

The couch had the qualities of its defects. It mercifully supported and gave cover for session-long silences where what I had to say was formed but could not come off the tongue while I gazed at Perls famous subway painting on the wall in front of me, strategically placed. He would at those times disappear for ten minutes at a time for an apparent piss call. The reality was he was bored silly and the ever-lit cigarette wasn't working. I was relieved he was out of the room. He never interpreted that or my arriving forty minutes late or not at all. He should have.

It seems incredible that there were long earnest discussions of the merits, if any, of face-to-face or rather chair-to-chair therapy. Laura and Paul Weisz had evolved to that long before and had settled it for themselves. I couldn't see what the fuss was about. There are times for couch or times for chair. Face-to-face gave me more opportunity to read direction and motive and get there betimes. As Perls said to Bob Wilson of Cleveland: "Dick? Ja, that one really knows what's going on!" I didn't trust even more than he didn't trust and so had all the right lines which happened to be true, but as Goodman said, were also rationalizations.

But the experiences added up. Somehow, feeling one's way in the dark revealed more and more clearly the bread crumbs on the ground that could blaze the path home. Allison Montague and I audited a Zen course at Columbia by Daisetz Sozuki which was mostly blackboards crammed full of derivations from the Sanskrit to the Chinese to the Japanese, somewhat interesting but the point was that we got there from the here of our fascination with the sound of one hand clapping, or finding, and ultimately showing, the face we had before we were born. The significant thrust was we could all burst into laughter with the right koan and rest on that. We did not have to seek further, to find out why.

We knew we would get it in time. The real intellectual in the group, Laura, said, "Things take time. And they have their own time." Thus, there was suffering, or from the gestalt view of suffering: to allow it to happen, which is of course, the Tao on which rests the theory of therapeutic or healing anxiety and its invitation and expectation. So again, rather than interpreting or anesthetizing panic anxiety away, the technical problem became how to get breath dished out and in, in teaspoons.

Again, to come full circle, excitement and growth in the human personality as contained to anxiety and stultification was, *mirabile dictu*, especially to be worked with therapists themselves who certainly had varying tolerance for freedom. Or, perhaps in "getting it," they "got" all they could contain, and went off to found their own schools. The Seventeenth Century divines pondered the problem of the degrees of heavenly grace the souls of the departed could expect from an all-loving God. They solved it ingeniously by comparing the souls to differing containers all full. So you got as much grace as you could hold.

As Paul Goodman said, "So far, so bad." But the work of "getting it" carries with it a nagging sense, perhaps an itch, that one has not "got" it. Inevitably then, one has to kill the teachers, leave the teaching behind and nail one's own flag to the mast of his theory, his boat. Thus, the schools, until recently, were reluctant to talk to each other.

But to continue with "getting it," let us forward (!) to the turn of the Twentieth Century and William James and pragmatism for a parallel case:

> If we said nothing in any degree new, why was our meaning so desperately hard to catch? (M.T. pp. 181) ... Where our ideas (do) not copy definitely their object, what does agreement with that object mean? Pragmatism asks its usual question. "Grant an idea or belief to be true," it says, "what concrete difference will its being true make in any one's life? What experiences (may) be different from those which would be obtained if the belief were false? How will the truth be realized? What in short, is the truth's cash-value in experiential terms?

> The moment pragmatism asks this question, it sees the answer: *True ideas are those that we can assimilate, validate, corroborate, and verify. False ideas are those we cannot.* That is the practical difference it makes to us to have true ideas; that therefore is the meaning of truth, for it is all that truth is known as.

Let us agree that truth is what one gets when one "gets" it. Or is synonymous with "getting" it? Therefore:

> The truth of an idea is not a stagnant property inherent in it. Truth happens to an idea. It becomes true, is made true by events. Its verity is in fact an event, a process, the process namely of its verifying itself, its verification. Its validity is the process of its validation. (M.T. pp. xxx)

Further, let us allow those who toil in the vineyards of psychotherapy to suffer the work of getting their own truth, cultivating their tender grapes in making themselves true by their events.

We can derive some hints for psychotherapy from James above. If true ideas are those we can assimilate, validate, corroborate, and verify; false ideas are those we cannot, *and this is a practical difference...* If true ideas are thus an achievement, as is the self, then the very delectable mountain for the correction, or learning away from false ideas, should be the teaching/learning/community, the healing part of which is psychotherapy. For it is the idea that cannot get on in the world, when the completion of its circuit of verification in action is interrupted, which instead becomes an arc, an interrupting or unaware blocking is sometimes called neurosis.

In gestalt therapy, we keep an eye out for normal interruptions when they shade into unaware ones and focus on the structure of the interruption. For example, stiffening the body and of course, choking the breath, is our definition of anxiety. Patient and therapist experiment together, focusing, developing awareness of these structures and support, not the process so much, but both the process and the field. Some therapists prefer to lead carefully from the front, others from the back of the process. Perhaps this is a personal choice, but whatever it is, the choice is supported by the faith and knowledge that we are involved in a whole phenomenon, a common experience. The interrupting, the diagnosis, the theory, and the praxis are one. The "plan of this book" is to direct attention to false splits and so to affect the healing process.

From page 2, we hear Frederick Perls exclaim that there is a possibility of a self-supported existential philosophy and that it comes from not a philosophy, but a psychology, gestalt psychology, which had its heyday in Germany in pre and post-World War II, first came to America fleeing Nazi oppression. It became established at the New School, Swarthmore, Chicago and perhaps Los Angeles. As we all remember, the names were: Wertheimer, Köhler, Koffka, Lewin, Gelb and Goldstein. In his regret that he did not pay enough attention to the gestalt goings-on in Frankfurt, being so preoccupied with psychoanalysis, let us keep in the minds' eye that Laura Perls wrote her dissertation on color constancy under Adhemar Gelb.

It makes a snarl in the mind's web to envision Frederick Perls preoccupied with psychoanalysis. (He spelled it with the hyphen). His primary reference to it was always perhaps, a sighing sarcasm, or outright attack: "Years, decades, lifetimes on the couch."

If we can picture the brilliant young psychoanalyst arriving at a conference to present a paper on oral aggression: he waits upon the master, Freud, to receive him in the doorway with: "If you do not believe in anal aggression, why don't you resign from the organization?" Perls had the door slammed in his face. His humiliation, disappointment and betrayal can only be approximated to those of childhood and the family. From preoccupation to despair. Frederick Perls kept an autographed picture of Freud on his office wall. Laura Perls kept a bronze head of her husband on a column in her living room.

As I wrote the above paragraph, I suddenly saw quite clearly the quiet support and enormous intellectual opportunity Laura must have supplied to her husband in that time. He had to have the architectonic of gestalt psychology in his wife; he could pick and choose, restate his original intuition in 1942 South Africa as *Ego, Hunger and Aggression.* He dedicated it to Laura Perls. She always said she had written the *Dummy* chapter and another which I can't remember. Perhaps, it was the background for the theory of dental aggression based on her observations of native children and her own nursing experiences. Perls dedicated the second edition to Max Wertheimer.

At his funeral oration for Perls, Paul Goodman, I thought grandly, said that Perls' only original contribution was, in fact, the theory of dental aggression. This set off an uproar from the loyalists who came to praise but not to bury. "We all know Fritz was a character, but that's not what we came here for." This from Perls' first patient in New York whom he privately told me he was unable to budge in therapy. Of course, it was *not* his fault; the impediment was the patient's loyalty to his lover.

The gestalt psychology which Goodman chose to found, *Excitement and Growth in the Human Personality,* was mostly from Willis Ellis', *The Source Book of Gestalt Psychology.* He describes his technique for researching in his diary published as *Five Years: Thoughts during a Useless Period.*

> I both respect and am ashamed of my way of doing research. I read a few books and reports, titles that seem promising, including always two or three standard text books, to see what they think is solid enough and comprehensive enough to teach academically. Most of this does not prove to be informative; but it serves to satisfy me that I know as much about the subject as some of the authors, naturally enough, since I would not be engaged with it if I were too dissatisfied with the usual opinions.
>
> With luck, I come on a few propositions that are novel or unexpected to me, and I theorize them into my general view. If

> my own theory thereby becomes tighter and simpler, my
> inventive faculty is aroused. (This is Aristotle's method of
> collection — experience — intuition.) (P.G., 1966, pp. 206)

My experience in intuition and collection in launching this section of the
lecture was that I wanted to set up the formal principles of gestalt
psychology and introduce Goodman's use of them in his adaptation to a
theory, of personality and psychotherapy, furthering the basis for Perls'
lament as I have called it. I knew somewhere in *Five Years,* Goodman
had described his way of doing research as he puts it. I searched through
my volume and found the entry pretty quickly on Page 207. This was
satisfactory, indeed a source of confirmation and intellectual flush of
pleasure.

Underneath *Five Years,* was *Here, Now, Next: Paul Goodman and the
Origins of Gestalt Therapy,* by Taylor Stoehr, and, lo, another delightful
shock of recognition and some chagrin, I found the same quotation of
Goodman's way of doing research. (Also, it has the elements of "stealing
one's thunder" which requires a reassessment of where one is and where
he is going in the libretto.)

Therefore, I have tried to flesh out the problem of the shaky philosophic
foundations of gestalt therapy and have traced a mini-history of its
development. My aim was to show that the founders had not the
conceptual tools to integrate adequately their intuitions and learning into
a coherent or perhaps ontic whole that "could stand on its own two feet."
The closest was, of course, Goodman's work on the theory, and his
restatement of gestalt psychology, further to show that gestalt
psychology itself cannot stand on its own two feet, which gives gestalt
therapy a shaky foundation in the first place. There is the adequate base
for theory, however, in the work of American Pragmatism, especially
James and Dewey, but uniquely George Herbert Mead.

Goodman always asserted the influences of James and Dewey but in
Gestalt Therapy does but barely mentions them. He is equally general in
his other works. He speaks in Stoehr of James as the "first gestaltist" but

there are few specifics. I have already referred to Dewey on dogma and Goodman's treatment of intrinsic and extrinsic evaluation that is but a paraphrase from *The Quest for Certainty*. There is never a reference to George Herbert Mead. I have been able to gather but two nods to him from conversation. (In the professional group on some matter or other, I remarked, "He's only obeying the rules of the game." There was much muttering and pipe-puffing and head-nodding and, I think, "Yes, he's only obeying the rules of the game." To a graduate student who was doing her dissertation on the self and seeking his advice, he said that she would have to "read Mead on that.") (Karen Humphrey, oral communication.)

We are entering the world of perception or rather the experience of perception in experimental psychology which is a universe before gestalt or configuration psychologists, of quills and quiddities of the so-called "old psychology," a world of retinas and mental contents; where realities are proved by recourse to illusions.

William James spoke to this when he talked of the difficulties of introspection and its safeguard "in the final consensus of our farther knowledge correcting earlier ones, until at last the harmony of a consistent system is reached."

> The English writers on psychology, and the school of Herbart in Germany, have in the main contented themselves with such results as the immediate introspection of single individuals gave, and shown what a body of doctrine they may make. The works of Locke, Hume, Reid, Hartley, Stewart, Brown, the Mills, will always be classics in this line; and in *Professor Bain's Treatises*, we have probably the last word of what this method taken mainly by itself can do — the last monument of the *youth of our science*, still non-technical and generally intelligible, like the chemistry of Lavoisier, or anatomy before the microscope was used. (James, P.P., Vol. I, pp. 192)

The italics are mine, above. They are there to point to a detail which is pathognomonic of the whole, that is, the mine of material, even locution, whose ore formed the bedrock of the work of the gestalt psychologists, but whose propagandists not only did not credit *The Principles of Psychology,* but like Frederick Perls himself referring to *Excitement and Growth in the Human Personality,* felt obliged to deny that it ever existed, or that "it is now obsolete." There are, I think, three references to James in Köhler's *Gestalt Psychology,* one wrong, the others having nothing to do with their work as if the *Principles* itself never existed.

(*Psychology as a Young Science* is a chapter in *Gestalt Psychology* and the locution is prated endlessly to deny, mostly to ignore, evidence to the contrary of the gestalt. We will return to this shortly as we (finally) conclude this section.)

But, let's continue with James's delightful outburst as he moves from introspection in the classic sense to the technical and "generally unintelligible" new psychology, hurling bolts of thunder and lightning from his Olympian heights. The reference is famous:

> ...But psychology is passing into a less simple phase. Within a few years what one may call a microscopic psychology has arisen in Germany, carried on by experimental methods, asking, of course, every moment for introspective data, but eliminating their uncertainty by operating on a large scale and taking statistical means.

> This method taxes patience to the utmost, and could hardly have arisen in a country whose natives could be bored. Such Germans as Weber, Fechner, Vicrodt, and Wundt obviously cannot; and their success has brought into the field an array of younger experimental psychologists, bent on studying the elements of *the mental life, dissecting them out from the gross results in which they are embedded, and as far as possible, reducing them to quantitative scales.* (Ibid)

The last sentence is basically heralding what will appear fifty years later in Köhler as his critical chapter, *Psychology as a Young Science,* from the starting point of physics.

> The simple and open method of attack having done what it can, the method of patience starving out and harassing to death is tried; the mind must submit to a regular siege, in which minute advantages gained day and night by the forces that hem her in must sum themselves up at last into her overthrow. There is little of the grand style about these new prism, pendulum, and chronograph-philosophers. They mean business, not chivalry. What generous divination, that superiority in virtue of which was thought by Cicero to give a man the best insight into nature, has failed to do, yet their spying and scraping, their deadly tenacity and almost diabolic cunning, will doubtless bring about. (James, Vol. I, pp. 193).

When most I wink then do mine eyes best see
For all the day, they view things unrespected.
But when I sleep, in dreams they look on thee,
And darkly bright, are bright in dark directed.
Then thou, whose shadow shadows doth make bright,
How would thy shadows form from happy show
To the clear day with thy much clearer light,
When to unseeing eyes, thy shade shines so!
How would (I say) in eyes be blessed made,
By looking on thee in the living day,
When in dead night thy fair imperfect shade
Through heavy sleep on sightless eyes doth stay!
All days are nights till I see thee,
And night bright days when dreams do show thee me.

— Sonnet 43

To pursue my goal, I will first try pull aside the curtain of gestalt psychology and see it in terms of a foundation for gestalt psychotherapy as a philosophical dead end. This is hard because it marks the undoing of what had been a tenet of faith perhaps, which as usual, succumbed to a more careful reading and a native skepticism of authority. I don't think that classical gestalt psychology can carry the burden of gestalt psychotherapy; in fact in the end, I will argue that it is gestalt therapy that will shoulder whatever influence the formal psychology has or will continue to make in the world.

Briefly, the "configuration psychologists," Mead's term, rebelled against what they considered the elementalism of their time and insisted that experience was of wholes, of figures against grounds, sharp figure against homogeneous grounds, and they experimented these phenomena in perception.

The whole and parts or figure/ground relation which became famous, appropriated informally by Perls and formally by Goodman, was a statement against the atomism of behaviorism and the purely logical relations of Introspectionism and attempted to establish a whole of perception experienced, the *percept unique*. That is, it depended upon the so-called dynamical relations of figure/ground. They described the conditions of the field that brought about the perceptions. Thus, the familiar constancies and generally the law of *prägnanz:*

> ...There are numerous instances of phenomenal facts that are not identical with the properties of things as physical analysis describes them though lawfully related to them...In terms of physics, it is as correct to say that the frame moves with reference to the line as to say the reverse. Our experience however, is more absolute, seeing the movement in one direction ...These strictly psychological processes have an important function: they demonstrate a tendency to perceive the surroundings in as clear a way as the conditions permit.
>
> This tendency to *prägnanz*, or to achieve maximum clarity, can function to produce either greater accuracy or quick but *inadequate organization*. In particular, we have shown that the

> forms of objects, the ways in which they are grouped and segregated, cannot be derived from the properties of the *parts taken in isolation* or from the individual relations *of* the parts. An effect observed at a particular point is not determined independently by local stimulation; what happens at a given point is a function of events in its neighborhood. By varying the illumination of the surroundings alone, we can change the appearance of a surface of constant brightness from white to black, as Wallach has shown. (Asch, pp. 59. Italics mine.)

Since I intend to compare these propositions with empirical analyses of the same experiences, let me add:

> We do not see an object in motion simply because its image on the retina changes position; physically stationary objects can, under appropriate conditions, be seen to move. (Asch, pp. 59)

It is important or rather crucial that the phenomena described be wholes of perception, that is, they be not learned, or as Köhler says, merely logical relations. As I understand it, the relation "2" in 1, 2, 3, is not serial but one of *betweenness*. He did it with three dots in a row with the whiteness between. I use this example because William James treated the identical one in his wide-ranging chapter on *Sensation* in the *Principles*.

As is now obvious, all this psychologizing rests or rather depends on one's theory of perception. I sound this note now in the melody because we will have to go deeply into the philosophic music somewhat later to get into the movements of our ontic symphony.

To return to a more specific example requires an accuracy with which we can tell horizontal and vertical to within one degree. How do we do this?

> This apparently narrow question will illustrate the differences between the elementaristic and gestalt interpretations. Most people when they first think about this problem (!) are likely to discover the following solution. A line may be said to consist of

points; if the image of the points on the retina is vertical, we see the line as vertical.

An elaboration of this explanation was in fact, proposed by the physiologist, Hering. The retina, he suggested, is like a coordinate system. Each point on it, when stimulated, has a particular "space value." Points directly above and below the center of the retina have a certain height value and zero width value; those directly right and left of the center have a particular width value and zero height value; similarly for other points. When contiguous retinal points are excited, the person reports seeing a vertical line; he reports a horizontal line when the retinal points excited all have the same height value. In short, Hering proposed to derive the orientation of a line from the sum of the elementary impressions of separate points.

This explanation, which has the merit of great simplicity, is a striking example of an elementaristic theory of psychological process. It reduces the given fact to its apparently simplest elements, notes their properties, and derives the former from the sum of the latter. (Asch, pp. 56)

Note that the parts are assumed already, and then the elements are summated to form the whole of perception. But we need more authority to examine these asseverations, so let us refer to the Master who treats of the identical matter in the *Principles of Psychology* about fifty years before Wertheimer's, *Untersuchungen zur Lehre von der Gestalt*, in the *Psycholgische Forschung* with its *prägnanz* in 1923. I will refer extensively to James, Vol. 11, Chap. XX, *The Sensation of Space.*

Let us go to the example of Hering's eye to which Asch referred above. Apparently, "an eye for an eye," and we all know what an eye is. But after describing the problem of local excitation, a touch anywhere on the *body* is moved from the member touched to its most sensitive tip, hand to fingertip and so forth, (my italics above).

...thus, arise lines of habitual passage from all points of a member to its sensitive tip. These are the lines most readily recalled when any point is touched, and their recall is identical with the consciousness of the distance of the touched point from the tip.

A point can only be cognized in its relation to the entire body at once by awakening a *visual* image of the whole body. Such awakening is even more obviously than the previously considered cases, a matter of pure association. (James, Vol. II, pp. 161)

(We will do more than well to keep this analysis in the eye of our minds for its resonance in our ears when we approach George Herbert Mead and his theory of perception within the Act as the unit of existence and his pellucid restatement of resistance.)

James then takes us to the eye in like manner describing the exquisite sensitivity of the center, the *fovea*, so that

> ...*whenever an image falling on the point P of the retina excites attention, it more habitually moves from that point towards the fovea than in any one other direction.* The line traced thus by the image is not always a straight line. When the direction of the point from the *fovea* is neither vertical nor horizontal, but oblique, the line traced is often a curve, with its concavity directed upwards if the direction is upwards, downwards if the direction is downwards. (James, Vol. II, pp. 162)

He asks one to make the simple experiment of having first "gazed at some point remote from the source of light, let the eye suddenly be turned upon the latter."

> The luminous image will necessarily fall in succession upon a continuous series of points, reaching from the one first affected to the fovea. But by virtue of the slowness with which retinal

excitements die away, the entire series of points will for an instant be visible as an after-image displaying the above peculiarity of form according to its situation …

We are incessantly drawing (these radiating lines) between the fovea and every point in the field of view…*The result of this incessant tracing of radii is that whenever a local sign P is awakened by a spot of light falling upon it, it recalls forthwith, even though the eyeball be unmoved, the local signs of all the other points which lie between P and the fovea.* It recalls them in imaginary form, just as the normal reflex movement would recall them in vivid form; and with their recall is given a consciousness more or less faint on the whole line on which they lie. (Ibid)

As you see, when Asch spoke of the "physiologist" Hering's analysis of retinal coordinates as "elements," he, of course, omitted the crucial point of incessant tracing of radii "whenever a local sign P is awakened by a spot of light falling upon it. It recalls forthwith, even though the eyeball be unmoved, the local sign of all the other points between P and the fovea," as above. Moreover, the recall in imaginary form, the entire human achievement of memory and imagery without which a whole and parts relation is even conceivable is suppressed in the service of founding the new gestalt psychology.

Further, in the above reference, we have the basis for retinal lag, consequently, the phi phenomenon and, further, an explanation for the induced movement in the experiment with the light in the dark box that seems to move when the frame is moved:

If one observes in a darkened room a point of light surrounded by a rectangular contour or frame which is slowly (!) moved to the right or left, he sees the point moving in an opposite direction to that of the frame which is seen as stationary. The movement is compelling and entirely indistinguishable from objective movement. (Asch, pp. 58)

This is Karl Duncker's "induced movement" experiment. If the movement is "entirely indistinguishable from objective" movement, what possible meaning of "objective" can he intend? Asch here can only be in complete agreement with Hering without realizing it.

James is serious in his title, *The Sensation of Space*. The extensive bibliography from the *Optikal* studies of the last half of the Nineteenth Century (already referred to) circled about space and objects within it:

> My own sensationalist account has derived most aid from the writings of Hering, A. W. Volkmann, Stumpf, Leconte, and Schön. All these authors allow ample scope to that experience which Berkeley's genius saw to be a present factor in all our visual acts. But they give experience some grist to grind which the soi-disant "empiristic" school forgets to do. (James, Vol. 11, pp. 282)

We move to another example from the theory of identity in perception:

> It was long assumed that identity (or similarity) of two objects is a function of the identity of their elements ... Three points of light are exposed simultaneously on a dark field; they are then replaced after a very brief interval by the Points D, E, and F. In physical terms, the Points b and c are identical with the Points D and E respectively; Point A had disappeared, and a new Point F had been added.

> What the observer sees however is the movement of the three Points A B C from left to right into positions D E F. It is instructive to see how different the physical situation is from the phenomenal facts. We see items move where there is no movement physically; B C are physically identical with and phenomenally different from D E, and a d are physically different and phenomenally identical. (Asch, pp. 55)

He then concludes that it is a function of the "structural relations" that makes "identity" intelligible and not the adding of the "elements."

James, remember the *Sensation of Space*, in a similar treatment to the shifting "identical" elements of the Wertheimer and Ternus experiment cited by Asch, reads:

> Every single visual sensation of "field of view" is limited. To get a new field of view for our object, the old one must disappear. But the disappearance may be only partial. Let the first field of view be A B C. If we carry our attention to the limit C, it ceases to be the limit, and becomes the centre of the field, and beyond it appears fresh parts where there were none before: A B C changes in short to C D E.
>
> But although the parts A B are lost to sight, yet their image abides in the memory, and if we think of our first object A B C as having existed or as still existing at all, we must think of it as it was originally presented, namely as spread out from C in one direction just a C D E is spread out in another. A B and D E can never coalesce in one place (as they could were they objects of different senses) because they can never be perceived at once: we must lose one to see the other.
>
> So (the letters standing now for "things"), we get to conceive of the successive fields of things after the analogy of the several things which we perceive in a single field. They must be outside and alongside of each other, and we conceive that their juxtaposed spaces must make a larger space. A B C + C D E must, in short, be imagined to exist in the form of A B C D E or not imagined at all. (James, Vol. 11, pp. 185)

James, as a sensationalist, is saying that far from being a function of structural relations creating identity, what we are experiencing is a new experience in which we are speaking of the "primitive chaos":

Nevertheless, throughout all this confusion, we conceive of a world spread out in a perfectly fixed and orderly fashion, and we believe in its existence...How is the chaos smoothed and straightened out?

Mainly by two operations: Some of the experiences are apprehended to exist both out and alongside each other, and others are apprehended to interpenetrate each other, and to occupy the same room. In this way, what was incoherent and irrelative, ends up being coherent and definitely related; nor is it hard to trace the principles by which the mind is guided in this arrangement of its perception in detail.

In the first place, following the great intellectual law of economy, we simplify, unify, and identify as much as we can. Whatever sensible data can be attended together, we locate together. Their several extents seem one extent. The place at which each appears is held to be the same at which the others appear. They become, in short, so many properties of ONE AND THE SAME REAL THING. This is the first and great commandment, the fundamental "act" by which our world gets spatially arranged. (James, Vol. II, pp. 183)

Again, we have the principle of *prägnanz* of Wertheimer a half-century earlier.

In *Gestalt Psychology*, Köhler specifically dismisses Hering's work as "merely logical" and regards it as a classificatory system. In Chapter 11, *Psychology as a Young Science*, he asserts Hering's work as faulty in order to found the gestalt psychological principle of "psychophysical isomorphism" in cases of spatial order.

Gestalt psychology works with a principle which is both more general and more concretely applicable than that of Hering and Müller. These authors refer to the merely logical order of experiences which for this purpose, are abstracted from their

context and judged as to their similarities. The thesis is that when
related physiological events are also taken from their context,
and also compared as to their similarities, the resulting logical
order must be the same as that of the experiences. In both cases,
it will be seen, the order in question is the order of dead
specimens as given the right places in a museum. But experience
as such exhibits an order which is itself experienced.
(Köhler, pp. 60)

To repeat from Page 19, where James relies heavily on Hering's work:

My own sensationalistic account has derived most aid and
comfort from the writings of Hering, A. W. Volkmann, Stumpf,
Lecont and Schön. All these authors allow ample scope to that
"experience" which Berkeley's genius saw to be a present factor
in all our visible acts. But they give experience some grist to
grind, which the *soi-disant* "empiristic" school forgets to do.
Stumpf seems to me the most philosophical and profound of all
these writers; and I owe him much. (James, pp. 282)

Clearly, James does not understand Hering as merely logical and
classificatory, but to give exactly the very long footnote that James feels
he must refer to:

Hering has well accounted for the sensationally vivid character
of these habitually reproduced forms. He says after reminding us
that every visual sensation is correlated to a physical process in
the nervous apparatus:

If this psychophysical process is aroused, as usually happens, by
light-rays impinging on the retina, its form depends not only on
the nature of these rays, but on the constitution of the entire
nervous apparatus which is connected with the organ of vision,
and on the state in which it finds itself. The same stimulus may
excite widely different sensations according to this state.

The constitution of the nervous apparatus depends naturally in part upon innate predisposition; but the ensemble of effects wrought by stimuli upon it in the course of life, whether these come through eyes or from elsewhere, is a co-factor of its development. To express it otherwise, involuntary and voluntary experience and exercise assist in determining the material structure of the nervous organ of vision, and hence the ways in which it may react on a retinal image as an outward stimulus.

That experience and exercise should be possible at all in vision is a consequence of the reproductive power, or memory, of its nerve-substance. Every particular activity of the organ makes it more suited to a repetition of the same ever slighter touches that are required to make the repetition occur. The organ habituates itself to the repeated activity.

Suppose now that, in the first experience of a complex sensation produced by a particular retinal image, certain portions were made the special objects of attention. In a repetition of the sensible experience, it will happen that notwithstanding the identity of the outward stimulus, these portions will be more easily and strongly reproduced; and when this happens a hundred times the inequality with which the various constituents of the complex sensation appeal to consciousness grow ever greater.

Now in the present state of our knowledge, we cannot assert that in both the first and the last occurrence of the retinal image in question, the same pure sensation is provoked, but that the mind interprets it differently the last time in consequence of experience; for the only given things we know are, on the one hand, the retinal image which is both times the same, and on the other, the mental percept which is both times different.

Of a third thing, such as pure sensation, interpolated between image and percept, we know nothing. We ought, therefore, if we wish to avoid hypotheses, simply say that the nervous apparatus reacts the last time differently, from the first, and gives us in consequence a different group of sensations.

But not only by repetition of the same retinal image, but by that of similar ones, examples awaken as it were, a stronger echo in the nervous apparatus than other portions. Hence, it results that *reproduction is usually elective;* the more strongly reverberating parts of the picture yield stronger feelings than the rest. This may result in the latter being quite overlooked and, as it were, eliminated from perception. It may even come to pass that instead of these parts eliminated by election a feeling of entirely different elements comes to consciousness — elements not objectively contained in the stimulus.

A group of sensations, namely, for which a strong tendency to reproduction has become, by frequent repetition, ingrained in the nervous system, will easily revive as a *whole* when, not in its whole retinal image, but only an essential part thereof, returns. In this case, we get some sensations to which no adequate stimulus exists in the retinal image, and which owe their being solely to the reproductive power of the nervous apparatus. This is *complementary (ergansende) reproduction.*

Thus, a few points and disconnected strokes are sufficient to make us see a human face, and without specially directed attention, we fail to note that we see much that really is not drawn on the paper. Attention will show that the outlines were deficient in spots where we thought them complete…

(Here we have the anecdote frequently enough cited by Köhler and attributed to Wertheimer, that the caricaturist captures the identity of his subject better than a camera.)

…The portions of the percept supplied by complementary reproduction depend, however, just as much as its other portions, on the reaction of the nervous apparatus upon the retinal image, indirect though this reaction may, in the case of the supplied portions be. And so long as they are present, we have a perfect right to call them sensations, for they differ in no wise from such sensations as correspond to an actual stimulus in the retina.

Often, however, they are not persistent; many of them may be expelled by more close observation, but this is not proved to be the case with all ... In vision with one eye ... the distribution of parts within the third dimension is essentially the work of this complementary reproduction, i.e. of former experience.

When a certain way of localizing a particular group of sensations has become with us a second nature, our better knowledge, our judgment, our logic, are of no avail. Things actually diverse may give similar or almost identical retinal images; e.g. an object extended in three dimensions, and its flat perspective picture. In such cases, it often depends on small accidents, and especially on our will, whether the one or the other group of sensations shall be excited ...

We can see a relief hollow, as a mold, or vice versa; for a relief illuminated from the left can look just like it would illuminated from the right. Reflecting upon this, one may infer from the direction of the shadows that one has a relief before one, and the idea of the relief will guide the nerve-processes into the right path, so that the feeling of the relief is suddenly aroused...

Whenever the retinal image is of such a nature that two diverse modes of reaction on the part of the nervous apparatus are, so to speak, equally, or nearly equally imminent, it must depend on small accidents whether the one or the other reaction is realized. In these cases, our previous knowledge often has a decisive effect, and helps the correct perception to victory. The bare idea of the right object is itself a feeble reproduction which with the help of the proper retinal picture, develops into clear and lively sensation.

> But if there be not already in the nervous apparatus a disposition
> to the production of that percept which our judgment tells us is
> right, our knowledge strives in vain to conjure up the feeling of
> it; we then know that we see something to which no reality
> corresponds, but we see it all the same. (James, Vol. II, pp. 261,
> citing from *Hermann's Hanb der Physiologic.* m. 1, pp. 565–
> 571)

I thought to summarize the above but instead wanted to make a few
comments about my personal experience in coming to terms with the
apparatus of argument that counters it. Köhler specifically cites Hering
and James as authorities wrong in their treatment of the organization of
visual perception. This is in his chapter *Sensory Organization* in *Gestalt
Psychology* where he must argue against Introspectionism and
Behaviorism (or Learning and Stimulus-Response) theory, as primary in
perception.

He wants to install gestalt psychology in their stead and also to
undermine James's sensationalism that obviously would be the end of
gestalt psychology. I remind you again that the *Principles* was published
in 1890 and many of its articles appeared earlier, e.g., Footnote 1 on page
16, referring to *The Spatial Quale* of 1879. Ewalt Hering died, I believe,
in 1896.

To give an example of the tortuosities besetting any attempt to follow the
route of Köhler's arguments, let me first refer you to *English and English
of 1958* and its surprisingly elegant and even witty definitions of
Psychological and Psychoanalytical Terms. Here's a definition for the
entry, "stimulus":

> 7. *Any phenomenon, object, aspect of an object, however
> conceived or described, which modified behavior by eliciting
> activity in a sense organ.* This deliberately inclusive and
> undiscriminating meaning is distilled from the loose usage that
> is, by far, the most prevalent.

It seems clear that stimulus, cannot in actual use, be effectively restricted either to a physicalistic or a mentalistic meaning. Much as one would like to see a stimulus restricted to its traditional meaning, it is probably too late, no delinquency being so incorrigible as a semantic one. Insistence upon the restricted meaning in formal definition has not kept the usage consistent; it has merely led to the fallacy of the ambiguous middle term: "A stimulus is a form of physical energy; the father's anger is the stimulus to the child's fear; therefore the father's anger is a form of physical energy.

Perhaps, however, stimulus can be held to a useful meaning as in (7) which combines the three basic ideas of stimulus set forth at the beginning of the entry: the ideas of (A) incitement, (B) external agent, (C) relation to sensory process." 3

It is impossible to resist their motto to the work on the frontispiece:

Ad-i-ad-cho-kin-e-si
Is a term that will bolster my thesis
That 'tis idle to seek
Such precision in Greek
When confusion it only increases.

To his credit, Köhler says, "Behaviorists use the term 'stimulus' in such a loose fashion ... in vision, for instance, the organism tends to respond to millions of stimuli at once; and the first stage of this response is organization within a correspondingly large field. In many cases, reactions of the effector organs will begin soon; but often even the first of these reactions depend upon the organization of the field as it develops in time...The right psychological formula is therefore: *pattern of stimulation-organization-response to the products of organization.*" (Köhler, pp. 165)

So now we have the unit; not the "stimulus," whatever it may mean; not the "mosaic," e.g., on the retina, but the pattern of stimulation-organization-response to the products of organization.

A further class of experiences to illustrate the "elementary nature of continuous wholes" is that in which adults blind since birth have had their cataracts removed.

> When they are shown objects they have known by touch, (he) can seldom give a *satisfactory response...he does* not recognize such forms when now *given only in vision. Obviously*, he has before him a specific entity to which he refers the question and which he *tries to name*. Thus, if the object has a simple and compact form, he need not learn what "aggregate of sensations" he must regard as one thing. Elementary visual organization seems to be given to him at once. (Köhler, pp. 150. My italics)

This is a class James has treated extensively. In one of his cases, the person with new vision was shown a sphere and a block as pieces of wood. He indeed could not name them but instantly recognized them by touch and was told their names and that was that. He had already the "aggregate of sensations" from his *imagery* of touch. I think that was classified by Aristotle in his notion of the common sensibilities, without which, of course, there would have to be as many senses as objects, which is absurd.

A telling and charming aside with this previously blind man is that he picked up this furry object walking about, hugged it, and said: "Now, Puss, I shall know thee the next time I see thee."

On the one hand, I present the literature to demonstrate what I called above Köhler's style of argument, here conflating "recognition" with "naming" and using examples that can be argued pro and con, there, that "elementary visual organization seems to be given to him at once." Well, he had it already.

The problem with imagery is that it is connected with memory and memory with the stream of thought and its characteristics according to James. Köhler speaks of the formal relations of "mutually independent local stimuli":

> Although the local stimuli are mutually independent, they exhibit formal relations such as those of proximity and similarity. In this respect, the stimuli copy corresponding formal relations among the surface (!) elements of the physical objects. These formal relations in the physical objects are preserved as corresponding relations among the stimuli, and since organization depends upon the latter, it must also depend upon the former. (Köhler, pp. 167)

> Pattern of stimulus-organization-response to the products of organization; or: The...nervous system...responds to a situation, first, by dynamic sensory events which are peculiar to it as a system, (!) i.e., by organization, and then by behavior which depends upon the results of the organization.

And as above,

> Although the local stimuli are mutually dependent, they exhibit formal relations such as those of proximity and similarity. (Köhler, pp. 167)

I appreciate that he is trying to analyze perception to an original act, but I cannot see that he has said more than a stringing together of synonyms or rather of parts-in-wholes and wholes-in-parts which is for the devil to sort out. Let us all agree that experience is of wholes of perception and that is the vision of the gestalt psychologists. Where is the good of repeating it endlessly without adding anything? James says of Hegel:

> Any author is easy if you can catch the centre of his vision ... But if Hegel's central thought is easy to catch, his abominable habits of speech make his application of it to details exceedingly

difficult to follow. His passion for the slipshod in the way of sentences, unprincipled playing fast and loose with terms; his dreadful vocabulary, calling what completes a thing its "negation."

For example; his systematic refusal to let you know whether he is talking logic or physics or psychology, his whole deliberately adopted policy of ambiguity and vagueness, in short: all these things make his present-day readers wish to tear their hair or his, out in desperation. Like Byron's corsair, he has left a name "to other times," linked with one virtue and a thousand crimes. (James, *A Pluralistic Universe,* pp. 85)

Exactly my sentiments, except I felt brain-damaged for two weeks trying to make sense of *Sensory Organization,* Köhler's Chapter V in *Gestalt Psychology.*

To further his case against "empiristic" solutions to the problem of the gestalt or the perception of wholes of experiences, Köhler must somehow destroy the notion that they can be acquired or learned, that is, "empirical." He resorts to the problem of illusion and its place in perception. Loosely, illusion means in this case that what is phenomenal experience is not the retinal experience; or, as in Asch above, not the science.

How then to account for the lively vividness of the so-called illusion? We have the notorious illustrations on the cover of every book or article about gestalt: the head profile/goblet; the staircase going up then going down, and so forth. We can all recall the famous ones. Apparently the same stimulus gives alternate perceptions that are striking in their clarity. We have already explicated this in the long quote from Hering, but James felt this was a crucial point in his Chapter XX, *The Perception of Space,* and I want to tie up the question with his analysis of the problem.

First, to give the background of the question, James, discussing that we have shape in almost all retinal experience as "perspective distortions,"

Out of the flux, however, one phase always stands prominent. It is the form the object has when we see it easiest and best; and that is when our eyes and the object both are in what may be called the normal position. No other point of view offers so many aesthetic and practical advantages. Here we believe we see the object as it is; elsewhere only as it seems.

Experience and custom soon teach us, however, that the seeming appearance passes into the real one by continuous gradations. They teach us, moreover, that seeming and being may be strangely interchanged. Now a real circle may slide into a seeming ellipse; now an ellipse may, by sliding in the same direction, become a seeming circle; now a rectangular cross grows slant-legged; now a slant-legged one grown rectangular.

Then, in a momentous treatment of optical signs to optical reality, James invokes Berkeley's theory, of vision, that is, sensations as signs of their significates as a parallel to thinking in words:

Almost any form in oblique vision may be thus derivative of almost any other in "primary" vision; and we must learn, when we get one of the former appearances, to translate it into the appropriate one of the latter class; we must learn of what optical "reality" it is one of the optical signs.

Having learned this, we do but obey that law of economy or simplification which dominates our whole psychic life, when we attend exclusively to the "reality" and ignore as much as our consciousness will let us, the "sign" by which we came to apprehend it. The signs of each probable real thing being multiple and the thing itself one and fixed, we gain the same mental relief by abandoning the former for the latter that we do when we abandon mental images with all their fluctuating character, for the definite and unchangeable names which they suggest. (!)

> The selection of the several "normal" appearances from out of
> the jungle of our optical experiences, to serve as the real sights of
> which we shall think, is psychologically a parallel phenomenon
> to the habit of thinking in words, and has a like use. Both are
> substitutions of terms few and fixed for terms manifold and
> vague. (James, Vol. II, pp. 240)

I use the term "momentous" for two reasons. First, it struck me that we
have here a biological if you will, or perhaps original, in the sense of
constituent, statement of the fundamental continuum in James of
sensation-percept-concept, that is the nature of humankind's evolution
and thus an analysis of its nature. Secondly, it sounds the death knell of
the evil of substituting names for processes since it gives the key to
unlock the doors hiding behind the names and opening the rooms behind
them to light and air to clean out the mustiness.

Correlatively, we see both in content and tenor why education fails: we
are coerced to learn the names and gabble of the so-called "field" without
a prior understanding of the unity of experience, thence, its
manifestations in science, mathematics, aesthetics and morality.
Everything is half-baked, authoritative, extrinsic and alien. There is not a
place to stand. It is *Compulsory Mis-education* standing on the backs of
turtles and elephants all the way down. To return to the libretto:

> This service of sensations as mere signs, to be ignored when they
> have evoked the other sensations which are their significates,
> was noticed first by Berkeley and remarked in many passages, as
> the following:

> Signs being little considered in themselves, or for their own sake,
> but only in their relative capacity and for the sake of those things
> whereof they are signs, it comes to pass the mind overlooks them
> so as to carry its attention immediately on to the things signified
> ... which in truth and strictness are not seen, but only suggested
> and apprehended by means of the proper objects of sight which
> alone are seen. (*Divine Visual Language*, Par. 12)

The foregoing are selections from sections *Sensations Which We Ignore, and Sensations Which Seem Suppressed,* which lead immediately to the classes of illusions that are used to deny a strictly sensationalist theory of perception which is, of course, James's position which would emerge fully in his *A World of Pure Experience* in 1904. (The paper was published first, then the book in 1910.)

The position is, of course, contrary to the popular notion of apperception or the theory, that there is some "sleeping power of the soul" of "psychic stimulus," *a priori,* synthetic unity of apperception that accounts for all human experience.

In our choice of visual reality, sensations which we ignore, and sensations which seem suppressed, as aforesaid, we must "learn," when we get (one form of appearance) to translate it into the appropriate one of the (primary) classes. Ignoring subjective optical sensations is fundamental in the classes of those that are not "signs of outer objects at all." These are the floaters, after-images, and double images, etc. And they divide themselves into groups: color perception, double images; after-images "distorted by projection onto oblique planes; and the instability of our judgments of relative distance and size by the eye." (James, Vol. II, pp. 240–282)

Again, all the points were covered in the long reference from Hering on Page 19. But in a more general way what the examples from the different classes are used to prove is that these phenomena arc not originally sensational but are mental affairs. Then, of course the transfer to the metaphysical phenomenon of the Apperception, Manifold, *a priori* Unity, Psychic Stimulus, Transcendental Unity, is inevitable. And it is, of course, the Kantian metaphysics.

Generally, all the cases can be analyzed in the manner of Hering:

>...The color contrast problem...In my opinion, Hering has definitively proved that, when one color is laid beside another, it modifies the sensation of the latter, not by virtue of any mere

mental suggestion as Helmholtz would have it, but by actually exciting a new nerve process, to which the modified feeling of color immediately corresponds.

The explanation is physiological, not psychological. The transformation of the original color by the inducing color is due to the disappearance of the physiological conditions under which the first color was produced, and to the induction, under the new conditions, of a genuine new sensation, with which the suggestions of experience have naught to do. (James, Vol. II, pp. 244)

And so it is with double images, also eliminated as cases of defective discrimination, "or as changes of one space-sensation into another, when the total retinal process changes." The cases I have called famous are the ones the gestalt psychologists have demonstrated in their effort to prove the physiological foundation of the whole-and-parts relation. They are the plane figures, stairs, cubes, tunnels, which give particularly vivid perceptual experiences as they flap back and forth.

The real object, lines meeting or crossing each other on a plane, is replaced by an *imagined solid which we describe as seen. Really, it is not seen but only so vividly conceived as to approach a vision of reality.* (James, Vol. II, pp. 258)

In these changes, the actual retinal image receives *different complements from the mind.* But the remarkable thing is that the complement and the image combine so completely that the twain are one flesh, as it were and cannot be discriminated in the result. If the complement be a set of imaginary absent eye-sensations, they seem no whit less vividly there than the sensation which the eye now receives from without.

The case of the after-images distorted by projection upon an oblique plane is even more strange, for the imagined perspective figure, lying in the plane, seems less to combine with the one a moment previously seen by the eye than to suppress and take its place. The point needing explanation...is how imagined sensation ... usually so inferior in vivacity to real ones, should in these few experiences prove to be almost or quite their match.

The following paragraphs are those which segue to the Hering passage at page 19 above and which contain the meat and potatoes of a sensationalist account of the mystery:

The mind uniformly uses its sensations to *identify things by*. The sensation is invariably apperceived by the idea, name, or "normal" aspect of the *thing*. The class to which all these experiences belong...are "perceptions" of definite "things" situated in tri-dimensional space...The peculiarity of the *optical* signs of things is their extraordinary mutability.

A "thing" which we follow with the eye, never doubting of its physical identity, will change its retinal image incessantly. A cross, a ring, waved about in the air, will pass through every conceivable angular and elliptical form. All the while, however, as we look at them, we hold fast to the perception of their "real" shape, by mentally combining the pictures momentarily received with the notion of peculiar positions in space. It is not the cross so held, the ring so held.

From the day of our birth, we have sought every hour of our lives to correct the apparent form of things, and translate it to the real form by keeping note of the way they are placed or held. What wonder, then, that the notion "so placed" should invincibly exert its habitual corrective effect, even when the object with which it combines is only an after-image, and make us perceive the latter under a changed but more "real" form?

The "real" form is also a sensation conjured up by memory; but it is one so probable, so habitually conjured up when we have just this right combination of optical experiences, that it partakes of the invincible freshness of reality, and seems to break through that law which elsewhere condemns reproductive processes to being so much fainter than sensations. (James, Vol. II, pp. 206)

In a final paragraph before the Hering account, James emphasizes and restates his sensationalist account with a criticism of the uses of these "imaginations of absent feeling" which were to become so fateful for the flurry of papers and experiments of the gestalt psychologists commencing about a half century later. "Fateful," because in their insistence on a physiological nature of the whole-and-parts relation, they were forced to retreat to a Kantian position that, in spite of Köhler's christening, or perhaps naming "psychology as a young science from the starting point of physics," it never achieved its goal .

Following is the paragraph immediately preceding Hering that I think comprehensively restates the problem, its explication and its solution together with a magisterial scolding of the use to which the optical experiences had been made. Afterwards, I will make a blessedly shorter summary:

> Once more, these (above) cases *form an extreme. Somewhere, in the list of our imaginations of absent feelings, there must be found the vividest of all.* These optical reproductions of real form are the vividest of all.

> It is foolish to reason from cases lower in the scale, to prove that the scale can contain no such extreme cases as these; and particularly foolish since we can definitely see why these imaginations ought to be more vivid than any others, whenever they recall the forms of habitual and probable things. These latter, by incessantly repeated presence and reproduction, will slough deep grooves in the nervous system.

> There will be developed to correspond to them, paths of least resistance, of unstable equilibrium, liable to become active in their totality when any point is touched off. Even when the

> objective stimulus is imperfect, we shall still *see* the full
> convexity of a human face, the correct inclination of an angle or
> sweep of a curve, or the distance of two lines.

> Our mind will be like a polyhedron, whose facets are the
> attitudes of perception in which it can most easily rest. These are
> worn upon it by habitual objects, and from one of these, it can
> pass only by tumbling into another. (James, Vol. II, pp. 260)

The general problem is that of the perception of space. How is it possible
that there is extension, thence time? Not having the tools of evolution,
i.e., a theory of development, the Idealists, with their backs to the wall of
an otiose theory of association, pronounced both space and time,
"transcendental, *a priori* synthetic, the understanding, psychical
synthesis, physical stimuli," and so forth. But their notion of Association
is a principle that produces nothing but "only knits together things
already produced together in separate ways." (James, Vol. II, pp. 271)
The Critique of Pure Reason irrupted in 1781 and *The Origin of the
Species* in 1853.

It is impossible to make clear under what form of sensation the original
spatial experiences discover themselves in consequence of Association.

> The space they speak of is a super-sensational mental product.
> This position seems to me thoroughly mythological." (James,
> Vol. II, pp. 273)

> "I call this view mythological, because I am conscious of no
> such Kantian mythological machine shop in my mind, and feel
> no call to disparage the powers of poor sensation in this
> merciless way. I have no introspective experience of mentally
> producing or creating space. My space-intuitions occur not in
> two times but in one. There is not one moment of passive
> inextensive sensation succeeded by another of active extensive
> perception, but the form I see is as immediately felt as the color
> which fills it out.

That the higher parts of the mind come in, who can deny? They add and subtract, they compare and measure, they reproduce and abstract. They inweave the space-sensations with intellectual relations; but *these* relations are the same when they obtain between the elements of the space-system as when they obtain between any of the other elements of which the world is made ...

The essence of the Kantian contention is that there are not *spaces,* but Space — one infinite continuous *Unit* — *and* that our knowledge of *this* cannot be a piecemeal sensational affair produced by summation and abstraction. To which the obvious reply is that if any known thing bears on its front, the appearance of piecemeal construction and abstraction, it is this very notion of the infinite unitary space of the world. It is a *notion* if there ever was one and no intuition.

Most of us apprehend it in the barest symbolic abridgement; and if perchance, we ever do try to make it more adequate, we just add one image of sensible extension to another until we are tired. Most of us are obliged to turn around and drop the thought of the space in front of us when we think of that behind. And the space represented as near to us seems more minutely sub-divisible than that we think of as lying far away. (James, Vol. II, pp. 275)

And so with Wundt and Helmholtz: Wundt for maintaining the impossibility of discovering the nature of the space "quality in consciousness;" he also says, "The antecedents thereof, are psychical and not cerebral facts;" Helmholtz, for an empiricism that relies on the illusory determinations in Experience to induce that "real" experience must also be the same, the psychic activity required being the association of ideas. The obvious problems remain of the infinite regress, that the first experience requires an antecedent experience which requires an earlier experience, etc., etc.; and the impossibility of "association (to) produce a space-quality not in the things associated."

And as for Wundt:

His theory is the flimsiest thing in the world. It starts by an untrue assumption, and then corrects it by an unmeaning phrase. Retinal sensations are spatial; and were they not, no amount of "synthesis" with equally spaceless motor sensations could intelligibly make them so. Wundt's theory is, in short, but an avowal of impotence, and an appeal to the inscrutable powers of the soul. It confesses that we cannot analyze the constitution or the genesis of the spatial quality in consciousness.

But at the same time, it says the antecedents thereof are psychical and not cerebral facts. In calling the quality in question a sensational quality, our own account equally disclaimed ability to analyze it, but said its antecedents were cerebral, not psychical, in other words, that it was a first physical thing. This is a question of probable fact which the reader may decide. (James, Vol. II, pp. 278)

Moreover, these brilliant experimentalists are led astray by conflating the "analysis of an idea with the means of its production." Here James gives the example of Lipps who "finds that every space we think can be broken up into positions, and concludes that in some undefined way the several positions must have pre-existed in thought before the aggregate space could have appeared in perception."

In the analysis of movement which "is the very meaning of space" as scope for it, we have a case of the "psychologist's fallacy" where the observer's observations about the experiment — his "mere acquaintance with space is treated as tantamount to every sort of knowledge about it, the conditions of the latter are demanded of the former state of mind, and all sorts of mythological processes are brought in to help." (James, Vol. II, pp. 281)

It must be obvious by now, perhaps through some *aperçu* or irritation, that I am analyzing and criticizing gestalt psychology from the standpoint of work done a half century before the mature work of those psychologists. Surely, this is a novelty. In the ordinary course, analysis would proceed in the reverse direction. In the coda to James's critique of the experimental method, he says:

> It must be said that in some of these fields, the results have as yet borne little theoretic fruit commensurate with the great labor expended in their acquisition. But facts are facts, and if we only get enough of them, they are sure to combine. New ground will from year to year be broken, and theoretic results will grow. Meanwhile, the experimental method has quite changed the face of the science so far as the latter is a record of mere work done. (James, Vol. I, pp. 193)

This is in the chapter, *The Methods and Snares of Psychology*, which has been famously chosen to describe James's antipathy to "sensation." But let me fast forward a hundred and twenty years to illustrate another method and snare of psychology in both Frederick Perls, Köhler and others, that of denying, sweeping under the rug, downright distorting, and ignoring to irrelevancy the ground on which they stand. In Perls' case, it was his gust for originality and what he called "simplicity." He really wanted to be famous, and simplicity was counter to "complicated," read "thinking" or "intellectual," against which he placed crucifixes in windows and wore necklaces of strung garlic.

In the case of the gestalt psychologists, it was impossible to admit the work of the *Principles* if their work was to stand and flourish since the authoritative treatment of the same experiences had been well and truly accomplished by William James and his extensive references both pro and con.

To forward also to 1991 and the *Library of Living Philosophers*, Volume XX, *The Philosophy of Charles Hartshorne*, where Wayne Viney writes Hartshorne's "approach to sensation would have been welcomed by James...For all his catholicity and tolerance, sensation was one area for which William James could generate little enthusiasm." This is simply wrong.

Indeed, Edwin G. Boring pointed out that James disliked the topic, found it unimportant, and neglected it as much as possible. Boring, quoting from R. B. Perry's biography of James, points out that "James did not mention color mixture in the *Principles*, and put the topic into the *Briefer Course* only under protest." James's attacks both on the questions investigated and the methods employed by German sensory psychologists are well known..."The German microscopic psychology..." etc. His even more scathing remarks on Fechner leave no doubt about his permanent disdain for the minutiae of such topics as thresholds, just noticeable differences, and after-images. (Viney, pp. 107)

We have Viney quoting Boring citing Perry describing James. To put it otherwise, 1991 to 1942 to 1935 to 1890. It is a wonder and marvelous to behold how positions can be misstated, picked up and cited and the citations become authority, the originals never perused.

Item: One of James's authorities, who he frequently cited, is of course, Hering, whose primary work was precisely in color perception and indeed the reciprocal influence of adjacent patches of color.

Item: His famous attack, as above, was leavened by his hope that eventually theoretic progress would arrive with accumulating enough experimental work.

Item: As for his "scathing" attack on Fechner, had Boring been lively enough to bestir himself from his dogmatic slumbers, he would have discovered a chapter in *A Pluralistic Universe* in which James wrote of Fechner in full and not less than adulatory language for his life work and statement and analysis of multiple consciousness levels. *Concerning Fechner* was given as part of the *Hibbert Lectures* at Manchester College, Oxford, in 1908, and published in 1909. James died early the following year. The irony of course is that the material referred to by Boring is in the chapter *The Method and Snares of Psychology*.

And there also, before he took on comparative psychology, James listed seven principal fields of experimental psychology: the psycho-physical connections and correlations; space analyzed to its sensational elements; the duration of simplest mental processes measured; the accuracy of reproduction in memory of sensible experiences and intervals of space and time; how simple mental states influence each other; the number of facts simultaneously discernible to consciousness; and the elementary laws of "oblivescence and retention."

In 1945 at Rutgers, where for my sins and naiveté, I was at first a psychology major, in fact, the text was eponymously Boring. I do not know how many of you were tortured by this tome but having very little self to get in the way, I managed to memorize enough for each exam to get by. Thorndike's famous dictum, "Reward stamps in and punishment stamps out," sometimes called the Law of Effect, obviously operated here. It also works with rats and chickens. (I must say my mother knew nothing of Thorndike or his law, but effectively understood it perfectly).

It is not conceivable that the mind of man could build a more adequate torture rack on which to twist and strain and wrench the minds and bodies of still hopeful student victims striving to ascend the delectable mountain of learning only to discover it was a brick wall. This brings us to James's delicious satire on comparative psychology which is the third of the new psychology's triumvirate: introspection, experimental and comparative.

> The comparative method, finally, supplements the introspective and experimental methods. This method presupposes a normal psychology of introspection to be established in its main features. But where the origin of these features, or their dependence one on another, is in question, it is of the utmost importance to trace the phenomenon considered through all its possible variation of type and combination.
>
> So it has come to pass that instincts of animals are ransacked to throw light on our own and that the reasoning faculties of bees

and ants, the minds of savages, infants, madmen, idiots, the deaf and blind, criminals, and eccentrics, are all invoked in support of this or that special theory about some part of our own mental life.

The history of sciences, moral and political institutions, and languages as types of mental product are pressed into the same service. Messrs. Darwin and Galton have set the example of circulars of questions sent out by the hundred to those supposed able to reply. The custom has spread, and it will be well for us in the next generation if such circulars be not ranked among the common pests of life. Meanwhile, information grows and results emerge. There are great sources of error in the comparative method.

The interpretation of the "psychoses" of animals, savages, and infants is necessarily wild work, in which the personal equation of the investigator has things very much its own way. A savage will be reported to have no moral or religious feeling if his actions shock the observer unduly. A child will be assumed without self-consciousness because he talks of himself in the third person, etc., etc. No rules can be laid down in advance.

Comparative observations, to be definite, must usually be made to test some pre-existing hypothesis; and the only thing then is to use as much sagacity as you posses and to be as candid as you can. (James, Vol. I, pp. 195)

Now, on page 30, I was a bit savage about experimental psychology and Boring and the reluctance of scholars to peruse the original texts. So I took myself to the New School Graduate Faculty Library and retrieved Boring's paper. (*Human Nature vs. Sensation: William James and the Psychology of the Present, The American Journal of Psychology 55* (1942): 310–327)

It is impressive, indeed, gentle, with some scholarly wit and appropriate distance. As before, I think him wrong but what is interesting is his analysis of the two positions, the old and the new psychology, into nativist and empiricist, between accepting the given, and reducing it to what makes it the given thus making a larger relation; between James's genetic sensationalism and what he would call "physiology."

Boring places Helmholtz, Lotze and Wundt on the side of the reductionists; Hering, Stumpf and James with the phenomenologists and also Köhler in *The Place of Value in a World of Facts*. That is, human value in a world of scientific fact.

> Starting with Newton, we can come on down the line of history. Goethe derided Newton because he used experiments to distort the obvious (white is a mix of color). Helmholtz ridiculed Goethe as a victim of his own vain obstinacy (Goethe had a prism in his hand and refused to use it). James found that Helmholtz's "indefinite and oracular statements about the part played by the intellect (in perception) have momentarily contributed to retard psychological inquiry." Sully objected to the "dazzling effect" of James' *Principles* as obscuring the sharp boundaries of scientific thought.

Since then, there has been the opposition between Watson and McDougall, and between behaviorism and gestalt psychology. The most famous opposition of this nature was however, the mutual disapproval of Helmholtz and Hering each for the other, an antagonism that gives us at once the key to the difficulty, for Helmholtz was an empiricist and Hering, a nativist. In this dichotomy, James, of course, belongs on the side of Hering as do also all the gestalt psychologists.

> It is usual to refer to the issue of nativism vs. empiricism as a dead and futile controversy of the late Nineteenth Century, but now we begin to see that the controversy is alive and still with us. The dislike of the gestalt psychologists for Helmholtz is

based upon his empiricism, his constant appeal to past experience for the explanation of present phenomena.

Similarly, the phenomenologists mistrust operationism because it goes beyond the given to the conditions of givenness, asserting that the given is not ultimate since the giving of it has to be understood. These operationists do not take experience as self-validating; they want to know what experience is and they answer their own question by submitting the process of observation to description. So there lies the issue: nativism vs. empiricism; phenomenology vs. reductionism. (Boring, pp. 322)

Thus, Boring indirectly points out that the original gestalt texts that insisted on the perception of the whole as a perceptual fact "from the starting point of physics" and not constructed, or apprehended, or for that matter cognized, had been abandoned. Wertheimer and Köhler had fired broadsides against that latter position in the early days. Indeed, it had to be so if psychology as a "young science" might accept that thin edge of the wedge known as "gestalt psychology" as entirely physiological or cerebral. The gradual development from the "starting point of physics" to "dynamical processes in the brain" as the psychology struggled to swallow the camels of isomorphism and eventually gulp the gnat of Apprehension, is a case study of the futility of a masquerade.

In a contemporary treatment of *The Gestalt Theory and the Problem of Configuration,* we have an exhaustive examination, theoretically, empirically, scientifically and ultimately philosophically by Bruno Petermann.

The beginnings of the gestalt controversy are, as a matter of fact, still concerned with nothing further than questions of detail. Mach in 1861, G.E. Müller in 1890, Husserl in 1891, von Ehrenfels in 1898 (even in so far as they take their stand, as a matter of course, independently of actual psychological work and more upon logical grounds) still have as their essential objective the further extension of our knowledge of the phenomena.

Even as with von Ehrenfels, this phenomenological analysis might result in emphasis upon the singularity and irreducibility of the "gestalt" facts, the cardinal significance of this with regard to the systematic conceptions of the time as yet receives no attention. (The "old" psychology.)

The same is true even of the delicate researches of Schumann in 1898, where for the first time a more thorough enquiry into certain fundamental manifestations of the gestalt problem is systematically carried out by means of careful experiments; or even of the first precisely set out theories, the Production theory (cf. e.g. Benussi), or the Coherence theory (G.E. Müller).

In its subsequent development, however, a narrowing down of the gestalt problem to questions about underlying principles ensues.

The most far-reaching claims in this direction are made by the school of Wertheimer, Kafka, and Köhler. To them, the word "gestalt" has become the symbol for a basic reorientation. So much so, that they put forward their theory as a fundamentally "new psychology," in radical opposition to all other work which has been done in psychology. (The subtitle to *Gestalt Psychology* is *An Introduction to New Concepts in Modern (!) Psychology.)*

But as indicated above, there was a progressive development in the old psychology: Cornelius and Lapps (Gestalt-quality, Complex-quality); Krueger ("wholeness" characteristic of psychic phenomena, 1905); and Volkelt's revision in *Complex-quality,* 1912. Goetz Martius had already criticized Wundt's work as an atomistic-synthetic psychology and

...in 1912, formulated in principle, at least, the central point of the present gestalt controversy, viz. the cleavage between the atomistic standpoint of the refuted theory and the characteristic closure (!), which the phenomena of form-perception manifest.

It is perhaps thus time to close this overly long treatise and I hope to do it somewhat in the manner of falling off a precipice. (Why didn't I say "cliff?")

Gestalt psychology has no original or even new foundation. Its works had been experimented, studied, explicated and published under the "old psychology" as far back as the mid-19th Century. The effort in the main, as I see it, had been to dress up the old in the gaudy garb of new labels in an unintelligible rhapsody. It cannot support itself. It certainly cannot support a psychotherapy to which it bears only a relation of figure and ground expressed otherwise as "figure/ground."

As usual, everyone tried to isolate "figure/ground" into two words to make sense of it. However, it is meant as one word in spite of the reams of scribble reading otherwise.

Without that awareness and its foundational connotations, gestalt psychotherapy has no meaning. I expressly do not mean the technical meaning of the word itself. I do mean it as an expression of that holism the psychotherapy was developed to fertilize and grow in a field otherwise sown to apparently irreconcilable splits.

After pointing out that the "anti-synthetic" and "immanent" positions as well as "gestalt tendencies" inherent in perception amount to "the complete ontologization" of all psychology and reflect in Krueger's words, "a numinous glitter," Petermann concludes with a prophecy:

> ...if we leave the question open as to whether there is or is not an apprehensional theory with an anti-synthetic orientation — the further difficulty remains that here obviously a "factor" in itself unknown, somehow and to some extent appears to enter in account like a *deus ex machina*...It is evident that here extremely serious discrepancies are involved...which must be taken seriously and as such not be brushed aside.

From this point of view, the present work can rest content with once more stressing two points...to pursue in any way possible, the analysis of the conditions involved in the genesis of definite gestalten, in quite concrete, specific studies of the circumstances of cognizance, i.e. of apprehension; ... (and not) take the problem to have been very simply and smoothly solved by the introduction of the concept of gestalt tendency...(in so far as this does not...in the last resort, amount to a apprehensional tendency)."

And finally:

> The singularity of the scientific position of the analyses put forward by the gestalt school, as a general glance at the multitude of recent works in the fields of perceptual, of thought, and of volitional life again and again confirms, and consists in this — that the correct reconciliation of these discrepancies remains for the future, and this will have to be a settlement in which both sides of the controversy received their due credit. (Petermann, pp. 319)

The irony is that Frederick Perls had it right in the first place. In the introduction to Perls, Hefferline and Goodman (*PHG*), he pointed out that to understand the book the reader had to have the "gestalt attitude;" but to have the attitude he had to understand the book. Further, that the attitude was not unique but was the natural way of mankind, then sundered by the splits.

But Perls' "lament" for ontology and pitch for it in gestalt psychology was an example of a classical collapse to authority of a not untypical rebel whose ears and eyes were closed to "thinking" and for whom all the world was a stage.

We will see in the next lecture how his partner in the effort, Paul Goodman, in a most brilliant exegesis, as well, cut, pasted and fudged, embraced contradictions and ignorances and perhaps unintelligibilities from time to time in the guise of wisdom.

But in the main, for them both, the "center of their vision" as William James says, was grand and true, fundamentally sound and stirring, a call to life in a saner and just society, where again after James, "something is doing in the universe. "

Epilogue

The association (of Paul Goodman and Kurt Goldstein) was brief and only the barest record of it survives ... Nonetheless, it was the beginning of Goodman's interest in gestalt psychology, which might be said to have arrived in America in 1934. That same autumn, Wolfgang Köhler was giving the William James' lectures at Harvard, lectures that became the best of the most philosophical of his books, *The Place of Value in a World of Fact,* and he, too, would soon be emigrating (a job was found for him at Swarthmore College along with Kurt Koffka (who went to Smith College), Kurt Lewin (the University of Iowa took him in), and Max Wertheimer (who ended up at the New School). (Stoehr, Taylor, 1950)

References

English, H.B. and English, A.C., *A Comprehensive Dictionary of Psychological and Psychoanalytical Terms.* Longmans, Green and Co., New York, 1958.

Mead, George Herbert, *The Philosophy of the Acts*, University of Chicago Press, 1938.

James, William, *The Sensation of Space.* The chapter is 158 pages, the authorities cited are extensive, broad and deep. Berkeley; J.S. Mill; Jas. Ferrier, A. Bain; H. Spencer; Mill on Hamilton; T.K. Abbott; A.C. Fraser on Abbott; J. Sully; J. Ward; J.E. Walter. "My present chapter is only the filling out with detail of an article entitled *The Spatial Quale,* which appeared in the *Journal of Speculative Philosophy* for January 1879 (XII. 64)".

Petermann. Bruno, *The Gestalt Theory and the Problem of Configuration*, Routledge & Regers Paul Ltd., London, 1932, Reprinted 1950

Stoehr, Tayor, *The Gestalt Theory and the Problem of Configuration*, Routledge & Regers Paul Ltd., London, 1932, Reprinted 1950

Synopsis of Fiftieth Anniversary Address

2003

Towards the end of his life and perhaps in expiation of the anti-intellectual side of his career, Frederick Perls, then Fritz Perls, lamented that gestalt therapy could not stand on its own two feet. He attributed that in part to his neglect of the Frankfurt gestalt psychologists where he ultimately thought a proper philosophical foundation could be sought. Further, his energies had been directed toward existentialism and making a living as a practicing psychoanalyst.

Today, Phil Lichtenberg has redirected the roots of gestalt therapy toward the political/radical side of psychoanalysis, particularly between the wars, and taking off from Freud's "scientific" complete experience of mother/child, impulse gratification interaction, in this case, the breast/sucking complete circuit. The circuit was in the field, initiated internally, and obviously completed socially and was probably a first gestalt as it integrated the field satisfactions in the so-called individuals.

Freud abandoned this first attempt at a scientific basis for psychoanalysis but its radical nature appealed to the psychoanalytic left and it is there that Phil finds the philosophical and political sources for gestalt therapy.

I have agreed with him and in my search have determined that (contrary to Perls' asseveration) the roots of gestalt therapy could not be found in gestalt psychology which itself lacked a coherent philosophy and consistent scientific basis. The roots could indeed be located in the radical politics of a generation earlier, particularly, the socialist politics of what became the American pragmatic philosophers at Chicago - John Dewey, George Herbert Mead, and arising out of his genius and the "old psychology," the "Principles" of William James.

That search arose out of the central field notion, indeed theory, of the "gestalt therapy" of Perls, Hefferline and Goodman of 1951 and its logic. However, the practice of the time seemed individual therapy, frequently in a group context, ignoring the group process. This therapy was founded on the programmatic four step theory of contact of Paul Goodman and most adequately practiced and elegantly taught by Isadore From. The so-called "interruptions to contact" with their consequent "loss of ego function" resulted in neurosis. The steps to contact were: fore-contact; contact a) and b); final contact; post contact. The interruptions were specific to the steps and were, I think, respectively: confluence; introjection; projection; retroflection; egotism. And this model guided the therapy and told the therapist "where to look."

Goodman had described the process as "a continuous sequence of figures and grounds." In practice, for example we had the famous: "The patient comes in for the first time" (!) and right-off-the-bat-present, divulges hair-raising material. It is clear (at least to the therapist) that the patient is in the clinch of an all-embracing confluence and does not have adequate orienting function, that is, ego function, and therapy must be directed to some inkling of awareness that there are, perhaps, for example, two people, more or less, in the room.

However, as in most enterprises, the model was embraced, altered, developed by some and rejected by others as its problems became clear. Chief among them was the central one that the terms and theory of Perls, Hefferline and Goodman could not themselves be used to cure the difficulties. Further, the contact model could easily become mechanical and itself introjected and an appliqué. One had to stand outside them. But where?

So about fifteen years ago, we began to study carefully for sources themselves of those terms. We went through Aristotle, the gestalt psychologists, particularly Köhler, Goodman's other writings, and his other influences: James ("I was brought up breathing the air of James' pragmatism"), Dewey, Reich, Freud. And in the doing, we tried to keep in balance Perls' first part of the book, his extremely valuable, indeed crucial experiments. Experimenting is the other chamber of the heart of gestalt therapy. I should note here that "thinking" can be experimented. I should note it forcefully.

In the course of our search, we serendipitously literally bumped into George Herbert Mead. Serendipitous because having realized I did not get the meaning of "meaning," I was browsing through a dictionary of philosophy where the entry before "meaning" was Mead, George Herbert. I read

> (Mead's) view of perception marks out a path somewhat similar to that whereby (the vocal) gesture led to symbolic meaning. In the case of perception, his point is that the *consummatory* phase of perception is *contact* so that perception can be said to be implicit *manipulability*. Thus the idea of substance is generalized from the sense of *resistance*. Space, time, and mass are derived from *contact* experiences."

I cannot describe to you in any better way my experience as I read except to say I felt my hair stand on end. I read on

> Stressing the importance of the *present*, Mead stressed also the ubiquitousness of *novelty* both in the *emerging present and the past and future, which likewise becomes novel in terms of the unique character of that present.*"

Now we all read in undergraduate sociology, *Mind, Self, and Society,* with the genesis of the self arising in the social act of the vocal gesture in the sounds and hearings that danced its infancy upon our knee; thus improving to play, and finally in taking the developing role of the other, learning the rules of the game, meaning and self-reflection. But we learned it in the way such things are learned in the shadows of the lecture hall, dimly. Goodman insists on the social nature of man in PHG and it is a noble attitude especially in his analysis (brief) of isolation, from Kafka, as an independence that is a lonely and senseless business. But what is that social *nature*? An explanation is not an analysis.

> His view of sociality led to a *perspectival* theory of the universe, centering in the *act* in which the present moment is pluralistic due to the multitude of perspectives taken with respect to that moment by different individuals. On the other hand, however, the individuality of these perspectives is reduced (that is, is objective) by the fact that each of us has the ability also to take the view point of the other."

That discovery led to Mead's *Philosophy of the Act*, which was based on lecture notes from his whole career at Chicago, 1892 – 1930 and papers written about the turn of the century to 1910. It was out of print and I copied its 667 pages, a chapter a week, for our seminar. My first reading is dated May 3rd 1996.

Mead's unit of reality is the process of the act itself which, of all things has four phases:

Impulse, Perception, Manipulation, and Consummation. Out of the attitude of readiness, `the impulse, sensitized with its opportunities in the environment, creates a more developed organism/environment field in which objects are handled and finally consumed. The process may be swift or checked as the hand in the manipulatory phase holds and explores the object in its crumbling process of analysis. No matter the rapidity, the process takes time — and space — and involves work of the distance experience that is the anticipatory co-explorations of the senses and the susceptibilities of the organism and their environmental opportunities.

Hence, Mead's famous "mantra" as we have learned to call it: The organism *logically* determines the environment through its senses and susceptibilities; the environment *causally* determines the organism through its opportunities. The relation is mutual but not convertible." The distance experience becomes referred primarily to the visual experience. Thus the object in perception is a collapsed act having in it all the phases and in its existence expressing the organism/environment relation.

It is central to grasp that in our restatement of *PHG*, we finally have a developmental analysis that grasps and makes clear the confusions and obscurings that have so beset us. This is not to say that we have not had explanations. We have. We have not had analyses at the fundamental or "primary" level. Does Goodman mean in the preceding sentence "primary" as "first," "most," or both? He uses it in all those senses. He "locates" boundary. As a phase in a process that is ongoing, it cannot be located. Hence the question, "Where is boundary?" becomes nonsense.

How did it come about? I have traced it to his early experience of the "Creator Spirit" and training at Columbia: "I am a Kantian," and his efforts at a significant sexual life while at Chicago during the period of the "rationalization" of the department of Philosophy from a power house of pragmatism to one of reactionary conservatism under the new Chancellor, Hutchins, and his friend, Mortimer Adler, heavily influenced by Jacques Maritain. The department of Philosophy became religious and probably anti-sexual and Mead died, broken, in early 1931.

Goodman's teacher at Columbia, Richard McKeon, went to Chicago in 1934 as part of the rationalizing and got Goodman a job in the Great Books there, and the opportunity to work on his doctorate. McKeon, a prodigious scholar, produced his 1928 two volume *Selections from Medieval Philosophers*, that is to say, the scholastic philosophers for whom the doctrine of agency is essential for God; and for the "synthetic unity of apperception" of the Kantians. I am saying there was a significant tension in Goodman that found its way into PHG in the form of ambiguities, confusions, misunderstandings that formed a wall around getting to a more coherent theory. For example, "The self is the system of contacts in the organism/environment field and the agency of growth." But the self does not grow, the organism does. (?)

The air of Jamesian pragmatism that Goodman breathed has in its mists and vapors "the constituents of the self." They are the material, social, spiritual selves and the pure Ego self

In this more complete examination in *The Consciousness of Self* in the *Principles of Psychology*, we have room to grow and places to stand. And what are we to make of organism in the "organism" grows? Is it the body? If so, the sentence is unintelligible. Is it half of the organism/environment field of which we make so much? The intelligibilities multiply.

The implication of Agency behind experience, that is *a priori*, is unavoidable and directly contrary to the "air of Jamesian pragmatism" that Goodman said he was bought up on. This is *Speaking and Language* in 1971 twenty years after *Gestalt Therapy*, and a year before his death. James, in the *Principles of Psychology* (Did Paul ever read it?) pointed out that Kant himself intended *a priori* Agency, but for his followers the fit became "paroxysmal as if they were going up in a balloon," as the self solved the subject/object contradiction.

Thus in an irony of history, the young philosopher radicals of the 19th century, fleeing the constrictions of evangelical Christianity in their American schools, returned from their German studies with their Social Democrat politics. They were to find themselves swamped a half century later by the reactionary forces they had earlier fled and were in command when the young Paul Goodman trained there.

And perhaps that has made all the difference.

Keynote Address before the New York Institute for Gestalt Therapy Fiftieth Anniversary Conference

2003

Some years ago, I conceived a structure within which to state gestalt therapy as I understood it, to restate it on a firmer base than its putative roots in gestalt psychology, specifically that of the pragmatism of the Chicago school, and to project where I thought the therapy had to go to continue its development and viability in the coming years.

The first fruit of that structure was an overlong paper titled *Three Lectures* which I think succeeded in displacing gestalt psychology as fundamental to the therapy and introduced William James, especially the *Principles of Psychology*; and George Herbert Mead's *Philosophy of the Act* as firm foundations on which to build the therapy.

Phil Lichtenberg has described an historical route of development of gestalt therapy from the radical branch of psycho-analysis. This branch was politically left and suffered the isolations typically enjoyed by the beneficent ministrations of the academy and such other establishment minions.

Paul Goodman attributed *his* influences to Freud, William James, Dewey and Reich, very much parallel to Phil's analysis, though not so strictly psychoanalytic. It is curious that James is not mentioned at all in Perls, Hefferline and Goodman (PHG) except in naming him in the James-Lange theory of emotions. We must remember for example that one does not experience fear and then run; but that the running includes the fear. The activity engenders the emotion. It had been thought that perception is prior to emotion which is a relation of cognition, an effect. Goodman thought this an inadequate analysis and approached it from his conception of a "field" point of view: that, e.g., it was not mere running but "running to." Nonetheless, this still preserves the perception/emotion splitting. We will come back to this relation, essentially dependent on one's theory of perception as we get further on. But for now as we trace the routes of those historical occasions known as William James, John Dewey and George Herbert Mead who were to become the famous "Chicago School" of Pragmatism, some biographical data are needed.

James was born in 1842, Dewey in 1859 and Mead in 1863. James became a professor at Harvard in the Seventies after post graduate study in Germany (he learned German to better understand *The Critique of Pure Reason* from the original text.) There was little opportunity to study psychology apart from the departments of evangelical religion in American universities, hence the flight to Europe where the "old" psychology was beginning to measure everything in sight, sound, smell, touch or taste as it strove to establish itself as a natural science. Dewey and Mead in exactly the same boat as James, followed his trail, the same schools and perhaps the same teachers in Germany, defining themselves, their politics and philosophy in those currents. Karl Marx, for example, was influential in the politics of France in that turbulent period.

Darwin's *Origin of Species* exploded on the world in 1859. It is a phenomenon of wonder that the battle of natural selection is still being fought fiercely by the so-called "creationist" conservative right who do so merrily and with a righteousness that would be laughable were it not so hideous in its deceptions and naked greed. Will there be *anything* left of the environment?

The political convulsions in America and in Europe in the mid to late 19th century deeply affected Dewey and Mead and completed their socialism and heady plans for the future back home where labor strife and robber barons and malefactors of great wealth co-existed uneasily.

Writing from Germany to his friend Henry Castle, 21 October, 1890, Mead said: "We must get into politics of course—city politics above all things because there we can begin to work at once in whatever city we settle because city politics need men more than any other branch—and chiefly because according to my opinion, the immediate application of the principles of corporate life—of socialism in America, must start from the city." (Joas, 1985)

Mead was offered a job at the University of Michigan and joined Dewey there in 1891 teaching physiological psychology. In 1894, Dewey was offered chair of Philosophy at the University of Chicago. He accepted providing, among other conditions, that he could take Mead with him and so it happened.

I do not know what the other conditions were but we must keep clearly in mind that The University of Chicago was founded in 1891 by John D. Rockefeller as a Baptist institution. My surmise is that as the faculty was being built, some brave souls insisted, Dewey among them, on academic freedom if within a religious institution.

Dewey's paper on the reflex arc in which he redefined the process as a circuit rather than an afferent/efferent stimulus/response splitting was from this period in 1896. The circuit was a complete unit and could not be split unless for purposes of analysis that also kept its integrity in the foreground. This was a very productive period for Dewey that solidified his pragmatism, instrumentalism, "learning by doing" and progressive theories of education which led him to Teachers College at Columbia University in 1904. He thus escaped the turbulence of urban Chicago and the dramatic shift of administration at the University that overwhelmed Mead, then chairman of the department of Philosophy, a quarter of a century later in 1928.

In a complete and incisive critique of George Herbert Mead, sub-titled *A Contemporary Re-examination of his Thought*, Hans Joas notes:

> Toward the end of the Twenties, the wave of reaction menaced even the *remnants* (my italics) of pragmatist thought at the University of Chicago. After teaching for almost 40 years at this university, George Herbert Mead died on April 26, 1931 generally unknown, esteemed by some colleagues and students as an extraordinary thinker, and deeply embittered by controversial changes in the university's internal politics that threatened to alter the nature of philosophy there, making it Catholic and reactionary in character. So great was Mead's bitterness that shortly before his death, he decided to leave the institution and the city that had been his field of action. It is probably not going too far to see a connection between this turn of events and Mead's death. (Joas, 1985, p. 28)

The wave of reaction and the controversial internal politics were detailed in a terse and memorializing footnote also by Hans Joas:

> David Miller has in his possession papers that show unequivocally that the reason for Mead's desire to leave Chicago and for his profound resignation lay in the policies of the new President of the University of Chicago, Hutchins, and in particular, in the appointment of the Neo-Thomist, Mortimer Adler, to a professorship there... Hutchins and Adler became important figures for the conservative emigrants from the Third Reich, for whom the University of Chicago became a gathering place—very much in contrast to the traditions of that university's first decades. (See Radkau's book, *Die deutsche Emigration in den USA*) (Düsseldorf 1971), where a characterization of Mortimer Adler appears by Thomas Mann

and others, who ascribe to him 'spiritual fascism'. (Joas, 1985, p. 221)

Hutchins became Chancellor of the university in 1929 and resigned in 1950. In the interim, the university had been given the rights to The Encyclopedia Britannica by Sears Roebuck, and Hutchins became chairman of the board of editors. Subsequently, he and his friend, Adler, edited the *Great Books* with its 54 volumes and "102 great ideas" and its two volume *Syntopicon* index.

This is also the period (1934) of Richard McKeon's move from Columbia University to Chicago. Paul Goodman had audited his courses and it was frequently said that Goodman "followed McKeon to Chicago." I had always assumed it was a contemporaneous event but obviously Goodman who would have been 17 at the time, did not get to Chicago until the late Thirties where the wreckage in the department of Philosophy had already been accomplished and McKeon had become a Dean.

Thomism and Pragmatism contrasted.

To present a view of the department of Philosophy at Chicago, let me give you an insider's opinion, that of Charles Hartshorne, who came from Harvard in 1928, heavily influenced by Whitehead with whom he was faculty, and Charles Peirce whose papers he and Paul Weiss edited:

> Both Whitehead's lectures that year in the class in which I was his assistant and Peirce's papers began to impress me more than any of my teachers so far had done.... (Hartshorne, p. 24)

> In the next academic year after I arrived in Chicago, Robert Maynard Hutchins became president of the University. (At age 30, he had been Dean of the Yale Law school. R.K.) Through two friends and admirers of his, Mortimer J. Adler and Richard P. McKeon, he soon brought about considerable changes in the

> way philosophy was taught there. Among the result(s) was the
> departure of Mead, who had been chairman.
>
> Mead soon after my arrival, lost his wife by death, and a year or
> so later, was terminally ill himself. I heard but one lecture by
> him. The few personal encounters were unimportant in my case.
> What was important was the argument between Hutchins, Adler,
> and McKeon, on the one hand, and the pragmatists and most of
> the faculty on the other. The dispute seemed, at first, far more
> than it really was, between partisans of neo-scholasticism or
> Thomism and the then dominant form of American philosophy.
> It led me to think more than I otherwise might have about the
> issue between medieval theology, represented by Jacques
> Maritain, friend of Hutchins (not a professional philosopher)
> who visited in Chicago and was introduced by another friend of
> Hutchins as the "greatest living philosopher." (One wondered
> how the introducer had ascertained this preëminence.)
> (Hartshorne, p. 30)

The arcana of corporate board's inter-relations seem to operate, like
God's, in mysterious ways their wonders to perform. You will recall that
Hutchins—as chairman of the board of editors—and Adler moved to
the Great Books, Hutchins, at least, still in the administration of the
University of Chicago. Adler had earlier been moved to the School of
Law because his thesis work had been in *evidence*. (The italics are
Hartshorne's). McKeon remained as Dean while Hartshorne became
Administrator. He lasted two quarters.

> In 1936, Goodman's teaching career took an academic turn when
> he was invited by McKeon to come and work in the "Great
> Books" (!) program at Chicago. While teaching he could also
> take a few courses and write a dissertation for his doctorate.
> (Stoehr, 1994, p. 28)

Now, here's a howdy-do! The man who is to describe his influences as
Charcot to Freud and Reich; James and Dewey, reports for work (and

presumably tuition exemption) at the invitation of a medievalist specialist at a school that has been "rationalized" from a bulwark of pragmatism to what Joas above had called reactionary in its increasingly religious bent.

He was here free to write his dissertation but not to act his ideals of sexual liberation. In 1939, he was fired because he refused to confine his foraging activities to off-campus fields. The University of Chicago had the Divinity School and three theological seminaries associated with it and some part of the budget of the department of Philosophy was funded through the divinity side. Probably *something* had to be done!

But let us see what our twenty five year old also brought with him to Chicago in his intellectual development. He had been auditing McKeon for years and presumably was enormously influenced by his mentor, who clearly was also impressed by his brilliant—can we say protege? — enough to reach out to bring him to Chicago. McKeon was an influential medievalist and you remember one of those of whom Hartshorne spoke as Neo-Thomist brought into the department of philosophy. His two volume opus was published in 1928 when Goodman was 17 and Paul must have learned considerable both in content and method. Let me excerpt from McKeon's introduction after he places his investigations as also an effort to connect the twelve hundred years from Augustine to Roger Bacon.

> The method of the later works… combined the virtues of the dialogue and the commentary… The method of the scholastics was to present a question, quote whatever had been said by authorities on either side, then resolve the question… (McKeon, vol. I, p. xiv)

> But the common criticism that scholastic problems were solved by reference only to authority is without foundation: a good scholastic was one who could find authority for either side of a question and who was convinced further that truth could be

discovered best by examining the interplay of such possible contradictory statements.

...But whatever the metaphysics or the theology of a writer, his appeal to authority was literally an appeal to what authors had in the past said on the subject: to be free from authority was to be unaware of the history of the problem discussed. And indeed, all the fresh starts in the history of Philosophy, even the fortunate ones have proved distressingly innocent of philosophical sophistication. (McKeon, p. xv)

(At this point, I have to interject a distressingly, perhaps too cynical note. I find both in my *Three Lectures* and so far in this work that it seems an inveterate habit in philosophical and psychological work to maintain one's innocence of his/her history and to trumpet one's "new" work from the roof tops. The foundation of the house must, of course be, and remain buried. Interminable and mind numbing conferences are founded on this flummery, R.K.)

Careful and meticulous readings; many technical aids as charts, tables, and contrasts; fine dialectical progressions and conclusions. One can imagine the razor of Ockham wielded surgically and the sufferings of fools in the scars on their flesh.

Therefore, Goodman brings a disciplined and well-trained mind to Chicago not without a religious turn. Indeed, as he was proud to announce in reference to his use of the synthetic unity of apperception, "I am a Kantian." We will analyze this further as we get to what else he brought with him to Chicago but of which we hear very little, namely the influence of William James.

But before that, to add more color to the emotional palette of this driven man, let me add this as a tentative uneasy equilibrium or perhaps existential juggling between the divine and the flesh

> Sex is our religion because it holds out the hint of Paradise, and we are its priests and votaries. (Goodman, 1966)

William James wrote to his brother Henry that he had to "forge every word in the teeth of stubborn and irreducible fact." He was speaking of his *Principles of Psychology*, an amazing tour de force from which "he laid down his pen in 1885" but was published to great acclaim in 1890.

> ...In spite of the exclusion of the important subjects of pleasure and pain and moral and aesthetic feelings and judgments, (I find no such "exclusions." R.K.), the work has grown to a length which no one can regret more than the writer himself. The man must indeed by sanguine who, in this crowded age, can hope to have many readers for fourteen hundred continuous pages from his pen. (James, p. v)

We will leap over three hundred pages to Chapter X, *The Consciousness of Self,* itself one hundred ten pages, to the pure Ego, one of the four constituents of self, the others being the material self, the social self and the spiritual self. (p. 292). The theories of the pure self are the Spiritualist, Associationist and the Transcendentalist.

And our focus is on the Spiritualist which immediately becomes the "Soul"

> ...At the end of the chapter (Chapter VI), we said we should examine the "Soul" critically in a later place, to see whether it had any other advantages of thought accompanying a stream of cerebral activity, by a law yet unexplained. (James, p. 343)

> The theory of the Soul is the theory of popular philosophy and of scholasticism, which is only popular philosophy made systematic.

Then in a long reference which I will quote, James gives the classical rationale or rather theory of scholasticism and his analysis as against the opposing "Stream of Thought". Thence to the Transcendentalist theory "which owes its origin to Kant." You remember, "I am a Kantian."

I am clearly aiming at what I see as a difficult double allegiance in Paul Goodman: the scholastic rigor with its Augustine and Aristotelian backgrounds with the Kantian Unity in back of everything. This is acceptable, indeed, a desideratum in the new department of Philosophy in Chicago as against the pragmatism of James, Dewey and Mead, which is most emphatically not. And I do not think it programmatic but as I said above an existential situation which Paul was uncomfortable with and which had fateful consequences for his treatment of theory in Perls, Hefferline and Goodman some fifteen years later.

The consequences are embedded in the key concepts he wrote into *Gestalt Therapy* which have influenced countless students and study situations. In her excellent book, Sylvia Crocker, has spoken of "ambiguities." I will speak of perhaps subconscious, though therefore not completely deliberate efforts to protect an intellectual persona that was not clear in the concepts and used an enlightened eclecticism, which as I think Taylor Stoehr says in *Here, Now, Next* in another context made possible varying views of the theory. Further, it thus provided a kind of a barrier to getting behind the concept to any meaning one could get hold of. Queries aimed at them bounced off as if from an invisible wall. Isadore From elevated this technique to a high art. (Incidentally, *Here, Now, Next* as a title has provenance in James's *de proche en proche* from the *Principles*, "next to next.")

To return to James and the theory of the Soul as scholasticism, he gives the classical argument from Saint Thomas. (p. 343)

> (The theory) declares that the principle of individuality within us must be substantial, for psychic phenomena are activities, and there can be no activity without a concrete agent. This substantial agent cannot be the brain but must be something *immaterial*; for its activity, thought, is both immaterial, and takes cognizance of immaterial things, and of material things in general and

intelligible, as well as in particular and sensible ways, —all which powers are incompatible with the nature of matter of which the brain is composed. Thought moreover is simple, whilst the activities of the brain are compounded of the elementary activities of each of its parts. Furthermore, thought is spontaneous or free, whilst all material activity is determined *ab extra*; and the will can turn itself against all corporeal goods and appetites, which would be impossible were it a corporeal function.

And then the conclusion from the objective reasons as above:

For these objective reasons, the principle of psychic life must be both immaterial and simple as well as substantial, must be what is called a *Soul*.

And for the reasons from the subjective side of the argument:

Our consciousness of personal identity assures us of our essential simplicity: the owner of the various constituents of the self, as we have seen them, the hypothetical Arch-Ego whom we provisionally conceived as possible, is a real entity of whose existence self-consciousness makes us directly aware.

I am separating the following from the paragraph although it is one in the text because the conclusions are dramatic for the theory of gestalt therapy and we will return to a fuller analysis from that point of view later in the discussion:

…The hypothetical Arch-Ego…is a real entity of whose existence self-consciousness makes us directly aware. *No material agent could thus turn around and grasp* **itself**—*material activities always grasp something else than the* **agent**. *And if a brain* **could grasp** *itself and be self-conscious, it would be conscious of itself as a brain and not as something of a altogether different kind.*

(The italics are mine except for the bold type which is originally italicized in James's text.)

To re-orient ourselves, remember from page 5 line 21, we were to study in Chapter X, *The Consciousness of the Self.* Here we are talking of the Soul as in the Spiritualist theory of "the pure self, or inner principle of personal unity." Spiritual has become Soul and Soul has become the Unity of perhaps Ego or perhaps Self.

> The Soul then exists as a simple spiritual substance in which the various psychic faculties, operations and affections inhere (Aristotle's powers and operations.)

> If we ask what a Substance is, the only answer is that it is a self-existent being, or one which needs no other subject in which to inhere. At bottom, its only positive determination is Being, and this is something whose meaning we all realize even though we find it hard to explain. The Soul is moreover an *individual* being, and if we ask what that is, we are told to look in upon our Self, (!) and we shall learn by direct intuition better than through any abstract reply. Our direct perception of our own inward being is in fact by many deemed to be the original prototype out of which our notion of *simple active substance in general* is fashioned. (My italics, R.K.)

And then the thumping conclusion that separates the Thomists from Chicago's Pragmatists as the department of Philosophy is "rationalized" by Hutchins and Adler and McKeon:

> The *consequences* of the simplicity and substantiality of the Soul are its incorruptibility and natural immortality—nothing but **God's direct *fiat*** can annihilate it—and its *responsibility* at all times for whatever it may have done.

The central point I am developing has a dual aspect. The first is that in Paul Goodman's soul, if you will, the Thomist and the Pragmatist maintained an uneasy truce, the reactive oppressions of which were worked off in his "Creator Spirit" activities; and secondly released, not as such, in his driven and rebellious iconoclasm for its own sake.

And further, that duality found its way into Perls, Hefferline and Goodman in the many-faceted aspects of the terms of its theory the examination of which will be the heart of this paper. There is classical authority for just such a duality: thus from James in the *Principles* of 1885 (!).

> This substantialist view of the soul was essentially the view of Plato and Aristotle. It received its completely formal elaboration in the middle ages. [*The Scholastics*]. It was believed in by Hobbes, Descartes, Locke, Leibnitz Wolf, Berkeley, and is now defended by the entire modern dualistic or spiritualistic or common-sense school. Kant's successors, the absolute idealists, profess to have discarded it, —how that may be we shall inquire ere long. (p. 344)
>
> *It is at all events needless for expressing the actual subjective phenomena of consciousness as they appear.* (James, p. 344)

What is James's candidate for expressing the "actual subjective phenomena of consciousness as they appear?" Nothing less than the famous stream of consciousness written as *The Stream of Thought* in the preceding sixty pages of Chapter IX, preceding that of Chapter X, *The Consciousness of Self*. James refers this chapter to an article he wrote in 1884 (!) *On Some Omissions of Introspective Psychology* in *Mind*.

Instead of starting with apparently simpler mental facts as sensations and building to higher ones, James begins the study of the mind "from within." This is as much as to deny the classical simplest mental fact is a sensation, thence synthetically constructing mind upwards. The series of classy verbal nuggets one after the other are too delicious to paraphrase even if it was possible.

"We now begin the study of the mind from within."

"No one ever had a simple sensation by itself."

"The notion that sensations, being the simplest things, are the first things to take up in psychology is (an) apparently innocent supposition that nevertheless contains a flaw."

"It is astonishing what havoc is wrought by [the flawed innocent suppositions] the consequences which develop and are irremediable."

"The first fact is that thinking of some sort goes on."

And from Chapter VII, *The Methods and Snares of Psychology*, as he seeks a term for states of consciousness merely as such, he hits upon "Thought"

"...(W)hich would be the best word by far to use if it could be made to cover sensations."

(Thought) immediately suggests the omnipresence of cognition (or reference to an object other then the mental state itself) (!)

"Which we shall soon see to be of the mental life's essence." (p. 186)

"It is a patent fact of consciousness that a transmission (The 'title' of a collective self) be passed from one Thought to another... Each pulse of cognitive consciousness, each Thought, dies away and is replaced by another. The other, among the things it knows, knows its own predecessor, and finding it 'warm,' greets it saying; 'Thou art *mine*, and part of the same self with me.' Each later thought, knowing and including thus the Thoughts which went before is the final receptacle — and appropriating them is the final owner — of all that they contain and own. Each Thought is thus born an owner, and dies owned

> transmitting whatever realized as its Self to its own later
> proprietor." (p. 339)

So the Thought knows, chooses, and appropriates all of the Thought that
preceded it and this "adoption is the foundation of the appropriation of
most of the remoter constituents of the self."

> Who owns the last self owns the self before the last, for what
> possesses the possessor possesses the possessed. (p. 340)

For contemporary authority and a statement of the turmoil in the souls of
the students at Chicago, we go the testimony of Joas:

> The alleged opportunist adjustment of the pragmatist, social-
> reformist intellectuals to the changed circumstances (the
> "reactionary wave") was a crucial experience for their students,
> and the cause of the rift between the latter and their teachers.
> One of Dewey's most gifted students, Randolph Bourne,
> searched for the causes of this adjustment in a polemical essay,
> which today's reader still finds gripping, and discovered them in
> pragmatism's central concept of adaptation. In Bourne's view,
> the technocratic consequences of pragmatist philosophy issued
> from its programmatic confinement to *ad hoc* reforms and its
> refusal to conceive of utopian alternatives to existing society. He
> readily admits that Dewey's "instrumentalism" was not an
> ideology of value-free technical knowledge, the use of which is
> to be guided only by arbitrarily chosen values, but that it was,
> rather, implicitly founded on humanistic values.

You will immediately recognize where Bourne is going, namely to the
necessary and supreme role of the *a priori*, which is behind everything;
that will take you to the one-for-one paralleling to the discussion of the
Soul in James above. You will no doubt track Bourne's argument in that
light and experience for yourself the personal conflict he is describing.

However, Bourne argues, the implicitness of these values had not sufficed. In Bourne's essay political radicalization is combined with a willingness to give up pragmatism in favour of a philosophy of a priori values. What emerges in the text is a (personal? R.K.) conflict that is of essential importance for understanding pragmatism. Bourne rejects a philosophy of adaptation, since its inherent limitation prevents it from making full use even of the available framework for social reforms.

He has wound up, and the fast ball now comes which in aim and target suggest the motive of striking the batter. Its expressive tone seems that of an underlying rage, one of whom it may be said his gods—or as in his title, his "idols" — have failed. Or rather betrayed him, and the fires of his rage and disappointment are unquenchable.

Let me read too much into my interpretation. I feel entitled. When after the arduous effort in *Three Lectures* to reply to Frederick Perls (now) famous lament: "Cannot gestalt therapy stand on its own two feet?," with his sturdy reaffirmation of the gestalt psychology of the Frankfort school where Perls had said the foundational theory (of gestalt therapy) lay, I discovered the construct fallacy in the psychology, I too was enraged. Then contemptuous. But not and not yet bitter. After all, what is another disappointment in a reality of them? I *have* survived.

But to return to Bourne and this is 1919, so the strife is early engaged:

> The defect of any philosophy of "adaptation" or "adjustment," even when it means adjustment to changing, living experience, *is that there is no provision for thought or experience getting beyond itself.* (This is absurd if one had read or perhaps understood James's *Stream* of 1880. R.K.)

> ...(O)pportunist efforts usually achieve less even than what seemed obviously possible... A philosophy of adjustment will not even make for adjustment. If you try merely to "meet"

situations as they come, you will not even meet them. (Joas, p. 29)

Joas is citing from Randolph Bourne, *Twilight of Idols* in: *Untimely Papers* (New York, 1919, p. 114 – 139)

We have come a long way from page 7 where James had analyzed the notions of Self to the passing perishable Thought that knows and appropriates the contents of the previous thought and so on. Thus the *a priori* nature of the Self becomes a myth. But Bourne's point must be taken seriously.

Since he was one of Dewey's "most gifted students," Dewey's analysis in the *Quest for Certainty* is appropriate. It is also the basis for Goodman's analysis of the collapse to authority in Perls, Hefferline and Goodman. The shock and confusion of the unsupported freedom leads to the false support of dogma which is no *sui generis* support at all. Of course, Santayana's observation, "When the end is lost sight of and the effort redoubled, we have fanaticism," is the adequate statement of the consequences of dogma. Ultimately, collecting faggots for the *auto da fe*.

One does not have to strain at the beam to swallow the mote of recognition that Bourne is using Dewey's own argument against dogma against Dewey himself.

I will group the *a priori* argument with the Soul argument which you have followed above in a summary statement from James, summary and prospective in the sense of the force of the Stream of Thought as more than adequate to contain and express the phenomena that the Soul theory purports to explain.

> *It is at all events needless for expressing the actual subjective phenomena of consciousness as they appear.* We have formulated them all without its aid, by the supposition of a stream of thoughts, each substantially 1) different from the rest,

but 2) cognitive of the rest, and 3) "appropriative" of each other's content.

...At least, if I have not already succeeded in making this plausible to the reader, I am hopeless of convincing him by anything I could add now.

The (1) unity, (2) the identity, (3) the individuality, and (4) the immateriality that appear in the psychic life (remember the scholastic argument) are thus accounted for as (a) phenomenal and (b) temporal facts exclusively, and with no need of reference to any more simple or substantial agent than the present Thought or "section" of the stream.

We have seen it to be single and unique in the sense of having no *separable* part—perhaps that is the only kind of simplicity meant to be predicated of the soul.

The present Thought also has being—at least all believers in the soul believe so—and if there be no other Being in which it "inheres," it ought itself to be a "substance." If *this* kind of simplicity and substantiality were all that is predicated of the Soul, then it might appear that we had been talking of the soul all along, without knowing it, when we treated the present Thought as (a) an agent, (b) an owner, and the like.

But the Thought is a perishing and not a immortal or incorruptible thing. Its successors may continuously succeed to it, resemble it, and appropriate it, but they *are* not it, whereas the Soul-Substance is supposed to be a fixed unchanging thing. (James, p. 345)

And then to get to the heart of the matter in the conclusion of the paragraph above which I have sectioned and semi-outlined for emphasis and clarity, (with James one tends to run with the elegance of the prose and then wonder what happened to the enormous weight of the mere *information and learning* of the thing that has romped so before him. This was psychologist Sully's complaint: that the beauty of the language got in the way of the technical psychology.) Again to the heart of the matter:

> By the Soul is always meant something *behind* the present thought, another kind of substance, existing on a non phenomenal plane.

This shuttlecock and battledore of the mind is what I have seized upon as the workings of Goodman's personal philosophy which he never really resolved or perhaps confessed. Are Creator Spirit and Eros synthetic *a priori, the pre-existence of which* constitute reality, and the absence of which make "pain in my breast" and "I am bitter"?

Therefore, before we wind up this section in the analysis of the Transcendental Ego of Kant, I want to present a few sentences from James, the tone of which runs through and through Goodman's thought in all his writing:

> The simpler formulation (than the Soul) says that the thought simply *comes*. (James, p. 345)

There is not some thing behind it or for that matter also in front of it, lying in wait or anticipation to receive the thought aroused by the correspondence of the brain processes.

> But what positive meaning has the Soul, when scrutinized, but the **ground of possibility** *of the thought?*

> ...And what is the (thought) but the ***determining of the possibility to actuality***?

> And what is this after all, but giving a sort of concreted form to one's belief that the coming of the thought when the brain-processes occur, has *some* sort **of ground in the nature of things?** (p. 345) (My emphases in bold-face, R.K.)

But once more to turn to the turns and swings from the Creator Spirit to his pragmatic "influence" in James and Dewey, most poignantly expressed in Five *Years: Thoughts During a Useless Period*. He was 45:

> ...The really desperate efforts for sexual happiness that I made got the reception that is given to desperate efforts in this line. But worst of all, I suffered from bleak hours of nothing to do or plan during lonely walks along the river or of nursing a beer in a bar.
>
> Or bluntly, the unlucky truth is that all my life I have existed in an interim, but only for those five years did I write in pocket notebooks.
>
> The truth is I feel like an Exile--from paradise; and I mean as will be clear in the following pages, a very bread-and-butter kind of paradise. (He quotes the Hebrew), "but because of our sins, we are exiled from our land." (Goodman, 1966, p. vii)

I hesitated; I wanted to italicize "sins" but in deference to the reader's smarts and the reality of my hesitation, I will let it stand.

In a startlingly frank analysis, Goodman reveals how he achieves "the snake-like suppleness of my style." The twists and turns which I long since ascribed to a dual allegiance and which in gestalt therapy unites in terms and names which though literary mandarin drive readers to despair.

> At Random House, Jason praises the "snake-like suppleness" of my style. How do I manage this continuity in motion? Primarily, by avoiding asyndeton. In almost every sentence, I use connective particles (but, nor, for), or connective references (this, such, the contrary), or connectives of attitude (of course, naturally, nevertheless!). Almost as frequently as in Greek. I get denseness, too, very carefully placing my "onlys" and "preciselys." But also, I get continuity and speed by often using

> an unexpected word choice that produces a further connection,
> e.g. a pejorative adjective when I seem to have been approving,
> or vice versa; or an unexpected emphasis by position; or even a
> rhythm, compression, expansion, sudden summation serving as a
> *premise of enthymeme*. The enthymeme is given in the texture of
> the words, without my having to state it in propositions. That is,
> I combine overfull motion of thought with a continuous run-on
> of connectives.

Now one has experienced these vice versas and the texture of the words
serving as unstated propositions or even parts of speech. They are wake
up calls *within* the composition and for me provide a sudden check to the
flow while I attempt to decipher it. It is sometimes not decipherable,
nonetheless intriguing.

Let me give you an example that racked me and my study groups for
years. It is from the heart of Perls, Hefferline and Goodman, Chapter
XIII, *Creative Adjustment: II. Final Contact and Post-Contact, Section I:
Unity of Figure and Ground.* This section is particularly difficult because
as one of my English professor patients said: "He is trying to show how a
thing can be one thing and another thing at the same time." There is
another dynamic: how to preserve the whole-and-parts relation central to
gestalt psychology in the theory of figure and ground. The relation is
obviously circular since you have to make wholes that are parts for there
to be parts. It depends on your theory of perception, your definition of an
"Object" in that theory, the Berkeleyan theory of signs and the workings
of imagery, developmentally. For an adequate analysis of that mouthful,
we will shortly turn to George Herbert Mead and his *Philosophy of the
Act.* But to return to the libretto and the example.

> ...In final contact, the self is immediately and fully engaged in
> the *figure* it has discovered-and-invented; momentarily, there is
> practically no background. The figure embodies all the concern
> of the self, and the self is nothing but its present concern, so the
> self *is* the figure. The powers of the self are now actualized, so

the self becomes something (but in so doing, it ceases to be self). (p. 416)

> Let us consider the nature of an awareness that has no environmental or body background, for awareness is a figure against a ground. Such awareness is possible only of a whole-and-parts, where each part is immediately experienced as involving all the other parts and the whole, and the whole is just of these parts. The whole figure could be said to be the background for the parts, but it is more than ground for *it* (My italics); it is at the same time the figure *of* the parts and they are ground. To put this another way: the experience does not allow for any more possibilities because it is necessary and actual; these parts at this moment cannot mean anything else.

This is not snake like. It is eel like. How does one get hold of it? I taught from that book for forty years in ongoing study groups and could never crack the nut of the italicized pronoun *it*. Where, what, is its antecedent? In my battered edition, I have a note with an arrow pointing to *it*. The note says, "Finally! 10/91." I *still* don't get it, or rather the why of it. I think it also entirely literary as the rest of the chapter becomes nothing less then soaring, beautiful, dazzlingly brilliant. Poetry.

Perhaps fifteen years ago, I determined to get to the bottom of the matter and brought the book to Isadore and Hunt at one of our frequent dinners. The combination of Isadore's expertise and Hunt's skills as a professional editor should see the task accomplished. Isadore perused the material standing up, the book on the dining table. He said: "It *is dense*" and we repaired to the office leaving the task to Hunt. After about five minutes, there was an uproar and smashing and banging in the kitchen. "I can't find an antecedent. I don't think there is an antecedent. And I don't give a damn. Fuck it!" It was authoritative and heroic.

Some years after I presented the passage to one of the most intelligent persons I knew who was also brilliantly free intellectually and a literateur. Almost immediately, excited, red-faced, with an intellectual flush of pleasure and delight in discovery came the diagnosis: "There is no antecedent. The whole paragraph is the antecedent!"

Well, one teaches by example. Remember page 12, line 9 onwards, where Paul says that he does not need to give the propositions of the premises but they are in the texture of the work itself as a literary device to achieve his snake like suppleness.

I still don't know what the antecedent is. I think, to repeat, Goodman was squirming, not like a snake but a like worm on a hook trying to keep parts and wholes, therefore figures and grounds without which his formidable and brilliant exegesis and adaptation of them to gestalt therapy personality theory falls apart.

On page 11 line 10, I suggested the preceding example of Goodman's artistic handling of the theory of the self; and also perhaps a feature of his dilemma, as a prelude to concluding this section with a treatment of "The transcendentalist theory (of the Self) which owes its origin to Kant." (James, p. 360)

My approach here will be from Perls, Hefferline and Goodman to James and not vice versa. In the early Fifties in the professional group there were frequent discussions in which everyone agreed that the theory of the Self was the weakest point in psychoanalytic theory. It seemed to me that Ego and Self were used interchangeably leading to less and more confusion. In Chapter XI, *Critique of Psychoanalytic Theories of the Self*, page 384, Goodman essays a masterly restatement. His attack rests on 1) a "critique of a theory that makes the self "otiose," and 2) a "critique of a theory that isolates the Self in fixed boundaries." (p. 387)

To the first, the otiose theory, he ascribes Anna Freud and *The Ego and the Mechanisms of Defense*. In the healthy situation, the ego does nothing and it is only in the neurotic situation when the defenses are breaking down that the ego can be seen at work, doing its synthesizing activity in producing the mechanisms (of defense against the unconscious knowledge.)

> Notice, here, that the tendency to synthesis is called another
> function of the available ego, mentioned in parentheses at the
> end of the chapter; but this tendency is what Kant, for instance,
> judged to be the essence of the empirical ego, the synthetic unity
> of apperception, and it is what we have been considering to be
> the chief work of the self, gestalt-formation.

There are parallels and, indeed, trenchant agreements with both Anna
Freud and Goodman in James's analysis in *The Consciousness of the
Self, The Transcendentalist Theory* "which owes its origin to Kant."
(James, p. 360)

Indeed, they are so marked that I could persuade myself that a not small
part of the reason that James is often cited as "influence" but it is hard to
track that influence in Goodman's opus, is that it is so close that he could
be swallowed up in James. And then what? Let me give what is not so
much an analysis as a pointed digression from Ralph Barton Perry, *The
Thought and Character of William James.*

> These (idealism and empiricism) are the currents and eddies of
> thought in which James found himself when he began to
> navigate his own philosophical craft in 1861. Toward the
> charting of his own course, he brought certain well-marked
> prepossessions, too general to commit him to any definite
> philosophical doctrine, but undoubtedly eliminating certain
> alternatives, and affecting the emphasis within those which
> remained. (Perry, p. 466)

Let us keep also focused on the twenty-five year old Paul Goodman at
Chicago. Further, although it is difficult to keep the span of time to the
fore: *The Critique of Pure Reason* was 1781; *The Principles of
Psychology*, 1890, completed in 1885; *Gestalt Therapy*, in 1951. I fully
realize I have placed our text in quite elegant company! To continue with
Perry and James:

Among these prepossessions, I count three as unquestionable. The first of these was his moralism. He was not a man to rest content with any philosophy which disparaged or enervated the will. Perhaps, the very fact that he did not engage extensively in the work of the world, but adopted an intellectual career, intensified this tendency. What he could not express in affairs found expression in a dramatization of life in which he cast himself in the role of moral champion. His second prepossession was in favor of variety and change, the intellectual counterpart of his restless disposition. It was not likely that a man who was bored by sameness, and who found routine intolerable, should be receptive to philosophical influences of the rationalistic type which emphasized identity and worshipped coherence. Thirdly, even though James abandoned art (Perry means 'painting' here, R.K.) he remained a man of artistic sensibility.

Literature and the plastic arts claimed a large part of his attention. He had the novelist's interest in character, the dramatist's interest in life and the poet's interest in nature. In other words, he was repelled by verbalism, logomachy, and abstractness. No philosophy could ultimately satisfy him that did not embrace an intuition of concrete realities, and exalt feeling and sensation above the intellect. (Perry, p. 467)

This is Perry in 1935 writing the history and biography of the young Paul Goodman in the shade of *The Thought and Character of William James*.

Returning to the analysis of the Ego, Goodman turns to Federn one of the "Ego" psychologists and his treatment of "boundary" as a phenomenon that arises when the principal method of analysis is introspection. He is quoting from Paul Federn, *Mental Hygiene of the Psychotic Ego*, *American Journal of Psychotherapy*, July, 1949, p. 356 – 371.

"Whatsoever is mere thought is due to a mental process lying *inside* the mental and physical boundary; whatsoever has the connotation of being real lies *outside* the mental and physical ego-boundary, (and;)

"The mental and the bodily ego are felt separately, but in the wake state always in such a way that the mental ego is experienced to be inside the body ego." (Perls, Hefferline and Goodman, p. 388)

Goodman circles around the problem of "inside" and "outside"...the "thought" and the "real".

...[I]f the contact system is essentially (rather than sometimes and as a special structure) the proprioception of one's individuality within distinct boundaries, then how possibly does one get into contact with a reality outside the boundaries?

In the present state of philosophy, this kind of formulation seems perfectly reasonable, but it is absurd. For how does one become aware of the distinction between the inside and the outside, the "thought" and the "real"? Is it not by awareness?

In *that* present state of philosophy more than fifty years ago, it could probably be entertained that fixed boundaries of inside and outside of the self, or that part of self called "Ego" could and its boundedness made sense. But now it appears a particularly irritating notion and Goodman's analysis of Freud and Federn a mind-numbing *Spitzfindigkeit*.

This is particularly the case when he concludes that in the case of the less restrictive "introspection" where one includes the field, (and also the body as "field") that instantly one has a unity and, of course, a heightened awareness, "boundary-ness(es)" if not "the" boundary.

Although he must have known better, my conclusion is that the Goodman notion of (his) body as also an environment was not well-formed or perhaps a comfortable concept. "I wish I wasn't so damn ugly, period." (*Five Years*). In any case, it is my (fairly solid) impression that

Laura Perls and I were very much in the van when we insisted and continued to insist on "thinking" as also contactful and contacting. This in spite of Frederick Perls to whom thinking was "why" talk and utterly displacement upward.

Goodman continues his analysis from the standpoint of the chronic low grade emergency which is the lot of mankind generally. If in the emergency, the body is in semi-paralysis, the breath restricted, the thinking is repetitious and obsessional, all of which must be in obedience to the Reality Principle,

> then the "objects of such an external world are such as require to be pushed about by an aggressive will (rather than interacted with in a process of growth), and cognitively they are alien, fragmented etc., such as to be known only by an elaborate abstract ratiocination." (p. 391)

However in aware experiment

> ...(T)he self, aware in middle mode, bursts the compartmenting of mind, body, and external world. (Therefore) must we not conclude that for the theory of the self and its relation to the "I," introspection is a poor *primary* method of observation, for it creates a peculiar condition?

> We must begin by exploring a wide range of concernful situations and behaviors. Then if we resume the introspection, the true situation is apparent: that the introspecting ego is a deliberate restrictive attitude of the psycho-somatic awareness, temporarily excluding the environmental awareness and making the body-awareness a passive object. (p. 389)

In treating of the exact same subject, James in *The Consciousness of the Self,* insists that the kernel of the Self is not an abstraction nor the body in the sense that they cannot be felt all alone in the stream of consciousness, "but always together with other things."

James is trying to experience by his introspection the possible meaning of the Spiritual Self prior to taking up his final analysis of the Transcendental Ego in Kant.

> But when I forsake such general descriptions and grapple with particulars, coming to the closest possible quarters with the facts, *it is difficult for me to detect in the activity any purely spiritual element at all. Whenever my introsopective glance succeeds turning around quickly enough to catch one of these manifestations of spontaneity in the act, all it can ever feel distinctly is some bodily process for the most part **taking place in the head**.* (p. 299)

Then he describes the movements as adjustments of the sense organ(s) to which it relates as for example, thinking in visual terms, the eyeballs rolling in as in sleep; in memory inwards from the periphery; in reasoning, he speaks of a kind of "vaguely localized diagram in my mind with the various fractional objects of the thought disposed at particular points thereof."

The movement of air is a powerful factor in his consenting or negating with his glottis as its "sensitive valve."

> In *effort* of any sort, contractions of the jaw muscles and of those of respiration are added to those of the brow and glottis, thus the feeling passes out of the head properly so called. It passes out of the head whenever the welcoming or rejecting of the object is *strongly* felt. Then a set of feelings pour in from many bodily parts, all "expressive" of my emotion, and the head-feelings proper are swallowed up in this larger mass.

> In a sense, then, it may be truly said that, in one person at least, *"the Self of selves" when carefully examined is found to consist mainly of the collection of these peculiar motions in the head or between the head and throat.*

> I do not for a mount say this is *all* it consists of, for I fully realize
> how desperately hard is introspection in this field. But I feel
> quite sure that these cephalic motions are the portions of my
> innermost activity of which I am *most distinctly aware.*

> If the dim portions which I cannot yet define should prove to be
> like unto these distinct portions in me, and I like other men, *it
> would follow that our entire feeling of spiritual activity, or what
> commonly passes by that name, is really a feeling of bodily
> activities whose exact nature is by most men overlooked.* (p. 302)

He concludes from this introspective analysis, this incessant opening and
closing of doors, adjustments and reactions that this is all there is and
that from Substantial, Spiritual, or Transcendental these motions are
ultimate and Objective.

> ...(T)hat this Objective falls asunder into two contrasted parts,
> one realized as "Self" the other as "not-Self;" and that over and
> above these parts there *is* nothing save the fact that they are
> known, the fact of the stream of thought being there as the
> indispensable subjective condition of their being experienced at
> all.

But far from concluding from this that there is a Thinker that is given as
a logical, postulate, e.g., Matter, he says such speculations "traverse
common sense;"

> I mean by this, that I will continue to assume (as I have assumed
> all along...a direct awareness of the process of our thinking as
> such, simply insisting on the fact that it is an even more inward
> and subtle phenomenon than most of us suppose. (p. 305)

There are striking (shall I call them non-parallels?) again in Goodman
and James.

...(T)he acts of attending, assenting, negating, making an effort, are felt as movements of something in the head. In many cases, it is possible to describe these movements quite exactly. In attending to either an idea or a sensation belonging to a particular sense-sphere, the movement is the adjustment of the sense organ, felt as it occurs. (James, p. 300)

Then in *Five Years*, Goodman describes his experience from an altered state of consciousness to a more alert state traversing levels from less to more reality, as he "recalls his sleepy behavior."

Lying half-asleep, I move my glasses or pipe out of harm's way. Later, though I recall my action, I am less willing to affirm it as real, and, of course, remember it less well. This seems to indicate that by "reality" we mean the object of *alert* sensation and motor behavior. (Not that the real is 'made of' sensations; rather, we affirm, believe in, alert sensations of the real.) (*Five Years*, p. 208)

To return to James as *he* recalls his introspective efforts to "detect in the activity any spiritual element at all":

In attending to either an idea or a sensation belonging to the particular sense-sphere, the movement is the adjustment of the sense-organ, felt as it occurs. (James, p. 300)

Many philosophers however, hold that reflective consciousness of the self is essential to the cognitive function of thought. They hold that a thought in order to know a thing at all, must expressly distinguish between the thing and its own self. (And in a foot note: "Kant originated this view").

This is a perfectly wanton assumption, and not the faintest shadow of reason exists for supposing it true. As well might I contend that I cannot dream without dreaming that I dream, swear without swearing that I swear, deny without denying that I deny, as maintain that I cannot know without knowing that I know.

I may have either acquaintance-with, or knowledge-about, an object O without thinking about myself at all. It suffices for this that I think O, and that it exist. If, in addition to thinking O, I also think that I exist and that I know O, well and good; I then know one more thing, a fact about O, of which I previously was unmindful. That, however, does not prevent me from having already known it a good deal. O *per se*, or O *plus* P, are as good objects of knowledge as O *plus* me is.

The philosophers in question simply substitute one particular object for all others, and call it the *object* par excellence.

It is a case of the "psychologist's fallacy". *They* know the object to be one thing and the thought another; and they forthwith foist their on knowledge into that of the thought of which they pretend to give a true account.

To conclude, then, *thought may, but need not, in knowing, discriminate between its object and itself.* (p. 274–5)

To return to Goodman: but having made that statement and noticing he has (of the pipe and glasses) he characteristically moves to the next step. It is vexatious for him to leave anything alone until he has written it or loved it or squeezed it dry. Phyllis Greenacre speaks of the "compulsive pulse takers and scab-pickers." But of what is the matter of philosophy if not the silent pulse or the grown over wound?

But the act by which I notice (!) my sleepy behavior, and am later aware of its perhaps-fantasy quality, gives me also another aspect of reality that is real and concrete but has a certain barrenness and vagueness. And I think that a part of what we call "generalization" or "abstraction" is the concrete but bare and

> schematic perception (?): the grasping of the object when we are as if half-asleep.
>
> ...In language it is expressed in the syntax, the kinds of construction allowable, rather than in the terms. In behavior it is expressed in the method and habit rather than the acts. (*Five Years*, p. 208)

This last is unintelligible. Describe for me the parsing of a sentence that is attributable to its syntax, method, and habit. And what of all things from a poet is "the kinds of construction allowable?"

(Actually, my comment above is unintelligible unless I tell you that I read "In language *behavior*, "four times before I realized language and behavior had been separated and Goodman was introducing "elements" of speech from the linguistic theorists of the period of the later *Five Years*. This was counter to all I knew of his general drift. I reread *Speaking and Language* and find on page 93 from 1971 year of publication

> And it is obvious that innumerable forms have come to be because of reasons of meaning, e.g. abstract words formed from concrete actions—"concept" is formed from a word for grasping, "abstract" from dragging, "comprehend" from taking hold...
>
> Language is behavior. [!])

This development from a distance of twenty years.

Continuing James's analysis of his introspection:

> I cannot think in visual terms, for example, without feeling a fluctuating play of pressures, convergences, divergences, and accommodations in my eyeballs. The direction in which the object is conceived to lie determines the character of these movements, the feeling of which becomes for my consciousness,

> identified with the manner in which I make myself ready to
> receive the visible thing. (James, p. 300)

To keep us oriented, remember we are considering the possible spiritual
nature of the Ego considered from as above the psychoanalytic point of
view, basically Kantian, or as in Goodman, arising in the development of
contacting and within the activity, though as I am contending, not
completely. He, Goodman, needs a Creator Spirit behind everything that
he cannot get his hands on.

> Such a concrete but bare schema is different from the logical
> abstraction of a name, e.g. "apple" as standing for apples, which
> is a definite rule for dealing with particular apples.

> My hunch is that Plato's ideas were, for him, concrete but bare
> reals of this kind, occurring in mystical experience that made
> them seem very vivid to him.

> I myself find it hard to think in logical abstractions, but I think
> readily and habitually in schemata. I am a Kantian (!).

And dancing back to James:

> In reasoning, I find that I am apt to have a kind of vaguely
> localized diagram in my mind, with the various fractional objects
> of the thoughts disposed at particular points thereof; and the
> oscillations of my attention from one of them to another are most
> distinctly felt as alternations of direction in movements occurring
> inside the head.

> In one person at least, *"the Self of selves," when carefully
> examined, is found to consist mainly of the collection of these
> peculiar motions in the head or between the head and throat...*I
> feel quite sure; that these cephalic motions are the portions of my
> innermost activity of which I am most *distinctly aware.*

If the dim portions which I cannot yet define should prove to be like unto these distinct portions in me, and I like other men, *it would follow that our entire feeling of spiritual activity, or what commonly passes by that name, is really **a feeling of bodily activities whose exact nature is by most men overlooked**.*

We will find this position taken over *in toto* and burnished with his glossary of systematic metaphysics by Alfred North Whitehead in *Process and Reality* as he, too, comes to "stubborn and irreducible fact" as he stands on the shoulders of William James, his "adorable genius."

Part II

We have reviewed the basic theory of gestalt psychotherapy as written by Paul Goodman in the second volume of *Gestalt Therapy, Excitement and Growth in the Human Personality*. We have established, I think, that far from a debt to formal gestalt psychology, the therapy is directly founded and shaped in the pragmatism of the Chicago School, C.S. Peirce, John Dewey, George Herbert Mead, and above all, the "master," William James.

Originally, as conceived in my *Three Lectures* (of which this is the last two) I intended to state—and did—the "bases of gestalt therapy" from the point of view of Mead's *Philosophy of the Act* which is itself a fuller and more thorough theory of contact than Goodman's schematic rendering. Mead is never acknowledged in Goodman and one searches about for a reason as many of his locutions seem identical.

He arrived at Chicago in 1936. Mead died five years earlier in April, 1931. There must have been something in the air of Mead. It appears the same curtain of silence that fell about James became a fortress encircling Mead.

As Hans Joas points out in James' "subjectivist" and Peirce's "scientific" pragmatism, what is one to think of a Mead who can write in *A Pragmatic Theory of Truth* about Peirce:

> The passage runs as follows: "If the Pragmatic doctrine is a logical generalization of scientific method, it cannot merge the problem that engages thought with a larger problem which denies validity to the conditions that are the necessary tests of the solution which thought is seeking." (Joas, 1987, p. 221)

In that vein and as part of "the Conditions," this part of the paper will examine basic concepts of gestalt therapy and try to restate them in terms that are more fundamentally grounded; that is to say, "can stand on their own two feet," according to the statement of what I have called Frederick Perls' lament in his *In and Out the Garbage Pail.*

The method will be to state the concept and within it its classical usage and finally a clarifying treatment designed to fit the case more cleanly.

The first of these will be the notion of Agency which is central in the development of the theory of Self and to which we can segue most smoothly from the analysis of the Kantian view of the Transcendentalist Theory of the Self.

The notion of agency or agent central in a theory of self is treated in the famous "The self is the system of contacts in the organism/environment field;" and "the agency of growth." Or elsewhere, "The self is the system of contacts and the agent of growth." And Goodman specifically states that the organism grows, but not the self and he provides a brilliant analysis of the sequence

> It is the organism and not the self that grows. Let us speculatively describe growth as follows: (1) After contact there is a flow of energy, adding to the energy of the organism the new elements assimilated from the environment. (2) The contact-boundary that has been "broken" now reforms, including the new energy and the "organ of second nature." (3) What has been assimilated is now part of the physiological self-regulation. (4) The boundary of contact is now "outside" the assimilated

learning, habit, conditioned reflex, etc., —what is *like* what one has learned does not touch one, it raises no problem.

He is distinguishing the need for contact from the physiological needs, i.e., the transitory need for novelty from the conservative self-regulation

> ...(I)t seems reasonable to define the physiological as the conservative, the non-aware, self-regulation, whether inherent or learned. The psychological is the shifting, transitory contact with novelty. The physiological "first nature," including non-aware neurotic interference with "first nature," has periodic recourse to contact need for novelty. The physiological "second nature" is contacted aperiodically—e.g., available memory is drawn on as a result of external stimulation. (*PHG*, p. 428)

And the "Agent," that ranging widely, finding and making the opportunities for contact and itself, is the self in its proper role.

(For years, I have tried to understand how the self cannot grow, certainly with the organism, and have tried to understand the relation as one between function and entity, That is, the organism actually physically "grows": accumulates, gets bigger, increases, expands; and the self gets stronger. But somehow, this is never satisfactory and I am caught in a dizzying circle.)

The confusion rests in at least two notions of Agency, mere selection or acting, and the *a priori* notion of the actor working for the synthetic unity.

On pages 6 and 7, we considered Agency from William James and his analysis of it within the scholastic tradition of substantial soul. And we thought that this was the rat behind the arras of Goodman's thinking as he built the formal theory of gestalt psychotherapy. That is, in spite of his theory of self occurring within a process of contact, there was always a synthesizer, of more or less ("diminished") self, depending on the "alert/real" character of one's activity.

To settle the question, James returns to a more decisive analysis of self as agent operating as, or better, in, a temporal sequence resting on an ambiguity in Kant's treatment

> The ambiguity referred to in the meaning of the transcendental Ego is as to whether Kant signified by it an *Agent*, and by the Experience it helps to constitute an operation;

> Or whether the experience is an event *produced* in an unassigned way, and the Ego a mere indwelling *element* therein contained.

> If an operation be meant, then Ego and Manifold must both be existent prior to that collision which results in the experience of one by the other.

> If a mere analysis is meant, there is no such prior existence, and the elements only *are* in so far as they are in union. (James, p. 364)

We remember we are concerned with a theory of Self which Goodman calls also the agent or agency of growth but which itself does not grow. It is the agent of growth for the organism. This is what it does.

> Now Kant's tone and language are everywhere the very words of one who is talking of operations and the agents by which they are performed. (Yet there is doubt; then what if the transcendental Ego *be an* agent?)

> Well, if it be so, Transcendentalism is only Substantialism grown shame-faced, and the Ego only a 'cheap and nasty edition' of the soul.

Then the analysis and objections to the Soul on pages 6 and 7 should be reviewed and the problem of the self as agent is discarded since the self ("Soul")

...(E)explained nothing, the "syntheses" which she performed were simply taken ready-made and clapped on to her as expressions of her nature taken after the fact

The Ego is simply *nothing*, as ineffectual and windy an abortion as Philosophy can show.

But if Kant himself thought the Ego did nothing it remained for his successors the post-Kantian idealists to "call it the first Principle of Philosophy"

...(T)o spell its name in capitals and pronounce it with adoration, to act, in short, as if they were going up in a balloon, whenever the notion crossed their mind. (James, p. 365)

Moreover this resemblance of the timeless Ego to the Soul is completed by other resemblances still.

The monism of the post-Kantian idealists seems always lapsing into a regular old-fashioned spiritualistic dualism. They incessantly talk as if, like the Soul, their All-thinker were an Agent operating on detached materials of sense.

It is needless to repeat that the connection of things in our knowledge is in no whit *explained* by making it the deed of an agent whose essence is self-identity and who is out of time. The agency of phenomenal thought coming and going in time is just as easy to *understand*.

In a coda that has resonance for modern times and its fascination for fancied paradoxes as the "Nothing naughts," or being "Hurled into the world,"

And when it is furthermore said that the agent that combines is the same "self-distinguishing subject" which "in another mode of its activity" presents the manifold object to itself, the unintelligibilities become quite paroxysmal, and we are forced to

> confess the entire school of thought...still dwells habitually in
> that mythological stage of thought where phenomena are
> explained as results of dramas enacted by entities which but
> reduplicate the characters of the phenomena themselves. (James,
> p. 369)

By way of putting "the agent or agency of growth" to rest in favor of the
passing Thought that knows the previous one, resembles, continues, and
appropriates it, I append a footnote from James where he analyzes
"potential thought" from Kant.

> It must be noticed, in justice to what was said (earlier: to know a
> thing the knower must also know itself), that neither Kant nor his
> successsors anywhere discriminate between the *presence* of the
> apperceiving Ego to the combined object, and the *awareness by*
> that Ego *of* its own presence and of its distinctness from what it
> apperceives. That the Object must be known to something which
> *thinks, and that it must be known to something which thinks that
> it thinks*, are treated by them as identical necessities, —by what
> logic, does not appear.

> Kant tries to soften the jump in the reasoning by saying the
> thought *of itself* on the part of the Ego need only be *potential*—
> the "I think" must *be capable* of accompanying all other
> knowledge—but a thought which is only potential is actually no
> thought at all, which practically gives up the case. (James, p.
> 361)

It is an intriguing and instructive notion, a "potential thought." Never
having thought about such an *avis rara*, I tried the experiment. I suggest
you try it now, right now: Think a thought that is a potential thought. But
keep your sense of humor. And then you will have the nub of Agency
and we can let the matter drop. Alfred North Whitehead says in *Process
and Reality*, that humankind does not have much tolerance for infinite
regressions.

We are now perhaps able to leave William James and turn to George Herbert Mead for our further development of a more grounded theory of gestalt therapy than we are used to in Perls, Hefferline and Goodman (*PHG*).

By way of transition, I want to present a brief and rough summary from Köhler's *Gestalt Psychology*, the chapter on *Behavior*. He tried to organize scientifically the problem of social behavior. How do we know, or rather what is the evidence comparable to what we have in ordinary perception, for what is going on inside another person. He dismisses the usual perceptions and readings off our own bodies and ends the chapter with a warning to psychological science to avoid social perception. Indeed, this was the basis for Paul Goodman's complaint that the gestalt psychologists had busied themselves with ingenious perceptual experiments but had neglected pressing human problems.

(Freud himself abandoned the incest theory except as a fantasy to insure that the new psychoanalysis would be politically palatable in Nineteenth Century Catholic Vienna.)

George Herbert Mead's work is vast but our influences will be *Mind, Self, and Society*, and *The Philosophy of the Act*. In the first, he develops a social genesis of the self; in the second he places reality in the structure of the act itself as in its phases, impulse, perception, manipulation and finally consummation or contact (!).

However, in the shift to Mead and in a introductory comparison, let us briefly delve into *The Philosophy of the Act*, the magnificent chapter, *The Process of Mind in Nature*. While we are scanning some lines there, we will keep the foregoing of Köhler's warning against social perception cut and pasted for comparison purposes.

> The (relation in immediate experience) that answers to that between mind and body (is that) between a social animal and its environment...The dividing-line between the environment and the individual is functional. The individual acts (!) and that upon

which he acts is the environment...That organism that effects processes is the individual.

The contents of the things in the environment are their colors, sounds, tactual qualities, colors, and tastes, their beauty or ugliness their meanings and values, including characters of past and anticipated experience that go to make up the object.

The content of the individual in immediate experience seems to shrink to the efforts and strains involved in attention, postures, and movements of the body, with such boundaries (!) as actual or anticipated contacts define.

This statement has reference to what are called physical things as distinguished from social things. The social environment is a narrower one than the physical environment.

The physical environment also includes the social environment, that is social things are also physical things.

And then the crescendo:

But persons, or selves, (!) are things in our immediate experience, and the individual in that social environment of things is himself a person, or better, a self (!).

The same distinction between things in the environment and the individual hold here that holds between the physical things and the physical individual in whose environment they lie.

This amounts to saying that social objects, or persons, are immediately present in experience, or, in customary psychological language, are perceived.

Insisting on the direct influence of the efforts and bent of social conduct as well as the characters of physical things that individuals possess,

Mead develops the social self as an object in immediate perception, and this is psychological evidence.

> It is important to note that in immediate experience the environment and the things within it extend both spatially and temporally, that things are therefore at distances from one another, that they change qualitatively and move, and that these relations of extension in immediate experience are always with reference to the here and now of the individual that answers to the particular environment.
>
> Things exist immediately at a distance, and they occur immediately before and after one another.
>
> Spatiotemporal intervals are judged and criticized in reflective experience, but, in order that they may be judged, they must exist immediately and in the organization centered about the here and now of the individual implied in the experience. (Mead, p. 361–362)

The organization of the individual and the environment and its determining relation in immediate experience for all the relevant fields is not otherwise than the usual evidential base in perception and thus is available for a scientific psychology, in spite of the science of the "configuration psychologists" as Mead called them, proceeding from the starting point of physics. This last obviously rules out social objects.

Moreover, Mead embraces the meaning of agent and agency as in James above: "If a mere analysis is meant, there is no such prior existence... and the elements only *are* insofar as they are in union.

> In immediate experience, the import of this determining nature of the relation between environment and the individual appears in the differences in all the forgoing *fields* which results from the different positions, sensings, and acts of attention of the individual.

> Furthermore, the meanings and other values of things are relative to the particular act which in immediate experience the individual exists as agent. The action of the individual in all fields of so-called experience is selective. The contents of things in immediate experience are in a considerable degree dependent upon the individual as acting, as an agent. (Mead, p. 363)

There is no *a priori* agent acting on the powers and the operations of the Soul. And further that being the case, there is then no need to seek for evidence of the existence of a self in experimental psychological terms to create a science of gestalt psychology. It is there already.

Again

> The action of the individual in all the fields of so-called (!) experience is selective. The contents of things in immediate experience are in a considerable degree dependent upon the individual acting (!), as agent. In this sense the environment of the individual is relative to the individual. (Mead, p. 363)

Even in the case of the illusions, the "illusory aspects of things are in the environment." This includes the imagery coming from memory as we recognize it in perceptual experience as we learned from the "old psychology" of the Nineteenth Century.

The striking example is in reading in a variation on Berkeley, we see words (names)

> ...light from which never reaches the retina...We see things hard and cold and smooth and succulent, and there are sensuous contents present that bear the same immediate relation to the individual as do those of vision. When we recall the tenuous images of a past vivid experience, these images are out there somewhere in the environment. in no way disturbing the vision of things we say to be actually there. (Mead, p. 364)

And all this is available for experimentation. It is always difficult to understand exactly what point Köhler is making, but here in the case of his "social perception," he has scuttled his own ship. Self must be accounted for and if it is accounted for by "apperception" and not by prägnanz, grouping, etc., and the other laws of gestalt perception what happens to the psychology? We are left with the "so-called judgment of perception."

Part III
In outlining the steps above in the formation of the self as an environmental, therefore a social object, and seeking to further the analysis, I found Mead contradicting himself, or rather denying his own thesis in part. The clue to the confusion came from Hans Joas, already cited. Joas points firmly to the development of Mead's thought after *The Definition of the Psychical* in 1903 in a series of articles to 1913.

My references were from *The Philosophy of the Act*, published in 1938, eight years after Mead's death. Further, the 1934, *Mind, Self, and Society*, and the 1932 *The Philosophy of the Present*, were also posthumous. The last was based on the Carus Lectures which Mead delivered at Berkeley in 1930 just prior to his death. You will remember that the turmoil at the University of Chicago during that period drained him and he was unable to give the lectures the attention he had anticipated.

Moreover, *Act* and *Mind, Self* were reconstructed from university course lecture notes from students notes and lack the precision of the articles. The point is that if the self exists as a social object, its origin must be social and how is this possible. We have had this before in Goodman's attack on psychoanalysis with its introspective method as a poor "primary" approach to therapy. ("Primary" is a cop-out. How is a primary approach different from an approach at all? It is like thinking a potential thought. R.K.)

Here we have Mead's analysis of "social objects...themselves also perceiving objects;" he particularly is attacking Draghicesco's notion that social objects are essentially conclusive of "necessary introspective certainty of the self, in contrast to the physical object, which is accessible to us only through analysis." (Joas, 1985, p. 92)

> From the psychological point of view, the question becomes this: does introspection present the knowing self to the knower, as a social content implying necessarily other selves, while the known physical object is subject to analysis into states that must be referred to this self? If this were the case, we might indeed deduce the whole cognitive process out of a consciousness which was primarily social and secondarily physical. But the fact is that this self which our introspection reveals is the so-called empirical self, and is just as much a construct as the physical object...

> ...A constructing self never appears as the object of introspection. He can no more be got on to the dissecting table than Kant's transcendental ego. It is true that we cannot construct empirical selves without constructing other selves. It is equally true that we cannot construct our physical bodies as objects without constructing other physical objects, and it is a piece of Berkeleyan idealism to refer the consciousness of physical objects to the consciousness of the empirical self, giving precedence in reality to the latter over the former. (Joas, 1985, p. 92–93)

The above is Joas quoting Mead from *Review of D. Draghiscesco*.

And we will remember from pages 15 to 19, James' subtle analysis of his own introspection as he strove to find any spiritual element at all in his awareness of self. This versus Goodman who in his analysis, announced "I am a Kantian," because he found thinking schematically his natural way of thought.

So now we have the constructing self referring all to the empirical self by a consciousness which itself is beyond examination in introspection, itself the more real. And the problem becomes how to get a unified self ultimately based in corporeality on which to erect an objective (scientific) social psychology in the genesis of self.

Apart from the problem of the "anthropology of an egotistical human nature which makes sociality inconceivable or restricts it tothe form of a common will, excluding the content," (Joas, p. 94), Mead had entree to the problem through McDougall's theory of social instincts, sexuality, parenting, perhaps cooperative community activities as food-gathering, etc. But McDougall is unable to come to a theory which makes self itself a datum on an equal plane with others and the problem of "how an individual with egotistical drives can become an altruist." (Joas, p. 94). McDougall's *Social Psychology* came out in 1908.

Mead is further influenced by Wundt's *Völkerpsychologie* as he realizes that individual psychology cannot account for the unique *capacity* for language of the human species. Especially, philology cannot account for it because of its concern for the "details" of the language rather then language capacity.

Mead takes over completely Wundt's notion of the gesture, and the vocal gesture, in which

> Mead summarizes completely uncritically, not only Wundt's interpretation of the gesture as an affective expression, but also the further implications of his conception of language.

> Wundt conceives of communication as having arisen out of a mechanism by means of which gestures call forth in a fellow species-member feelings that are identical with the affects triggering those gestures.

It must be becoming clear by now, the associationist theory that language was invented and the elementarist psychology is swept away in a developing theory of action which can become good science without begging a transcendentalist Soul to bail it out of its epistemological muddle.

But Wundt cannot get past a notion of apperception which you will remember from *Three Lectures* was the downfall of the gestalt psychologists' quest for a science "from the starting point of physics." He ultimately tries to account for apperception from associations rather then accounting for associations within a theory of action.

The work that accomplished this was the series of articles from page 25

> *Social Psychology as Counterpart to Physiological Psychology*, *Psychological Bulletin 6* (1909).
>
> *Social Consciousness and the Consciousness of Meaning*, *Psychological Bulletin 7* (1910).
>
> *What Social Objects Does Psychology Presuppose*, *Psychological Bulletin 7* (1910).
>
> *What Social Objects Must Psychology Presuppose, Journal of Philosophy 7* (1910).
>
> *The Mechanism of Social Consciousness, Journal of Philosophy 9* (1912).
>
> *The Social Self, Journal of Philosophy 110* (1913),

It remains to summarize the distinct steps above into a coherent whole of Mead's thought. He has done this in *Mind, Self, and Society*. It is my experience that, like James' *Principles of Psychology*, this seminal work has disappeared, certainly in the general import of a coherent functional theory of humankind in James; and more certainly in an objective theory of the social nature, the constitutive, the originary social nature of humankind in Mead.

(While Goodman insisted on the social nature of humankind in *Gestalt Therapy*, he never came near the precision that Mead and James developed in spite of his frequent assertions of influence of, at least, thereby James, leaving key concepts standing in swamps. We will come to these shortly. But we owe to Laura Perls, the obligation to clear conceptualization and statement that will in some measure screen the endless "gestalt-ands" that beset us. Goodman *never* refers to Mead.)

We will remember from James and his exquisite peeling back of the onion of introspection to feelings as delicate bodily feelings—literally, "feelings" — principally, cephalic, glottal, those of breathing. These become the habitat of the body which are the emotions. Whitehead takes this over in *Process and Reality*, and speaks of feelings as "lures to theory" which makes sense if you will take two minutes to think about it. Whitehead is radical about perception and experience.

> ...(A)ccording to Humian principles what has happened in experience has happened in experience and that is all that can be said. (The way in which one actual entity—subject—is qualified by other actual entities...is the experience of that subject).

> Everything else is bluff, combined with fraudulent insertion of "probability" into a conclusion that demands "blank ignorance."

> The difficulties of all schools of modern philosophy lie in the fact that, having accepted the subjectivist principle, they continue to use philosophical categories derived from another point of view.

> These categories are not wrong, but they deal with abstractions unsuitable for metaphysical use. The notions of "green leaf" and "round ball" are at the base of traditional metaphysics.

They have generated two misconceptions: *one* is the concept of vacuous actuality, void of subjective experience; and the *other* is the concept of quality inherent in substance.

In their proper character, as high abstractions, both of these notions are of the utmost pragmatic use.

In fact, language had been formed chiefly to express such concepts. It is for this reason that language, in its ordinary usages, penetrates but a short distance into the principles of metaphysics.

Finally, the reformed subjectivist principle must be repeated:

(T)hat apart from the experiences of subjects there is nothing, nothing, nothing, bare nothingness. (!) (Whitehead, p. 167).

I appreciate that the last is "the curfew that tolls the knell of parting day" but let us retrace the path that got us here. We remember as gestalt therapists from Perls, Hefferline, and Goodman, (*PHG*), the first words of the book

I
The Structure of Growth
1: The Contact-Boundary

Experience occurs at the boundary between the organism and its (!) environment, primarily the skin surface and the other organs of sensory and motor response. Experience is the function of this boundary, and psychologically what is real are the "whole" configurations of this functioning, some meaning being achieved, some action completed. (PHG, p. 227)

Noting that "organism" and "human" organism and "animal" are murkily synonymous but this is not a major sin; most theorizing in this line must always leave a primary animal model for a basis, "instincts", "alimentary function," "sexuality," and so forth all of which can be experimented, really empirical, which in humans would be unethical. But it is not until the later paragraphs of this section that the content becomes specifically human.

It is specifically winding up to a theory of self which had always been the "weakest part of Psychoanalytic theory" as was often discussed in the Fifties' professional group. And further, unless we decide the boundary functions of the amoeba are not included in "experience occurs at the boundary", etc.; and that "social" constituent in "self" does not include the bees and the termites, we shall not have to speak of the "self" of the lower organisms.

As I write this, I see from my window armies of human organisms presumably walking their dogs. I very frequently see the dogs tugging their humans. Also, one human organism will speak to his/her dog organism as interlocutor for a co-dog organism walker's dog organism: "Spot, here is Muffin, say hello to Muffin. Aren't you glad to see Muffin?"

Well, Samuel Johnson had a fit on the same subject when Boswell said, "Really, Sir, one does not know what to think when one sees a very intelligent dog." Responds the great Cham of literature: "And one does not know what to think when one sees a very stupid fellow!"

Johnson had very long conversations with his cat, "Hodge," as he fed him in his lap his favorite oysters.

(Mead makes the distinction within the division of labor as represented in the somatic/biological differentiations of the organism: queen, drone, pollen gatherers, workers [ventilation] and so forth. The human organism with the achievement of self developmentally accomplishes the meaning and techniques of life in the social capacity of "taking the role of the other.")

The rough schema is the co-caring activities of parenting/child-ing interaction from the first including, in my view intra-uterine. (For heuristic purposes, this last can be conceived as an oxymoron.) From the first, the parent/child organism is making co-internal reciprocal and imitative pre-speech sounds. "Goo-goo" and "Da-da," and without doubt, "Ma-ma," are not too exaggerated forms of this educating. It shuttles back and forth with smiles and beams and motes as they reward the others' accomplishment. We have only to study the great series of Madonna-and-child paintings of the Renaissance to see its total make-over of the human environment. There is one where the Virgin holds the infant Jesus while He peers challenging, and daringly and directly into the face of the viewer with his face also of a very tough, masculine, wise young man. It is an amazing painting in the prophecy of taking the role of the entire social other as the Redeemer who in assuming the sins of the world pays for them in the sacrifice of the crucifixion, to redeem the others from eternal damnation. And so as in any mythic transformation, the entire *condition humaine* is re stated and re-enforced.

From the burbling and gurgling where what is heard is what is sounded and what is sounded is what is heard, the fundamentals of communicative human speech are learned as a product of natural social interaction. Notice we have the same organs systems involved in the push and the pull of making the environmental interaction called sound.

So "sounding and hearing" are the same.

A perhaps further step is in the finding and making of boundedness in the environment. This is emphatically not "boundary" in Goodman's sense or that of the gestalt psychologists with their between-ness in the figure and the ground interaction. And further Mead's analysis give us gestalt therapists finally a coherent and rational approach to "contact" the notion of which as such is stated drives one to despair.

For an example of the treatments of the interaction of the organism/environment field as the necessary background for any theorizing in perception to "contact," let us turn first to Goodman in Perls, Hefferline and Goodman (*PHG*)

Interaction of Organism and Environment:

Now in any biological, psychological or sociological investigation whatever, we must start from the interacting of the organism and its environment. It makes no sense to speak, for instance of an animal that breathes without considering air and oxygen as part of its definition, or to speak of eating without mentioning food, or of seeing without light, or locomotion without gravity and supporting ground, or of speech without communication.

There is no single function of any animal that completes itself without objects and environment, whether one thinks of vegetative functions like nourishment and sexuality, or perceptual functions, of motor functions, or feeling, or reasoning. Let us call this interacting of organism and environment in any function "the organism/environment field"; and let us remember that no matter how we theorize about impulses, drives, it is always to such an interacting field, and not to an isolated animal.

Where the organism is mobile in a great field and has a complicated internal structure, like an animal, it seems plausible to speak of it by itself--as, for instance, the skin and what is contained in it--but this is simply an illusion due to the fact the motion through space and the internal detail call attention to themselves against the relative stability and simplicity of the background. (PHG, p. 228)

At the distance of fifty years, I notice with more than a mild irritation that the foregoing seems a strung-on necklace of synonyms and obvious platitudes to which who but an imbecile could say nay. (And indeed in the next section, Goodman says as much but concludes to an analysis of the "contact boundary" in its broadest sense). We will return to it.

But first, going backwards in time to perhaps pre-World War I or so, we return to George Herbert Mead to his first chapter in the *Philosophy of the Act.*

Stages in the Act: Preliminary Statement

A. The Stage of Impulse

1. Sensitivity as a Function of Response

> Perception as such involves not only an attitude of response to the stimulation but also the imagery of the result of the response. A perception has in it, therefore, all the elements of an act—the stimulation, the response represented by the attitude, and the ultimate experience which follows upon the reaction, represented by the imagery arising out of past reactions.

> ...The process of sensing is itself an activity. In the case of vision this is most evidently the case. Here the movement of the eyes, the focusing of the lens, and the adjustment of the lines of vision of the two eyes require a complicated activity which is further complicated by the movements of the eyes which will bring the rays of light coming from all parts of the object upon the center of clearest vision.

(This will come as no surprise to those of us who have been studying in James' *Principles of Psychology* published a more than a century ago; completed in 1880. Also, *his* sources in the "old psychology" of the mid-Nineteenth Century, Hering, Helmholtz, Müller, etc.)

> The process of perceiving a object through the eyes (and this may be called the normal perception, since our perception through other organs of sense is so largely mediated through the imagery of vision itself) is thus an activity of considerable proportions.

The perception by the hand (My italics) is also one that involves such movement in the exploratory processes of hand and fingers and the movements the skin. Hearing involves at least the fixing of the head (and the whole body as the basis for the movement of the head) and the innervation of the minute muscles which stretch the eardrum. Smelling involves the drawing of the air over the olfactory surfaces by means of the processes of inspiration plus the placing of the head in such a position as to make the smelling most effective. Tasting, in so far as it is to be distinguished from tactual perception, involves the bringing of the fluids of the mouth in continually changing contact with the taste buds through the process of mastication. In normal perception, however, all the processes of hearing, smelling, tasting and temperature-feeling are referred to some presentation of vision as that which is the source of the stimulations of the other senses

...The sensing of the object as so located that the organism takes a definite attitude toward it, involving possible movement toward or away from the object, is thus a part of the process of perception. (Mead, p.4)

I offer the two treatments of interaction in the organism/environment field for comparison both in specificity and foundation, for therapeutic purposes in directing experiment and for shoulders the philosophizing therapist can stand on. It is significant that Goodman in arguing against the "isolation" of the animal from its field says to repeat from above

Where the organism is mobile in a great (!) field and has a complicated internal structure (?) like an animal, it seems plausible to speak of it by itself (!)—as, for instance, the skin and what is contained in it—but this is simply an illusion (!) due to the fact that the motion through space and the internal detail (?) call attention to themselves against the relative stability and simplicity of the background.

We have the problems of the broad brush in painting over the details: how is it known as a "great" field and a "complicated" internal structure. Is it not resistance putting insides to things? And does not this hold true also for "of it by itself" although how that leads to "an isolated animal" is beyond comprehension unless we consider that we have given a name to an oft repeated experience that has become an "object" and then deduce and use all kinds of attributes of the name as the reality of the object. This is a direct statement of Berkeley's theory of vision and equally directly leads to James' theory of the "psychologist's fallacy" where observer and observed agree upon the object and the experimenting and the reality of the perception is farther and farther removed from the experiment.

Further, it is difficult to understand Goodman's use of "illusion" here unless you first postulate the animal isolated from its background. If you take the position of the gestalt psychologists of perception from the "starting point of physics" and of "psychology as a young science," you do indeed start from the "objects" of perception and then everything falls apart. There is no place to stand and everything falls into the trap of "appercepion" which is necessarily denied in the first place.

Then, what is the nature of an illusion? It was a favorite device of the gestalt psychologists to argue from the illusions the creative process of the figure and the ground founded in the gestalt fundaments of closure and the tendency to completion.

James in his analysis of illusions ascribed them to the imagery of countless experiences requiring the barest stimulation to bring them forth so there would be the alternating perceptions so common to them.

In the common example of the ellipse seen as a circle, the famous penny seen on the ground, Mead, through the "perception by the hand," speaks of the pragmatic principle whereby the use the penny is to be put to— "fingering it in your purse" —determines its perceived circularity.

And throughout the ghost of Goodman's inadequate sense of the body also as a physical thing with the confusion of "inside and outside" and the boundary "primarily at the skin surfaces" returns as the uninvited guest at the feast of contact and breaks the good meeting in the most admired disorder.

For example, if as stated, "contact is at the boundary in the organism/environment field," and the "self is the system of contacts in the organism/environment field," the question immediately presents itself in any examination of the proposition, what and where is the boundary?

Laura Perls always insisted the boundary was the experience of the "other" or perhaps the experience of other, which in her case, was usually embarrassment. The etymology of "embarrassment" takes to the experience of being barred or embarred. One can conceive of a reciprocal organism/environment process of pre-reaching-out-not-yet-in-motion. But it will immediately become clear in the process that boundary is not a location and as George Herbert Mead says in *The Philosophy of the Act*, in another context, but which I apply directly here: "The boundary can be marked but it cannot be located."(!)

We had the example from sounding and hearing the primary and constitutive experience of communication and speech. What is offered us as a building process in the analysis of the boundedness of things?

Mead proposes the primary and constitutive activity of Resistance which arises socially primarily within the infant (even pre-uterine?) pushing of one hand against the other. You see at once the relation of the hearing and sounding organs: it is one not two experiences when one hand pushes and the other is being pushed and vice versa by exactly the right amount of pressure to accomplish what ever the total process demands in the now so-called organism/environment field.

This phenomenon of resistance is of profound importance in perception since in the four phases of the act, impulse, perception, manipulation and consummation or contact and the distance experience within the whole act creating the object, we have known already how much intention or effort perhaps to give and take within the process. The object in that sense is a "collapsed act" of perception.

Further, and crucially, the experience of resistance is the experience of learning to put insides to things. That experience is crucial because in its absence we would merely accumulate more surfaces in reality rather than creating a living breathing reality in also the social inanimations as we and the world evolve together.

We understand immediately what I called the crucial nature of resistance in any possible or common-sense understanding of "boundary", or then "contact at the boundary." The awareness through resistance of the touch-not-touching which immediately gives marking to the [boundary] but not its location.

In the collapsed act where we have a, or rather the, perception of a thing that is about to be an object, we have the experience of an object at a distance and the phases seem to occur at once. But since it is at a distance, it takes time however swift and space however short, and action at a distance in terms of perception rather than electromagnetic dynamisms is impossible unless one can take the role of the other. Not in a Zen-like way, but to stand with the object and one's self and see both from the perspective of the other. Or, to put it another way, to be "objective."

It is impossible to bring this to the theoretical table without proceeding developmentally and so we have the progression of the infant from sounding what he hears and hearing what he sounds; and pushing against what pushes him/her which is his own resistance as we saw. This activity improves to the role of play, perhaps as in the "This little piggy went to market, and this little piggy stayed home." And not getting any roast beef the last little piggy "cried: 'Wee, wee, wee, all the way home.' " The whole theory of self flowing in a nursery rhyme! We are accustomed to these common-sense and folk tales and their cosmic personality and anthropological fundamentals when we consider that Sleeping Beauty was put to sleep by a prick and awakened with a kiss.

But in play, the child talks to himself and then replies to himself in the famous soliloquy and is in both, not yet "roles." It is only when this process improves to the game where the child can take the role of the generalized other, that is, to say all the roles of the game, that we have achieved self acting in all the roles.

The famous formula is the individual arouses in the other by his response to the other what he has aroused in himself. Then by way of the generalized other he responds to that response. This last step is usually overlooked; without it a self is impossible.

So the usual demonstration of perception and field and dynamic interaction with an object, so to speak, like a "brown rock" is far more powerful than it at first seems since it also demonstrates openly what is occurring implicitly, namely, that we are asking ourselves to take the role of a brown rock itself and experience our co-resistance with it and so assert the universe.

> At the risk of belaboring the point, I wish to insist that the self does not transfer *its* (My italics) kinesthetic sensation to the object, but that, through the tendency to push as a physical thing against one's own hand in the role of another individual, one has become a physical object over against the physical thing.

> Such a development of the physical thing over against the physical self is an abstraction from an original social experience, for it is primarily in social conduct that we stimulate ourselves to act toward ourselves as others act toward us and thus identify ourselves with others and become objects to ourselves.

> The identification lies in the identity in the conduct of others toward ourselves with that conduct toward ourselves which we have tended to call out in our own organisms.

The child by his cry has called out a tendency in his own organism to soothe himself. The identity in kind of this with the sympathetic response of the parent is the identification of the child with the parent. (Mead, p.428)

To return to the presentation and analysis of the brown rock as a physical field or percept constituted by atom, molecules and fields of forces; (Whitehead uses a "gray stone"):

The earliest objects are social objects, and all objects are at first social objects.

Later experience differentiates the social from the physical objects, but the mechanism of the experience of things over against a self as an object is the social mechanism.

It is definitely not the scientific object in the sense of the scientific materialism of particles in motion within an ether or stuff

The difficulty with (the) mechanical statement, which places the reality of the object in the physical particles in motion (a presentation which includes the physiological organism), and leaves the distance characters and those belonging to the object as within the life-process *hanging without organic relations to the perception* (My italics), (placed either in a field of so-called consciousness or in a world of subsistence)

(L)ies in an implication of the mechanical statement that the object of perception and scientific conception is logically prior to the earlier stage of experience out of which perception and reflection arises, and that this scientific analysis reveals the reality of nature, *not only as it was but as it remains in experience, to the exclusion from the same field of reality of all from which this mechanical statement abstracts.* (My italics) (Mead, p. 439)

It seems that the abstractions from the gestalt therapy theory of contact such as confluence, introjection, retroflection, projection, egotism, etc., etc., as well as the famous, "It tells you where to look," for orientation within the session, is precisely just such a mechanical statement that leaves the characters of the life process "hanging without organic relations."

What remains is a Gordian knot of abstractions in the shadow of the therapist's brain that is called the patient. This is another example of William James' psychologist's fallacy or perhaps a elevated version of the *folie à deux*.

We are now closer to an answer to the question where is boundary in "contact at the boundary in the organism/environment field?" We are closer because we have been able to restate the unit of reality, that is to say, "contact", or if you will, "self" for our purposes.

The classical theory of contact in gestalt therapy is outlined on page 403 of the text:

1. Fore-contact: the body is the ground, the appetite or environmental stimulus is the figure...

2. Contacting:

   a. the excitement of appetite becomes the ground and some "object" or set of possibilities is the figure...There is an emotion (!).

   b. There is choosing and rejecting of possibilities, aggression in approaching and in overcoming obstacles, and deliberate orientation and manipulation. These are the identifications and alienations of the Ego.

3. Final Contact: Against a background of unconcernful environment and body, the lively goal is the figure and *is in touch*. (My italics)

4. Post-Contact: There is a flowing organism/environment
    interaction that is not a figure/background: the self diminishes.
    (PHG, p.403)

In the commentary that introduces this famous schema (Remember, "I
am a Kantian), Goodman asserts the general "continuous sequence of
grounds and figures" which is supported by the further basic assumptions
of gestalt psychology namely the drive toward closure, (socially,
"unfinished business") and gestalt formation.

He also introduces an energetic component that comes from both "poles
of the field, both the organism and the environment." This is of course
the Reichian notion of the release of bound energy. Goodman's model of
action is sexual/libidinal; Perls' is dental/alimental.

Reich, however, situated his energetic theory in a positivist pseudo-
science with voodoo measurements and scientistic hocus-pocus, and it
can not be isolated from that system. The energetic reality in its nature
can only be realized in the act that leads to possible contact or
consummatory reality.

(It is very difficult to analyze Paul Goodman's prose: everything and
everywhere is included so in his pages where one could point to the gaps
or the potential for reification, one can also refer to specific mention that
covers the points. For example, in spite of his cautions, the four step
contact sequence has been reified into "cycles of awareness" and
"interruptions" of contact, and in general a reference point for "where to
look" for orientation in clinical practice. Experiment has suffered not so
benign neglect.)

At the outset, Lichtenberg identified a radical branch of psychoanalysis
with a leftist politics as a strong influence, indeed a root of gestalt
psychotherapy. I contributed a further influence in the Social Democratic
politics of those who became principals in American pragmatism
namely, John Dewey and George Herbert Mead of the Chicago School.
The social activism of both the radical psychoanalysis and the

pragmatism was paramount in their psychology and philosophy and culminated in the one in *Gestalt Therapy: Excitement and Growth in the Human Personality*, with its unifying concept in a four-step theory of contact as above.

With continuing frustration arising out of the aporiae and broad strokes of *Gestalt Therapy*, and ultimately realizing that in spite of Frederic Perls' ultimate eagerness to find an ontic base for gestalt therapy theory in gestalt psychology, I discovered that, indeed, gestalt psychology itself lacked a firm philosophic base. It could not support itself except by blotting out or ignoring the great work of the previous century, the "old psychology" and especially and specifically the magnum opus of that century, *The Principles of Psychology* of William James which was the foundation for his pragmatism.

Pragmatism offered a adequate theoretical structure it seemed to me especially with the discovery of *The Philosophy of the Act* of George Herbert Mead. Far more rigorous and subtle than Goodman's work the similarity of locution and structure is frequently amazing, often uncanny.

For example, Mead, too, has a four stage theory, impulse, perception, manipulation, and consummation or contact (!) to his theory of the Act, which is his unit of reality:

1. Impulse.

> This first stage has behind it an attitude, a stance, of being with the "withness" of about-to-be-perception as the ranging organism, in the active attitude "picks out certain characters in the field of stimulation." This is the agency of mere selective attention without the implication of "agency for." A partial description of the activity was given on page 30. "The mechanism of this selection is frequently found in the anticipatory presentation of the object which is of importance"; and which runs into the next stage, that of

2. Perception

"The perceptual object is primarily the organization of the immediate environment with reference to the organism." (Mead, p. 16) The object is the statement of the relation of the organism/environment world of the individual, viewed in its social perspective, the social being prior to objects which arise out of it. Perception is mediated by the senses, including the bodily senses as a physical thing, which give the distance values to the process and thus the promise of contact or consummation in the creation of the thing to be possessed.

3. Manipulation

This is the phase of matter and science and measurement possessed by the human animal by way of hand and arm, which holding the process studies it primarily with the crumbling process of hand and fingers which in imagination can range from atoms to galaxies. And of course draws from and further contributes to the imaginary stores as the foreground/background is activated for solutions to the problem presented by the failure of the emerging hypothesis. This is not an "interruption" in the gestalt sense of the "interruptions of contact with loss of ego function." It is a temporary checking in the search for the hypothesis that will solve the problem of the failing object and the creating of the new one. It is the human statement of the scientific method in process and human existence. To the extent we can speak of "neurosis" and "psychotherapy," we are speaking of temporary normal functioning checked by the musculature and it is to the abstraction we call the "body" that we must turn to for the opening we call the experiment.

4. Consummation or Contact (!)

The perceptual reality of the object "comes in between the beginning of the act and its consummation." It is not the end of the process in contact that initiates the process. As in 2 above it is the distance values mediated by the sense organs and the capacity to see the promise in the object by taking its role in the social process. The leading distance stimulation is vision and the organization of the perceptual world is referred "To the visual experience."

But consummation is of things not distances. "The physical thing, then, as distinct from a stimulus, is a hypothetical, hence future, accomplishment of an initiated process, to be tested by the contact experience"...

...(I)f it sets free the initiated process, e.g., driving the nail, it is a hammer." (Mead, p. 15)   It is there to be seized, i.e., contacted, consumed.

It is of critical importance again to return to our distinction between "mediate" and "immediate," between the beginning of the act and its consummation which confirms the reality of the initiated hypothesis. So the future as James pointed out is in the smallest current of the stream of consciousness, consciousness in all its connotations.

Every act, however, is moving on from its physical objects to some consummation. Within the field of consummation all the adjectives of value obtain *immediately*. (My italics, R.K)

There objects are *possessed, are good, bad, and indifferent, beautiful or ugly, and lovable or noxious...*

In the physical things these characters are only mediately present...[They] are means, and means for ends which often have to be discovered. (Mead, p. 14)

To contrast or perhaps integrate the gestalt therapy theory of contact with the theory of consummation/contact in the pragmatic theory of the act let us take a humble (and humbling) experience.

It is October of 1949. I am returning from my second or third session with Frederic Perls. I don't know what is going on. I have been assigned home work. I am to chew my food to a fluid mass before I swallow it. In Pennsylvania Station [before the real estate Huns destroyed it], at the end of the glorious promenade before the escalators to the magnificent Stanford White waiting room there is a Savarin coffee shop. I sit at the counter and order a tuna on rye toast, lettuce and lots of mayo and so embark for my first voyage on the wine-dark sea of the theory of dental aggression about which, again I knew nothing. (Incidentally, I was prone to seasickness and other various and sundry and weird visual experiences: the Holland tunnel unrolled itself under my car as my car remained still).

Diligently masticating, I experience the pre-heaving and the nausea simultaneously. Slyly and desperately I manage to mouth the contents into my paper napkin and escape ransoming my exit with a shameless but regrettable over tip.

So, physical thing, tuna on rye with mayo. Chewing or eating, the process of consuming or contacting. As for the regurgitating experience which came out of nowhere:

> What we are going to do determines the line of approach [to the distant stimulus, the sandwich] and in some sense its manner...It is the later process already aroused in the central nervous system, controlling the earlier, which constitutes the teleological character of the act...

> And the past is also in the act, for facility and familiarity are products of past reactions. The physical thing, then, as distinct from a stimulus is a hypothetical, hence future accomplishment of an initiated process, to be tested by the contact experience. If it sets free the initiated process, e.g., driving the nail, it is a hammer. (Mead, p. 15)

Now it is no small thing to imagine my mother and teleology bound in tuna on rye toast but there it is. All the great series of "Don'ts" in life that seemed to encapsulate my early training (I can't seem to remember *any* "Do's).

To complete the tale fast forward the next week to Perls' upstairs office in the brownstone. I report the experiment to my therapist who seems delighted and eager in an almost child-like way

R.K. "But I got even with you. I lived on bananas and soup for the rest of the week."

F.P. "Oh, please, please, go back to chewing. In this one case, you can be as obsessional as you like."

A resounding "Do" but I still didn't know the theory of dental aggression.

To gather together my long ramble from "Where is the boundary?" in "contact at the boundary in the organism/environment field" or even "*self* is the system of contacts in the organism/environment field," we conclude that there is no "where." The boundary can be marked but not located.

Developing from the basic notion of resistance originating in the pressure of one hand on the other, thereby putting insides to things thus creating the object in the act of perception and also taking the role of the object and responding to that response, we see boundary as a subphase of a *process* called the Act. A separate boundary is impossible except conceptually in an-after the-experience analysis.

Mead's insistence that without resistance in the sense of putting insides to things we are merely multiplying surfaces thereby making human experience impossible, is directly at variance to Goodman's boundary at the inside/outside continuum, especially at the skin surfaces. It is an impossible doctrine and as I have said before rests on his inadequate awareness of the body as a physical thing.

Another emphasis in gestalt therapy theory and practice is "here and now." It is a refreshing redirecting from Freud's archaeological digs into "causation" and the layering activity of repression with the recovery of the causal memories.

We are immediately at "ground." For the moment, I want to divorce it from "Figure/ground." The latter arose from the organization of the gestalt and its analysis in the experimentations of those psychologists. It was the genius of Paul Goodman to work it into a formal theory of personality. I have always taken figure/ground as one word and still do. But in that emphasis the far more important notion of ground as the result of past experience and an imaginatively active function that contributes fully fifty percent to the process of perception within the act, has been swept aside.

If we take the "foreground" in paraphrase from Whitehead as "conscious apprehension"

> When we survey the chequered history of our own capacity for knowledge, does common sense allow us to believe that the operations of judgment, operations which required definition in terms of conscious apprehension, (i.e., are figural, R.K.), are those operations which are foundational (i.e., ground), in existence either as an essential attribute for an actual entity, or as the final culmination whereby unity of experience is attained? (Whitehead, p. 161)

In swift reversal, Whitehead shows us again that we have the cart before the horse.

> The general case of conscious perception is the negative perception, namely, "perceiving this stone as not grey." The "grey" then has ingression in its full character of a possible

> novelty, *but in fact by its conformity emphasizing the dative grey, blindly (!) felt*

And in general, we again see the broad brush strokes in the *pentimento* of Perls, Hefferline and Goodman must give way to the whip of sharper analysis as we guide our way to a place on which to stand, firmly to do our psychotherapy.

He is using "datively" as the adverbial form from "datum," the singular of "data." He means by it the original, or originary of perception. To continue:

> Consciousness is the feeling of negation: in the perception of "the stone as grey," such feeling is in the barest germ; in the perception of "the stone as not grey" such feeling is in full development.
>
> Thus the negative perception is the triumph of consciousness. It finally rises to the peak of free imagination, in which the conceptual novelties *search through a universe in which they are not datively exemplified* (!). (My italics)

Astonishingly, the emphasis should not have been on the activity of choosing which we seem to feel as we identify with the developing sense of effort. The background more exactly represents itself in the negative function of integrating all the possibilities for rejection.

For an example in therapy, let us go to a classical negation.

> Patient: "I feel (!) empty, dead, nothing."
>
> Therapist: (attitude of ?).
>
> P: "I am (!) numb"
>
> T: "Can you show me where you experience (!) 'numb' "?
>
> P: (Points to abdomen.)

    T: "Can you place your hands on your numb area, please?"

    P: (Does).

    T: "What is your experience now" (!).

    P. "I feel my hands slightly pushing. The numbness is more localized."

    T: "Is your abdomen pushing back?"

    P: "Yes. I am breathing." (!!).

I leave the interpersonal psychohistory to your speculations, e.g. "Who is your numbness?"

The nothing does not naught in spite of Heidegger. The experience of resistance, the body as physical thing (as opportunity), as the boundedness of experience; the taking the role of the other in the numbness, the breath of life, the apparent opposite of numb/dead/empty. This has all been called paradoxically a paradox. I have never understood why except as a verbal conceit. The real paradox if it existed would surely be that life did not lead to life.

The ground in this sense is a less mysterious and more directly active in its selective negativity than, I think, Goodman dreamt of in his "Fertile Void."

To sum up the opportunities in the *negativity* of the ground we return to Whitehead:

> The consequences of the neglect of this law, that the late derivative elements are more clearly illuminated by consciousness than the primitive elements, have been fatal to the proper analysis of an experiment occasion.

> In fact, most of the difficulties of philosophy are produced by it. Experience has been explained in a thoroughly topsy-turvy fashion, the wrong end first.
>
> In particular, emotional and purposeful experience have been made to follow upon Hume's impressions of sensation. (Whitehead, p. 162)

"How do you feel here and now?" This became a mantra that sounded around every moment of the session. I asked Perls what he meant by *here and now*? I was frankly baffled. Obviously, as one answers the question it is already "there and then." In my own early imitation of a therapist I asked a student the same question. Long silence, then: "Here and now, there and then, I…" etc., etc.

But how to date experience? Or rather what does it mean?

> The analysis of perception does not, then, take us to a reality which lies outside an actual or possible perception. It does take us to contact experiences which may have any dimensions required. These *imaginatively* presented contact objects are freed from the peculiarities which different distance perceptions give them, both our own and those of others, and it gives to them the uniformities which all must recognize, since the contact experiences of different persons are identical in the superpositions of measurements and the effective occupation of space, and since we place ourselves in the places of other observers. (Mead, p. 23)

Accepting the theory of the act and within in it, taking the role of the other, that is of arousing in the other what you have aroused in yourself and responding to that response it is clear that there must be an identity of content in both you and the other. The identity is not exact but individual and given the uniformities within species can be counted on. It therefore is objective, the "same" experience from varying perspectives. It is thus dated and oriented in both. It is here and now.

This difference has huge implications for psychotherapy. "Are you [patient] having a similar experience to mine (therapist)"? Or better, "At the moment, my experience is this. Can you say what yours is?" The contrasts, not the differences, will indicate time and space and co-individuality and level the playing field to a shared contour. The patient finds out with the therapist who the Wizard of Oz is.

We have examined many of the central and basic, perhaps the unifying concepts of gestalt therapy theory, principally those of our text from Perls, Hefferline and Goodman. We were compelled to restate them in the light of fifty years experience in the New York Institute for Gestalt Therapy. As experience accumulated especially in group work we found that work proceeded in the early days by ignoring its own logic.

For example, the context was totally ignored and the work was leader and technique bound as one on one individual therapy was done in a group setting. This was unsatisfactory and eventually the group as such was taken seriously with a flexible and various shifting individual/group, group/individual.

This became theoretically possible with a social theory of self and an awareness that "individual" was an impossible conception even as physical thing except as an abstraction from "isolation," itself a further abstraction, defensively, from an existentially ridiculous notion of independence.

Practically, group work was accelerated and enriched by a much more sophisticated leadership theory which, as so often in our development turned the one on one or individual therapy on its head.

Replacing the "leader," whatever that means apart from its authoritative fascism, was the shifting leadership that the processes in the group called out as the varying talents of the members were needed to bring the group to its group contact and within that dynamic, to release the members to their own growth. Once can see the sensitivities of group dynamics training at work here.

A fruitful development in theory was the discovery some years back that the royal road to leadership talent lay in precisely the individual vulnerabilities. What one was most protective of therefore afraid or timorous became, with group support and heartening courage, that diagnostic sensitivity to process without which no group can generate and regenerate its energies and movement to its recreative contact novelties and be reborn.

The entire revolution was brought to a temporary resting place as the Institute turned itself into a self teaching and learning community. With the invention of process groups to examine and chew the "inter-personal" dynamics of the individuals, usually conferring an interest topic, and separate task groups to work the content of the topic, the possibility, indeed "the sure and certain hope of the resurrection" respites in a larger group interest, namely a supported sense of one's and one's group's sense of fittingness in the political and social whole.

And gestalt therapy revolutionizes itself again to its humane and radical origins.

References

Goodman, P. (1966). *Five Years*. New York: Random House.

Hartshorne, C. (1991). *The Philosophy of Charles Hartshorne*. vol. xx. La Salle, II: Open Court.

James, W. (1890) The Principles of Psychology.

Joas, H. J, (1985). Cambridge: The MIT Press.

Perry, R. P. (1935) *The Thought and Character of William James*. vol I. Boston: Little, Brown and Company.

Mead, G. H. (1904) The Relations of Psychology and Philology. *Psychological Bulletin 1*.

Mead, G. H. (1905) Review of D. Draghiscesco, Du rôle de l'individu dans le déterminisme social, and D. Draghiscesco, Le problème du déterminisme, déterminisme biologique et déterminisme social. *Psychological Bulletin 2*.

Mead, G. H. (1938) *The Philosophy of the Act*. Chicago: University of Chicago Press.

Stoehr, T. (1994). *Here Now Next*. San Francisco: Jossey-Bass. (p. 28)

Whitehead, A. N., (1978). In Griffin, D. R.; Sherburne, D. W. (Eds.), *Process and Reality*. New York: The Free Press.

Part II

2003

The notion of agency or agent central in a theory of self is treated in the famous statement, "The self is the system of contacts in the organism/environment field"; and "the agency of growth." Or elsewhere, "The self is the system of contacts and the agent of growth." Goodman specifically states that the organism grows, but not the self and he provides a brilliant analysis of the sequence:

> It is the organism and not the self that grows. Let us speculatively describe growth as follows: (1) After contact, there is a flow of energy, adding to the energy of the organism, the new elements assimilated from the environment. (2) The contact-boundary that has been "broken" now reforms, including the new energy and the "organ of second nature." (3) What has been assimilated is now part of the physiological self-regulation. (4) The boundary of contact is now "outside" the assimilated learning, habit, conditioned reflex, etc. — what is like what one has learned does not touch one, it raises no problem. (*PHG*, p. 428)

He is distinguishing the need for contact from the physiological needs, i.e., the transitory need for novelty from the conservative self-regulation.

> ...It seems reasonable to define the physiological as the conservative, the non-aware, self-regulation, whether inherent or learned. The psychological is the shifting, transitory contact with

novelty. The physiological "first nature," including non-aware
neurotic interference with "first nature," has periodic recourse to
contact need for novelty. The physiological "second nature" is
contacted aperiodically — e.g., available memory is drawn on as
a result of external simulation.

And the "Agent," that ranging widely, finding and making the
opportunities for contact and itself, is the self in its proper role.

(For years I have tried to understand how the self cannot grow, certainly
with the organism, and have tried to understand the relation as one
between function and entity, that is, the organism actually physically
"grows": accumulates, gets bigger, increases, expands; and the self gets
stronger. But somehow this is never satisfactory and I am caught in a
dizzying circle.)

The confusion rests in at least two notions of agency, mere selection or
acting, and the a priori notion of the actor working for the synthetic
unity.

Previously, we considered Agency from William James and his analysis
of it within the scholastic tradition of substantial soul. We thought that
this was the rat behind the arras of Goodman's thinking as he built the
formal theory of gestalt psychotherapy. That is, in spite of his theory of
self-occurring within a process of contact, there was always a
synthesizer, of more or less ("diminished") self, depending on the
"alert/real" character of one's activity.

To settle the question, James returns to a more decisive analysis of self as
an agent operating as, or better, in, a temporal sequence resting on an
ambiguity in Kant's treatment:

> The ambiguity referred to in the meaning of the transcendental
> Ego is as to whether Kant signified by it an Agent, and by the
> Experience it helps to constitute an operation; confess the entire
> school of thought...still dwells habitually in that mythological

stage of thought where phenomena are explained as results of
dramas enacted by entities which but reduplicate the characters
of the phenomena themselves. (James, pp. 369)

By way of putting "the agent or agency of growth" to rest in favor of the
passing thought that knows the previous one, resembles, continues, and
appropriates it, I append a footnote from James where he analyzes
"potential thought" from Kant:

> It must be noticed, in justice to what was said (earlier: to know a
> thing the knower must also know itself), that neither Kant nor his
> successors anywhere discriminate between the presence of the
> apperceiving Ego to the combined object, and the awareness by
> that Ego of its own presence and of its distinctness from what it
> apperceives. That the Object must be known to something which
> thinks, and that it must be known to something which thinks that
> it thinks, are treated by them as identical necessities — by what
> logic, does not appear.
>
> Kant tries to soften the jump in the reasoning by saying the
> thought of itself on the part of the Ego need only be potential —
> "the "I think" must be capable of accompanying all other
> knowledge" — but a thought which is only potential is actually
> no thought at all, which practically gives up the case. (James, pp.
> 361)

It is an intriguing and instructive notion — a "potential thought." Never
having thought about such an *avis rara,* I tried the experiment. I suggest
you try it now, right now: Think a thought that is a potential thought.
But keep your sense of humor and then you will have the nub of Agency
and we can let the matter drop. Alfred North Whitehead says in *Process
and Reality* that humankind does not have much tolerance for infinite
regressions.

We are now perhaps able to leave William James and turn to George
Herbert Mead for our further development of a more grounded theory of

gestalt therapy than we are used to in Perls, Hefferline and Goodman. (*PHG*)

By way of transition, I want to present a brief and rough summary from Köhler's *Gestalt Psychology*, namely the chapter on *Behavior*. He tried to organize scientifically the problem of social behavior. How do we know, or rather, what is the evidence comparable to what we have in ordinary perception, for what is going on inside another person? He dismisses the usual perceptions and readings off our own bodies and ends the chapter with a warning to psychological science to avoid social perception. Indeed, this was the basis for Paul Goodman's complaint was that gestalt psychologists had busied themselves with ingenious perceptual experiments but had neglected dealing with pressing human problems.

(Freud himself had abandoned the incest theory, except to describe it as a fantasy of his female patients, in order to insure that his new psychoanalysis would be politically palatable in Nineteenth Century Catholic Vienna.)

George Herbert Mead's work is vast but our influences will be *Mind, Self, and Society,* and *The Philosophy of the Act.* In the first, he develops a social genesis of the self; in the second, he places reality in the structure of the act itself as in its phases, impulses, perception, manipulation and finally consummation or contact.

However, in the shift to Mead and in a introductory comparison, let us briefly delve into *The Philosophy of the Act,* the magnificent chapter, *The Process of Mind in Nature.* While we are scanning some lines, there we will keep the foregoing of Köhler's warning against social perception cut and pasted for comparison purposes.

The organization of the individual and the environment and its determining relation in immediate experience for all the relevant fields is not otherwise than the usual evidential base in perception and thus, is available for a scientific psychology, in spite of the science of the "configuration psychologists" as Mead called them, proceeding from the starting point of physics. This last obviously rules out social objects.

Moreover, Mead embraces the meaning of agent and agency as in James above:

> If a mere analysis is meant, there is no such prior existence ... and the elements only are insofar as they are in union:

> In immediate experience, the import of this determining nature of the relation between environment and the individual appears in the differences in all the forgoing fields which results from the different positions, sensings, and acts of attention of the individual.

> Furthermore, the meanings and other values of things are relative to the particular act which in immediate experience the individual exists as agent. The action of the individual in all fields of so-called experience is selective. The contents of things in immediate experience are in a considerable degree dependent upon the individual as acting, as an agent. (Mead, pp. 363)

There is no *a priori* agent acting on the powers and the operations of the Soul. And further that being the case, there is then no need to seek for evidence of the existence of a self in experimental psychological terms to create a science of gestalt psychology. It is there already.

Again:

> The action of the individual in all the fields of so-called (!) experience is selective. The contents of things in immediate experience are in a considerable degree dependent upon the individual acting (!), as agent. In this sense, the environment of the individual is relative to the individual. (Mead, pp. 363)

Even in the case of the illusions, the "Illusory aspects of things are in the environment." This includes the imagery coming from memory as we recognize it in perceptual experience as we learned from the "old psychology" of the Nineteenth Century.

The striking example is in reading in a variation on Berkeley, we see words (names):

> ...light from which never reaches the retina...We see things hard and cold and smooth and succulent, and there are sensuous contents present that bear the same immediate relation to the individual as do those of vision. When we recall the tenuous images of a past vivid experience, these images are out there somewhere in the environment. In no way disturbing the vision of things we say to be actually there. (Mead, pp. 364)

All this is available for experimentation. It is always difficult to understand exactly what point Köhler is making, but here in the case of his "social perception," he has scuttled his own ship. Self must be accounted for and if it is accounted for by "apperception" and not by *prägnanz*, grouping, etc., and the other laws of gestalt perception, what happens to the psychology? We are left with the "so-called judgment of perception."

Part III

2003

Apart from the problem of the "anthropology of an egotistical human nature which makes sociality inconceivable or restricts it to the form of a common will, excluding the content," (Joas, pp. 94), Mead had entree to the problem through McDougall's theory, of social instincts, sexuality, parenting, perhaps cooperative community activities as food-gathering, etc. But McDougall is unable to come to a theory, which makes self itself a datum on an equal plane with others and the problem of "how an individual with egotistical drives can become an altruist." (Joas, pp. 94)

Mead is further influenced by Wundt's *Volkerpsychologie* as he realizes that individual psychology cannot account for the unique capacity for language of the human species. Especially, philology cannot account for it because of its concern for the "details" of the language rather than language capacity.

Mead takes over completely Wundt's notion of the gesture, and the vocal gesture, in which Mead summarizes completely uncritically, not only Wundt's interpretation of the gesture as an affective expression, but also the further implications of his conception of language.

> Wundt conceives of communication as having arisen out of a mechanism by means of which gestures call forth in a fellow species-member feelings that are identical with the affects triggering those gestures.

As it must be becoming clear by now, the associationist theory that language was invented and the elementarist psychology is swept away in a developing theory of action, can become good science without begging a transcendentalist Soul to bail it out of its epistemological muddle.

But Wundt cannot get past a notion of apperception that you will remember from *Three Lectures,* was the downfall of the gestalt psychologists' quest for a science "from the starting point of physics." He ultimately tries to account for apperception from associations, rather than accounting for associations within a theory of action.

References

Goodman, P. *Five Years*. Random House, New York. 1966.

Hartshorne, C. *The Philosophy of Charles Hartshorne, The Library of Living Philosophers, Vol. XX.* Open Court, La Salle, Ill. 1991.

Joas, Hans. *Pragmatism and Social Theory*. University of Chicago Press, Chicago. 1993.

Perry, R.P. *The Thought and Character of William James,* Vol. I, Little Brown and Company, Boston. 1935.

Developmental Theory in the Light of Pragmatism and Interruptions of Contact: An Integration

2003

Argument: The paper is somewhat divisible in seven sections. The first section sketches the work of the early gestalt psychologists and their attack on the elementalist psychology of their time. They demonstrated perception in whole and parts configurations and illustrated the figure/ground and its contour and modeling properties and postulated a neural isomorphism based on psycho-physical parallelism. The problem of direct social perception remained but field, process and context were established.

Building on that work, the gestalt therapy of Frederick and Laura Perls took the "unfinished business" of Kurt Lewin (and the tendency to complete those unfinished situations), combined it with homeostasis, organically the same thing perhaps, and created a psychotherapy ultimately to be called gestalt therapy with concentration experiments within a unifying theory of contact at the boundary in the organism/environment field. A central feature was the restatement of aggression as oral and native, an original and revolutionary intuition, and its accompanying theory of dental aggression.

In 1951, in collaboration with Paul Goodman, the theory of contact was fully developed and formalized. He developed the Perlses' original insights, focused aggression as a force toward contact in social and language behavior, and analyzed the so-called neurosis of normalcy as a pitiful resignation of the self to contemptible standards as he dissected unnatural coercion in a local politics seen as a social psychotherapy. In an awareness continuum where therapy is directed to the interruptions of contact to the achievement of a strong gestalt, the figure/ground in contact is itself the creative integration of experience. The diagnosis is the interruption; the therapy is to the interruption in awareness. The therapy and the diagnosis, the theory and the therapy are the same.

However, the ontological problem remained: how to ground their theory, adequately without the mind/body problem that persists in an impossible solipsism ideally or empirically, the inevitable consequence of parallelism. In a here and now therapy of experience founded on a psychology that largely experimented, the conditions of perception, the question of direct experience imperatively, social experience was left dangling. Renaming stimulus/response as dynamic relations in the field and so forth does not solve the problem. What is perception? What is experience? Perception cannot be assumed in a theory of perception.

Dewey had set the stage in 1896 analyzing the reflex arc model of stimulus/response as a snippet of a circuit, a whole, in which the response was included in the stimulus. George Herbert Mead restated the unit of experience as the act prior to the social and the self out of which they were achieved. Resistance, primitively the pushing of one hand on another, the vocal gesture arousing in oneself the attitude aroused in the other then responding that response; development of the self and the other in play, and learning the rules of the game where one can place oneself in the role of the generalized other, should have completed the analysis.

Perception was mediate and perspectival, a collapsed act set in motion by the spatio-temporal nature of action as impulse/perception/manipulation with — as in gestalt therapy — finally, with consummation or contact. The human hand with its crumbling activity at the manipulatory phase was the mediation as the indefinite possibilities of the human cortex patterned and organized competing hypotheses toward completion. Within evolution, the form determined the environment logically; the environment determined the form causally. The relation is strictly mutual but not convertible.

The developmental implications of this pragmatism seemed experimented in Daniel Stem's work as he grounded the interpersonal world of the infant in the emerging, social, verbal or narrative self and core senses of the self, ongoing, not attached, dynamically and reciprocally proceeding throughout life. The self/narrative is perhaps a pathoformic indicator. That is not the point here. How to rewrite the narrative as a whole activity, as figure/ground in contact is the point. And we must be careful that the style of the narrative does not interrupt closure itself as the theory of narratology asserts. The possibilities of a hermeneutic circle in group where the group writes its own and its members' narrations, as the narratable, not the narrative, appears to be an apt therapeutic tool. The New York Institute has been aggressing this method for years, always in struggle and frequently productive conflict, reflecting its founders' very strong personalities and friendships.

I. The gestalt psychologists in their attack on behavioral psychology changed the emphasis in perception from elements summating to a whole of perception to a whole-and-parts configuration or gestalt. The figural or formed component contoured against the formlessness of the ground had been pointed out by Rubin in 1896. To overcome the problem of direct experience of perception, they further postulated a brain or neural functional isomorphism with the environment based on a psychophysical parallelism to make whole the subject/object mind/body problem.

Köhler distinguished figural perception, immediate perception and direct social understanding and warned of the pitfalls of using "common social understanding as evidence in psychological work." (Köhler, 1947, pp.

246–247) The vocabulary became field oriented as organization, whole, demand nature of figure against ground and interaction became central in gestalt psychology research.

II. In 1942, Frederick Perls revised psychoanalytic theory with his intuition of oral aggression combining organic homeostasis, the tendency to complete unfinished situations, figure/ground formation and introduced contact at the boundary in the organism/ environment field as a unifying concept in his psychotherapy (Perls, 1969). With ego functioning at the boundary, the central place of field in Frederick and Laura Perls' psychotherapy was established. Boundary functioning led directly to experiments phenomenally selected and structurally aimed to exercise and strengthen that functioning. Logically, this was the end of interpretation as such, since clear and unclouded functioning within the experimental work empowered the individual, a trainee in psychotherapy, was free to make his own interpretation. The central place of transference in psychotherapy thus also was swept aside.

Equilibrium is perhaps a more subtle and fertile notion than Perls' zero point of homeostatic as the resting place after the contact, the gestalt achieved. In the tendency to complete unfinished situations or to reach equilibrium, the debt to Lewin, obvious in his theory of quasi-needs, was specific (Perls, 1969, pp. 101). Lewin's measurement was topological rather than linear and quantitative.

Equilibrium as the result of calibrated forces, seen as vectors above and below the level achieved, had the advantage of a more finely tuned mechanism than mere balance. It also enabled the clarity of systems models within gestalt therapy theory, which as always were reified *in situ* and resulted in baroque intricacies as a theory of contact became a revisionist cycle of experience.

In 1924, Mead wrote of Dewey, "In the *Outlines of Ethics*, we find the will, the idea, and the consequences all placed inside of the act, and the act itself placed only within the larger activity of the individual in society." (Mead, 1938, pp. 9)

As the simplest and first reality, Goodman defined contact itself as "in touch, touching." He identified four phases of the process within the typology of a single behavior in order to conveniently divide the contacting activity. They were fore contact, contacting, final contact, and post-contact. Translating to the vocabulary of psychoanalysis, they were respectively, the given or id of the situation; the developing appetite and environment and objects within it, perhaps the stimulus/response perceptual phase of the circuit or the adjustments of the ego. Finally, in gestalt therapy, contacting the lively goal in unitary touch and bright awareness, "in the figure of the You" and flowing organism/environment interaction in the whole experience of diminished self.

From another aspect, the poet sets the scene, states the conundrum that is balking him, approaches the possibilities and restates them, and moves thumpingly to his point as a new reality. The process is a passage from past to future, the artist at work, the self in aware creativity.

This is a brilliant exegesis and an adequate theory of psychotherapy especially given the difficulties of exposition that attempt to describe Unity and Awareness and to bring them to the field of action and experiment. The key is of course the *structure* of experience within the guiding field of therapy, not the content "so much" as the *how* of the feelingful, physical, emotional, perceptual, aware interaction; and attention is concentrated as these areas become figural. For example, the brilliant work of Reich analyzing the character structure and its maintenance in muscular armoring was directly influential on Perls and Goodman. It opened the language of the body to the therapy.

Again, what is experience? The gestalt psychologists skillfully experimented the conditions of experience in perception but their formal basis was an isomorphic parallelism that inevitably led to a solipsism that cannot found an holistic theory of perception, nor be the basis for an holistic psychotherapy as gestalt therapy is. To maintain that in perception there is in the neurons a dynamic and relational equivalent to the object of perception leaves always the question how does this come about? And what is the mechanism?

The neurology is itself a perception and cannot be used primarily to explain perception. The problem remains even under a strict phenomenal approach; that is, without a real unity, immediately the problem of the *noumena* looms. The thing-in-itself is where Kant came to philosophic grief.

Charles Hartshorne felt that an "utterly presuppositionlessness consciousness" as Husserl postulated for his phenomenology was naive. Husserl's influence became profound in gestalt therapy theory, but the ontic space implicit in it indeed became occupied by cognition, or an uncreative awe in the contemplation of the spiritual or perhaps the transpersonal. One feels many nagging questions but the principal one is on what firm unity does all our work rest? Frederick Perls said that gestalt therapy had to "stand on its own two feet" or it would never survive.

IV. Paul Goodman identified his influences psychotherapy as Charcot, Freud, Reich. Intellectually, he always acknowledged his debt to Dewey and indeed pragmatic meaning discovered in the consequences, thus the effects of one's acts, was central to his theory of education as an active process in which the children were partners in also learning by doing. He did his graduate work at Chicago in the late Thirties when Dewey was long gone to Teachers' College. Mead, the Chairman of the Department of Philosophy, died at the beginning of 1931.

Pragmatism stressed the consequences of acts rather than will and action or the practical of Kant. Their criterion of meaning was stated in the maxim of C. S. Peirce: "Consider what effects that might conceivably have practical bearings, we conceive the object of our conception to have. Then our conception of these effects is the whole of our conception of the object." The theory of evolution was accepted which replaced essences with process and events and the dynamism of development.

The experimental method of science in which hypotheses were tested and verified or reconstructed was essential grounds. George Herbert Mead wrote *The Philosophy of the Present,* summarizing the importance of the present as the theater of action but also insisting on interdependence of past, present and future. (Mead, 1934) His theory of self and its social origins is crucial for gestalt therapy and any theory of intersubjectivity, or to Köhler's warning about direct social experience as evidence in psychology. Mead did his greatest work in social psychology and establishing the act itself as the unit of experience. (Mead, 1938)

He insisted on a continuum of development as a result of contact in the final or consummatory phase of the act and the genesis of the self in that uniquely human capacity to arouse in her/him/self the gesture she/he has aroused in the other, then to respond to that response. The basis for that is found in the self's unique capacity to have itself for an object. The mechanism is found in the speaking and hearing apparatus operating as vocal gesture so what one sounds, one also hears; the sounds arouse equivalent sounds in the other who then arouses them in the individual ultimately responding to that response. The parent/infant babbling play with its imitative to-ing and fro-ing play through the vestibular hearing and speech apparatus arouses in the infant what he has aroused in the parent. This is the genesis of the self. The infant learns to speak but the self ultimately speaks in the other's individual voice.

A similar process occurs in the evolution of play where the infant ultimately learns the rules of the game and is thus able to take all the parts of the whole process as she learns what is expected of her. She is able to see in herself the generalized other and become a member of the group. An exquisite picture of this process is given in Daniel Stem's, *The Interpersonal World of the Infant.* There he describes such processes as "affective attunement."

For Mead, particularly fateful for growth, is the development of resistance. The genesis of resistance is found in the pushing and pulling (or the "in touch touching"), especially of one hand on the other where the experiences are also felt on the inside. Therefore, it is an activity that puts insides to things so for example in perception, the object not only is there with its bounded surfaces but its gesture invites us to its activity. Thus, we feel from the inside of it, the sitting-downness of the chair. It is important that we perceive not merely figure against ground or surface since that would lead to an indefinite number of subdivisions and we would never get to the insides of the object. Experience would be frozen.

In his own words:

> When the individual assumes the attitude of pushing a heavy object, its character as ponderous is more than stimulation to exercise effort. It is a sense of the pressure or inertia which the body will exert upon the individual. It is true that memory images of past expenditures of effort upon it or like objects may arise, but these images will be of the efforts expended aroused by the stimulation of what we call the resistance of the object. They do not of themselves carry with them the location of the resistance in the object, nor is this location of the resistance given in the definition of the boundaries of the object through sight and touch. What has taken place is the "feeling one's self into" the object.

> What are the conditions of this attitude? There must be that in the position, I will say the gesture, of the object which arouses in the individual a resistance of the same sort as that which the body will exercise. I take it that it is the ability of the limbs to act upon the organism which endows the organism with this capacity to feel itself into the physical thing. When one sees the object to be pushed, it is first of all, a stimulation to the pushing.

> Then the awakened tendency to push against the object calls out in the organism the tendency to resist one's own effort as in the pressure of one hand upon the other. One, then, identifies the mere stimulation to exercise more effort, with the expenditure of force on the part of the object because this playing of the role of

> the heavy object has excited one's response in advance of the
> actual contact with the object. There is a dramatic rehearsal of
> what one is advancing to do.
>
> There is doubtless behind this a social attitude which is explicit
> at times, especially in childhood and moments of irritation. And
> this social attitude is of profound importance in the origin of this
> physical thing. (Mead, 1938, pp. 310)

Resistance in the classical sense was resistance to the analyst's interpretation. The Perlses restated resistance as the life of the patient and within the restatement of aggression as oral, and the opportunities for creative experiment in the session developed resistance as the royal road to contact by experimenting its conditions. Blocked contact, frozen resistance, the muscular armoring of Reich, awakening the sleeping insides of self and things, developed levels of awareness leading to contact...From physical things to the insides of things from and to which we give take and make leverage, assistance and support.

Although I have not been able to find any reference to George Herbert Mead in Goodman's works, the similarities border on the uncanny. For example, Mead also analyzes four phases of the act as impulse, perception, manipulation and contact or consummatory, and makes a much finer discrimination within them.

In impulse, perception, and manipulation are the invitations to experience that the organism's sensitivities and susceptibilities logically determine the environment and are causally determined by the environment in its opportunities. The determining relation is completely mutual but not convertible. The invitation to action is by the distance characters that are in all perception, including matter and extension as well as the so-called secondary characteristics of sound, odor, taste, color and shape, and touch.

Perception arises within the phases of the act as competing hypotheses aroused in the organism and the environment recede as the act proceeds and better organized hypotheses lead the process until in contact the object is seized, eaten, enjoyed or valued as in aesthetic appreciation.

The consummation is the final phase of the act which is invited through impulse, perception and manipulation with their distance characters to its futurity. Thus, perception is a "collapsed act" that has with it all the elements that the final phase promises, thus its future leaning. The act itself is in the perspective of the individual, but in its congruence with the distance promise and with the experience of others who could experience the same object, it is also objective as a generalized other.

Let us to turn to an example from the constancies in perception of the gestalt psychologists, the penny seen as a circle rather than optically in its various ellipticities. Mead says:

> Here is found the much labored penny that is seen as round though the contour that is presented to the eye is an oval or a line. A favored perspective practically supplants that which is immediately given in the so-called *sense datum*.

> The problem which is involved in this (mediate) phase of perception is that it cannot be accounted for by a mere fusing of one content with another. One cannot fuse an oval with a circle. Nor is it a mere substitution in the fashion which the visual deliverance of one retina is substituted for that of the other in certain situations.

> For in this case, one can recover the image which is rejected and hold also that which is selected for perception, and this cannot be done in this case. One cannot hold over against each other in the perception the oval penny and the round penny as actual so-called sense. This can be stated in terms of interpretation, in terms of Berkeley's theory, of vision.

> The datum in this case is there never was a mere visual content, *but as an indication of the experience of manipulation, and our*

> *percept of the penny is then in terms of the action under the*
> *conditions of most advantageous conduct.* However, they are
> interpreted, the two contours are facts of experience. One can see
> the oval, and one can see the circle. One does not fuse them, and
> one does not push aside and see the other." (Mead, 1938, pp.
> 128)

> "From one position, we see the penny as round, even though it is
> an oval form that registers upon the retina, because its oval
> character is the stimulus *to the movement which will bring it into*
> *what is the standard form for our conduct with reference to the*
> *penny*...The content of ellipticity is there not as a resultant but as
> stimulus to bring about the normal content which imagery may
> supply.

> The selective power of perception reduces ellipticity from a
> resultant to a mediate character of our spatio-temporal
> environment which is organized to lead up to a certain goal...
> Changing the goal of our attitude toward an ellipse at once places
> the present visual form of the penny in a final instead of a
> mediate situation. We make the mistake of assuming that it was
> there in that character in the earlier situation. (Mead, pp. 132–
> 133)

This is a many times more satisfactory statement of the mechanism of the
constancies than to say merely that they depend on the cues in visual
experience in the environment of the object of the perception.

Moreover:

> The difficulty is enhanced by the fact that we act so much in a
> field of a fifth dimension of the social symbol, the field of
> language, leaving action so largely to trained automatism. Still it
> remains true not only that the world of physical things arises out
> of locomotor responses to distance stimulation and our contact
> responses (especially of the hand), but also that it is just these

varied possible responses which the physical things hold in experience which offer the primitive logical field within which the social symbol can operate.

The multitude of possible responses which constitute mediate things that lie between our impulses and their consummations opens up the field of indication and reference out of which language can arise, though the two processes undoubtedly work together. (Mead, pp. 137)

The theory of resistance and the mediate character of perception developing in the spatio-temporal environment lead one directly to the experiments and work of the developmentalists. Daniel Stern's examples of the child with its attentive and peremptory gaze seems to state the spatiotemporal environment. Also, affect attunement, for example, is an exquisite illustration of the vocal gesture at work in achieving the developing self and communication. Habituation and dishabituation as the infant demands novelty is a striking feature. (Stern, 1985)

The baby will avert its gaze from that which it becomes used to. There is something delicious in the notion that the human being comes into the world with a native capacity to be bored by its parents. That seems a far more fruitful battle than the resolutions of the libido within the Oedipal strivings.

Ruella Frank's work, perhaps training in resistance, that is, putting the insides to things, finally states the relation of limbs to the organism as a whole. Or to put it in another way, takes seriously the organism as an environment of the organism as an exploratory field of experiment to restore the blocked and balked individual's awarenesses of "insides." Perhaps, a novel way to state neuroses would be hyper-concern with the indefinite divisibility of surfaces.

In Goodman's famous 1951 letter to Köhler, after explaining the distortions of simplicity in the unity of behavior in the therapeutic situation, the conditions become foreground, and the dynamic relation

and sequence of figures and grounds is reformulated, he cited
Goldstein's *Organism*:

> ...we are taking up Goldstein's therapeutic indication that in any
> malfunction (for example, a disabled and retracted limb), we
> must alternately regard the protected part as the figure or the
> ground. The bother with Goldstein's position, if I may go off on
> a tangent, is that he continually tends to defeat himself with his
> remarkable prejudice that extensor behavior is less "dignified"
> and less "human" than in drawing behavior ...
>
> The result of this is that the environment is effectually ruled out
> as a source of *curative energy* despite the fact that he
> occasionally mentions, generally in a parenthesis, that the
> environment does lend energy to forming the figure. That is, he
> condemns himself to a mere physiology just as most other gestalt
> psychologists restrict themselves to a perceptual or interpersonal
> psychology. In our book, we try to reintegrate these divisions.
> This leads to considerable metaphysical adventuring, very much
> at variance with popular conceptions... (Stoehr, 1994, pp. 101)

To be sure, it was not until much later that the awareness of the body as a
physical thing, or to put it another way, as an environment of and for the
organism as whole, became well-founded. Emphasis on contact at the
boundary in the organism/environment field and, "in touch touching"
with its inevitable skin focus and out-thereness and so called
interpersonality, had long suppressed the interactive physicality of the
organism, e.g., its limbs and their dynamic relation to the organism as a
whole, their resistances and insides and use of implements in offering
and taking leverage, assistance and support.

> It is important to recognize that the insidedness of the organism's
> activity could not be placed within the organism as a perceptual
> object until the act had placed the organism over against some
> outer position. Now the action of, say, an implement in the hand
> does place the hand and the organism of which it is a part over

against the implement. What the implement does in the cooperative process serves to place the hand and the organism-as-a-
whole as one of the perceptual objects in the field. It is
impossible to start off with the organism as an object and project
its contents into other perceptual objects.

The organism becomes a perceptual object only after the act is in
some sense located outside the organism. This is, of course, the
basis for reflective activity in which the organism becomes an
object to itself. Resistance as an activity is a fundamental
character which is common to all physical objects, including the
organism. From the standpoint of the resistance of physical
things, we resist them, but it is still necessary to describe an act
originating in the organism that can be so located outside the
organism so that the organism can become an object. (Mead, pp.
143)

The socializing infant is an adequate primary model for group work and
group therapy. A relation, a group that is a whole and parts dynamism
that is also completely intrinsic and is replicated in its parts, is uniquely
human and as Goodman never tired of reminding us, the social out of
which they are developed is prior to the ego and the self. Indeed, the
phases or stages of most developmental theory can be dated in their
social context.

Therefore, it is in the unfinished business or the interruptions of the
contact socially where the pathoformic sticking point is maintained and
must be recovered. The comment of Freud of the layering of the
personality and the analogy to archeology in uncovering the original
ruined city or social group is notorious.

V. A case in point is the phase at which the child is able to tell a story
about herself which occurs in the second year of life.

The advent of language ultimately brings about the ability to
narrate one's own life story with all the potential that holds for

changing how one views oneself. The making of a narrative is not the same as any other kind of thinking or talking. It appears to involve a different mode of thought from problem solving or pure description. It involves thinking in terms of persons who act as agents with intentions and goals that unfold in some causal sequence with a beginning, middle and end. (Narrative-making may prove to be a universal human phenomenon reflecting the design of the human mind).

This is a new and exciting area of research, which it is not yet clear how, why or when children construct (or co-construct with a parent) narratives that begin to form the autobiographical history that ultimately evolves into the life story a patient *may first present to a therapist.* The domain of verbal relatedness might, in fact, be best subdivided into a sense of a categorical self that objectifies and labels, and of a narrated self that weaves into a story elements from other senses of the self (agency, intentions, causes, goals, and so on). (Stern, pp. 174)

In *Ego, Hunger and Aggression*, Frederick Perls cites Kurt Lewin's findings that "contrary to what one would expect from the libido theory," the memory for unfinished interrupted tasks was firmer than for the completed ones. He used this as a launching pad for a discussion of the repetition-compulsion and obsession ritual where the thing is never finished.

As I commented above, the surfaces are indefinitely divided without getting the resistance, the life, the consummation or contact. Unfinished business became a big deal in gestalt therapy and experiment in the mantra: "Where is the interruption of contact?" and to concentrate awareness there. Thus, the diagnosis and the therapy! Thus, also confluence, projection, retroflection, and perhaps, egotism are the mechanisms of the unfinished business and tension of the balked contact process.

Further research led to the effect reflected also in the completion of unfinished tasks and ultimately in the completion of the interrupted task by a partner in the experiment, provided however, the task made sense in a common or group effort. It is always the case that the group makes a more intelligent and efficient solution to problems than would be expected of the individuals natively. It is a perfect statement of the rules of the game culminating in the experience of the generalized other, that is to say, an expression of novelty which the parts of the whole (the individuals) could have at best only dimly foreseen.

If it is a better, more satisfactory solution, what is the almost universal resistance to organizing the task that is in front of us as part of a group effort to find and make the coming solution? Apparently, it is the case that instead of feeling more support in a group context, the individual at first, feels less, and therefore, is almost group phobic.

VI. In an evolutionary development, the New York Institute has attempted to democratize group therapy/theory primarily from the point of leadership. Starting from the perhaps Socratic notion that the members are the possessors of knowledge essential to the life process of the group, we have redefined leadership from position, perhaps person, to function. That is to say, from the point of view of the act. As Mead might have said: "What act is necessary at this point to move the process, perhaps the hypotheses, through impulse, perception, manipulation, thence to consummation or contact?"

We can then state the functions of leadership as processes arising from a level of support that values every voice, every member's contributions as it moves along. Or again, in Mead's terms as the competing hypotheses contribute and recede in the motion of the act, it is important that the hypotheses that fall away are not merely discarded. They go into the structure of the personal and group biography, the awareness of the generalized other that makes up background that becomes the pattern of group relating.

Perhaps, as Goodman has it, "the unaware background of the aware background of experience," that confluence is available to awareness but which we take for granted as the support for all our conduct. Morality, or right conduct, is grounded here.

So we try to support the group individual to his/her own contact within the group contact process. Remembering that courage is the support for all the other virtues (another way of saying the circuit of action of which the mere arcs are stimulus and response as Dewey pointed out) we respect our fears, hesitancies and cowardices. Further, the small group is always seen in its relation to the larger and to society so the opportunity for large group interaction with its cohesion in a further whole-and-parts relation is an objective.

Thus, the basic nature of group activity as a political one is revealed in the movement toward small changes within larger structures. Paul Goodman's aim was to tinker, here a little, there a little, biting off what one could chew rather than the grand things where the means/ends relation is too widely separated and one resigns in despair.

We think the model is appropriate for many clinical populations but the research has yet to be done, although clearly the process is self-evaluating. One of our members, Charles Myswinski, has interesting findings in large group therapy with twenty-five or so former substance abusers at the lowest socio-economic and personal resources scale.

Apropos, attempts to evaluate such a population with objective scales of depression, for example, Beck's, are impossible since the group members do not understand the questionnaire, or for that matter, the questions or even the terms of the question. The questionnaire culture is radically different from the *anomie* of their daily lives.

Clearly, what we are attempting to do is to rewrite the narrative. The nature of narrative however, is not always as Stern has it, the biographical story with a beginning, middle and end, perhaps not even natively. The style of the narrative can get in the way of the resolution or contact. The pathoformic point where the story does not move on to resolution betrays a frozen linearity. It may be in life that movement is spiraling. Certainly, that seems to be the experience in the group circle.

The theory of narratology makes clear the problem of the structure of the narrative is getting in the way of the narration itself. In *Narrative and Its Discontents, Problems of Closure in the Traditional Novel*, D. A. Miller has brilliantly analyzed Jane Austen, George Eliot and Stendahl and their triangularity in handling the problem of resolution.

> In the last analysis, what discontents the traditional novel is its own condition of possibility. For the production of narrative, what we called the narratable, is possible only within a logic of insufficiency, disequilibrium and deferral, and traditional novelists typically desire worlds of greater stability and wholeness than such a logic can intrinsically provide.

> Moreover, the suspense that constitutes the narratable inevitably comes to imply a suspensiveness of signification, so that what is ultimately threatened is no less than the possibility of a full or definitive meaning. Thus, novelists such as Jane Austen and George Eliot need to situate their texts within a controlling perspective of narrative closure, which would restore the world (and with it, the word), to a state of transparency, once for all released errancy and equivocation.

And in a footnote:

> Grivel accepts Derrida's position that there is no full meaning in a text, but only *différance* (difference, deferment). Yet for him the novel is precisely the mode in which *la différance existe pour faire cesser la différence*. (Miller, 1981, pp. 265)

Miller asserts the general truth that there must be conflict drive a story and resolution to end it. He compares this to the child in Freud who makes his toy disappear the more to savor its restoration.

> The seemingly binary opposition on which the child's game is founded, is, in fact, radically asymmetrical. The anxiety of disappearance is intrinsically stronger than the gratification of return, for the former is not merely a moment in the game, it is the underlying inspiration for the game itself. Even the gratification of return belongs to the logic of disappearance, since the toy stands in place of a primary but irrevocably lost satisfaction (total possession of the mother).

Does the anxiety of disappearance stronger than the gratification of return equal a subset within Lewin's tension of quasi-needs or unfinished business?

And further:

> Similarly, I have implied the narratable is stronger than the closure to which it is opposed than the closure to which it is opposed in an apparent binarity. For the narratable is the very evidence of the narrative text while closure (as precisely, the non-narratable) is only the sign that this text is over. (Miller, 1981, pp. 266)

VII. In 1890, George Herbert Mead transferred from Leipzig and Wilhelm Wundt to Berlin where he studied with Dilthey and Ebbinghaus among others. This experience introduced him to the controversy "between an 'explanatory' psychology oriented to the natural sciences and employing reductionist procedures... Ebbinghaus... and a 'descriptive' psychology using the interpretive methods of the humanistic sciences, represented by Dilthey..." (Joas, 1985, pp. 18)

Dilthey lacked a theory, of intersubjectivity and seemed to find in Husserl's "meaning" (*Bedeutung*) a bulwark against the "relativism of a purely psychological foundation of the human sciences..." and to open the way to their "hermeneutic" grounding in Dilthey's theory, of expression. In a footnote in his 1985 re-examination of Mead's thought, Hans Joas comments:

I have great difficulty with the distinction between a psychological and a hermeneutic phase in the development of Dilthey's thought on which Gadamer and Habermas base their interpretations. It is my opinion that in this distinction, several dimensions overlap one another: the merely empathic hermeneutics versus a hermeneutics directed to the understanding of meaning, and a relativist versus normative method of understanding.

In addition, this distinction suggests that hermeneutics itself does not require more than a linguistic grounding, whereas it must also be grounded in philosophical anthropology. Helmuth Plessner saw this, and used it to justify his hermeneutics of non-linguistic expression. Habermas' *Erkenntnis and Irteresse* opposes Peirce and Dilthey far too much on the basis of the distinction between instrumental and communicative action, which results in the slightly unjust treatment of both of them. (Joas, 1985, pp. 223)

Mead, however, was radical in his assertion of the social constitution of the self in communication and meaning.

The effective occupation of space involves not simply different degrees of effort in reacting to things but also an experience of the resistance which the object itself offers to these efforts. This implies the identification of the individual organism with the object for resistance which finds its expression in the kinesthetic experience of pushing and pressing against solids.

The effective occupation of space involves the identification of the individual organism with the object, for resistance which finds its expression in the kinesthetic experience of effort can appear in the object only in so far as this effort if located in the object. This has been explained by the transfer of the experience of the two hands, or any two opposing efforts of the organism to the object and has had a wider statement in Lipps' doctrine of *Einfühlung*.

It is the fact of the transfer that is of importance here…the fact is very fundamental in our attitudes toward all physical objects …The basis for the attitude of identifying one's effort with the experience of the thing can be most naturally found in the individual's exciting himself to react as the other acts toward him by his own response, and the mechanism for this is found in social conduct.

There the individual, in stimulating the other to an impulsive response, may arouse the same response in his own system if he is affected directly by his attitude as the other form is stimulated. This takes place notably in the use of the vocal gesture or any gesture which can be used for language…Through the tendency to push as a physical thing against one's own hand in the role of another individual, one has become a physical object over against the physical thing…

Such a development of the physical thing over against the physical self is an abstraction from an original social experience, for it is primarily in social conduct that we stimulate ourselves to act toward ourselves as others act toward us and thus identify ourselves with others and become objects to ourselves. (Mead, 1938, pp. 427)

In *Hermeneutics, Gestalt Therapy and Literary Text*, Sichera has argued very much the same thing. The break in the hermeneutic circle of therapist and client caused by the split between the scientific and the relational must be restored. This seems the split described above between Ebbinghaus and Dilthey, explanatory methods of natural science and Dilthey's humanistic sciences and their interpretive or hermeneutic methods.

Sichera writes:

> Above all...we have the opportunity to exploit the inherent
> potential of the gestalt method which, on account of its particular
> hermeneutic nature, makes us, as subjects involved in
> interpretation, recognize the otherness of the text. Ultimately, it
> is the text which will assume an autonomous semantic being as
> such and not as the surfacing of undeclared profound structures,
> basically coinciding with the psyche of the author...gestalt
> therapy encourages me to grasp the No's of the text, an
> indispensable sign of the sanity of my relationship with it. (A.S.
> pp. 63)

His analysis appears to me as a perfect example of the resistance we have
been discussing, putting the insides to things, in this case a text to get our
teeth into, arising out of the basic social attitude and which is never the
mere divisibility of surfaces.

After a discussion of the comic against humor, which rests on the
Aristotelian enthymeme, Sichera illustrates beautifully the theory of the
generalized other with Pirandello's *Six Characters in Search of an
Author*. As the characters wander about freeing themselves from the
control of the writer/father, they are gradually writing their own
characters.

This is purely perspectival. "He has only to make himself an instrument
so that the other who is growing inside his imagination can feel as he
really feels and be as deeply as he wishes to be." (A.S. pp. 68) (This, by
the way, was Paul Goodman's way, especially in *The Empire City*, to let
the personae take over and write themselves. He was critical of Musil's
Man Without Qualities for this reason. Thus, probably the title. A
depersonalized, therefore strangely omniscient narrator would be eerily
empty.

I am proposing a different context for the narrative, namely that of the group; also that the group be part of a larger group to which it relates more or less regularly. The task of the group is to restart the process of narration as the individuals relate and therefore so restate their tales, and make a group narrative as well, to support the members' efforts. For example, the game in which a sentence is written by one person and the next by another and so forth comes to mind.

The dynamical relations are part of the text and will be identified by the members as editors as the group moves to contact within their proper authorship. Relating to the larger group, of which the subgroups are a part, is a powerful support as similarities and differences (the "yes" and "no") figurally, are articulated and background patterns assert themselves. Again, the process is self-evaluating, the intrinsic, the process, that which moves the group toward felt contact, is supported and comparison to extrinsic standards fall away, one of the functions of inter-group relating. The video record of such a process is a compelling learning instrument.

In an illuminating moment at a recent conference in New York City, some experiments were developed based on Mead's theory of resistance such as the crumbling action of the fingers, one hand pushing on the other, etc., and social perception, e.g., experiencing in the same way hand in hand with the others…and visually, "I see you seeing me," and, "When I see you seeing me, I see…" One of the members, Mary Lou Shack, said: "I didn't know I was thinking it until you said it, but as you said it, I was thinking it."

References

Joas, Hans, (1985), G.H. Mead: *A Contemporary Re-examination of his Thought*. Cambridge, MA. MIT Press.

Köhler, Wolfgang, (1947), *Gestalt Psychology*. New York: Liveright Publishing Corporation.

Mead, George H. (1934), *The Philosophy of the Act*, Chicago, IL

Miller, D.A. (1981), *Narrative and Its Discontents*, Princeton, NJ

Perls, F. S. (1951), *Gestalt Therapy: Excitement and Growth in the Human Personality,* New York, Julian Press.

Perls, F. S. (1969), *Ego, Hunger and Aggression*. New York: Vintage Books.

Sichera, A. (1992), Hermeneutics, Gestalt Therapy and Literary Text. *Quaderni di Gestalt* 1, 61–69.

Stern, Daniel N. (1985), *The Interpersonal World of the Infant*. New York: Basic Books.

Stoehr, Taylor (1994), *Here Now Next: Paul Goodman and the Origins of Gestalt Therapy*, San Francisco, Jossey-Bass.

Group as Self, Self as Group

2005

Not for these I raise
The song of thanks and praise
But for those obstinate questionings
Of sense and outward things,
Fallings from us, vanishings;
Blank misgivings of a creature
Moving about in worlds not realized,
High instincts before which our mortal nature
Did tremble like a guilty thing surprised.

— Wordsworth
Ode: *Intimations of Immortality from*
Recollections of Early Childhood,
Stanza 9

In preparation for creating this paper within the New York Institute's continuing tradition of monthly presentations, I was sufficiently tentative to review the *Compendium* from the 50th Anniversary Conference. It remains an important document and justifies close reading. I think we should all be pleased that we were able to bring the conference off at all and to have as product (otherwise than the process work itself and presentations, however grand) as *residuum* or perhaps *vade mecum*, a refreshing, rich, handy document, readily available as testimony to the once and future Institute. It is a work of history, scholarship, authentic and serious effort, and should be so read.

I have taken the title above from Lee Zevy's presented paper and collapsed it, I trust rhythmically, to one word, or perhaps a process word since what I will be saying here is not new. Indeed, it is even ancient, implicit in Aristotle's insistence that if his auditor will only "say something," that is, respond within the beginning dialogue, then we can get on. If he will say nothing, then he is no "better than a vegetable" and it is better to abandon him. The social statement here is obvious and good provenance.

Experiment I
However, to fill in the blanks somewhat, it is also the case that we have over the years struggled with the notion of self/other, I and Thou — not from Buber but from our own discoveries and inventions in these very presentations — and the myriad manifestations of self-struggling in our group work. Perhaps, this is what we meant by the awkward yet persistent locution, "selfing."

I ask you merely at this very moment in your reading to STOP! and go within/without and experience what your present understanding means by "self"; without (!) examination, just as its flux makes and feels itself. Perhaps, the foregoing should be called appropriately:

Experiment I and only
With this step, we will have made the first of a series of experiments that we hope will energize and enliven whatever the didactics are that we will print on these blood, sweat and tears pages.

The questions are, as in Aristotle: Who is my audience? Who am I, then? And they? Who are they? And she who must be obeyed? And that vague, shadowy presence, hovering, perhaps lurking, available at best as shadow, is this, too, background? The famous background and foreground? What is that in your present experiencing? Or is it (!) a "that"?

Are the suppositious distinctions blurring as indeed they always are? This is great grist for an enormous mill that we're asking you to grind from just a moment of breath and examination. It has to be tremendous: It is the Universe … SELF.

This meeting has been variously described within the title *Self as Group*; Obviously, you will entertain the notion it could equally be within the rubric, *Group as Self*. (See PREP above). It is in that seesaw that we are attempting, all of us together, to stand the usual understanding, usually developed from the individual psyche, on its head. That is, let us limit our fortress of individual/group prejudice and stay with what is going on. As William James says, "Something is doing in the Universe."

Experiments II, III, and IV
Experiments II, III and IV will begin. Each series of experiments (3) will run for approximately a half-hour each. We will start by counting off in threes at the beginning and forming three large groups within which we can form triads with one observer for each dialogue between two, then rotating so that each person becomes part of the dialoguing and observing.

Experiment II
Actually, we should have titled this subsection, *Theory and Experiment II*, since what we are striving for is the intimation of the beginning of developing theory/praxis from our activity itself. Of course, this within the format necessarily means to and from our hard work of group process. (Cf. Whitehead indicates process as the hard substance of reality.) Hence, it stands the usual genetic account on its head.

Therefore, for starters, as suggested, *Experiment II* could be the experience and the manifestations of what we mean by the amazing abstraction, "individual."

Now separate "group" into triads. Address each other. Try to be an "individual." Even exaggerate the symptom. Derive what is salient from the experience for your record. Or perhaps you have already selected a volunteer/observer for that. (In which case, you will have already made your triads.) How? In the usual partition, have pair interaction with observer, and then rotate positions so each member of the triad has been in each role. It is essential that you share with your triad "what you got from *Experiment II*."

Experiment III

When you regroup your subgroup, let the process rip. Remember, we are learning what we mean by the "amazing abstraction — individual." Perhaps, it has resonance in Camus' equally amazing, "the ridiculous habit of life." Is "individual" a habit? Therefore, consult yourselves. See how "used" you are (habit?) to being an individual. Consult your "feeling" of habit with your subgroup. By this, we mean feeling: that which seems to point to "satisfaction." ("Habit" might be called, after Alfred North Whitehead, "lure for feeling.") It is not too soon to notice, record, and reciprocally communicate within.

Experiment IV

What is different within feeling and satisfaction in the experience of individual and group interaction? What changes and shifts do you make if your communication has a group intentionality or an individual leaning instead? Do you adjust and censor? Can you share this? Why so? Why not? Or is there no difficulty at all?

For Experiments V, VI and VII

Within each triad, please choose a group reporter who will enter a fishbowl or hub and continue the discussions. Members outside who wish to enter the discussion and bring the outside inside and inside outside can tap a member's shoulder and exchange places or not as the desire manifests.

Experiment V

Group support; keep in mind, at least as I understand it, that is, support. We are talking of "carrying from below or underneath." We are not talking of foundation. We are most definitely talking of an activity, arduous and therefore rewarding.

It is canard that the "getting-to-know-each-other" is a necessary phase of the "beginning group." Does it not mean "getting-to-know-who's-who?" and is quite authority-bound. But is this necessary? Therefore, what happens when you have fun with the sociologistical "roles" and "positions" of your colleagues?

What happens to the favorite ducklings of existential psychotherapy when you can experiment with the "getting-to-know?" (By the way, a "canard" is a duck.) And these are its ducklings:

- Authenticity

- Mutuality

- Dialogue

- I-Thou

- Meeting

Maybe the anagram is ADAM, I AM. Can those ducks get in a row? Try to keep in mind but do have the sense to be distracted so you are able to return refreshed, that all this arises from your group interaction and the stepping-stones are feeling and satisfaction, therefore:

Experiment VI
Experiment VI which takes us to our favorite gestalt therapy ducks.

- Unfinished business

- Here and Now

- Figure and Ground or

- Figure/ground

- Contact

- Foreground/Background. (Perhaps as in individual/group?)

- Dominance

- Need

Dip every one of these birds into the litmus sauce of your group and your group's experience and see if they change color. You should be clearer or not that we are here approaching learning from the inside of experience itself, the shared group experience and your group/self/individual experience, what behaviorally means. And this is PROCESSIVE CONCRETENESS.

Experiment VII

Experiment VII, the actuality. Presumably, the end and aim of contact, which we'll promote to a goose along with "awareness" in George Herbert Mead's fourfold unit of reality in the Act,

1. Impulse;

2. Perception;

3. Manipulation;

4. Consummation (or Contact).

Don't forget "excitement and growth".

For this experiment, we will need breath. Can you as a group experience breath? Perhaps in unison, as processive concreteness, which Alfred North Whitehead calls the "Actual."

Experiment VII: Can you breathe together? Perhaps even in unison? What happens — do you notice — when you share breathing?

Reprise

It should be clear or clearer now, that in our subgroup findings, we in a closer approach to developing self and these findings or experiences are preparation for reporting to the group-as-a-whole and to the body politic in our Teaching/Learning Community.

When we remember with Alfred North Whitehead that experience is di-polar, conceptual and physical (remember the "satisfaction" and "lure for feeling"), we can pair it with two other di-polarities, Teaching and Learning.

Thus, we have come full circle from our explorations in the *Self as Group* from Experiment I to our result in Experiment VII.

Self and Society

2006

The Soul selects her own Society
Then - shuts the Door -
To her divine Majority
Present no more

Unmoved - she notes the Chariots — pausing
At her low Gate
Unmoved - an Emperor be kneeling
Upon her Mat

I've known her - from an ample nation
Choose One
Then - close the Valves of her attention -
Like Stone

— Emily Dickinson

That is, the Self selects its own society; or better, selecting its society, makes it her own and social. It is in that sense an achievement must be worked so it can speak in the other's voice and also in its own, encompassing multitudes and thus, its contradictions. So it is with organizations.

The New York Institute, constituted by those magnificent "outcasts" with their differences, even contradictions, but united in their effort to create a new psychotherapy, also created an organization that from the beginning shut the door to emperors kneeling on the mat and insisted on excitement and growth in the human personality. Now there's a credo! They also knew it could not be achieved without aggressing and experimenting in the present case, directly from the thrust contacting at the boundary in the organism/environment field. And so they did.

And the years went by. Ones were chosen and the valves of attention were not closed to novelty, the emerging that said it is this way, not that. We will do this! There were many Chariots that paused and then went on. The gate was too low. The Institute was a membership organization from the beginning. The impedimenta of degrees, certifications, grades and costly credits could not get their bulk through the gate and their porters went elsewhere as we kept at the task.

The time came; that time of which the present is the present of that past and the future of that present, coming into being. And as the creators left us, the Theses did not begin but the experimenting went on as the organization began to mean itself. The interested new members with their training in social and group work were able to take seriously the social nature of humankind, and not without famous battles, moved that tenet of gestalt therapy to the foreground in group work that eventuated in the leader as facilitator. The autocracy of leadership was disestablished to person rather than position as the various gifts were called based on their *afforderungs charakter* within the interacting.

As that present from its past became its future, in experiment, it became clear that to actualize the gifts of these novelties, an organizational restatement was needed. And the Institute evolved a model of group development with small group interaction — triads, e.g., within traditional size groups, themselves reciprocally integrating with quite large groups so the fibers of support improved to the warp and woof of the design; this is itself a living expression, indeed a dramatic affirmation of what had become to be called the "aesthetic criterion" from the original "autonomous criterion."

In the first stage of its development, the Institute was directed by a Board of Fellows which re-elected the existence of the Institute annually. This was a requirement of the documents of incorporation. The provision was created to keep the organization from being "taken over" presumably by the Emperors and Chariots. It kept the gate low. The Fellows had the further obligation to present a paper, demonstration, and so forth at the monthly meeting during the academic year. They rotated this task for years, ultimately exhausting the process and turning to the Members.

No power, no work! The members rebelled, the remaining Fellows repealed the notorious self-perpetuating amendment and organizational democracy reigned as all degrees of membership got the vote and, except for existing ones where it is merely an honorific, the title "Fellow" was retired, Emeritus status remained for those no longer active in the Institute. It is clear that the revolution was created out of "leader as facilitator. The autocracy of leadership was disestablished to person rather than position as the various gifts were called based on their (demand nature) within their interacting." (Par. 4 above) *Mirabile dictu*: an organization acting what it means.

During all this time, we continued to read within our basic text and cooperatively discover what we were talking about. Individuals, while remaining true to an ongoing theory of gestalt psychotherapy, developed special emphases: somatic, group, and significantly what had always been true in New York, the arts, music, fine art, dance, theater. Further, we organized a third Wednesday of the month meeting to process in action what had been the formal first Wednesday regular meeting. The first Wednesday meeting has been going on for fifty years. We are all proud of that.

After a year of planning, the Institute presented a conference in 1991 at the Roosevelt Hotel. It was designed to demonstrate what has come to be known as the New York Model which developed out of organizational work I had developed beginning in the late Fifties and early Sixties at

Columbia, the late Sixties and early Seventies at New York University, and with Amtrak in the early Eighties.

As in paragraph 5 above, the model brought the large group of conferees together, developed task or interest groups, and introduced the novelty of "process" groups, seen as the "self" of the conference, to work on their own group process apart from the task groups. All these entities were mutually and reciprocally interactive and supportive. Two hundred and fifty people attended. That was the size of the last or plenary group, perhaps the first time a plenary group was ever done. This model has now been adopted all over the world and it is unthinkable to conference without some possibility of process grouping.

Within that period under the presidency of Joe Lay, we began quite formal and serious presentations that were documented, recorded and now exist as potential publications in the archives of the Institute. Logically growing out of that effort was the notion that we should reach out to other disciplines to counter perhaps, a parochial self-congratulatory smugness. We invited leaders from science, social, theater, to present at our monthly meetings. We learned a lot, forgot much, and returned to the task that presented itself, a revision of gestalt therapy theory as we knew it and a revisiting of its bases, a phase we are finally formalizing. This was the foundation for our Fiftieth Anniversary Conference in 2003.

Finally, the Italian Gestalt Institute reached out to us in New York and we now have close relations with that organization. Margherita Spagnuolo Lobb and Giovanni Salonia have been here and many of us have visited Italy in a rewarding cross-fertilization.

Es ist genug.

The Ecology of Contact Seminar

2007

"Contact" may be the most widely regarded word used in gestalt therapy. It may also be the least examined. A rounder view of it seems imperative and that is what I propose to do in this venture.

"Contacting at the boundary in the organism/environment field," is perhaps the friendliest sentence in gestalt therapy, having achieved the status of a mantra. It has several theories mixed within it. For example, the basic notions derived from gestalt psychology — the figure/ground (parts and wholes) and the movement, indeed the propulsion, towards closure. They are modeled from the perceptual experiments of gestalt psychology, including the field notions of Kurt Lewin.

Can they be transferred from one to the other? Or are they cobbled unaware from an inevitable *deus ex machina*? Or better: proceeding from the plan of *Perls, Hefferline and Goodman* (*PHG*, pp. 236) contact is intended to heal the basic neurotic dichotomies of theory as the following:

- Body/Mind

- Self/External World

- Emotional (subjective)/ Real (objective)

- Infantile/Mature

439

- Biological/Cultural

- Poetry/Prose

- Spontaneous/Deliberate

- Personal/Social

- Love/Aggression

- Unconscious/Conscious

It is touching, indeed, somewhat quaint, that these names now seem so completely old-fashioned, and even antique, when we have about us such formidable correlatives as:

- Subjectivity/Facticity

- Intersubjectivity/Intentionality

- Originary/Historic

- Mirroring/*Meconnaissance*

- System/Process

- And don't forget, Self/Other, and so on and so forth.

The method of my discussion here will be to subject the above to a contextual method of argument. Synonymously, this will become a "gestalt analysis," or later, will morph, or perhaps develop into a field analysis, the method itself requiring just such an analysis. But first, is this, the "cobbling" I referred to above? — to offer just such work, first more closely describing just these analytic tools. (Concepts are tools; they must be applied?)

This takes us to "will," of course; if the tools must be inhabited, worked, applied, it is clearly a volitional phenomenon. At last, we can approach more tightly, one of my more fortunate locutions, namely, *doing theory*. Perhaps, in doing so, we have innocently healed the so-called theory/practice split minus the *Spitzfindigkeit*. Thus, my over-riding effort of this lecture/workshop is to approach more closely and endearingly, the foundational *Denken* of gestalt therapy.

The term "ecology" is chosen to give force and structure to such an approach; to limn the combinations and permutations that have accumulated and freighted those original thoughts; to otherwise enlighten those gathering shadows, and to offer more complete and firmer bases for them. There are many aspects to ecology. As an introductory metaphor and guide, the insights and fundaments of geology will be used. We may speak of the geology of teaching/learning within the strata of contact.

In the preliminary notes for an opera of this *Ecology of Contact* seminar, we must start with the overture to *Excitement and Growth in the Human Personality*, *(PHG)*. This is sounded in my ears like a harmonious, yet eerily quiet resonance of the brasses in the orchestra. Here is the opening line in the chapter, *The Structure of Growth*, within the section on the contact-boundary:

> "Experience occurs at the boundary between the organism and its environment, primarily the skin surface and the other organs of sensory and motor response." (*PHG*, 1994. pp. 3)

And in the oval field of vision ("the seeing of your eyes"):

> "Notice, then, how in this oval field, the objects begin to have aesthetic relations of space and color-value. And so you may experience it with sounds "out there": their root of reality is at the boundary of contact." (*PHG*, 1994. pp. 4)

So let me propose some experiments for us to do here.

Experiment I:
Removing our shoes, we will experience the floor in foot-touch. This is the ground on which we stand; that which George Herbert Mead calls our stance or attitude. We should close our eyes for this primary experience.

Having touched our ground as fully as possible for now, let us try to see with our feet, thus repeat, in experiment the instruction from gestalt therapy in the paragraph above: "Notice, then, how in this oval field, etc."

What do you notice in this second "noticing?" We can suggest topics for discussion: aesthetic relations, space and color value, "out there" (their root or foot foundation?) of reality. Finally, what you would call *your* boundary experience now?

Further, and heralding the depth of meaning that characterizes the theory, but almost shamefully sliding it in:

> Now the purpose of all the practical experiments and theoretical discussions in this book is to analyze the function of contacting and to *heighten awareness of reality* (My italics). We use the word "contact" — "in touch with" — objects as underlying both sensory awareness and motor behavior. This states the interaction at the boundary in the organism/environment field. And this states reality:

> "Contact" is awareness of the field or motor response in the field. It is for this reason that contacting, the functioning of the mere boundary of the organism can nevertheless, pretend to tell reality…every kind of living relation that occurs at the boundary in the interaction of the organism and environment. (*PHG*, 1994, pp. 6)

There is earlier provenance for gestalt therapy's definition of contact/reality: "In touch touching." But what is touch? In *Book II:* Ch. 2 of Aristotle's *De Anima* we have:

The primary form of sense is touch, which belongs to all animals. Just as the power of self-nutrition can be isolated from touch and sensation generally, so touch can be isolated from all other forms of sense. (By the power of self-nutrition we mean that departmental power of the soul which is common to plants and animals: all animals whatsoever are observed to have the sense of touch)...Soul is the source of these phenomena and is characterized by them, viz. By the powers of self-nutrition, sensation, thinking, and motivity...for where there is sensation, there is also pleasure and pain, and, where these are, necessarily, there is also desire.

...If any order of living things has the sensory, it must also have the appetitive; for appetitive is the genus of which desire, passion, and wish are the species; now all animals have one sense at least, touch. Whatever has a sense has the capacity for pleasure and pain and therefore has pleasant and painful objects present to it, and wherever these are present, there is desire, for desire is just appetition of what is pleasant. Further, all animals have the sense for food (for touch is the sense for food); the food of all living things consists of what is dry, moist, hot, cold, and these are the qualities apprehended by touch only indirectly... All animals that possess the sense of touch have also appetition.

The matter is of extreme importance for Paul Goodman and if we fast forward to the chapter of Perls et al., *Verbalizing and Poetry* speaking of the effort to reform language without reference outside the ongoing processes:

...If it is once understood, as should be obvious, that feelings are not isolated impulses but structured evidence *of reality*, namely, of the interaction of the organism/environment field for which there is no other direct evidence except feeling; and further, that a complicated creative achieving is even stronger

> evidence *of reality*...then every contactful speech is meaningful.
> (*PHG*, pp. 111)

His concern here is to establish "contact" as a marker and essential for reality, its nature and the level of reality, whatever the "level" of reality can mean. What is reality is a problematic of philosophy for centuries and it is clear that "being real" is central to any process of psychotherapy. Various powerful thinkers have addressed it in varying terms. For example, and roughly, reality can be characterized by system. We have systems theory as our guide in therapy as in the Cleveland School of gestalt therapy. They speak of the internal, external, and group systems. But let us take a more formidable protagonist:

> By architectonic, I understand the art of constructing systems. As systematical unity is that which raises common knowledge to the dignity of science, and changes a mere aggregate of knowledge into a system, it is easy to see that architectonic is the doctrine of what is really scientific in our knowledge, and forms, therefore, a necessary part of the doctrine of method.

As Professor Kant develops his notion of reality and the unity of knowledge from a "mere aggregate of knowledge" and builds to a system, we understand why the chapter is titled, *The Architectonic of Pure Reason*. He is affecting an edifice of knowledge and needs the architecture to plan it from his schema, his plan.

> Under the sway of reason, our knowledge must not remain a rhapsody (the "aggregate", RK) but must become a system, because thus alone can the essential objects of reason be supported and advanced. By system, I mean the unity of various kinds of knowledge under one idea. This is the concept given by reason of the form of the whole in which both the extent of its manifold contents and the place belonging to each part are determined *a priori*. This scientific concept of reason contains therefore, the end, also the form of the whole which is congruent with it.

And then in a surprising *volta face* (turn-about), surprising because one expects him to be supportive positively, he uses the beam of a negative in the unity of the structure to move his schema along. The unity of the end to which all parties relate and through the ideas which are related to each other, enables us to miss any part, if we possess a knowledge of the rest and prevents any arbitrary additions or vagueness or perfection of which the limits could not be determined *a priori*.

Thus, the whole is articulated (*articulatio*), not aggregated (*conservatio*). It may grow internally (*per intus susceptionem*), but not externally (*per appositionem*), like an animal body the growth of which does not add any new member, but, without changing their proportion, renders each stronger and more efficient for its purposes.

We see in the above, the clear and distinct statement of what becomes a central tenet of gestalt psychology, namely, the tendency to completion of the incomplete, finish the unfinished and its propulsive force provided only and imperatively as in the schema, that the whole is already apperceived. We will return to the above when we reach a fuller discussion of George Herbert Mead here for "resistance" and "multiplying surfaces."

We are talking of nothing less than the nature of reality, its level in depth and height with its criteria as awareness and level of contact. However, instead of tunneling through the mountain of philosophy let us take a longer cut from *The Critique of Pure Reason* as the good philosopher of Könisgsberg warns us of the perils and snares of shallow philosophy: If I take no account of the contents of knowledge, objectively considered, all knowledge is, from a subjective point of view, either historical or rational. Historical knowledge is *cognitio ex datis*, (from the data) rational knowledge *cognitio ex principis* (from the principles).

Whatever may be the first origin of some branch of knowledge, it is always historical, if he who possesses it knows only so much of it as had been given to him from outside, whether through immediate experience, or through narration, or by instruction also (in general knowledge).

Hence, a person who in the usual sense has *learned* a system of philosophy, for instance, the *Wolfian*, though he may carry in his head all the principles, definitions, and proofs, as well as the division of the whole system, and have it all at his fingers' ends, possesses yet none but a complete historical knowledge of the *Wolfian* philosophy. His knowledge and judgments are no more than what has been given him. If you dispute any definition, he does not know whence to take another, because he formed his own on the reason of another.

But the imitative is not the productive faculty, that is, knowledge in his case, did not come from reason, and though objectively, it is rational knowledge, subjectively, it is historical only. He has taken and kept, that is, he has well learned and has become a plaster cast of a living man. Knowledge, which is rational objectively (that is, which can arise originally only from a man's own reason), can then only be so called subjectively also, when they have been drawn from the general resources of reason, from which criticism, nay even the rejection of what has been learnt, may arise.

> ...Till the image, which has so often proved a failure, has become like the original type as human power can ever make it ...Till then we cannot learn philosophy, for where is it, who possess it, and how shall we know it. We can only learn to philosophize, that is, to exercise the talent of reason, according to the general principles, on certain given experiments, however, with the reservation of the right of reason of investigating the sources of these principles, and of either accepting or rejecting them, (Immanuel Kant's *Critique of Pure Reason*, Second Part, F. Max Müller's translation, London, Macmillan and Co., 1881, pp. 714 & 719)

But let us first take the notion of field, which paradoxically, in these modern times seems to have been rediscovered as a trenchant component of therapeutic doctrine. It is hard to theorize a sense of field. We would find it necessary to get outside it to another field to treat it and that would bring us to ontology prematurely. We will later call that the "field of being." But staying with ecology, which is presumably more workable. What as an introduction does *PHG* tells us:

> Every contacting act is a whole of awareness, motor response, and feeling, a cooperation of the sensory, muscular, and vegetative systems, and contacting occurs at the surface-boundary in the field of the organism/environment. (*PHG*, pp. 34)

> We say it in this odd way, rather than "at the boundary between the organism and the environment, because … the definition of an animal involves its environment. It is meaningless to define a breather without air, a walker without gravity and ground, an irascible without obstacles, and so on for every animal function.

> The definition of an organism is the definition of an organism/environment field; and the contact-boundary is, so to speak, the specific organ of awareness of the novel situation of the field, as contrasted, for instance, with the more internal "organic" organs of metabolism or circulation that function conservatively without the need of awareness, deliberateness, selection or avoidance of novelty. (*PHG*, pp. 35)

Notice in the foregoing, that "animal" and "organism" are distinguished presumably because the former more closely, perhaps exclusively, involves the environment, while organism involves the "specific organ of awareness of the novel situation of the field, the contact-boundary." The foregoing launches Goodman to a treatment of consciousness, the functional nature of it and the quality of interaction at the boundary.

Simple, easy, lessened "awareness, reflection … motor adjustment, and deliberateness; but where it is difficult and complicated, there is heightened consciousness." (*PHG*, pp. 35) Notice in the above two linkages: 1) awareness as more than vaguely synonymous with consciousness, and 2) the difficult/complicated constellation of "heightened consciousness."

Moreover, this is attributed to William James who meant, of course, "the interrupted reflex-arc," which is attributed to the "result of a delaying of the interaction at the boundary." Again, notice that we have synonymity, peculiarly: a) reflex (arc)/interaction at the boundary in the organism/environment field which b) is foundational in the theory of contact.

I use the word "peculiarity" because this is not my reading of James and consciousness at all. I think for his purposes in explicating a simpler theory, perhaps an easier theory of contact, Paul stirred up a dust storm, dervishes and all.

From his own words in *Five Years*, we have (one of my favorites): "Life is not complicated and hard; life is simple and hard," which seems to amplify and at the same time deny Goodman's facile analysis in the service of his theorizing.

Further, that, "(E)very contacting act is a whole of awareness, motor response, and feeling, a cooperation of the sensory, muscular, and vegetative systems, and contacting occurs at the surface in the field of the organism/environment.") is not tenable. Although the reference turns on the meaning of "between," which is the "peculiarity" as in the boundary between the organism and environment on which he is establishing his field foundation, I think it obscures more than it funds.

Perhaps, "every contacting acting" is a whole, etc. etc., and would be closer to the bone. But to make these *aporiae* (gaps) in a section in which he discusses in a parenthesis, the "verbal embarrassments that are deep in our language," is *de trop,* that is too much).

Moreover, Dewey had settled the matter authoritatively in his 1896 discussion of the reflex arc. He points to the arc as an arbitrary cut in what is a complete circuit. Even as arc, it could not be selected in the first place were it not for its position in the whole configuration. This was a major contribution to the Decennial papers of the University of Chicago where Goodman was to study some forty years later. We may fairly conclude this is at least an irony. Goodman's exposition of James and consciousness is simply wrong.

In the great *Does Consciousness Exist?* (1904), James made the specific statement that it does indeed exist, not as an entity but as a function! The function of consciousness *is* knowing. As Mead later is to affirm, the etymology of consciousness is a "knowing together" which gives the social mill more grist to grind.

On this basis, James put to rest the centuries old bifurcation of nature: mind/matter, *res extensa/res cogitans*, perception/thought that had bedeviled philosophy. It was this that led Alfred North Whitehead in *Science and the Modern World* to christen William James, "that adorable genius."

Of course, again a further irony is from the beginning, the gestalt definition of neurosis was based on the splits or bifurcations which gestalt therapy was designed to heal. The further irony is Goodman's comment above that James meant consciousness as a result of delaying in the interruption of the reflex-arc, but let us here move in a gestalt theory.

We left touch in spite of its crucial nature in a theory of contact with many points still untouched. To recall, we spoke of foot-touch and visual touch. But as a segue and for further development, let us go to:

Experiment II:

1. Rub gently, touch together your thumb and forefinger of each hand, noting your observations

2. Do the same thing with first one hand on the other, then the other on the one. Is there a difference(s)? Remember to put eyes in your fingers. Do you now see more than you *see?*

3. Reach out and touch, take the hand of your neighbor. Note your sensations and now your feelings, if you can stand them.

This will be a very intensive experience for some involving even the digestive process. It *is* a digestive process. Touch, we begin to see, is constitutive of assimilation and accommodation that was pointed out in the previous reference of *De Anima*. Parenthetically, we see the seeds of the theory of dental aggression of Frederick Perls, which you will remember, Paul Goodman ascribed as Perls' only "original contribution" to psychotherapy theory.

In another parenthesis, we should treat assimilation more closely, of which Aristotle wrote, "the unlike is made like." I think we need some partitive language here, perhaps, the *"somewhat* unlike is made *somewhat* like."

It is possible that a theory of accommodation is a more productive notion in that we could conceive of novel accumulations and thus conserve the rejected constituents, yet not as mere introjections.

Further, then the partial structures of contact become richer, and the stages of contact in the famous page 403 of the 1951 *PHG* emerge not as "interruptions of contact," but as creative *pauses* in the accommodation of pregnant and constitutive negatives. In this sense then, "the interruptions to contact" apprehend a sterile notion. My hunch is that the question, "How are interruptions to contact possible?" is fruitful and generative of clinical theory and practice, the neglect of which can lead to an absolutistic energetic theory of human life. Perls himself, in 1969, spoke of the "physical aspect" as foundational, even ontological, although I cannot remember any instance of the word "ontology" passing his lips.

At this point, you will have already conjured that we are developing a notion of touch as foundational in the theory of contact which will lead to further consequences in the field we call gestalt therapy. We are doing it for ourselves from our own experimenting, thus de-structuring, or better destroying, Kant's caricature of the well-learned (from history) as plaster casts. Continuing therefore with:

Experiment III

Put your hands together and feel the mutual pressures of one against the other. Press stronger and less so, alternately, then simultaneously. Can you sense how one hand anticipates the resistance of the other? What does that mean to you? What is the mechanism of this form of contact-action?

We will return to this shortly. First, however, it is perhaps sleeker if we go to other authorities for their research. Can we begin to think of ourselves as experts in touch from our own research as we *do* theory? So in what we may call the epistemological approach, we have:

Movement and Touch

Perhaps the most important recent contribution to the problem of how touch mediates awareness of its objects was made by David Katz in *Der Aufbau der Tastwelt*. Summarizing Katz's conclusions, Merleau-Ponty expresses the crux of the matter as being that, "the movement of one's body is to touch what lighting is to vision...When one of my hands touches the other, the hand that moves functions as subject and the other as object. There are tactile phenomena, alleged tactile qualities, like roughness and smoothness, which disappear completely if the exploratory movement is eliminated.

Movement and time are not only an objective condition of knowing touch, but a phenomenal (!—RK) component of tactile data. They bring about the patterning of tactile phenomena, just as light shows up the configuration of a visible surface. (*The Encyclopedia of Philosophy*,

1967, Vol. 8, pp. 151, Crowell Collier and Macmillan). The citations to Merleau-Ponty and David Katz are in the bibliography of that article.

So we have here the research of gestalt psychologist David Katz and the father of existential phenomenology, Maurice Merleau-Ponty, from his *Phenomenology of Perception*. Taking ourselves seriously as original researchers, what are our findings in comparison to Katz and Merleau-Ponty? For myself, just the doctrine that one hand is subject and the other object, is already a confabulation abstracted from the spectator theory of knowledge directly from Descartes' *Meditations*. It is of the order of another brick placed in the wall of the building block universe and of a piece with mind/body, subject/object, empiricism/rationalism, and so forth and so forth.

Experiment IV
Place your left hand over your right; make various movements to feel your right hand. Repeat the process with your right hand on your left. Note your findings. At what point does the difference disappear? Can you get the rhythm of the pulsations of unity? The chiasm is a term from classical rhetoric. It refers to parallel sentences in which the second reverses the terms of the first and there is one. Classical examples abound in Shakespeare, especially in the sonnets and in popular culture, e.g., in baseball, "When the going gets tough, the tough get going."

Less obvious (in the style of George Herbert Mead), is the self finds the other; and so the other becomes itself. In our example of one hand on the other, we found the reciprocal and mutual activity of the organism-environment interaction in its logico/empirical function of life. Thus, our experiment takes us to the *chiasm of mutuality*, the developed awareness of the activity of resistance *within the activity*. And so, we build up/out reality from the inside where we have summoned the resistance of life to being. That is, instead of locating figure in the surfaces of objects that only accumulates more lines and angles, i.e. geometry, we have put the insides to things and so respond to their response in another chiasm. This analysis is direct from Mead and his description of the developmental activity from birth and infancy of the action of one hand on the other and the unity of the central nervous system.

That activity is coeval with the development of sound and vocal gesture in, let us say, the language behavior in the co-imitative function where they, in another chiasm, learn to take the role of the other, to play, to learn the rules of the game in the role of the generalized other. This is, of course, to say that the self has learned from itself to be in every role at once and thus, the problem of the unity of the many and the one is solved in a perspectival theory, from the attitude of one's stance, at once individual and co-objective/subjective.

At this point, we will pause in genuflection to Immanuel Kant and reaffirm his note from page 5:

> Thus the whole is articulated (*articulatio*), not aggregated (*conservatio*). It may grow internally, (*per intus susceptionem*), but not externally (*per appositionem*), like an animal body, the growth of which does not add any new member, but without changing their proportion, renders each stronger and more efficient for its purposes.

I would add in a tentative supplement the substitution of "organ" for "member" which would make the objects of intentionality even more inclusive in their emphasis. In short, the "inexistence" in "intentional inexistence" is non-existent. To return to chiasm and Merleau-Ponty and thereby return to our founding notion of contact, within the unifying activity/concept of touch, we earlier spoke of Merleau-Ponty as the "father" of existential phenomenology.

You will remember that Husserl originally took up the notion of pre-suppositionless consciousness and through the "Copernican revolution or conversion" from the transcendental reduction to the *epoché* and bracketing, proceeded to wrest the Cartesian *cogito* from its perch as the be-all and end-all where Descartes had placed it (Hence, his title as *Cartesian Meditations*). Instead of working through the scope of the *cogito* consciousness to reality, he proceeded to empty consciousness of its presuppositions and tacit prejudices. Proceeding on this bedrock, he made this new approach to philosophy.

To put it another way, the safe and secure ego of the *cogito* was threatened. The threat came from the world that *The Meditations* tried to shut out and we were left with an ego with nothing to relate to. So the *cogito* and the doubting promised much but were able to deliver little except more of itself.

But consciousness is always of something, about something and the world was still there and would not be shut out. And "intentionality" remained as that process whereby objects were referred by the active egology. It was the area that both the philosophy and the psychology share:

> ...(H)e stressed the need to abandon the "old mistrust," (still controlling even the author of the *Logical Investigations of Psychic and Egological Reality*). This done, one could examine the remarkable relationship between phenomenological and psychology ontology which permits the former to find its place in the latter and again, in a certain manner, also permits the latter, like all ontological disciplines, to find a place in the former. (Maurice Merleau-Ponty: *Between Phenomenology and Structuralism.* James Schmidt, 1985, St. Martin's Press, New York. pp. 31).

There is the *chiasm* with the parallelism in the psychology and the phenomenology that opened up and through which Merleau-Ponty crawled to bring them into the world. As rough synonyms, read; "object" > "body" > "flesh" > "incarnate" > "world." It is to these the targets of intentionality that cements the parallelism above and aims its propulsion or its teleology. I will maintain that the gestalt therapy concept of contact is a species within the genus of intentionality and so seen, is a richer and more productive *Weltanschauung* than what I have come to believe is the murky and more restrictive notion and use of contact and its interruptions.

The notion of the centrality of the *chiasm* was introduced by Paul Valery in response to Sartre who had introduced his panoramic vision in which the interrelatedness of being and nothingness were opposed and "unambiguous." From that high altitude, it was possible to be blind to the "inherence of being in nothingness and of the nothingness in being." Sartre (who, by the way was wall-eyed) just didn't get it. He was still bound in the trap of the Cartesian *cogito* and its splits (Schmidt, pp. 90–91).

Before we leave these French philosophers, we should essay a summary of where we are within the ecology and the unifying activity of touch with which we started as the primary and the constitutive activity of contact: We began with the activity of touch personally, individually, subjectively. It immediately became intersubjective as we touched others; thus, it is social.

The two sides of this activity, 1) the subject/object, and 2) the unity in the chiasm were represented in Sartre and Merleau-Ponty respectively. Sartre was seen as the last of the Cartesians since his position reflected the *tacit cogito* and its spectator theory of perception and reality and the primacy of thought: "I think, therefore I am."

Husserl working his way toward a conversion from the Cartesian in his phenomenology, began with Descartes but never really worked out of it until his maturity when he realized that intentionality without real objects was a contradiction. We posited that rejecting a theory of contact (in touch, touching), we could perhaps include contact as a species of the genus of intentionality. This now, too, seems untenable and we are faced with the classical question: What are you going to replace it (contact) with?

Merleau-Ponty made the unification incarnate in the body which becomes the "agency" of the other. In the experience of the chiasm, he made his unity of reality. And so the contradictions disappear. Figure/ground, the demarcation of contour and modeling and the homogeneous ground emptying into the figure as the drivenness of unfinished business morphs into an analysis of the lines about which the object rotates rather than oscillates.

Thus, that analysis is process unification and one speaks of "hinges" and process interrogation. The classical example of the rabbit-duck-rabbit-duck oscillation is rather an example of something going on in the universe that requires some *interested regard* rather than elements/part/whole/more-and-different-and-greater-than/the-sum-of-its-parts and the great Unfinished.

But let us return to a further analysis of the chiasm that became central for Merleau-Ponty in his re-examination and rejection of Sartre. In much the way we have been using touch, Valery included vision in the famous *regard d'autrui*, the look of the other, and the "crossing" of the gazes. We should also speak of the "crossing of the touchings" in our earlier researches of fingers and hands, that is, self and other.

The word *chiasm* denotes an X shaped figure (notice the crossing) which is ubiquitous in nature and the world and in its shape, both includes itself and cancels its members. We have it in "X marks the spot," as in "Put your X here (signature)," Railroad crossings ("Do not cross when red lights are flashing") and anatomically, and interpersonally. (Valery's) use of the term *chiasm* — a word that denoted X-shaped configurations of the sort frequently encountered in anatomy (for example, the interweaving of optic nerves) and by extension referred to all those interweavings, reciprocal interpenetrations, and crossings that Merleau-Ponty had sought to evoke through his use of rhetorical *chiasmata* — suggested an alternative to Sartre's panoramic vision (Schmidt, pp. 91).

We should not lose sight of the topic of our meeting. We are concerned with gestalt therapy, and in Isadore From's famous query: "Now just what has all this to do with gestalt therapy?" We should be concerned with the central role of intentionality as we are developing it as we re-examine and re-analyze in its ecology, the diminished role of contact and its interruptions in our clinical work.

Anne Teachworth in her work on the social psychology of interpersonal choice has given us an outstanding example of "why" we choose the people we do as mates, lovers, friends/enemies and exes — all of the above. It seems that she has determined and can predict those factors of the "why." In her presentation I attended, I thought what she was saying was all the choice factors were there in both parties, like eggs being brooded by malevolent fowls. And when the chiasmus, I-in-you/you-in-me, hatched its malevolent chicks, it was obvious that those individual eggs had been lying in wait to cross themselves in an X. We have it in "star-crossed lovers" and "double-crossed" and "crossing (someone) up" and on and on.

There is, of course, the famous illustration of Leonardo's nude circumscribed, legs spread and arms aloft touching everywhere the circumference of the wheel to which he is bound. Is this the wheel of life? The visual chiasm is obvious in the crossed X of arms and legs.

Again clinically, we have the work of Ruella Frank as she works out the neural and developmental chiasms that accompany us through life and that require a more muscular disentanglement in the process of gestalt psychotherapy.

My work in group has always had a geometric fascination for me as the members work out their logic of disentanglement. The even more interesting nodal point is that these chiasms are underneath, or as Paul Weisz was wont to say, "overneath."

Thus, in a large sense, the group members at first don't know what they are doing and much of that work is centered (X'd) around premature pacification *within* the false conflict of objects in the foreground. The real conflict in the background is the wish to remain uncrossed, to maintain the mask, to be torn apart in the great unwantedness.

Here again, is the task of psychotherapy: to maintain the two *foci* of apparent foreground and background as the mills of God grind slow, but exceeding fine. In Merleau-Ponty's elegant rhetoric, the work is to disentangle the chiasm and so arrive at awareness of the thrust of unity from the inside; just so, the task of psychotherapy. In the gravely, funebral, defiant and heartbreaking tones of Johnny Cash, the master, "We walk the line." In the *chiasm*, the line walks us.

Experiment V

Let five or six or so choose *yourselves* into a fish bowl group. Can you let yourselves be so the entanglements on the surface of the group and interpersonal chiasms can float to the top where they can become aware in their mutuality and so be welcomed? I should have said, "addressed" but I mean it in the Eighteenth Century sense of quality of presentness.

Can you and we in you, and you in we, bracket the urge to come to the points of crossing and overcome the tyranny of the figure in its determination of the process toward contact?

BREATHE.

We have a direct example in my instruction above where the second "we" is not grammatical. Since the preposition "in" precedes it, the pronoun would be "us." I actually hesitated in the servitude and slavery of the Rule. But obviously, it does not work as a chiasm (it tears it apart) and is ridiculously pedantic. It is ridiculous, period.

So again emphasizing ourselves as originary authorities in the first ever (?) seminar on the *Ecology of Contact*, let us abandon the rule and flee to the comfort of the great pragmatic imperative of action founded on meaning and ultimately, Truth.

The term "pragmatism" was adapted from Kant by C. S. Peirce. Kant had distinguished the practical — relating to the will and action — from the pragmatic — relating to consequences. Peirce derived a theory of meaning from this idea. The criterion of meaning was the pragmatic maxim: "Consider what effects that might conceivably have practical bearings, we conceive the object of our conception to have. Then, our conception of these effects is the whole of our conception of the object." He made this theory of meaning central to his philosophy. (W. L. Reese, *Dictionary of Philosophy and Religious Thought*. 1980. Humanities Press Inc. Atlantic Highlands, NJ, pp. 453).

The extension to truth is from William James: Since the criterion can exclude false hypotheses, truth from meaning becomes obvious. Let us make a new beginning with "in touch touching"; and let us use as our touchstone the work of George Herbert Mead (1863–1931) in Chicago in the first fifth of the Nineteenth Century. And further, our emphasis will be on his *Philosophy of the Act*.

In this seminal work, Mead worked out the basis and implications of the act itself as the unit of reality. Its basis is a transformation of the developing process of the act as *impulse; perception; manipulation; consummation.* Further, an astonishing restatement of the self within a theory of touch/touching developing from infancy, based not only on the activity of one hand on the other, but also on the other gesture, the *vocal* gesture, in the social field of being in which the infant/parent organism generates itself and turns back on itself.

Mead opens his theory of the development of the self with the primitive act of touch. That is to say, with the action of one hand on the other. Since in the human organism, they are connected (X'd) in the central nervous system, what one hand experiences is simultaneously experienced in the other, there is quite obviously, "a putting of insides" into what may be called objects. Mead calls this resistance and it is central to his theory.

Experiment VI

You have already experimented with touch individual/social/world. Repeat with your two hands pushing one on the other. Feel your reciprocal resistances to your own pressures. Notice how finely tuned your adjustment can become so that very quickly, you can gauge the hand/ounces of energy you need to contact and resist.

Now turn to your neighbor and with palms up as in "patty cake," and approach the other's palms but do not touch. Stop at the point where you feel your co-resistances are in equilibrium. Estimate that distance and note it since it will be useful for us when we encounter what we may call "social distance." What do you *know* now that you didn't know before the experiment? What is knowledge in the light of the experiment?

With very little excogitation, we can come to a quantifiable experience of the phenomenon of empathy. Or to place it within the theory of the act and therefore the development of the self in "taking the role of the other," we get a firmer sense of the social nature of humankind. We are not alone! That said, what are the specific steps in the development?

We demonstrated the stages in the gestural workings of what became the individual/social hands. Mead introduced (after Wundt) the vocal gesture. At first, in the burblings of infant and parent and their *imitative* vocal gestures, we have the originary template of taking the role of the other. Co-developing is the child's play (think of Piaget's "soliloquy.") Finally, from *playing* all the roles, the child *learns* the rules of the game and from there arises its sense of the *generalized other*. Now we have the social embedded so to speak in the self/other/self *chiasm.*

Further, there is the stratum then of group therapy and what I have called a place on which to stand for modern gestalt therapy. Perhaps, I should say for modern gestalt group therapy theory. But if there is a creative taking of roles of the generalized other, we see the nexus of the social in the individual.

Indeed, as in the drama, a frequent and effective technique has been to separate the roles embodying them in different individuals and letting the "shit hit the fan." It has been said in the drama in the first act, you get them up the tree, in the second, have them thrashing about as the branches twist in the wind, and in the third, you get them down from the tree. So we get the psychology, the phenomenology, the society, the aesthetic…and gestalt therapy.

To return to the question of knowledge from the above experiment and what it means in terms of the "social dimension," let us go to the *The Philosophy of the Act* itself. In its *Introduction*, we have:

> …Knowledge is not contemplation of meaning or existence, but discovery of the unknown through hypotheses put to test of action in an unquestioned world of things. (pp. xv)

Please put that sentence in italics in your mind, and in your serendipitous wanderings, let its enormous weight press on your understanding. Continuing:

> This position would be acceptable only if experience itself had a social dimension, and that this is so is one of Mead's basic and most fruitful claims. He not only argues that observation never reveals the self of the observer on a different status than surrounding things or persons, but concentrates his efforts on showing how the subjective or mental appears within the common world as a *stage* of its reconstruction. (My italics)

The debates we have even now within the discussions of phenomenology, viz., subject/object, subjectivity, intersubjectivity, dissolve in a startling exegesis: The private, as opposed to the subjective, is that which belongs to the experience of the individual as such. The private is not subjective, since it belongs, as Mead says, to the world that is there, and, as a *polar concept*, the private has meaning only over against that which is common. (My italics)

Just as Mead began his matured social psychology with the social rather than with the individual act, so his cosmology and epistemology begin with an unquestioned world within which the subjective or psychical is set off as the mental or symbolical phase of the act, and the private is interpreted as that portion of experience which belongs to the individual as individual in contrast to that which is common.

To establish the provenance of this theory, we must recall what appears in a footnote to the second paragraph of this excerpt: This theory of the mental as the stage of the hypothetical reconstruction of the act is found in *The Definition of the Psychical*, University of Chicago Decennial Publication, III (1903), pp. 77–112, except that the concept of the act as social has not yet been developed (*Introduction*, pp. xvi).

The error shared by both the traditional rationalists and the empiricists resides in making ubiquitous the spheres of the private and the mental, to the neglect of the common and the unquestioned. When "experience" is used in the (C.I.) Lewis' sense, as including the given, plus interpretation or meaning, the doctrine that experience has both individual and social dimensions, implies that there are individual and social aspects of the given, of meaning, and of knowledge (*Introduction*, Charles W. Morris). The reference to C. I. Lewis is to his *Mind and the World Order*. New York: Dover Publications, 1929.

We recall Husserl in 1929 as he speaks of Descartes as the "Father of Phenomenology": Descartes had shown phenomenology the path it must follow:

> Anyone who seriously considers becoming a philosopher must once in his life withdraw into himself and then, from within, attempt to destroy and rebuild all previous learning (*Paris Lectures*).

Saint Augustine had urged (and Husserl quoted, in Latin); "Do not wish to go out; go back into yourself. Truth dwells in the inner man." (pp. 39). (Remember, we are always referring to the development of the social dimension in American philosophy at the turn of the Nineteenth Century).

Three decades later, (1960) in Geneva, Claude Levi-Strauss called on the city's native son for aid in exorcising the spell the patriarch of phenomenology had cast over the human sciences:

> To attain acceptance of oneself in others (the goal assigned to human knowledge by the ethnologist), one must first deny the self in oneself. To Rousseau, we owe the discovery of this principle, the only one on which to base the sciences of man. Yet, it was to remain inaccessible and incomprehensible as long as there reigned a philosophy which, taking the *cogito* as its point of departure, was imprisoned by the hypothetical evidences of the self. Descartes believed that one could proceed directly "from a man's interiority to the exteriority of the world"; he forgot that societies, civilizations — in other words, the worlds of men — place themselves between these two extremes. (Schmidt, pp. 14)

Having gone as far as we can go without starting to plow a dust bowl, we leave the intellectuals and *literati* to *The Deux Magots*, the apricot cocktails in Monparnasse, the Gauloised atmosphere and the popped Benzedrine, while we return to American pragmatism.

We have already introduced George Herbert Mead in his *Definition of the Psychical* of 1903, which contained the seeds of his mature theory of the act. He conceived of the stages of the act as impulse, perception, manipulation and consummation. For our purposes, we will consider impulse and manipulation, but first, the *Stages of the Act,* beginning with the stage of impulse and "sensitivity as a function of response."

All perception involves an immediate sensuous stimulation and an attitude toward this stimulation that is that of the reaction of the individual to the stimulation. Notice that the stimulation and the attitude are immediate. I did not at first, really get the import of this statement, but I now regard it as startling. One is so used to stimulus, then response, then even after knowing better, the stratum somehow maintains its foundational nature for us. Hence:

> This reaction, in so far as the perception does not go out into instantaneous overt activity, *appears in consciousness* only as an attitude, but as such, it is the first stage in the complete response or group of responses which the stimulation in question calls out. (pp. 3, My italics).

Furthermore, some imagery accompanies this attitude of the response, which is taken from past experiences in which the responses have been carried out, leading to the final experiences to which such a stimulation naturally leads. That is, a perception as such involves not only an attitude of response to the stimulation but also the imagery of the result of the response. A perception has in it, therefore, all the elements of an act — the stimulation, *the response represented by the attitude*, and the ultimate experience which follows upon the reaction, represented by the imagery arising out of past reactions. (My italics).

There then follows a long paragraph that emphasizes the "process of sensing itself as an activity," not merely, or rather simply, "from the standpoint of presentation, the presence of material." He reworks for a page, the field of sensitivity and the adjustment of the sensing and responding organs and the total body. The sensing of the object as so located that the organism takes a definite attitude toward it, *involving possible movement toward or away from the object, is thus apart of the process of perception.* (My italics, pp. 4) The perception by the hand is also one that involves (activity of considerable proportions) in the exploratory processes of hand and fingers and the movements of the skin.

So we have a restatement of our first experiments in touch. But let us suppose a clinical situation. The patient is excessively cerebral and worse, excessively verbal, and you the eager psychotherapist, who wants to help, feels his blood being drunk by the cupful. In your own mind, you want to try the experiment of one hand on the other or the finger and thumb activity. Your thinking of displacement is probably accurate but what is displaced and from where? That route looks like a dead end. But suppose the hand and finger experiments are done and we remain merely in the attitude of immediate sensuous stimulation? What happens?

Experiment VII

My hunch is as we try the experiment, we will find silence in the perception of the hand and for perhaps, even a nanosecond, the patient might find some peace, like still waters, and things can be different. What are *your* research findings in this experiment? In any case, returning to the area of attitude, I find this the geography (perhaps geology) of ontology, that area in which Gabriel Marcel and Maurice Merleau-Ponty found that containerless pond into which reality pours over as it generates itself.

Manipulation

Usually the perceptual act "goes off," so there is no experience of delay in the perception of the object. But there is a need for the object to be located and dated. In other words, the act/object must have a "here" and a "now." More completely stated, it must have a "here-and-there" and a "now-and-then." How to accomplish this while the process continues? Mead finds the mechanism for this process in the unique construction of the human hand and its capacity for offering and receiving resistance, perhaps for offering and receiving effort and its gestalt psychology experimentation.

Especially important is the crumbling talent that is the human correlate to particle theory, that is, any bit of matter can always be conceived smaller. In the event the process is inhibited, held in the human hand while it continues locating and dating, the act continues, yet pauses, in the manipulatory phrase. Clearly, there are levels of act that continue while others move at a different rate.

This takes us to the social dimension again and the place where one can be everyone with just a slight change in perspective so the experience remains objective. Perspectives are in the world. Thus, Mead's criticism of "phenomenalism" that it is too individual, too subjective, and so one finds oneself sinking into those "phenomenal (quick) sands." Here, too, gestalt therapy's theory of figure/ground is inadequate. When the "roads less traveled" are rejected, they "sink into the background." But that is a very rich and varied area, quite active differently, which later makes all the difference and needs closer examination and experimentation (like the "interruptions").

> It is just the character of human reflective experience that it is social, i.e., the individual regards his own perspective from the standpoint of others. If he so regards his own perspective, he must regard himself as well, for while within a perspective, the field is simply there for the individual and excludes the individual himself. He could not be both determining and determined.

> But if he can regard the perspective of another, he must enter into the other to reach his perspective, and yet, as it is another for him, he must be regarding the other as well. This must be equally true of his experience of his own perspective and of himself in the role of another or of others. We call this self-consciousness. (PA, pp. 202)

> A further requisite is that this commencing to act as the other does should become a value in carrying out the common act, so that planning a common undertaking arises. Through this type of social conduct, the individual becomes all the members of the group, and thus, in some sense, the group itself, over against the group perspective, but he does it by both entering the attitude of the other and finding himself in this attitude with its perspective within his own perspective.

> It is a deliberative attitude in which the individual indicates situations to himself by indicating them to others, insofar as he assumes the attitudes of the others as the result of his own gesture. It is a process by which he puts an inside into the other who is otherwise only a distant social object. (PA, pp. 204)

Experiment VIII
Goodbye and thank you.

The Experiment Phenomenology

2007

The first of this seminar series, *The Ecology of Contact,* introduced itself with the experiment of touching. It was the key to the unity of the act-as-process and introduced the notion of processive concreteness as the antidote to the misconception that so fluid a concept as process could provide any firm place on which to stand for praxis of psychotherapy. Alternatively, the famous and usual Paul Goodman theory of contact in gestalt therapy theory was absorbed in the pragmatic doctrine of the *Philosophy of the Act* of George Herbert Mead. Abandoning the usual stages of fore-contact; a) contact and b) final contact and post contact from *PHG,* we proposed the more rigorous stages: Impulse, Perception, Manipulation, Consummation, from Mead's four-stage theory.

We noted the sometimes eerie connection, perhaps influence, of Mead on the Goodman model, equally with total silence on that *aporia* and as developed subsequently in a paper that established the pragmatism of James, Dewey, Mead, as well-founded foundational thinkers for a modern gestalt therapy.

To escape the snares of the ambiguities so pronounced in *PHG,* many theoreticians have fled to the lure of phenomenology as the be-all and end-all of theory and the appearances of things; (obviously the phenomena) will be a standpoint from which to view the tapestry of gestalt therapy theory and praxis, fundamentally and proactively.

But phenomenology, whose? Phenomenology, when? Phenomenology, how? The famous Ws: Who? What? When? Where? Why?...cry out for examination and we have projected this effort as *The Experiment Phenomenology* as an earnest of the rigor above.

The phenomenon has been around since ancient days. Plato in *Book VII of the Republic* introduces the parable of the cave with the well-known prisoners bound to witness only their shadows projected on the facing wall of the cave. The shadows were projected from light backlit on them of which they were unaware. Hence, they were perceiving only the appearances on the wall-screen.

They were aware only of the phenomena until Socrates liberated one of them and brought him to the patch of light at the far end entrance to the cave. Where dazzled by the light, that is, reality, he was led by Socrates to renounce mere appearances and to turn always to the light. Actually, the dialogue is with the usual Socratic straight man in this case. "Dear Glaucon," who is led to the truths in the preceding sentences, perhaps perceptually: solidity, modeling, thickness, foreground/background, simplicity of the whole, in short the *prägnanz* of the classical gestalt psychologists, and in value: the preference for reality, truth, inquiry, casting probabilities, science and art, especially craftsmanship and philosophy, truth and reason.

Further, Socrates asks Glaucon if it would not be the case that once being habituated, through much discomfort, probably vertigo, to the light of the sun, the former prisoner would no longer be satisfied with the shadows of the ordinary commerce of life such as occurs in courtrooms and legislatures, the discourses of the Sophists who offered to teach anything for a fee, the lies of the politicians, the usual hypocrisies that get us through another lousy day? Would they not all be rejected in favor of the true light?

Glaucon replies that he most certainly would not be satisfied; and besides the Sophists sweat in a most disgusting manner. It would be obvious that the freedman should, and perhaps would, always look upward for the light.

EXPERIMENT I

Let us begin again with touch as in Goodman's "in touch, touching." Let your right hand clasp your left until you've "got it." Then let the left hand clasp the right. Try to experience the resistance of one on the other as you tentatively push and resist in the process of getting it. Can you feel the insides of things and all of what is you, putting your insides there? And that this is not an additive which would only multiply the surfaces, but that it is a living process? Further, can you sense that in the experiment, we may be close to the thing-in-itselfness that Kant said as *noumenon* cannot be experienced, but that impossibility can be acknowledged as a limit in the criticism of pure reason? Can you experience the unity of touch, perhaps your touch in the universe?

The *noumenon*, of course, is the logical imperative to the acknowledgment of the phenomenon, which is all that can be known. Clearly, with our prisoner we are moving towards the light. The light in the parable becomes the Good, which every thinking person will henceforth prefer to the comfort, warmth, darkness and thin-dimensioned shadows of the cave. This is the same light that Gabriel Marcel is to reach two and a half millennia later as he arrives at *disponibilite* or availability as his *summum bonum* in his existentialism.

But to continue with the development of phenomenology, let us return to Plato and the cave, remembering that he is here developing a theory of education leading to the governance of the state by the training of the future philosopher kings. On the march from the data to the chiefest thing, the student must be led to closer and higher levels eventually to purity, hence clarity, for example in Section 524 of *Book VII*:

> In inviting reconsideration of confused quality by the calculating reason whether each of things reported is one or two ...and if it appears to be two, each of the two is a distinct unit... and if then, each is one and both two, the very meaning of "two" is that the

soul will conceive them as distinct. For if they were not separable, it would not have been thinking of two, but of one. ("Right," says Glaucon).

Sight to see the great and the small, we say, not separated, but confounded. Is not that so?...and for the clarification of this, the intelligence is compelled to contemplate the great and small, not thus confounded, but as distinct entities, in the opposite way from sensation...and it is not in some such experience as this that the question first occurs to us? What in the world, then, is the great and small?...and this is the origin of the designation intelligible for the one, and visible for the other.

Of course, we are aiming at an example of the famous Husserlain reduction or *epoché* which is essentially modern phenomenology which everyone gabs about especially from the epistemological side with its analysis of definitions which doesn't lead to much beyond more confusion.

But some contradiction is always seen coincidentally with it (unity)...there would forthwith be need of something to judge between them...and thus the study of unity will be one of the studies that guide and convert the soul to the contemplation of true being.

The contemplation of true being ontology.

The state should induce those to enter upon that study of calculation and take hold of it, not as amateurs, but to follow it up until they attain to the contemplation of the nature of number, by pure thought, not for the purpose of buying and selling as if they were preparing to be merchants or hucksters...but for facilitating the conversion of the soul itself from the world of generation to essence and truth. (*Book VII*, 526, c)

The foregoing was from Edith Hamilton's and Huntington Cairns' Eds. (1961) *The Collected Dialogues of Plato, Bollingen Series LXXI;* Princeton University Press. Since the point we are making has to do with comparison and unity, let us see what the Victorian, Benjamin Jowett, tells us with more texture and authority. His *Dedication* is to his students at Balliol College, Oxford, in gratitude for their attachment and friendship during fifty years.

We are reflecting back on the concept of unity and to clarify it further, Socrates invites Glaucon to an experiment. Glaucon asks him to explain:

> I mean to say that objects of sense are of two kinds; some of them do not invite thought because the sense is an adequate judge of them; while in the case of other objects, sense is so untrustworthy that further enquire is imperatively demanded... When speaking of uninviting objects, I mean those which do not pass from one sensation to the opposite; inventing objects are those which do; in this latter case, the sense coming upon the object, whether at a distance or near, gives no more vivid idea of anything in particular then of its opposite.

> An illustration will make my meaning clearer...here are three fingers...a little finger, a second finger, and a middle finger... Each of them equally appears a finger, whether seen in the middle or at the extremity, whether white or black, or thick or thin, it makes no difference; a finger is a finger all the same.

> In these cases, a man is not compelled to ask of thought, the question what is a finger? For the sight never intimates to the mind that a finger is other that a finger...Hence, nothing invites or excites intelligence...In these cases, the soul summons to her aid calculation and intelligence, that she may see whether the several objects announced to her are one or two.

> If two, he asks if each is not one and different; and if each is one, and both are two, she will conceive the two as in a state of

> division, for if they were undivided they could only be conceived
> of as one...The eye certainly does see both small and great, but
> only in a confused manner; they were not distinguished...
> Whereas, the thinking mind intending to light up the chaos, was
> compelled to reverse the process, and look at small and great as
> separate and not confused. (*Book VII*, Sec. 524.)

This is our twenty-five-hundred-year old reduction which Husserl took
over to craft his Twentieth Century phenomenology, but from which we
have a lot to learn still. And apropos, there is a rather lengthy
commentary which belongs in this record, perhaps tangential but
nonetheless for its humane grace. Socrates calls on his old friend, now
the very much aged Cephalus, whom he has not seen for a long time and
has missed him:

> At my age, I can hardly get to the city, therefore, you should
> come oftener to the Piraeus. For let me tell you, that the more the
> pleasures of the body fade away, the greater to me is the pleasure
> and charm of conversation. There is nothing which for my part I
> like better, Cephalus, than conversing with aged men; for I
> regard them as travelers who have gone a journey which I, too,
> may have to go, and of whom I ought to inquire, whether the
> way is smooth and easy or rugged and difficult.
>
> And this is a question which I should like to ask of you who have
> arrived at that time which the poets call "the threshold of old
> age." Is life harder towards the end, or what reports do you give
> of it?

Cephalus recites the woes of his friends: diet restrictions, slights by
relations, and so forth and so of the many evils that their old age is the
cause:

> But to me, Socrates, these complainers seem to blame that which
> not really is at fault. For if old age were the cause, I, too, being
> old, and every other old man, would have felt as they do. But this

is not my own experience or that of others whom I have known. How well I remember the aged poet, Sophocles, in answer to the question, "How does love suit with old age, Sophocles? Are you still the man you were?" Edith Hamilton gives this as, "Your relation to Aphrodite."

Sophocles in an elegant put-down to the young snot:

"Peace," he replied, "most gladly have I escaped the thing of which you speak. I feel as if I had escaped from a mad and furious master." His words have often occurred to my mind since, and they seem as good to me now as at the time when he uttered them. For certainly, old age has a great sense of calm and freedom; when the passions relax their hold, then, as Sophocles says, "We're freed from the grasp not of one mad master only, but of many."

The truth is, Socrates, that these regrets, and also the complaints about relations, are to be attributed to the same cause, which is not old age, but men's characters and tempers; for he who is of a calm and happy nature, will hardly feel the press of age, but to him who is of an opposite disposition, your nature and age are equally a burden. (Jowett, 1892, Vol. I. pp. 592 sec. 328–329)

EXPERIMENT II

Developing our notion and process of touch as unity, can you turn to a neighbor and reach out to touch his or her hand but do not complete the act. STOP! There will be a distance between your reaching out hand and the other's. What is that distance and its palpability? Can you experience with clarity the frustration of your intention? I say "frustration" and "intention" to emphasize the strain side of the germ of Lewin's unfinished business.

One of the great discoveries of psychology was the intentionality of Brentano as a psychological fact available for study and experimentation. Although not physical, which would be a datum for the sensationalist psychologists, it was nonetheless objective. To cover the non-sense of intentionality, the expression "intentional inexistence" became the fig leaf obscuring the genitalia of generation. The analysis of intentionality led to a bottomless churning of the objectivity of phenomenology. However, remember William James: "No one ever experienced a single sensation." There you have a spurious unity.

It must be clear at this point in our discussion and more importantly in our experimenting, that we are talking about experimenting good old fashioned gestalt psychotherapy "Contact" in its vanilla incarnation harking to our first paragraph in this exegesis.

> Primordial experience is the experience where the body is revealed as an organ of perceiving and is implicated in the percept. To know what this revelation is, let us shift our attention from the thing constituted through the organ-function and relate it to the local sensations which the body bears.

> Here we come upon the psyche just at the point of the organ-function. The case of double contact is the most revelatory: as I touch my left hand with my right, my body appears twice, once as what explores and once as that which I explore. (Ricoeur, 1967, Husserl, *An Analysis of His Phenomenology*, Northwestern University Press, Evanston, IL)

I doubt that we can come upon the psyche just at the point of organ-function. I think the sentence is unintelligible. I further doubt that the body can appear twice, explore/exploree. I think we have demonstrated that in our experimenting so far; thus double contact cannot be demonstrated except as a very elaborate series of abstractions and a lot left over.

Ricoeur goes on to "interrogate the sensation of contact":

> It has a very remarkable dual function. (Only if first separated. RK) The same sensation "presents" the explored thing and

reveals the body. Every touch in the broad sense (superficial touch, pressure, warmth, cold, etc.) is open to two "apprehensions" (*Auffassung*) where two sorts of thinghood (*Dinglichkeit*) are constituted. The extension of the thing and localization of the sensation are elaborated by a kind of superimposition.

On one side, adumbrations are elaborated into a flowing sensual schema which in turn moves beyond itself into the identical object. On the other side, sensation announces its belonging to a psyche and simultaneously reveals my body as mine ... The first experience attests to the privileged position of touch in the constitution of the animate body. (Ricoeur, 1967, pp. 61)

EXPERIMENT III
Referring back to Experiments I and II, where we felt the unity in touch and our doing of it, certainly not a dual reaction, and with that unity, the further unity of one-and-the-other, can you experience the joy of doing theory in experimenting? Can you grasp with both hands the excitement of making a body of theory and that body is you and you with other? Can you breathe into the strength that is inherently yours to make what seems to be solely intellectual so intentional that you can stand on your own two feet, also in the shoes of the other? "And this," as Sylvia Crocker says, "is good science

Many professional philosophers gave up trying to understand Husserl. Charles Hartshorne could not understand the possibility of completely presuppositionlessness and "didn't know what he was talking about." One of Husserl's students describes his standing and lecturing while one hand flapped back and forth "like a watchmaker gone mad."

Morton White, Professor of Philosophy at Harvard, synopsizes:

But the point is that I can also be experienced and treated as the result of a phenomenological reduction just as an appearance of a cube can be. (By the way, the analogy is direct from *Plato's*

Cave.) It is just (!) a matter of concentrating on the subject, rather than on the cube.

But this, upon which one might concentrate, is what Husserl calls "psychical subjectivity" and therefore, is still a matter of mere empirical concern, of interest to phenomenological psychology. There is a deeper I, he says "which for want of language we can only call... 'I myself.'" This is transcendental phenomenology, i.e. philosophy. It is the hidden I to which the psychical I is present. It is the end product of the most stringent reduction of all, along with another product which Husserl calls "transcendental intersubjectivity" which this writer cannot understand well enough to expound — a fault he shares with philosophers older and wiser and more trained in bracketing.

Presumably, by examining the structures of these obscure things, we arrive at the most profound philosophical truths by "presuppositionless" methods. (White, Morton, 1955, *The Age of Analysis, Mentor Book*, The New American Library, New York. pp. 104)

Can this awareness aid in our turning from the quills and quiddities of the "this-was-a-first-position Husserlian" gust after essence and reduction, to an utterly presuppositionless attitude of beginning?

The dualism in function of contact in touch suffers from the same conundrum of the early classical gestalt psychologists, namely for the duality, they must first separate (unlike Plato) the parts and then point to the dual reaction. Yet, I think we have established experimentally with the bark on the unity we are striving for, especially as we see unity in the flux of adumbrations. Peirce speaks of imperceptible shadings one into the other of the adumbrations: "The creative abductions of scientific endeavors shade into perceptual judgments without any sharp line of demarcation between them." (Peirce quoted in

Rosenthal, S. B., 1986, *Speculative Pragmatism*, pp. 12, University of Massachusetts Press, Amherst.)

As Ricoeur says, "All of phenomenology is not Husserl, even though he is more or less its center." (Ricoeur, 1967, pp. 3)

> The merit of phenomenology is to have elevated the investigation of the appearing to the dignity of a science by the "reduction." But the merit of Kantianism is to have been able to coordinate the investigation with the limiting function of the in-itself and with the practical determination of the in-itself as freedom and as the totality of persons. Husserl did phenomenology, but Kant limited and founded it. (Ricoeur, 1967, pp. 201)

Before leaving Husserl and his phenomenology, let us briefly return to an earlier analysis from the *Cartesian Meditations*. Ricoeur points out that Descartes abandoned his conversion too soon. From the doubting, he went to the cogito, thence to thinking, thence to existence: *Cogito ergo sum*; I think, I am; *Je pense donc je suis*. An egology without ontology. But as they say, he there "seems to have hit bottom." And it goes to the essence of intentionality, "the consciousness of." Thus, the object and "objectivation."

He should have continued the conversion *cogito/est* to *sum/est*: I am/it is which states the truth of intentionality and its synonymity with phenomenology as implicating reality, or finally, I am; what is? Now we have an egology generated from the ego itself with ontology.

Before bridging to yet another strand in the tapestry of phenomenology and prior to further development of *The Experiment Phenomenology*, let us return to Experiment III and its commentary. There we seemed to rejoice in the freedom of unity in making and doing our reality in Act and in that unity, perhaps arriving at an originary beginning (if there is such a thing) as ground on which to stand and stride in the horizon.

However, the return to the context of everyday or "lived" experience is never a brute return, for, as Dewey continues, "We cannot achieve recovery of primitive naïveté. But there is attainable, a cultivated naïveté of eye, ear, and thought, one that can be acquired only through the discipline of severe thought." (Dewey, 1981, *Experience and Nature*, pp. 37, quoted in Rosenthal, S., 1986., pp. 11.)

Continuing with Rosenthal, as she speaks of the "creation of scientific meaning:"

...Such scientific creativity arises out of the matrix of ordinary experience, and in turn, refers back to this everyday ordinary "lived" experience. The objects of systematic scientific creativity gain their fullness of meaning from, and fuse their own meaning into, the matrix of ordinary experience.

Though the contents of an abstract scientific theory may be far removed from the qualitative aspects of primary experience, such contents are not the found structures of some "ultimate reality" but rather abstractions, the very possibility of which requires and is founded upon the lived qualitative experience of the scientists. As Mead observes, "Controlled senuous experience is the essential basis of all our science."

Further, the ultimate touchstone of reality is a piece of experience, found in an unanalyzed world...We can never retreat behind immediate experience to analyzed elements that constitute the ultimate reality of all immediate experience, for whatever breath of reality these elements possess has been breathed into them by some unanalyzed experience." In Dewey's terms, the refined products of scientific inquiry 'inherit their full content of meaning' within the context of actual experience. (Rosenthal, 1986, pp. 11)

This is the direction I want us to move within as we grapple in our Experiments, that we are doing science, the science of gestalt therapy theory in a *novum organon*. It is further, of course, my *apologia* as I approach the "the threshold of old age."

The literature of phenomenology is vast. In Louvain, the Husserl archive is of thirty thousand shorthand pieces of hand-written manuscript never published. For me, this is evidence of Husserl's patience and integrity to arrive at a true beginning, the "primordial experience," a doomed effort, but which neither did he feel he could leave off as a dedicated and trustworthy toiler in the epistemic/phenomenologic sands.

To his everlasting credit, he never fell into the relativistic trap of treating individual experiencing as that person's reality. That is the trap-too-often for psychotherapy and it dooms the patient to the famous "rhapsody of individual experiences." Further, to the interminable descriptions, perhaps, the soliloquy of those experiences in the transference. The patient is left with nothing of the unity of the ground on which to stand, of something solid she/he can get the teeth into.

Moreover, that something can be made a solid abstraction that the field can come to and that the patient can paste in his hat brim, as they say, and from time to time, consult it to witness his travails and triumphs as the horizon spreads and recedes before.

One is touched by the image of the senior Husserl, side-lined by the Nazis, which he had predicted as a general social consequence in his *Crisis of European Science*, even as his pupil, Heidegger, is rising in the party, quietly resting in his knowledge of the unity and his light which could never be taken away from him in the eye of eternity.

EXPERIMENT IV
We speak of horizons. Let us try to experience "horizoning." Look to your field of people, perhaps your group by now.

Can you experience them experiencing you as you experience them?

Quietly. Quietly.

Let one of each pairing stand.

Regard each one.

Can horizon be vertical?

Or do you notice a sudden hierarchical shift from the democracy of horizons to the positioning in verticality, perhaps Hegel's master/slave?

 Is it possible for you to witness the traversings and intersectings so to speak of your group as group, as well as individuals within it?

And the rhythms and sequence of that sequencing?

Above all, can you sense the unity and then the futility of language to express it?

And the suggestion of poetry and music and art to capture it?

And with it, the light and its creative silence?

Is this what we have been calling contact?

And rest?

Colloquium Speech:
The Cycle of Experience
Contrasted

2008

The phases of the Cycle of Experience are: Sensation/awareness, Energy/mobilization, Movement or action, Contact, Resolution/closure, and Withdrawal.

They are variously sequential as they interact with the Levels of System that are essential to the interpretations and interventions that the Cycle requires. Thus, in the system-based theory, attention is directed toward the: Intrapersonal level, Interpersonal level, Dyadic or subgroup level, and Group level.

The system levels are straight-forward and intuitively obvious. Clearly, the theory operates sequentially and within the famous unfinished business strait A>B>C>D. The attention and intervention are directed by the leader/therapist and the budding leadership, as in the "gatekeeper" of individuals, is subsumed to role theory. It is thus possible to develop a handbook of examples to apply to any level and in Huckabay's chapter in Nevis' *Gestalt Therapy Perspectives and Applications,* there are convenient tables to guide reference.

The New York Model

I ask you to direct your attention to our model which is bottom-up, rotating leadership, shifting group and small group nodes and modalities, and welcoming, for example, vulnerability, not as intra-psychic, (if there is such a thing), but as inclusive, *e pluribus unum.*

The model shifts attention to the Group as figure in figure/ground. This is the result of long maturation trying to resolve the frustrations I felt as Frederick Perls modeled individual therapy in a group context, very rarely, and towards the end using the members as projections for the then current member with whom he was working.

In a therapy that has as foundational: Contact, Context, Figure/ground, Leadership, Organism/environment field, Politics, Resistance, Sociality, and Structure (meaning), it becomes impossible to theorize without explicit attention to the group context within which it occurs.

The theorizing as experimental becomes therapy and the theory/practice false dichotomy is healed in an attitude of group contact in a new yet familiar holism, a new gestalt. We become trainees in psychotherapy. And clearly that attitude fosters the new awareness of leadership as community where central is the shedding of leadership to the group as the opportunities for power in the individual talents open to the various members, supported within the group. So the group becomes *sui generis* and the partial structures to which we give names are emergent of the process, temporary resting places of the processive concreteness.

This result did not bloom full blown from my head but with various opportunities as in faculty teaching. Typically, within the course content, interest clusters were manifest. These clusters became small groups that met during the class. The requirements were three: to be present; to do a group presentation; to do an individual paper arising out of their work in their group. Everybody got an A. As one student wrote me, "I never worked so hard in my life, and learned more."

With more experiences in differing venues, sub-group problem solvings emerged. Their necessity became clear directly from the logic of group as source and solution, and the logic of emergent leadership, the usual leadership becoming more and more background and perhaps housekeeping. The model fully matured about thirty years ago when I fell into an organizational situation willy-nilly.

Amtrack

A client who went from Post Office trucker to patient to student to Ph.D. to friend introduced me to the Vice-President directing passenger relations for the National Transportation Railroad. (I sat as an outside reader for his dissertation defense). The railroad was studying a proposal from a McKinsey-type organization for an employee survey: you know, survey and identify (accumulate); develop and implement; and so forth and so forth, conclude, file away.

I read the screed and met with the Vice-President in her corner office with her underlings. She regarded me and said: "Well?" I told her and them the proposal, was classical, well done, and outlined. The only problem was it would not work. "Why?" she said.

As per their $250,000 proposal and their schedules for their survey, they had allotted all of forty-six seconds for each employee interview. Mind you, the math was all there if anyone had half the wit that God gave the geese, and only they looked for it.

Well, she threw everybody out and we two were commanded to lunch, not in the company cafeteria. The windup was I was hired to do the work; the activity was to be entirely in house which delighted the Vice-President. She gagged on the outrageous *per diem* for which I had asked, hoping it would get me off the hook, but as you all know, when you control a budget, miracles can happen. After all, had I not just saved them a quarter of a million dollars?

I trained some regular workers in process sensitivity, who then went back to their home bases and trained others; set up the frame work of a company-wide conference, and some two hundred and eighty employees showed up in Washington, D.C., for two weeks of work in the conferring. It was exhausting, exhilarating, tremendous and a triumph.

The Contrast

Now, why have I gone through all this? When I tried to study the Cycle, I could detect very little that was that different from the Sequence of Contacting, but realized that there appeared crucial shifts in emphasis. The Cycle appeared leader-bound, or could be, depending on the actual (leader) work; the emphasis on the systems. While it was extremely comforting to one who could founder in the process morass, it could become mechanical, hence hypostatized, as the gears got shifted, Intra, Inter, Group. I felt very much the "Hutt! Hupp! Hipp!! Hawpp!" marching orders from my days as an infantry duty soldier in training in 1946. Hence, a protected and cemented authority hegemony scrolling "overneath," as Paul Weiss was wont to say. (If you examine his videos carefully, you will see the South African Army Captain Frederick S. Perls, M.D.)

Claire Stratford's Therapeutic Milieu

There is the very excellent chapter of Claire Stratford's, *Gestalt Thinking and the Therapeutic Milieu,* in which she stresses the focus on the environment as essential in any treatment process. The environment is the staff and the organization that is being staffed and also the population that is being serviced. Her example is the psychiatric hospital.

With their differing demand loyalties, the staff is squeezed by the institution and its politics; the institution is squeezed by government; the patients are squeezed by everybody. (These are, of course, the "systems.") The symptoms are well-directed, ambient confusion, underlying and pervasive "isometrics," as Nevis says, where the activities are contradicted by foundational but unexamined normative structures. The diagnosis is burnout.

> But more to our point, is training or rather learning how to think and do process and what is their optimum vehicle. "The larger craziness of our current culture do not support the maintenance of subsystems that behave with integrity. (pp. 350)

The ability to articulate and acknowledge what is sensed but not spoken, is as effective at a larger system level as at a personal level. The degree to which speaking the unspoken is supported at a general system level will allow individuals to begin to feel it in the air, and observe and experiment for themselves. *Speaking the unspeakable, articulating what is taking place, naming feelings, and making space for differences, are all powerful medicine.*

Experiencing one's impact supports a sense of realness and potency. All of these processes and norms develop and persist when introduced and supported through administrative style, staff policy, and procedures, rather than as process discontinuities that front-line troops have to maintain in the face of the larger system influences. (pp. 350)

I wish I had said that!

RICHARD'S
FAVORITE POEMS

Ave Atque Vale

Through many countries and over many seas
I have come, Brother, to these melancholy rites,
to show this final honour to the dead,
and speak (to what purpose?) to your silent ashes,
since now fate takes you, even you, from me.
Oh, Brother, ripped away from me so cruelly,
now at least take these last offerings, blessed
by the tradition of our parents, gifts to the dead.
Accept, by custom, what a brother's tears drown,
and, for eternity, Brother, 'Hail and Farewell.'

— Gaius Valerius Catullus

Thanatopsis

To him who in the love of nature holds
Communion with her visible forms, she speaks
A various language; for his gayer hours
She has a voice of gladness, and a smile
And eloquence of beauty; and she glides
Into his darker musings, with a mild
And healing sympathy that steals away
Their sharpness ere he is aware. When thoughts
Of the last bitter hour come like a blight
Over thy spirit, and sad images
Of the stern agony, and shroud, and pall,
And breathless darkness, and the narrow house,
Make thee to shudder, and grow sick at heart; —
Go forth, under the open sky, and list
To Nature's teachings, while from all around —
Earth and her waters, and the depths of air —
Comes a still voice. Yet a few days, and thee
The all-beholding sun shall see no more
In all his course; nor yet in the cold ground,
Where thy pale form was laid, with many tears,
Nor in the embrace of ocean, shall exist
Thy image. Earth, that nourished thee, shall claim

Thy growth, to be resolved to earth again,
And, lost each human trace, surrendering up
Thine individual being, shalt thou go
To mix forever with the elements,
To be a brother to the insensible rock
And to the sluggish clod, which the rude swain
Turns with his share, and treads upon. The oak
Shall send his roots abroad, and pierce thy mold.

Yet not to thine eternal resting-place
Shalt thou retire alone, nor couldst thou wish
Couch more magnificent. Thou shalt lie down
With patriarchs of the infant world — with kings,
The powerful of the earth — the wise, the good,
Fair forms, and hoary seers of ages past,
All in one mighty sepulchre. The hills
Rock-ribbed and ancient as the sun, — the vales
Stretching in pensive quietness between;
The venerable woods — rivers that move
In majesty, and the complaining brooks
That make the meadows green; and, poured round all,
Old Ocean's gray and melancholy waste, —
Are but the solemn decorations all
Of the great tomb of man. The golden sun,
The planets, all the infinite host of heaven,
Are shining on the sad abodes of death
Through the still lapse of ages. All that tread
The globe are but a handful to the tribes
That slumber in its bosom. — Take the wings
Of morning, pierce the Barcan wilderness,
Or lose thyself in the continuous woods
Where rolls the Oregon, and hears no sound,
Save his own dashings — yet the dead are there:
And millions in those solitudes, since first

The flight of years began, have laid them down
In their last sleep — the dead reign there alone.

So shalt thou rest — and what if thou withdraw
In silence from the living, and no friend
Take note of thy departure? All that breathe
Will share thy destiny. The gay will laugh
When thou art gone, the solemn brood of care
Plod on, and each one as before will chase
His favorite phantom; yet all these shall leave
Their mirth and their employments, and shall come
And make their bed with thee. As the long train
Of ages glides away, the sons of men —
The youth in life's fresh spring, and he who goes
In the full strength of years, matron and maid,
The speechless babe, and the gray-headed man —
Shall one by one be gathered to thy side,
By those, who in their turn, shall follow them.

So live, that when thy summons comes to join
The innumerable caravan, which moves
To that mysterious realm, where each shall take
His chamber in the silent halls of death,
Thou go not, like the quarry-slave at night,
Scourged to his dungeon, but, sustained and soothed
By an unfaltering trust, approach thy grave
Like one who wraps the drapery of his couch
About him, and lies down to pleasant dreams.

— William Cullen Bryant

Hamlet's Soliloquy

To be, or not to be, that is the Question:
Whether 'tis Nobler in the minde to suffer
The Slings and Arrowes of outragious Fortune,
Or to take Armes against a Sea of troubles,
And by opposing end them: to dye, to sleepe
No more; and by a sleepe, to say we end
The Heart-ake, and the thousand Naturall shockes
That Flesh is heyre too? 'Tis a consummation
Deuoutly to be wish'd. To dye to sleepe,
To sleepe, perchance to Dreame; I, there's the rub,
For in that sleepe of death, what dreames may come,
When we haue shuffel'd off this mortall coile,
Must giue vs pawse. There's the respect
That makes Calamity of so long life:
For who would beare the Whips and Scornes of time,
The Oppressors wrong, the poore mans Contumely,
The pangs of dispriz'd Loue, the Lawes delay,
The insolence of Office, and the Spurnes
That patient merit of the vnworthy takes,
When he himselfe might his Quietus make
With a bare Bodkin? Who would these Fardles beare
To grunt and sweat vnder a weary life,
But that the dread of something after death,
The vndiscouered Countrey, from whose Borne
No Traueller returnes, Puzels the will,

And makes vs rather beare those illes we haue,
Then flye to others that we know not of.
Thus Conscience does make Cowards of vs all,
And thus the Natiue hew of Resolution
Is sicklied o're, with the pale cast of Thought,
And enterprizes of great pith and moment,
With this regard their Currents turne away,
And loose the name of Action.

> — from William Shakespeare's Hamlet,
> Prince of Denmark (written about 1600),
> Act III, Scene I

Macbeth Act V

Tomorrow, and tomorrow, and tomorrow,
Creeps in this petty pace from day to day,
To the last syllable of recorded time;
And all our yesterdays have lighted fools
The way to dusty death. Out, out, brief candle!
Life's but a walking shadow, a poor player,
That struts and frets his hour upon the stage,
And then is heard no more. It is a tale
Told by an idiot, full of sound and fury,
Signifying nothing.

— William Shakespeare

Lycidas

"Yet once more, O ye Laurels, and once more
Ye Myrtles brown, with Ivy never-sear
I come to pluck your Berries harsh and crude,
And with forc'd fingers rude,
Shatter your leaves before the mellowing year.
Bitter constraint, and sad occasion dear,
Compels me to disturb your season due:
For Lycidas is dead..."

Author: John Milton

Es ist genug

English translation

> *It is enough!*
> *Therefore, Lord, take my spirit*
> *from here to the spirits of Zion;*
> *undo the ties , that gradually are tearing me apart;*
> *set free this mind*
> *that yearns for its God,*
> *that daily laments and nightly weeps:*
> *It is enough!*
>
> *There is enough*
> *of the misery that crushes me!*
> *Adam's greed for the apple, the poison of sin*
> *have all but smothered me;*
> *nothing good dwells in me.*
> *What miserably separates me from God,*
> *what each day marks me out as polluted*
> *- of this there is enough.*
>
> *There is enough*
> *of the cross that almost*
> *breaks my back;*
> *how heavy, O God, how hard is this burden!*
> *Many nights I soak*
> *my hard bed with my tears.*

How long, how long must I yearn?
When is it enough?

It is enough
only when my Jesus wills.
He indeed knows my heart;
I wait for him and meanwhile keep calm,
until by him all the sorrow
that gnaws away at my sickly breast
is put aside and he says to me:
It is enough!

It is enough!
Therefore, Lord, take my spirit
from here to the spirits of Zion;
undo the ties , that gradually are tearing me apart;
set free this mind
that yearns for its God,
that daily laments and nightly weeps:
It is enough!

It is enough,
Lord, when it is pleasing to you,
then grant me release.
May my Jesus come!
Now good night, o world.
I am going to heaven's house,
I go confidently from here with joy;
my dismal sorrow remains down below.
It is enough!

Author: Franz Joachim Burmeister
Composer: Johann Rudolf Ahle

RICHARD'S
LATER FAVORITES

1. The Sonnets

2. Paul Goodman's Poetry

3. Paul Goodman's "Kafka's Prayer"

4. Gerard Manley Hopkins' "Windhover / Pied Beauty"

A Lexicon for the Reader

appetitive: adjective relating to appetite

asseverations: to declare seriously or positively, to affirm

asyndeton: the omission of conjunctions in sentence structure in which they would normally be used

Ave Atque Vale: means "hail and farewell." Poem by Gaius Valerius Catullus

awarely: adverb of aware – to be conscious of; to notice a change

chiasma: crossing as that of the optic nerves at the base of the brain

cogredient: mathematical term

digredient: mathematical term

diremption: a sharp division into two parts; separation; disjunction

egology: subjectivity of one's set of beliefs

eponymous(ly): giving one's name to a tribe, place, i.e. Romulus founded Rome

errancy: deviating from an accepted standard

Es ist genug: means "it is enough." It's the title of a chorale from
      Johann Sebastian Bach

funebral: pertaining to a funeral

guerdon: a reward, recompensation

irrupted: to break in or burst in, to increase rapidly

lexicon: the vocabulary of a particular language, field, social class,
      person, etc.

limn: to describe, to depict by painting or drawing

noumenon: the object, itself inaccessible to experience, to which a
      phenomenon is referred for the basis or cause of its sense content

oblivescence: the process of forgetting

ontic: possessing the character of real rather than phenomenal
      existence; nuomenal

PHG: Refers to the "Bible," *Gestalt Therapy, Excitement and Growth in
      the Human Personality*, written by Frederick Perls, MD, Ph.D.,
      R.F. Hefferline, Ph.D. and Paul Goodman, Ph.D: The PHG, of
      course, stands for "Perls, Hefferline and Goodman," since the
      authors' names or initials became a substitution for the title of
      the book.

polemical: a controversial discussion, involving dispute, controversial

prated: to talk

praxis: accepted practice of custom

prehension: the act of seizing or grabbing; mental apprehension

presuppositionlessness: the state of being in absence of a antecedent condition

quiddities: the essence of a person or thing, what makes the thing what it is

quod erat demonstradum "Q.E.D.": literally "that which was to have been demonstrated." The phrase is written in its abbreviated form at the end of a mathematical proof or philosophical argument to signify that the last statement deduced was the one to be demonstrated, so the proof is complete.

res ipsa loquitor: a legal term meaning literally "the thing speaks for itself" and further details are unnecessary; the proof is self evident

screed: a long usually tiresome piece of writing or speech on a scrap of paper

severally: separately or respectively, distinctly (all went their several ways)

sundered: to break into parts

tome: a book, especially a very heavy, large, learned book; a volume forming a part of a larger work

Already Published Works

Book Appearances

Kitzler, R. (1984). Bread From Stones. In E. M. Stern (Ed.), *Psychotherapy and the Abrasive Patient* (pp. 39) Haworth Press.

Kitzler, R. (2001). Foreword. In Perls, R., & Ain, Dr. Eileen J., *Those Who Came After*. New Orleans, LA: Gestalt Institute Press.

Kitzler, R. (2003). Creativity as Gestalt Therapy. In M. S. Lobb, & N. Amendt-Lyon (Eds.), *Creative License: The Art of Gestalt Therapy* (pp. 101–112) Birkhäuser.

Kitzler, R. (2008). The Gestalt Group. In B. Feder, & J. Frew (Eds.), *Beyond the Hot Seat: Revisited* (pp. 111–123). New Orleans, LA: Gestalt Institute Press.

Journal Appearances

Kitzler, R., Perls, L., & Stern, M. (1982). Retrospects and Prospects: A Trialogue between Laura Perls, Richard Kitzler and E. Mark Stern. *Voices, 18*(2), 5–22.

Kitzler, R. (1996). Isadore From: A Critical Appreciation. *Studies in Gestalt Therapy, 4*(5), 19–45.

Kitzler, R. (1998). Return to Novelty. *Gestalt Review, 2*(3)

Kitzler, R. (1999). Developmental Theory in the Light of Pragmatism and Interruptions of Contact: An Integration. *Studies in Gestalt Therapy, 8*, 182–197.

Kitzler, R. (2006). The Ontology of Action - A place on which to stand for modern gestalt therapy theory. *International Gestalt Journal,* vol. unknown.

Kitzler, R. (2007). The Ambiguities of Origins: Pragmatism, the University of Chicago, and Paul Goodman's Self. *Studies in Gestalt Therapy: Dialogical Bridges, 1*(1), 41–63.

Miscellaneous Appearances
Kitzler, R. "Dialogue with Isaac." Unpublished talk delivered at the New York Institute for Gestalt Therapy, November, 1990.

REQUIEM TO RICHARD

The Ancestor Tree

The giant redwoods stand in circles.
The center of those circles is not empty.

Within it is a mound of humus morphing to soil.
It is the remains of the ancestor tree
From whose seeds, the ring of giants grew.

Richard was our ancestor tree.
He touched the sky in places
To which we can only dream
And towards which
We must continue to try to reach.

— Dan Bloom
New York, 2009

From Dan Bloom

Richard Kitzler (b. 1927) died January 2, 2009, in New York City.

Richard was there at the very beginning of gestalt therapy, and continued teaching, supervising, and practicing gestalt therapy until his death.

He was among Fritz Perls' early patients. He later studied with him and Paul Goodman. Richard helped type the manuscript of *Gestalt Therapy (PHG)* by Perls, Hefferline, and Goodman. He was one of the founders of the New York Institute for Gestalt Therapy and was associated with Laura Perls, Isadore From, Patrick Kelley, Paul Weisz, and Eliot Shapiro.

He was a fellow of the New York Institute for Gestalt Therapy and a formidable part of its community until his death. Richard also was guest faculty at the Istituto di Gestalt HCC in Italy and was involved in collaborations between that institute and the NYIGT.

For many years in his seminars in New York City, Richard conveyed the complexity of gestalt therapy to generations of students through a careful line-by-line reading of *Gestalt Therapy (PHG)*. His teaching of this model became the basis for his interactive gestalt therapy group process, which he implemented in small and large groups in the United States and Europe.

He was integral to the formation of the Association for the Advancement of Gestalt Therapy. Richard was an outspoken presence at gestalt therapy conferences in the United States, Canada, and Europe. His personality made it impossible for him to utter an uncomplicated sentence or an uncontroversial idea.

Richard's mind was ceaselessly curious. As he continued to study gestalt therapy, he became increasingly dissatisfied and began a careful re-evaluation of its theoretical and practical basis, a project he continued until his death. Richard was broadening gestalt therapy into phenomenology and, especially the American pragmatism of William James and George Herbert Mead. Richard was convinced that Mead's theories of the self and of the "act" were a sounder basis for gestalt therapy than anything else.

Our journal, Studies in *Gestalt Therapy: Dialogical Bridges*, was fortunate to publish one of Richard's final essays, "The Ambiguities of Origins: Pragmatism, the University of Chicago, and Paul Goodman's Self," in Issue 1/1, the Inaugural issue. The book, *Eccentric Genius*, a collection of Richard's writings from the 1980s to 2008, is being published by The Gestalt Institute Press (www.teachworth.com).

We who have been close to Richard have lost a friend. He was an uncompromising teacher and an unrelenting advocate for his students.

We, who were his students, have lost a mentor. He was our ground. Such a foundation changes with his death, but cannot disappear.

From Renate Perls

I have nothing to offer but tears. Richard was part of my family for nearly fifty-eight years and I cannot imagine life without him either in the background or the foreground regaling us with his astounding insights and memories.

With whom can I now share those special moments sitting on somebody's front steps in the summer speaking not of anything particularly intellectual, but of our childhood, of our parents, of the earlier years and the beginnings of gestalt therapy?

"Do you remember…?" he would say, invariably telling me things I had long forgotten, or perhaps experiencing memories from his childhood which he had not thought of for years.

I will celebrate his life and honor his passing. And I most certainly will miss him.

From Anne Teachworth

Editing and publishing *Eccentric Genius* was a labor of love for me. I treasure the many many hours I spent with Richard working on his book over the last two years. He was so easy to work with and we had such fun laughing and sharing stories. The time just flew by sitting in Richard's art-filled apartment with him commenting on each article he'd written or the people mentioned in it. I am so sad at the loss of my dear friend's elegant, astute, witty and well-spoken presence. I wish I had audio-taped all my visits with him so I could hear him over and over again now.

I began the book project because I truly wanted Richard to be more widely recognized and acknowledged in the greater gestalt community worldwide, and especially that his wisdom be not limited only to those of us who were lucky enough to spend time with him. Richard Kitzler made me think past my own gestalt and philosophical limitations and certainly, past my own vocabulary. He had an uncanny knack for amazingly accurate questions and insights combined with a genuine acceptance for both himself and others...as is...here and now, right smack at our individual growing edges.

We hurried the first edition of *Eccentric Genius* to get it ready for the AAGT conference in Manchester, but unfortunately, Richard was too sick to fly there to England with me. On my return, we went over the book again and made some changes and additions for the Revised 2nd Edition, to be printed by May 2009. He wanted particularly to add the picture of 7 year old Joe, his childhood friend, who had recently died. Joe's memorial service had weakened Richard's spirit and from that point on, his stately strength ebbed out of him.

Richard loved reading over the book, especially the articles from long ago. Often, he would have forgotten what he had written until he came across a particular line he really liked and he was thrilled that he had said that... and in that way! His genuine enjoyment of the book was all that mattered to me then. Now, after his death, what matters to me is that through this anthology, Richard's many contributions will become a part of the treasury of gestalt history... that makes me happy now.

I edited and published *Eccentric Genius* because I wanted Richard to live forever and now he will for others who did not have the incredible opportunity to know him personally.

The last time I saw Richard, we (Renate Perls, Dan Bloom, Ora McCreary and I) sat at his long dining room table and shared a meal. I can still see him there at the head of the table... Regal, witty, strong of spirit and weak of body. "My dear..." he always said as he touched my arm, "The book is finished. Thank you."

It was a goodbye...

I join you all in fond remembrances of Richard Kitzler, Master Gestalt Therapist.

From Ansel Woldt

My heart sobs as I try to find words to express my sadness in learning of Richard's death. My heart goes out to all who cherish having been touched by this Gestalt Therapy Giant.

As some of you know, I dearly missed Richard at our last AAGT conference in Manchester. The conference felt incomplete without his presence. Learning of the reasons for his absence being due to an accident on his way to the airport also broke my heart — and Nancy's — as we dearly loved the man. He always teased me about how a Marine officer could possibly make the transition to gestalt therapy, and I loved every bit of his teasing.

I am so glad we chose to honor Richard with the special interview of distinguished gestalt therapists at our 2006 AAGT Conference in Vancouver. When I shared the DVD of that interview with my gestalt therapy graduate class last year they were very taken by Richard, many remarking about his sense of presence and solidarity, the clarity of his thinking about gestalt therapy, his humor and his humility.

In fact, it was during that Vancouver interview with Jon Frew when Nancy went to get Richard a glass of water when he was coughing—the kind of thing my lovely wife is known to do. She never thought any more about it and then one day, weeks after returning home to Kent, this stunningly beautiful artistic card arrived in the mail. Amazingly, it was inscribed by Richard with some of his wit and very sentimental words of appreciation for Nancy having attended to him in a time of need. That to me was Richard, through and through — attending to the obvious, honoring one's presence and articulating his love and appreciation with eloquence.

Ever since first meeting Richard at one of the early Gestalt Journal Conferences in the 70s, I always looked forward to our time together, he being one of the people I'd hope to join for a fine dinner. He was such a brilliant man. While I quaked in my boots every time he attended one of my presentations, I always experienced his sensitivity, support and kindness. I recall his challenging me and my doctoral advisees on the statistics we used to validate one of the gestalt personality tests we were using to measure contact styles. It was a presentation by me with a couple of my doctoral advisees at the Provincetown Inn on "Re-Searching Gestalt Therapy." Even though it had been several years since Richard's own statistics courses, he was as knowledgeable as the stellar statistician on the program. In the end Richard thanked us profusely for our efforts at applying factor analytic, Q-sort and normative statistics to examine basic gestalt constructs in our Kent State graduate program. Of course, he also used some words I didn't know were in the dictionary.

Another fond memory was from the Group Therapy Symposium in NYC when he asked me to volunteer to be in the demonstration group where he contrasted his gestalt approach with that of a therapist from England. That was a very moving experience for me and some of the other members of the group. In fact, some of us still talk about it when we meet at conferences.

One more thing I need to mention is that Richard was a "monster" during the authoring of AAGT's constitution and by-laws. While there may not have been a single phrase or paragraph that he didn't challenge or offer alternative language, his heart was golden in every step of the way. Yes, we had an argument or two over what I was trying to say, but his presence was always golden in forming the gestalts that developed the foundation on which AAGT stands.

My heart goes out to all the Fellows, friends and colleagues at the NYIGT and elsewhere who will dearly miss the grandeur of this glorious gestalt giant—Richard Kitzler.

Ansel Woldt, Ed.D., *is an Emeritus Professor of Counselor Education at Kent State University and is a psychologist in private practice in Kent, Ohio. He developed the Gestalt Therapy* Archives and Research Collection *which contains original manuscripts, video-tapes, photographs and films of gestalt therapy's history plus over 300 dissertations and theses on gestalt therapy research. Ansel was the founding Secretary and incorporating officer of the Association for the Advancement of Gestalt Therapy (AAGT), and continues to serve as Archivist and Continuing Education Officer. He and Sarah Toman co-edited the contemporary textbook,* Gestalt Therapy: History, Theory and Practice *(2005), Sage Publications and he's also Associate Editor of the* Gestalt Review.

Books from Gestalt Institute Press

ECCENTRIC GENIUS; AN ANTHOLOGY OF THE WRITINGS OF MASTER GESTALT THERAPIST, RICHARD KITZLER $40
Richard Kitzler

BEYOND THE HOT SEAT REVISITED:
Gestalt Approaches to Group $30
Edited by Bud Feder and Jon Frew

WHY WE PICK THE MATES WE DO $20
Anne Teachworth

GESTALT GROUP THERAPY $20
Bud Feder

A FUNNY THING HAPPENED ON THE WAY TO ENLIGHTENMENT $20
Lenny Ravich

THOSE WHO COME AFTER $20
Renate Perls with Eileen Ain

THE BRIDGE: DIALOGUES ACROSS CULTURES $40
Edited by Talia Levine Bar-Yoseph

SUFFERING IN SILENCE:
THE LEGACY OF UNRESOLVED SEXUAL ABUSE $20
Anne Schutzenberger and Ghislain Devroede

To Order, contact Anne Teachworth, Publisher:
THE GESTALT INSTITUTE PRESS
433 METAIRIE ROAD, SUITE 133, METAIRIE, LOUISIANA, 70005 USA

Phones: 1.800.786.1065 or 504.828.2267
E-mail: ateachw@aol.com
Order by Paypal at www.teachworth.com
Fax: 504.837.2796   VISA/MC/AMEX ACCEPTED

CPSIA information can be obtained
at www.ICGtesting.com
Printed in the USA
BVHW041433200820
586925BV00010B/117

9 781889 968001